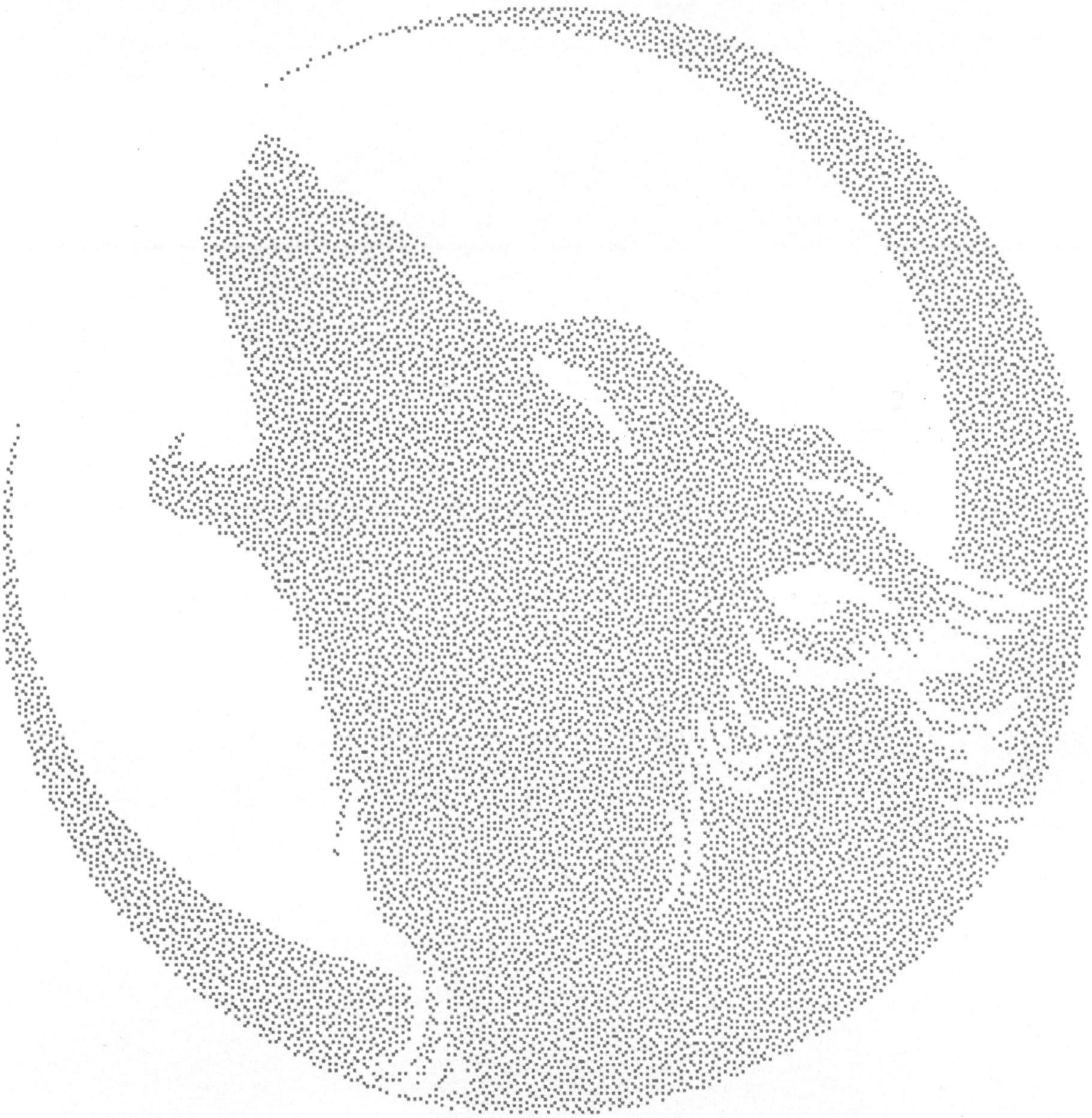

NEW BLOOD

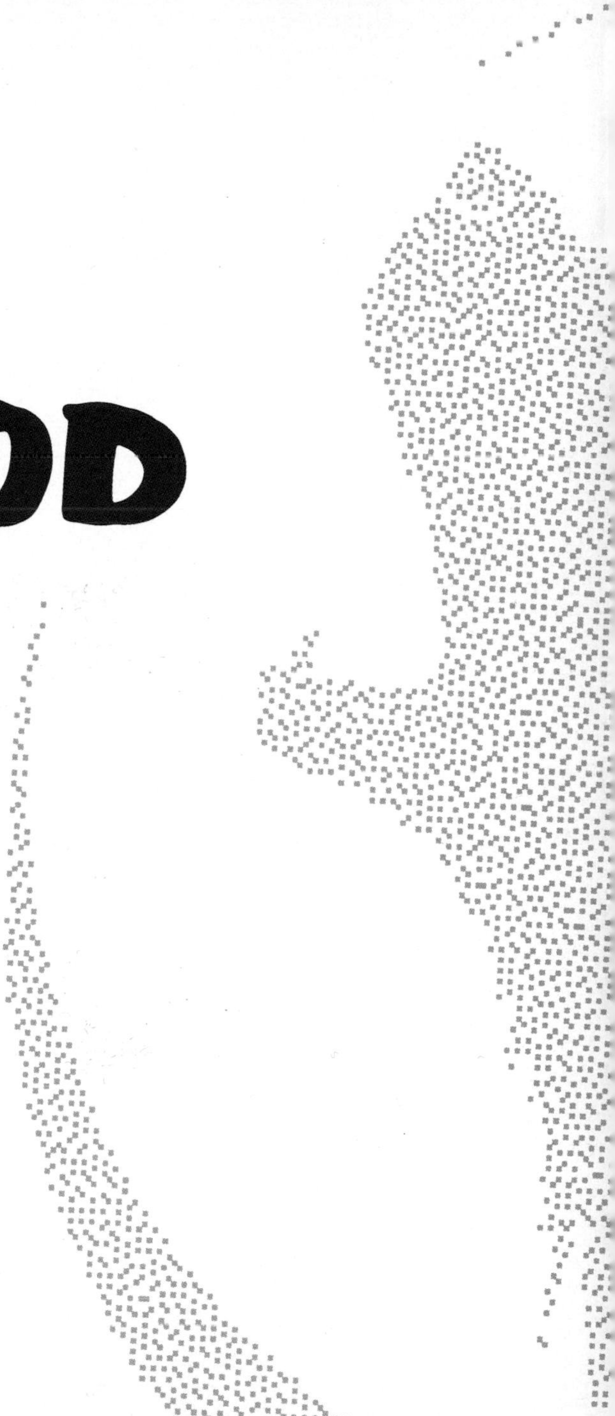

original visions of ELFQUEST
edited by Wendy & Richard Pini

WHAT IS HERE...

Elfquest - New Blood

(Previously published in
single magazine issues as
Elfquest: New Blood 1-5.)

Published by Warp Graphics, Inc.,
under its Father Tree Press imprint.
43 Haight Avenue
Poughkeepsie NY 12603

Printed in U.S.A.
First printing.
ISBN 0-936861-31-2

For a catalog of Elfquest
books, graphic novels, and music,
call 1-800-288-2131.

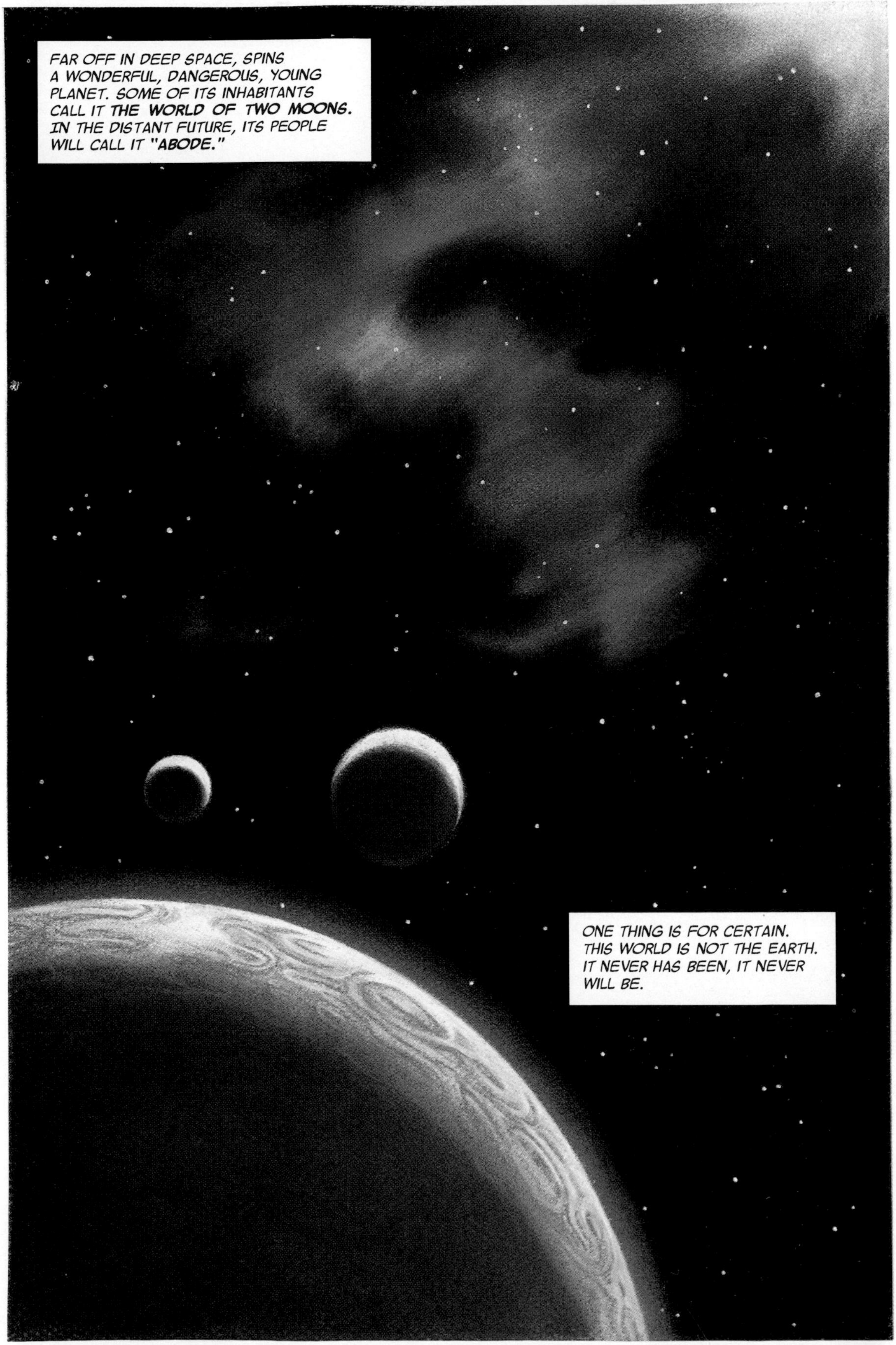
FAR OFF IN DEEP SPACE, SPINS A WONDERFUL, DANGEROUS, YOUNG PLANET. SOME OF ITS INHABITANTS CALL IT **THE WORLD OF TWO MOONS**. IN THE DISTANT FUTURE, ITS PEOPLE WILL CALL IT "**ABODE**."
ONE THING IS FOR CERTAIN. THIS WORLD IS NOT THE EARTH. IT NEVER HAS BEEN, IT NEVER WILL BE.

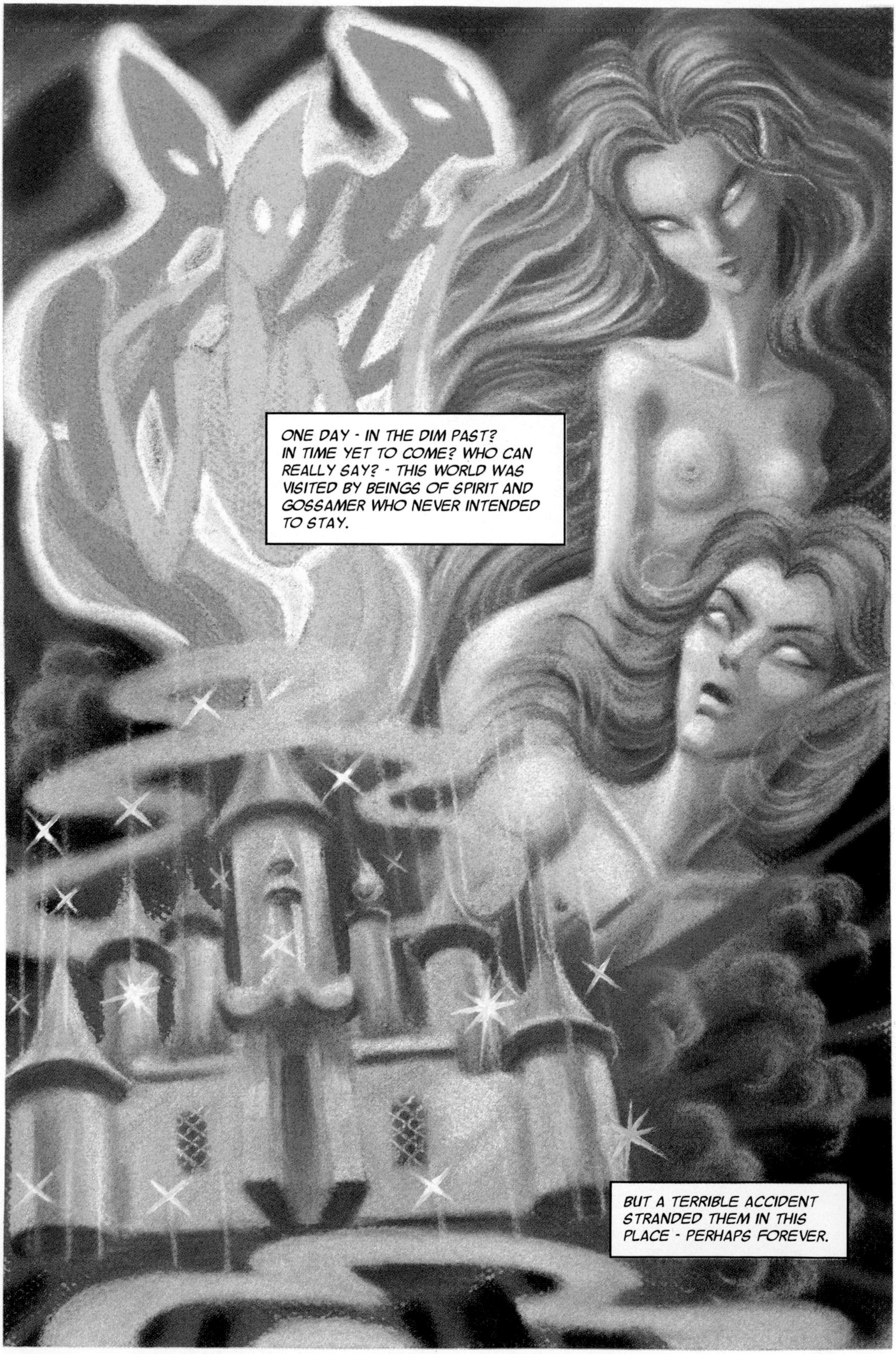
ONE DAY - IN THE DIM PAST? IN TIME YET TO COME? WHO CAN REALLY SAY? - THIS WORLD WAS VISITED BY BEINGS OF SPIRIT AND GOSSAMER WHO NEVER INTENDED TO STAY.
BUT A TERRIBLE ACCIDENT STRANDED THEM IN THIS PLACE - PERHAPS FOREVER.

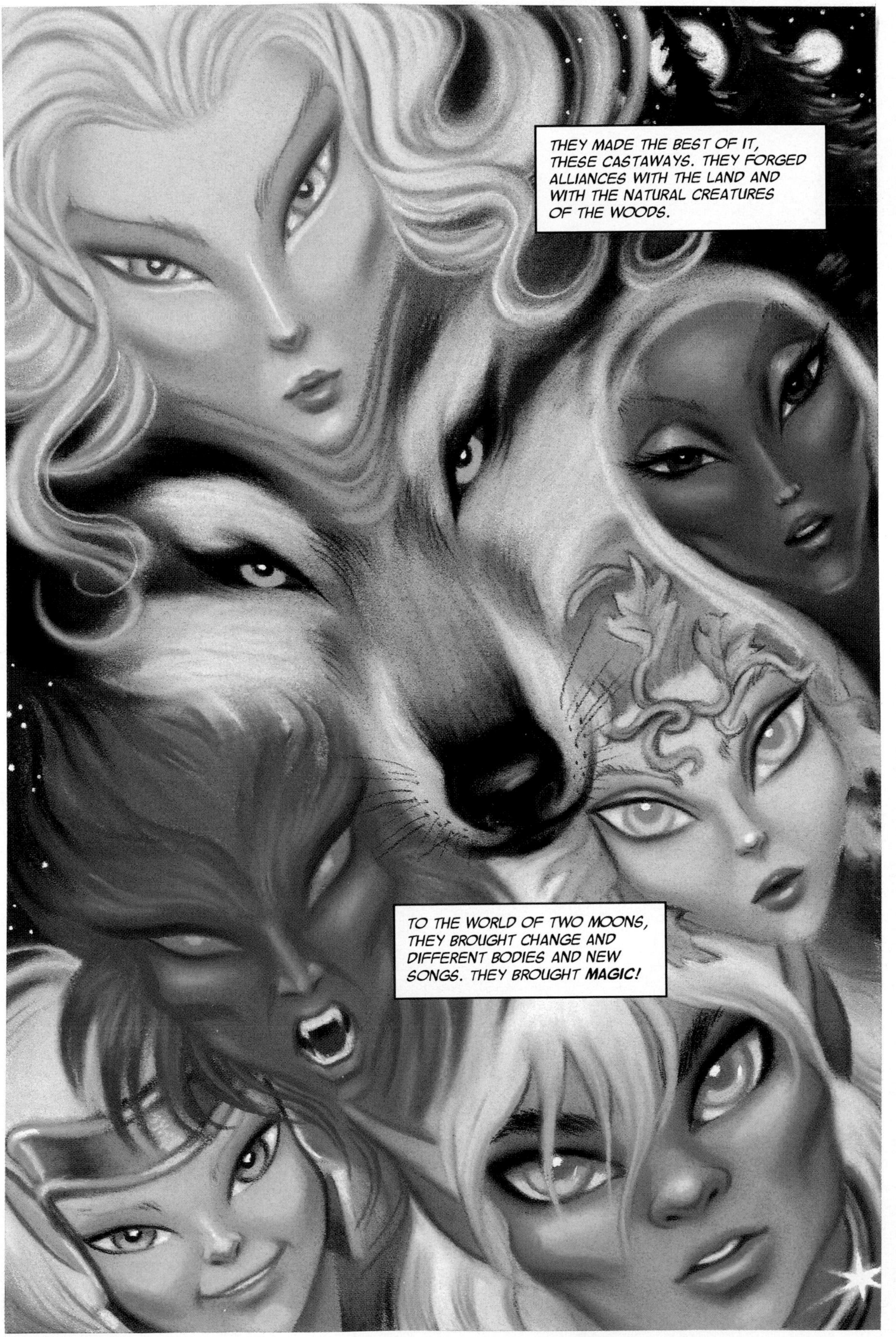
THEY MADE THE BEST OF IT, THESE CASTAWAYS. THEY FORGED ALLIANCES WITH THE LAND AND WITH THE NATURAL CREATURES OF THE WOODS.
TO THE WORLD OF TWO MOONS, THEY BROUGHT CHANGE AND DIFFERENT BODIES AND NEW SONGS. THEY BROUGHT **MAGIC!**

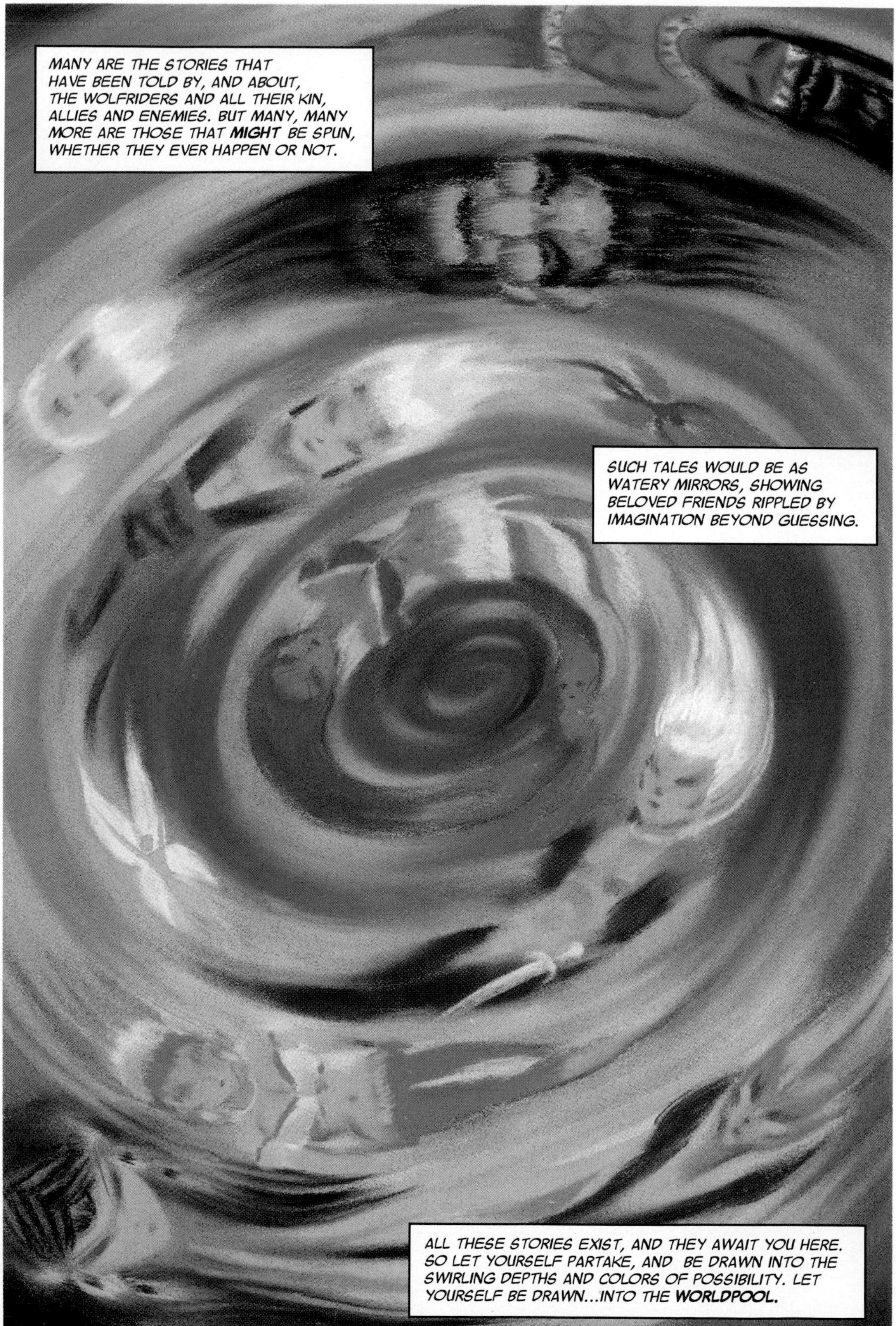
MANY ARE THE STORIES THAT HAVE BEEN TOLD BY, AND ABOUT, THE WOLFRIDERS AND ALL THEIR KIN, ALLIES AND ENEMIES. BUT MANY, MANY MORE ARE THOSE THAT **MIGHT** BE SPUN, WHETHER THEY EVER HAPPEN OR NOT.
SUCH TALES WOULD BE AS WATERY MIRRORS, SHOWING BELOVED FRIENDS RIPPLED BY IMAGINATION BEYOND GUESSING.
ALL THESE STORIES EXIST, AND THEY AWAIT YOU HERE. SO LET YOURSELF PARTAKE, AND BE DRAWN INTO THE SWIRLING DEPTHS AND COLORS OF POSSIBILITY. LET YOURSELF BE DRAWN...INTO THE **WORLDPOOL.**

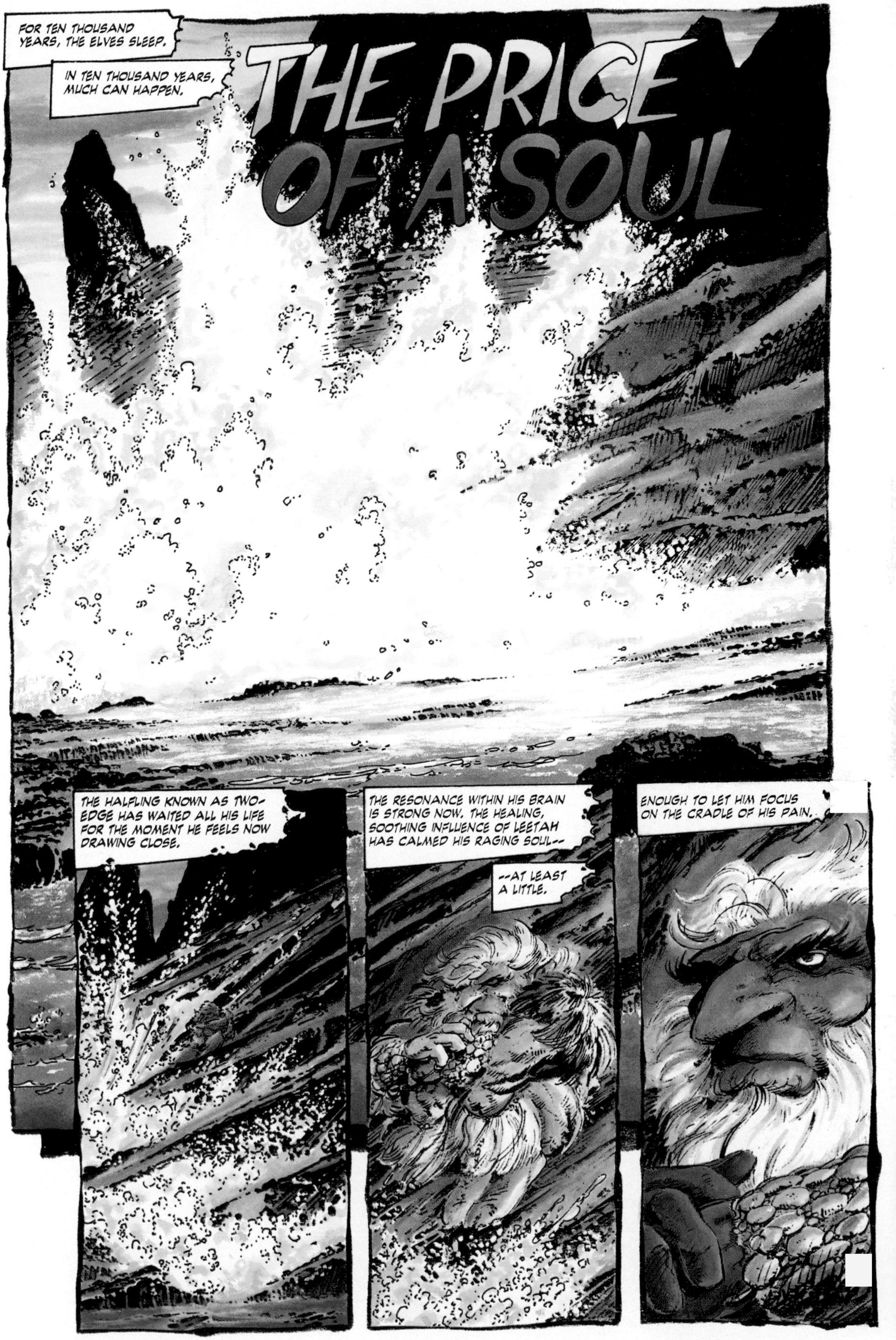
FOR TEN THOUSAND YEARS, THE ELVES SLEEP.
IN TEN THOUSAND YEARS, MUCH CAN HAPPEN.
THE PRICE OF A SOUL
THE HALFLING KNOWN AS TWO-EDGE HAS WAITED ALL HIS LIFE FOR THE MOMENT HE FEELS NOW DRAWING CLOSE.
THE RESONANCE WITHIN HIS BRAIN IS STRONG NOW. THE HEALING, SOOTHING INFLUENCE OF LEETAH HAS CALMED HIS RAGING SOUL--
--AT LEAST A LITTLE.
ENOUGH TO LET HIM FOCUS ON THE CRADLE OF HIS PAIN.

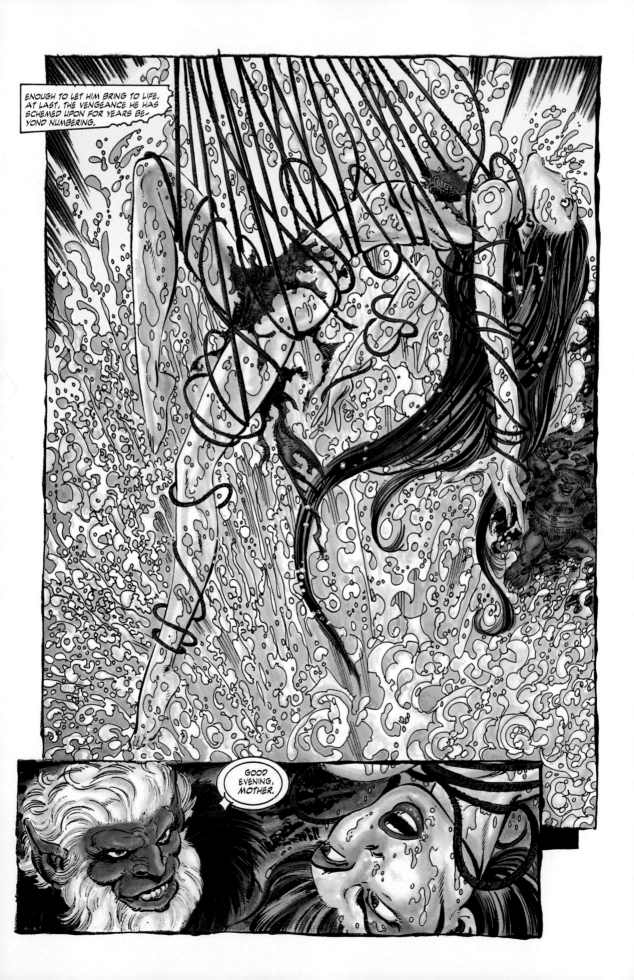

ENOUGH TO LET HIM BRING TO LIFE, AT LAST, THE VENGEANCE HE HAS SCHEMED UPON FOR YEARS BEYOND NUMBERING.

GOOD EVENING, MOTHER.

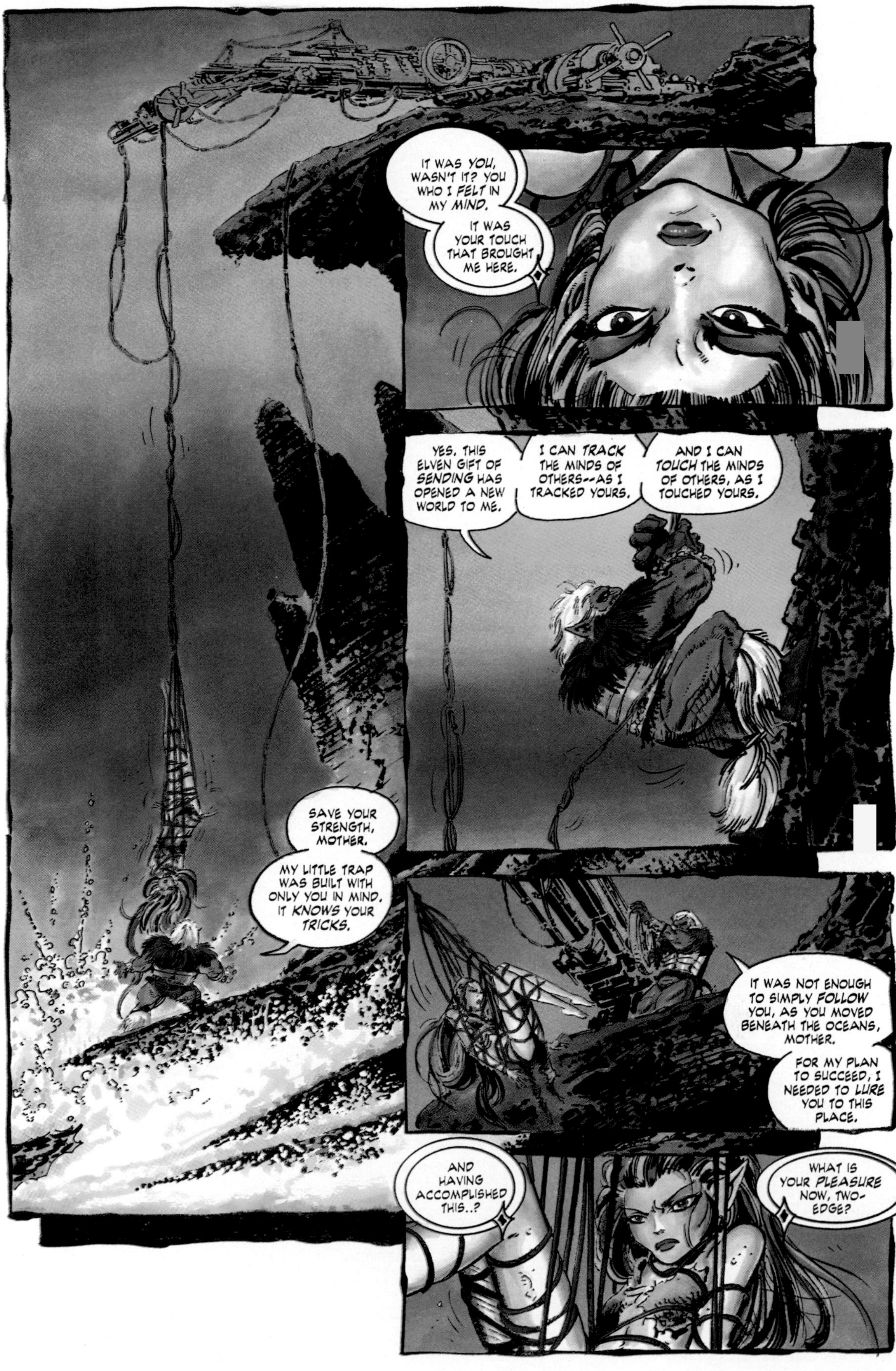
IT WAS YOU, WASN'T IT? YOU WHO I FELT IN MY MIND.
IT WAS YOUR TOUCH THAT BROUGHT ME HERE.
YES. THIS ELVEN GIFT OF SENDING HAS OPENED A NEW WORLD TO ME.
I CAN TRACK THE MINDS OF OTHERS--AS I TRACKED YOURS.
AND I CAN TOUCH THE MINDS OF OTHERS, AS I TOUCHED YOURS.
SAVE YOUR STRENGTH, MOTHER.
MY LITTLE TRAP WAS BUILT WITH ONLY YOU IN MIND. IT KNOWS YOUR TRICKS.
IT WAS NOT ENOUGH TO SIMPLY FOLLOW YOU, AS YOU MOVED BENEATH THE OCEANS, MOTHER.
FOR MY PLAN TO SUCCEED, I NEEDED TO LURE YOU TO THIS PLACE.
AND HAVING ACCOMPLISHED THIS..?
WHAT IS YOUR PLEASURE NOW, TWO-EDGE?

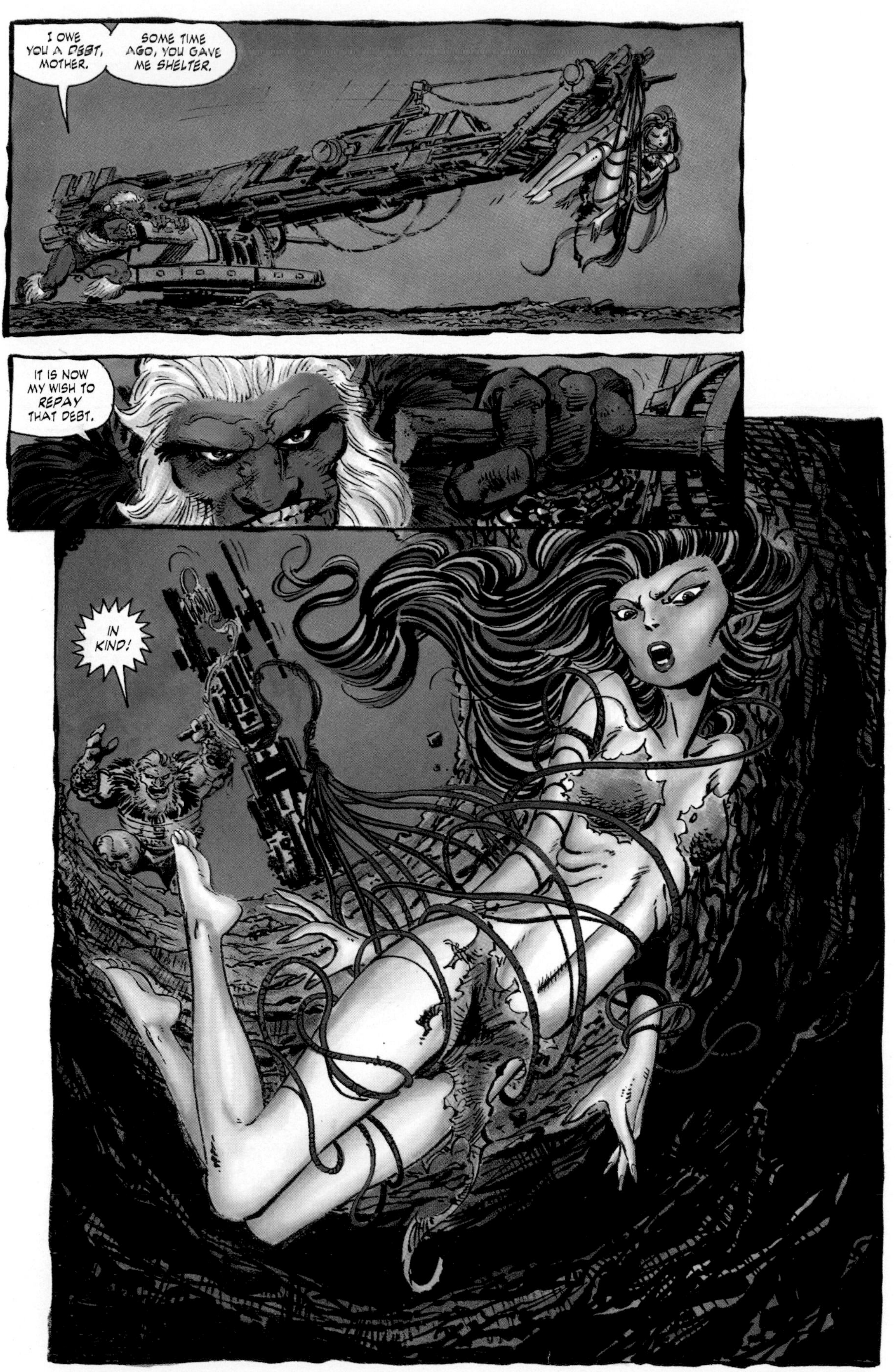

I OWE YOU A DEBT, MOTHER.
SOME TIME AGO, YOU GAVE ME SHELTER.
IT IS NOW MY WISH TO REPAY THAT DEBT.
IN KIND!

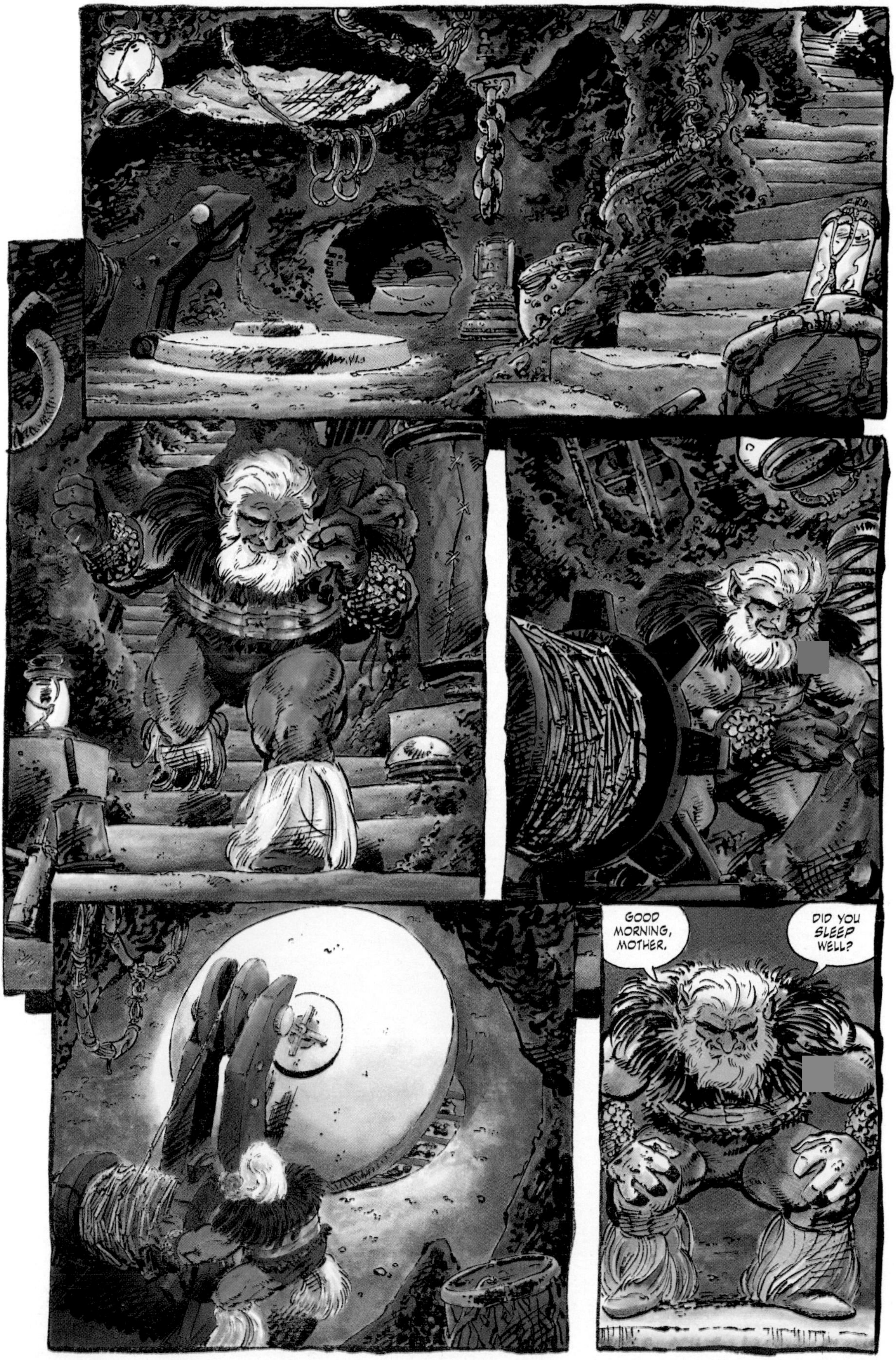
GOOD MORNING, MOTHER.
DID YOU SLEEP WELL?

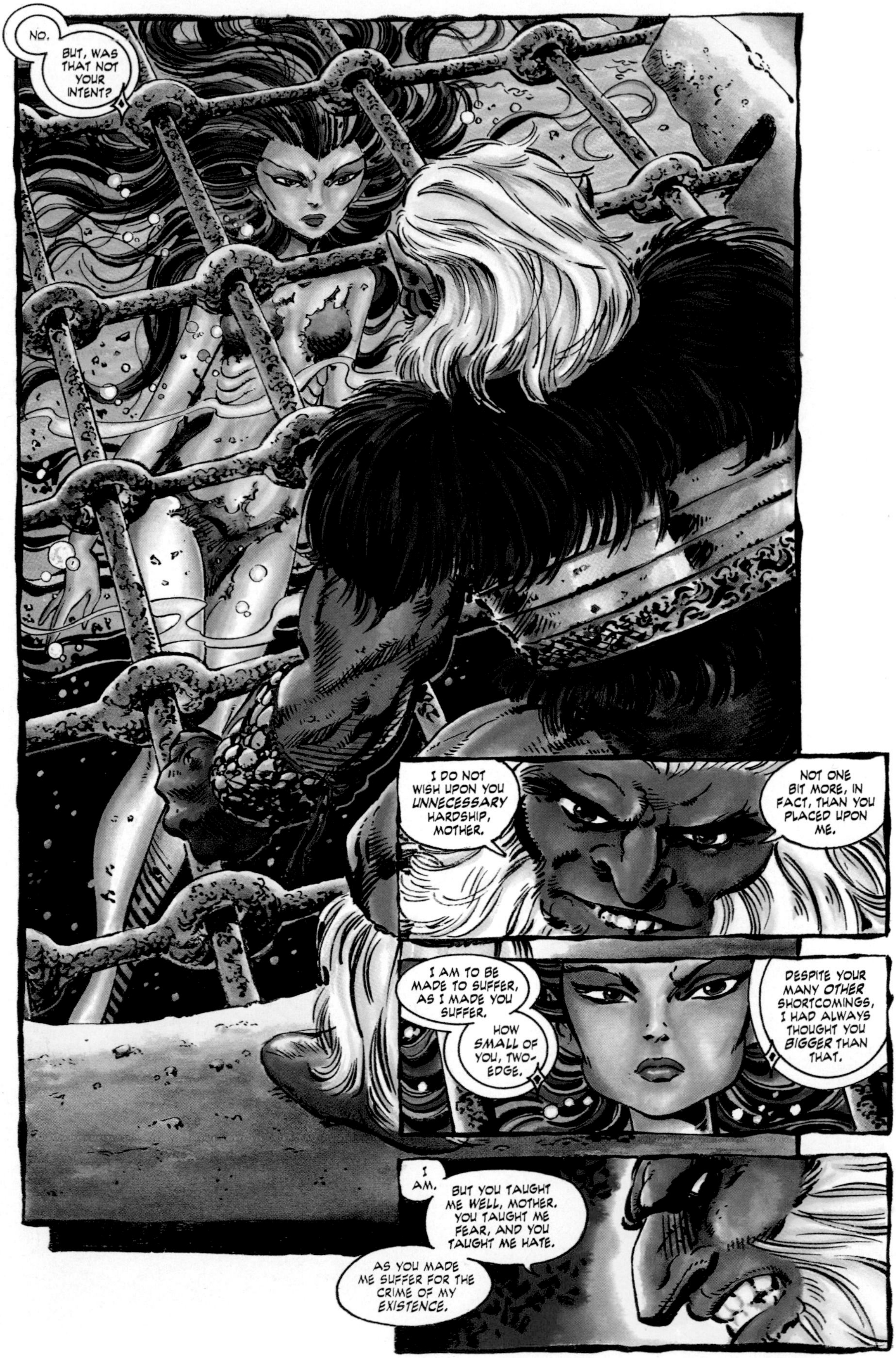
NO.
BUT, WAS THAT NOT YOUR INTENT?
I DO NOT WISH UPON YOU UNNECESSARY HARDSHIP, MOTHER.
NOT ONE BIT MORE, IN FACT, THAN YOU PLACED UPON ME.
I AM TO BE MADE TO SUFFER, AS I MADE YOU SUFFER.
HOW SMALL OF YOU, TWO-EDGE.
DESPITE YOUR MANY OTHER SHORTCOMINGS, I HAD ALWAYS THOUGHT YOU BIGGER THAN THAT.
I AM.
BUT YOU TAUGHT ME WELL, MOTHER. YOU TAUGHT ME FEAR, AND YOU TAUGHT ME HATE.
AS YOU MADE ME SUFFER FOR THE CRIME OF MY EXISTENCE.

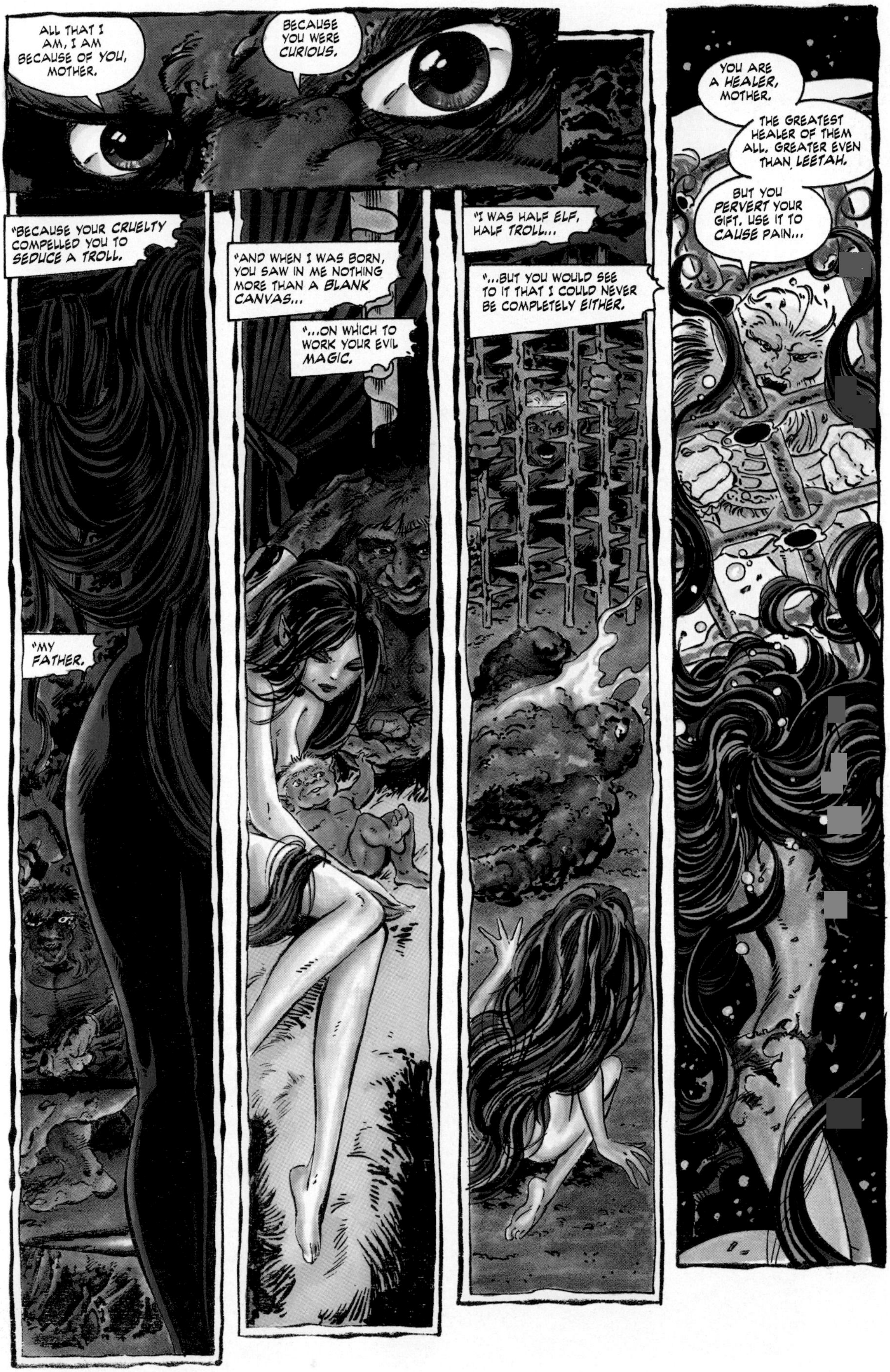
ALL THAT I AM, I AM BECAUSE OF YOU, MOTHER.
BECAUSE YOU WERE CURIOUS.
"BECAUSE YOUR CRUELTY COMPELLED YOU TO SEDUCE A TROLL.
"MY FATHER.
"AND WHEN I WAS BORN, YOU SAW IN ME NOTHING MORE THAN A BLANK CANVAS...
"...ON WHICH TO WORK YOUR EVIL MAGIC.
"I WAS HALF ELF, HALF TROLL...
"...BUT YOU WOULD SEE TO IT THAT I COULD NEVER BE COMPLETELY EITHER.
YOU ARE A HEALER, MOTHER.
THE GREATEST HEALER OF THEM ALL, GREATER EVEN THAN LEETAH.
BUT YOU PERVERT YOUR GIFT. USE IT TO CAUSE PAIN...

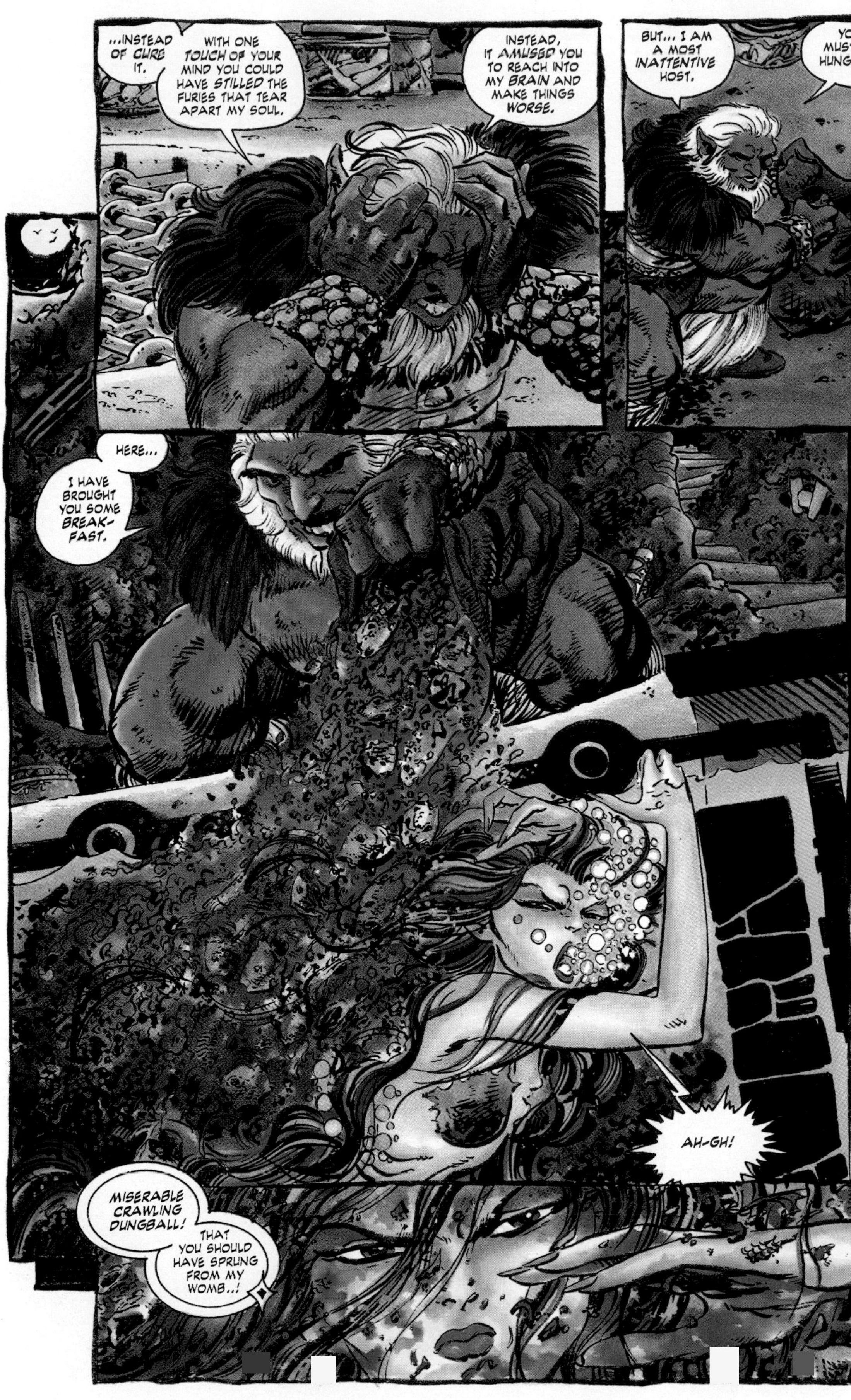
...INSTEAD OF CURE IT.
WITH ONE TOUCH OF YOUR MIND YOU COULD HAVE STILLED THE FURIES THAT TEAR APART MY SOUL.
INSTEAD, IT AMUSED YOU TO REACH INTO MY BRAIN AND MAKE THINGS WORSE.
BUT... I AM A MOST INATTENTIVE HOST.
YOU MUST BE HUNGRY...
HERE...
I HAVE BROUGHT YOU SOME BREAK-FAST.
AH-GH!
MISERABLE CRAWLING DUNGBALL!
THAT YOU SHOULD HAVE SPRUNG FROM MY WOMB..!

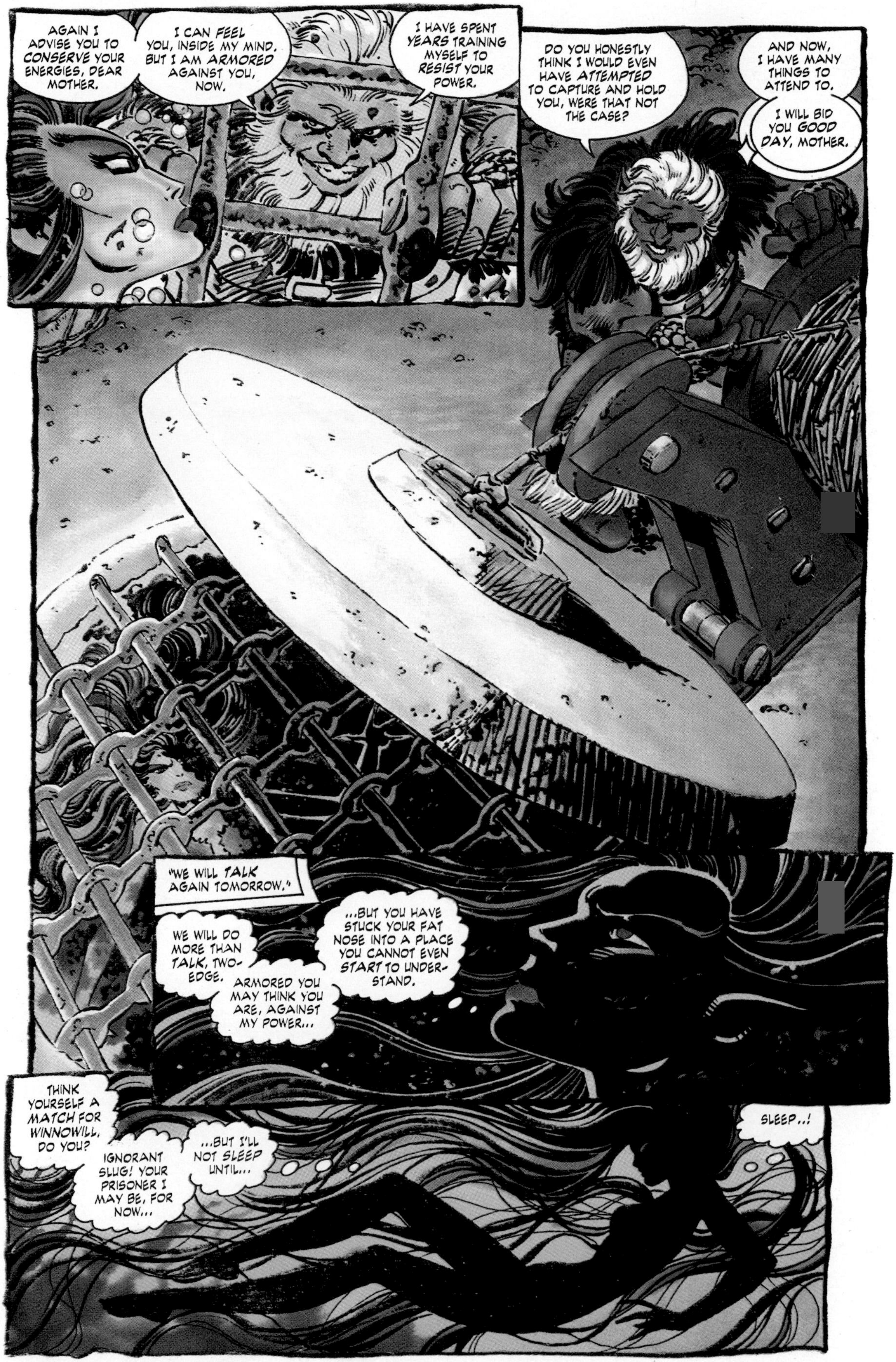
AGAIN I ADVISE YOU TO CONSERVE YOUR ENERGIES, DEAR MOTHER.
I CAN FEEL YOU, INSIDE MY MIND. BUT I AM ARMORED AGAINST YOU, NOW.
I HAVE SPENT YEARS TRAINING MYSELF TO RESIST YOUR POWER.
DO YOU HONESTLY THINK I WOULD EVEN HAVE ATTEMPTED TO CAPTURE AND HOLD YOU, WERE THAT NOT THE CASE?
AND NOW, I HAVE MANY THINGS TO ATTEND TO.
I WILL BID YOU GOOD DAY, MOTHER.
"WE WILL TALK AGAIN TOMORROW."
WE WILL DO MORE THAN TALK, TWO-EDGE.
ARMORED YOU MAY THINK YOU ARE, AGAINST MY POWER...
...BUT YOU HAVE STUCK YOUR FAT NOSE INTO A PLACE YOU CANNOT EVEN START TO UNDERSTAND.
THINK YOURSELF A MATCH FOR WINNOWILL, DO YOU?
IGNORANT SLUG! YOUR PRISONER I MAY BE, FOR NOW...
...BUT I'LL NOT SLEEP UNTIL...
SLEEP..!

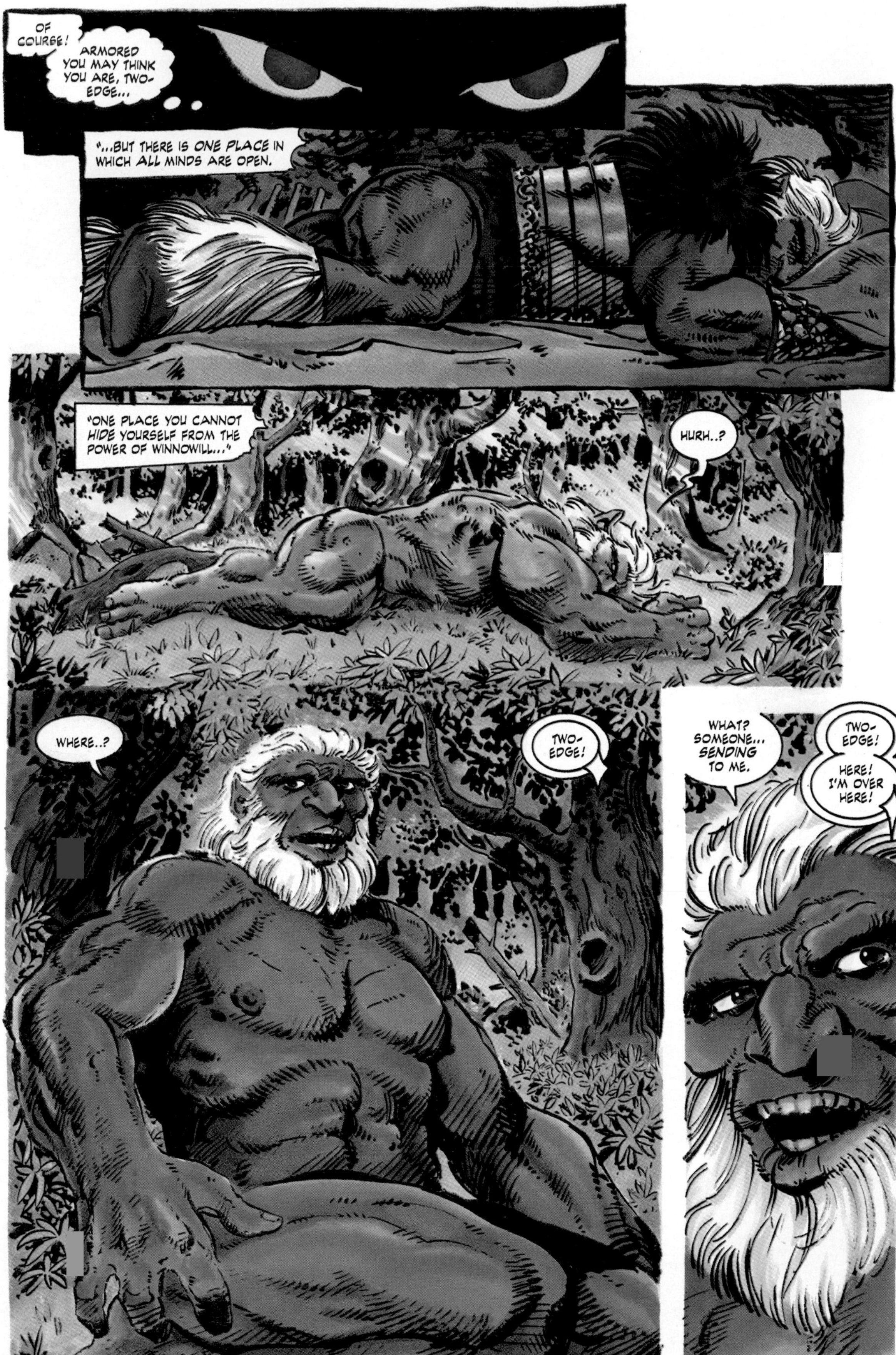
OF COURSE!
ARMORED YOU MAY THINK YOU ARE, TWO-EDGE...
"...BUT THERE IS ONE PLACE IN WHICH ALL MINDS ARE OPEN.
"ONE PLACE YOU CANNOT HIDE YOURSELF FROM THE POWER OF WINNOWILL..."
HURH..?
WHERE..?
TWO-EDGE!
WHAT? SOMEONE... SENDING TO ME.
TWO-EDGE!
HERE! I'M OVER HERE!

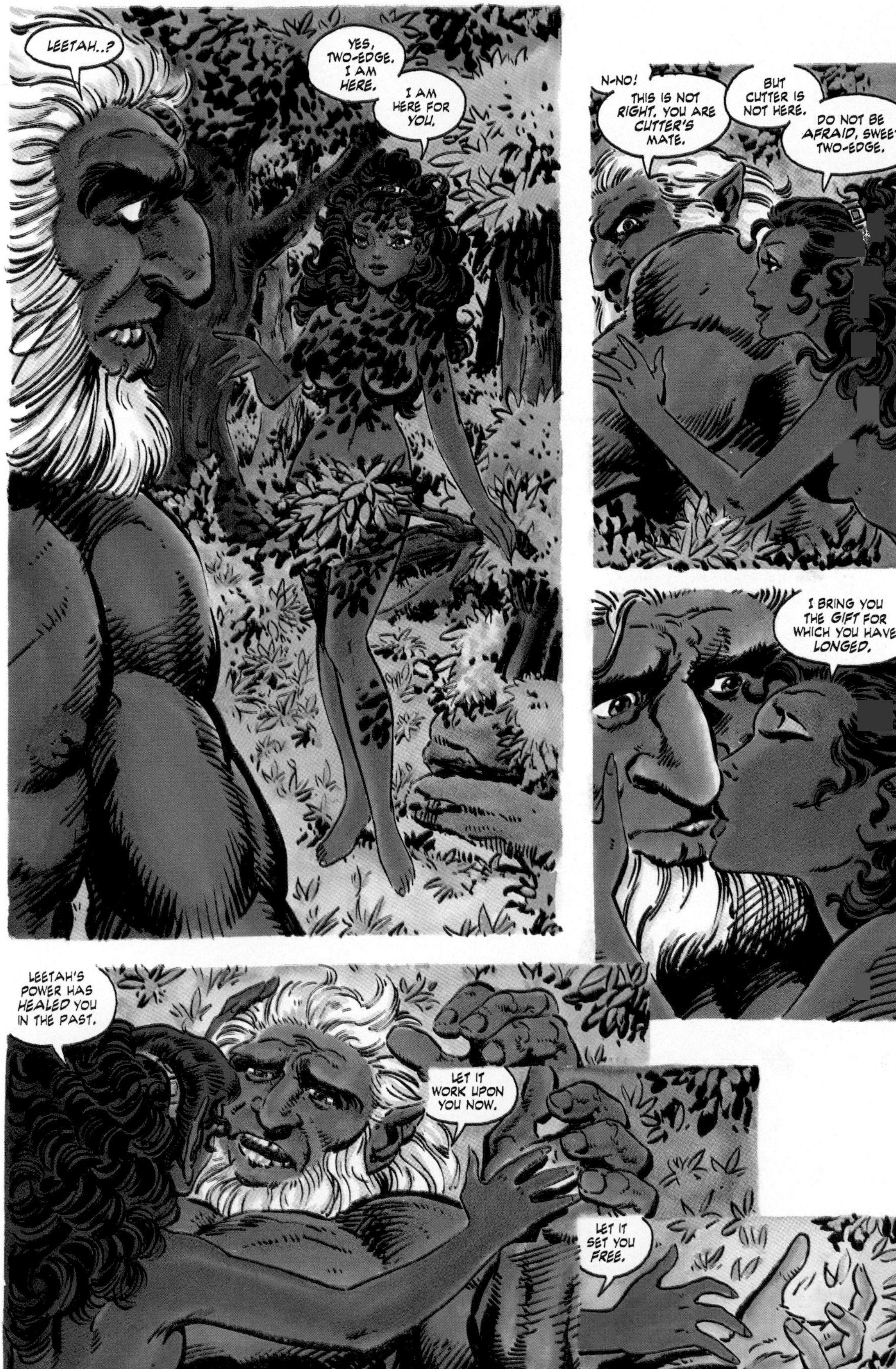
LEETAH..?
YES, TWO-EDGE. I AM HERE.
I AM HERE FOR YOU.
N-NO! THIS IS NOT RIGHT. YOU ARE CUTTER'S MATE.
BUT CUTTER IS NOT HERE.
DO NOT BE AFRAID, SWEET TWO-EDGE.
I BRING YOU THE GIFT FOR WHICH YOU HAVE LONGED.
LEETAH'S POWER HAS HEALED YOU IN THE PAST.
LET IT WORK UPON YOU NOW.
LET IT SET YOU FREE.

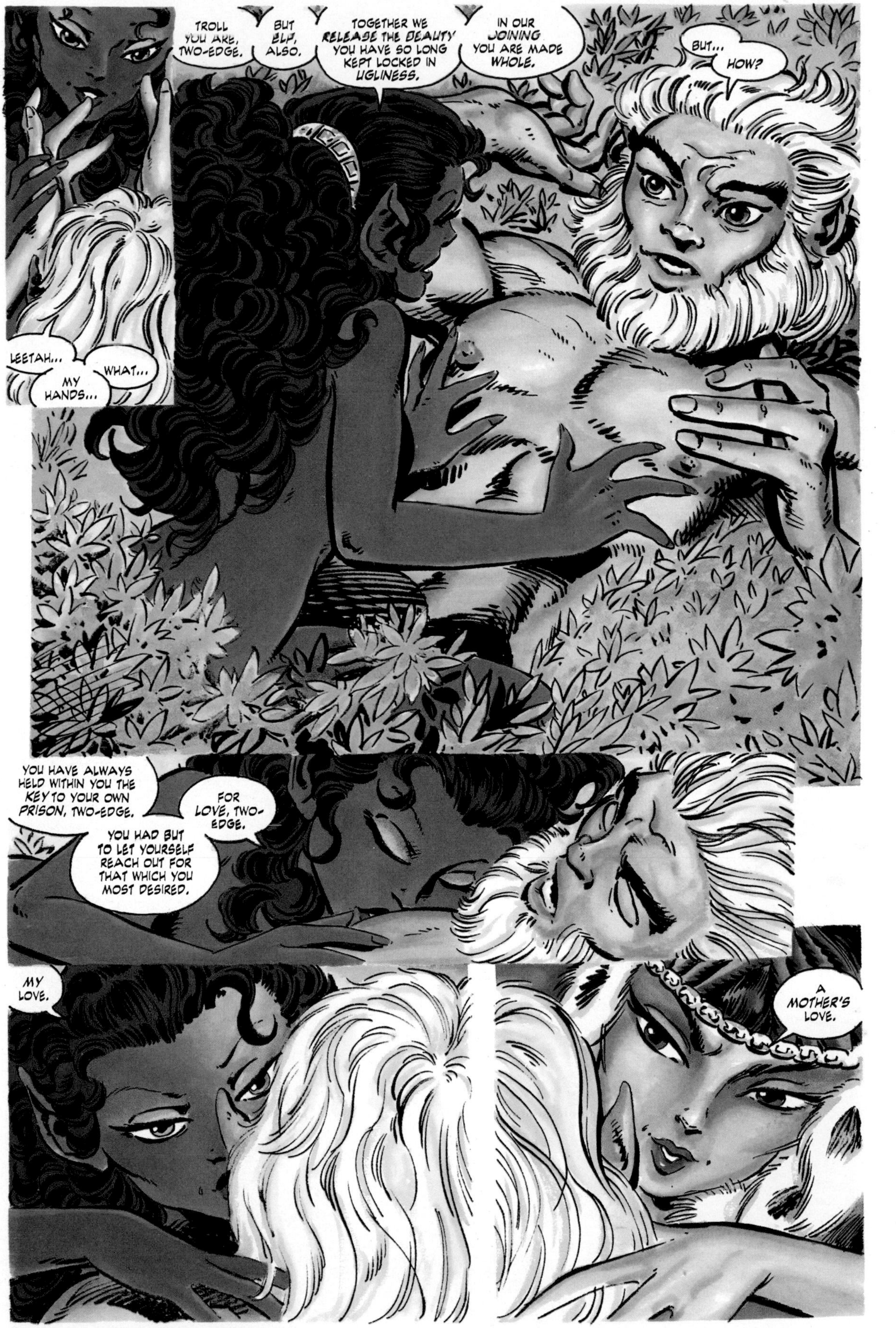
TROLL YOU ARE, TWO-EDGE.
BUT ELF, ALSO.
TOGETHER WE RELEASE THE BEAUTY YOU HAVE SO LONG KEPT LOCKED IN UGLINESS.
IN OUR JOINING YOU ARE MADE WHOLE.
BUT... HOW?
LEETAH...
WHAT...
MY HANDS...
YOU HAVE ALWAYS HELD WITHIN YOU THE KEY TO YOUR OWN PRISON, TWO-EDGE.
YOU HAD BUT TO LET YOURSELF REACH OUT FOR THAT WHICH YOU MOST DESIRED.
FOR LOVE, TWO-EDGE.
MY LOVE.
A MOTHER'S LOVE.

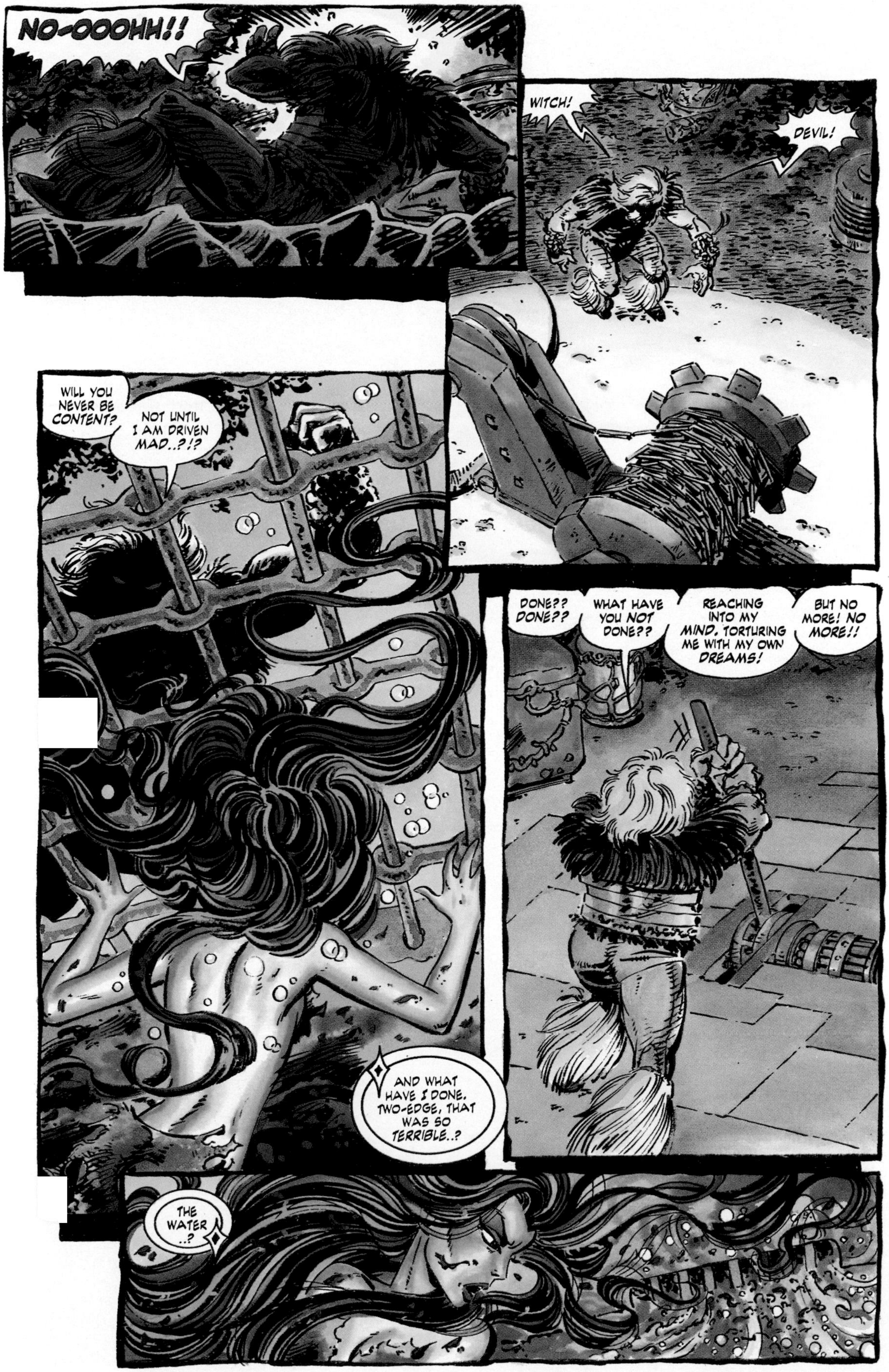
NO-OOOHH!!
WITCH!
DEVIL!
WILL YOU NEVER BE CONTENT?
NOT UNTIL I AM DRIVEN MAD..?!?
DONE?? DONE??
WHAT HAVE YOU NOT DONE??
REACHING INTO MY MIND, TORTURING ME WITH MY OWN DREAMS!
BUT NO MORE! NO MORE!!
AND WHAT HAVE I DONE, TWO-EDGE, THAT WAS SO TERRIBLE..?
THE WATER ..?

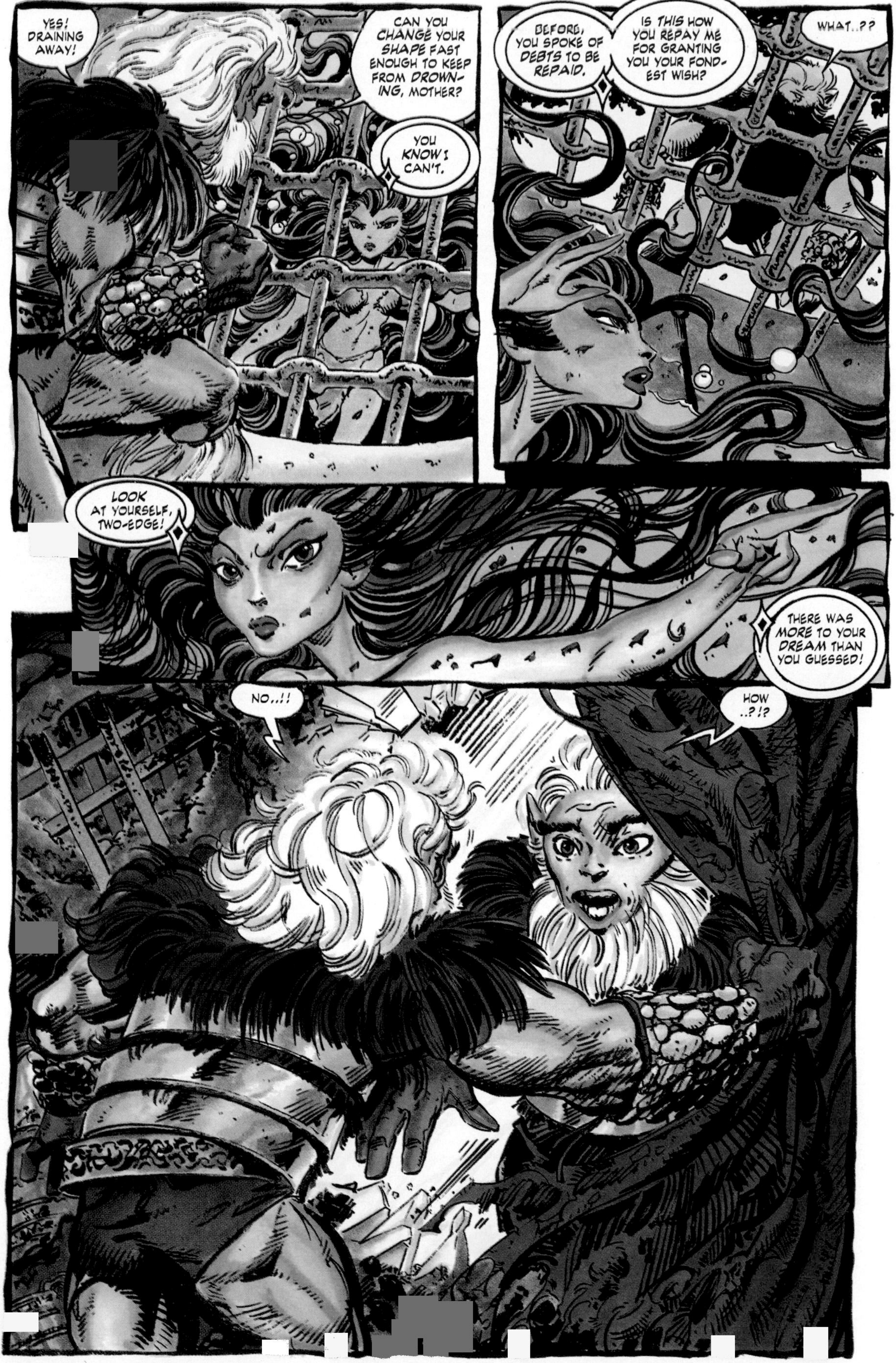

YES! DRAINING AWAY!
CAN YOU CHANGE YOUR SHAPE FAST ENOUGH TO KEEP FROM DROWN-ING, MOTHER?
YOU KNOW I CAN'T.
BEFORE, YOU SPOKE OF DEBTS TO BE REPAID.
IS THIS HOW YOU REPAY ME FOR GRANTING YOU YOUR FOND-EST WISH?
WHAT..??
LOOK AT YOURSELF, TWO-EDGE!
THERE WAS MORE TO YOUR DREAM THAN YOU GUESSED!
NO..!!
HOW ..?!?

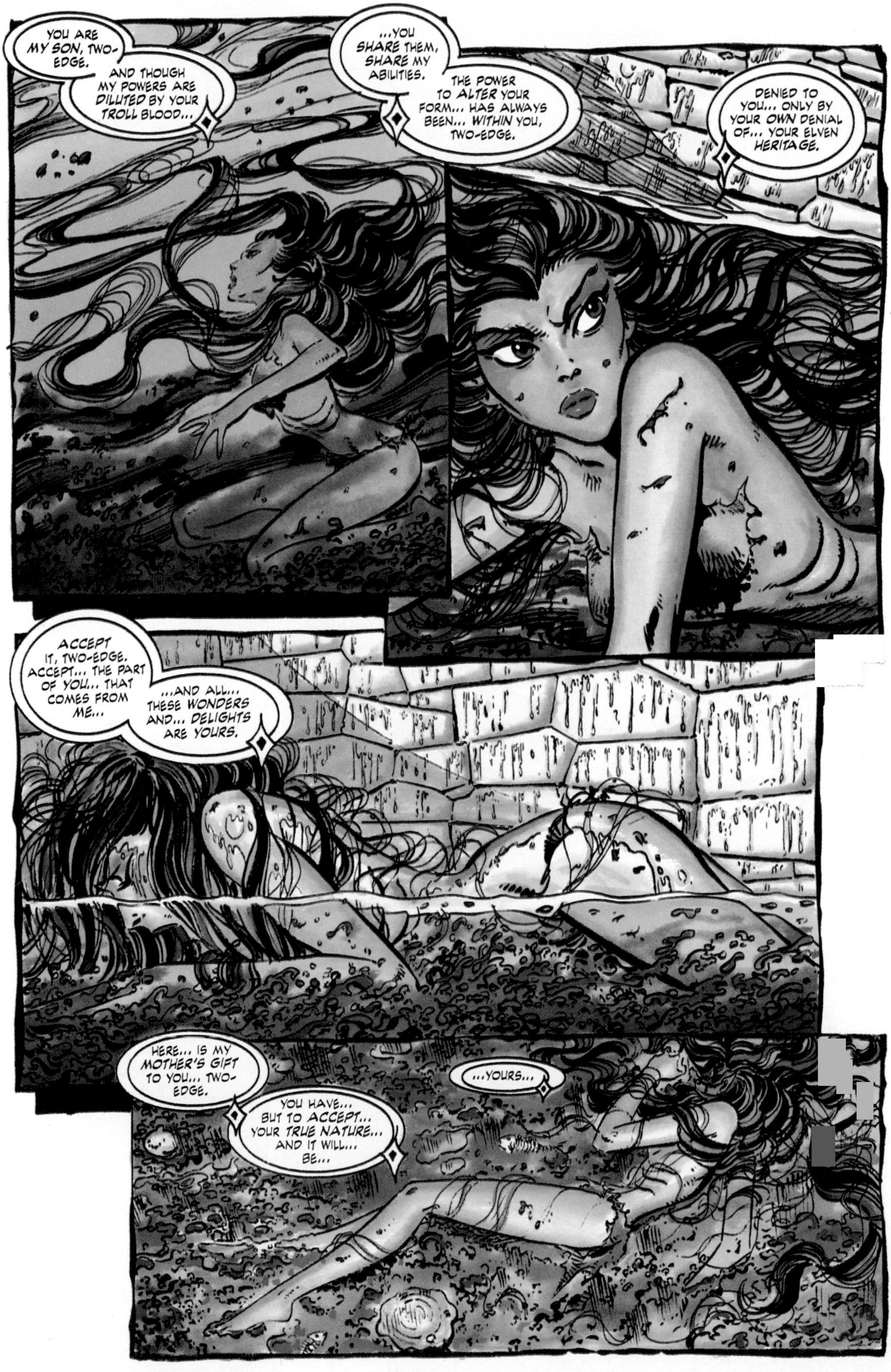
YOU ARE MY SON, TWO-EDGE.
AND THOUGH MY POWERS ARE DILUTED BY YOUR TROLL BLOOD...
...YOU SHARE THEM, SHARE MY ABILITIES.
THE POWER TO ALTER YOUR FORM... HAS ALWAYS BEEN... WITHIN YOU, TWO-EDGE.
DENIED TO YOU... ONLY BY YOUR OWN DENIAL OF... YOUR ELVEN HERITAGE.
ACCEPT IT, TWO-EDGE. ACCEPT... THE PART OF YOU... THAT COMES FROM ME...
...AND ALL... THESE WONDERS AND... DELIGHTS ARE YOURS.
HERE... IS MY MOTHER'S GIFT TO YOU... TWO-EDGE.
YOU HAVE... BUT TO ACCEPT... YOUR TRUE NATURE... AND IT WILL... BE...
...YOURS...

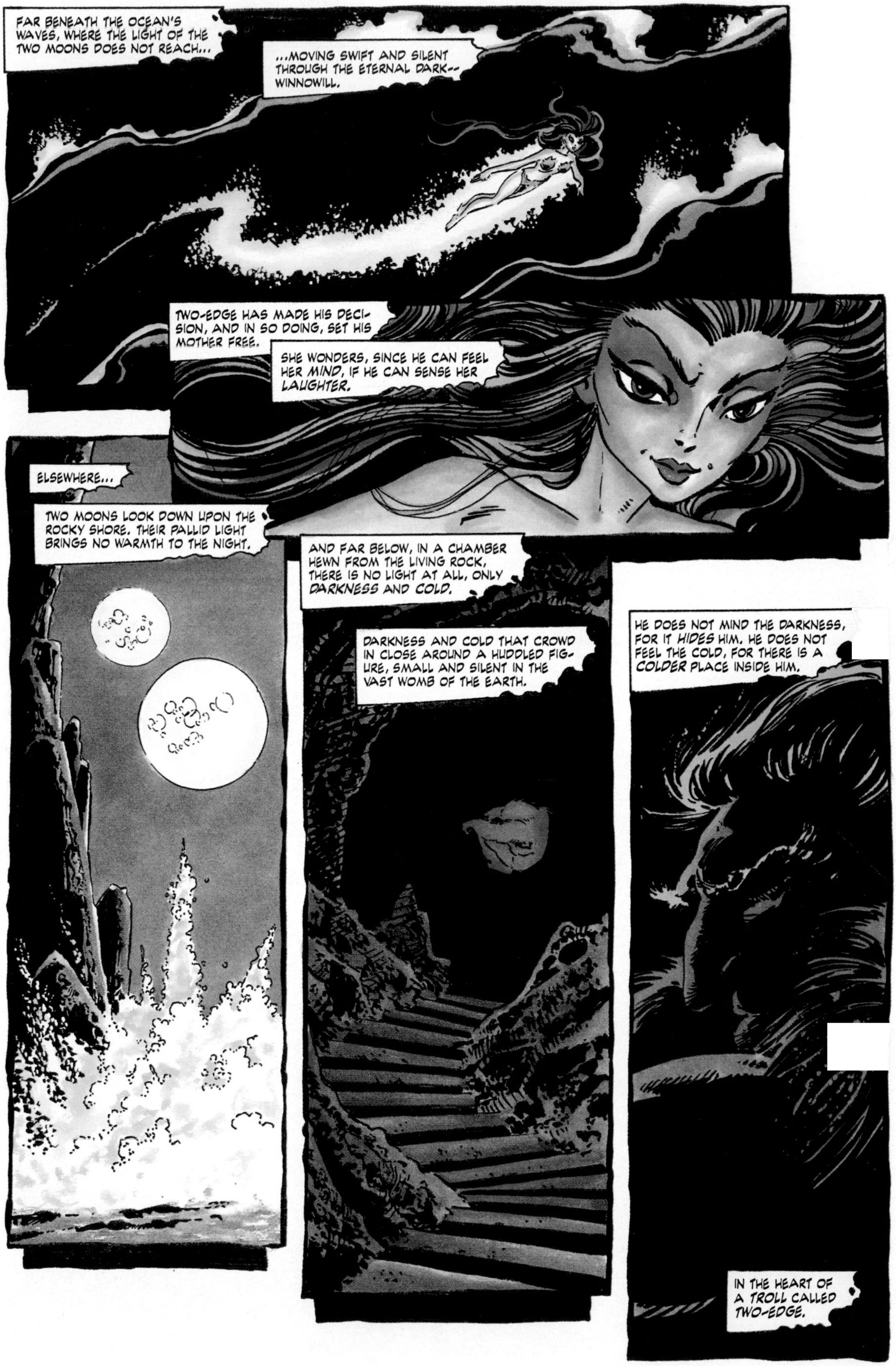
FAR BENEATH THE OCEAN'S WAVES, WHERE THE LIGHT OF THE TWO MOONS DOES NOT REACH...
...MOVING SWIFT AND SILENT THROUGH THE ETERNAL DARK-- WINNOWILL.
TWO-EDGE HAS MADE HIS DECISION, AND IN SO DOING, SET HIS MOTHER FREE.
SHE WONDERS, SINCE HE CAN FEEL HER MIND, IF HE CAN SENSE HER LAUGHTER.
ELSEWHERE...
TWO MOONS LOOK DOWN UPON THE ROCKY SHORE. THEIR PALLID LIGHT BRINGS NO WARMTH TO THE NIGHT.
AND FAR BELOW, IN A CHAMBER HEWN FROM THE LIVING ROCK, THERE IS NO LIGHT AT ALL, ONLY DARKNESS AND COLD.
DARKNESS AND COLD THAT CROWD IN CLOSE AROUND A HUDDLED FIGURE, SMALL AND SILENT IN THE VAST WOMB OF THE EARTH.
HE DOES NOT MIND THE DARKNESS, FOR IT HIDES HIM. HE DOES NOT FEEL THE COLD, FOR THERE IS A COLDER PLACE INSIDE HIM.
IN THE HEART OF A TROLL CALLED TWO-EDGE.

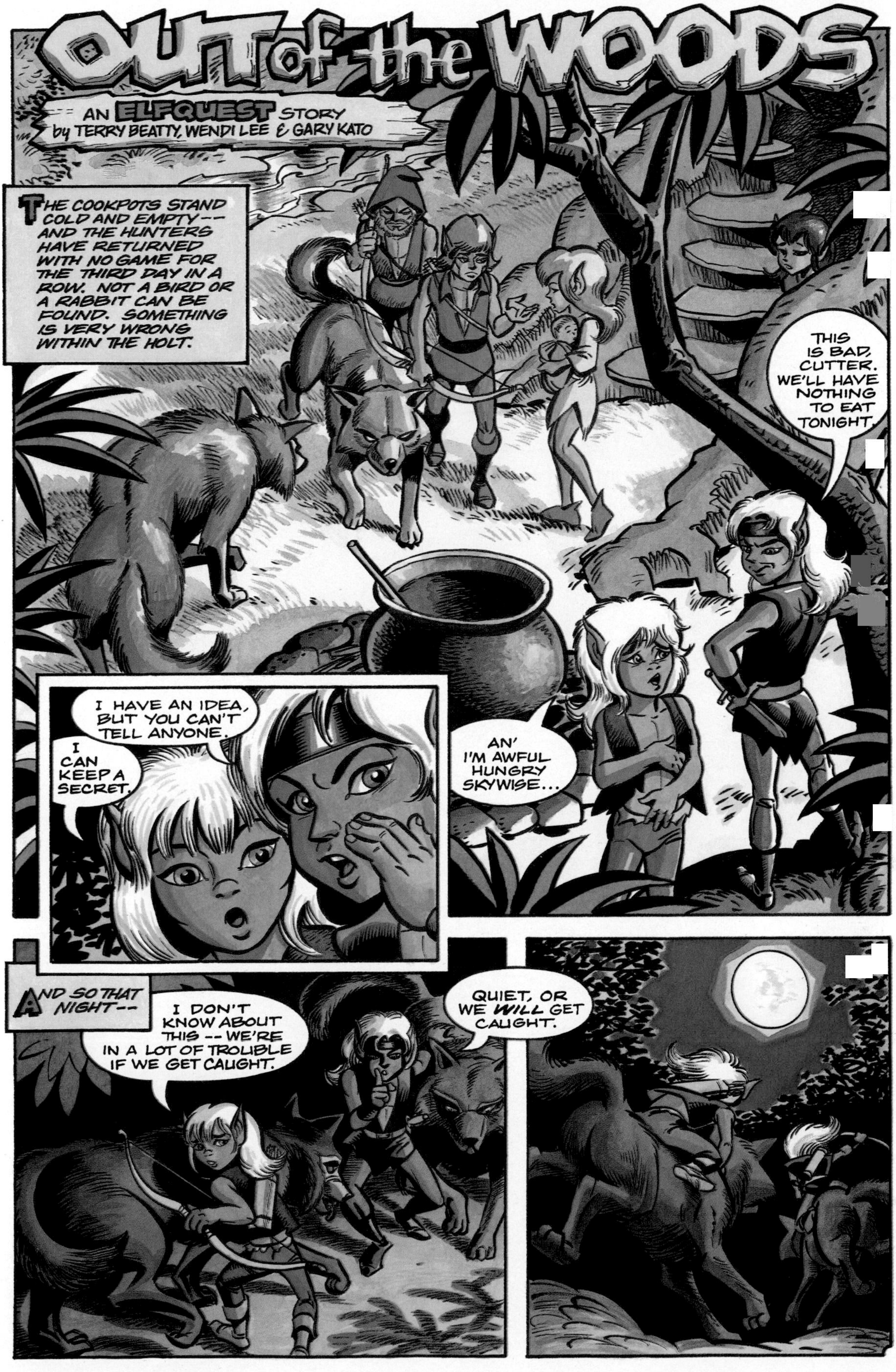
OUT of the WOODS
AN ELFQUEST STORY
by TERRY BEATTY, WENDI LEE & GARY KATO
THE COOKPOTS STAND COLD AND EMPTY -- AND THE HUNTERS HAVE RETURNED WITH NO GAME FOR THE THIRD DAY IN A ROW. NOT A BIRD OR A RABBIT CAN BE FOUND. SOMETHING IS VERY WRONG WITHIN THE HOLT.
THIS IS BAD, CUTTER. WE'LL HAVE NOTHING TO EAT TONIGHT.
AN' I'M AWFUL HUNGRY SKYWISE...
I HAVE AN IDEA, BUT YOU CAN'T TELL ANYONE.
I CAN KEEP A SECRET.
AND SO THAT NIGHT --
I DON'T KNOW ABOUT THIS -- WE'RE IN A LOT OF TROUBLE IF WE GET CAUGHT.
QUIET, OR WE WILL GET CAUGHT.

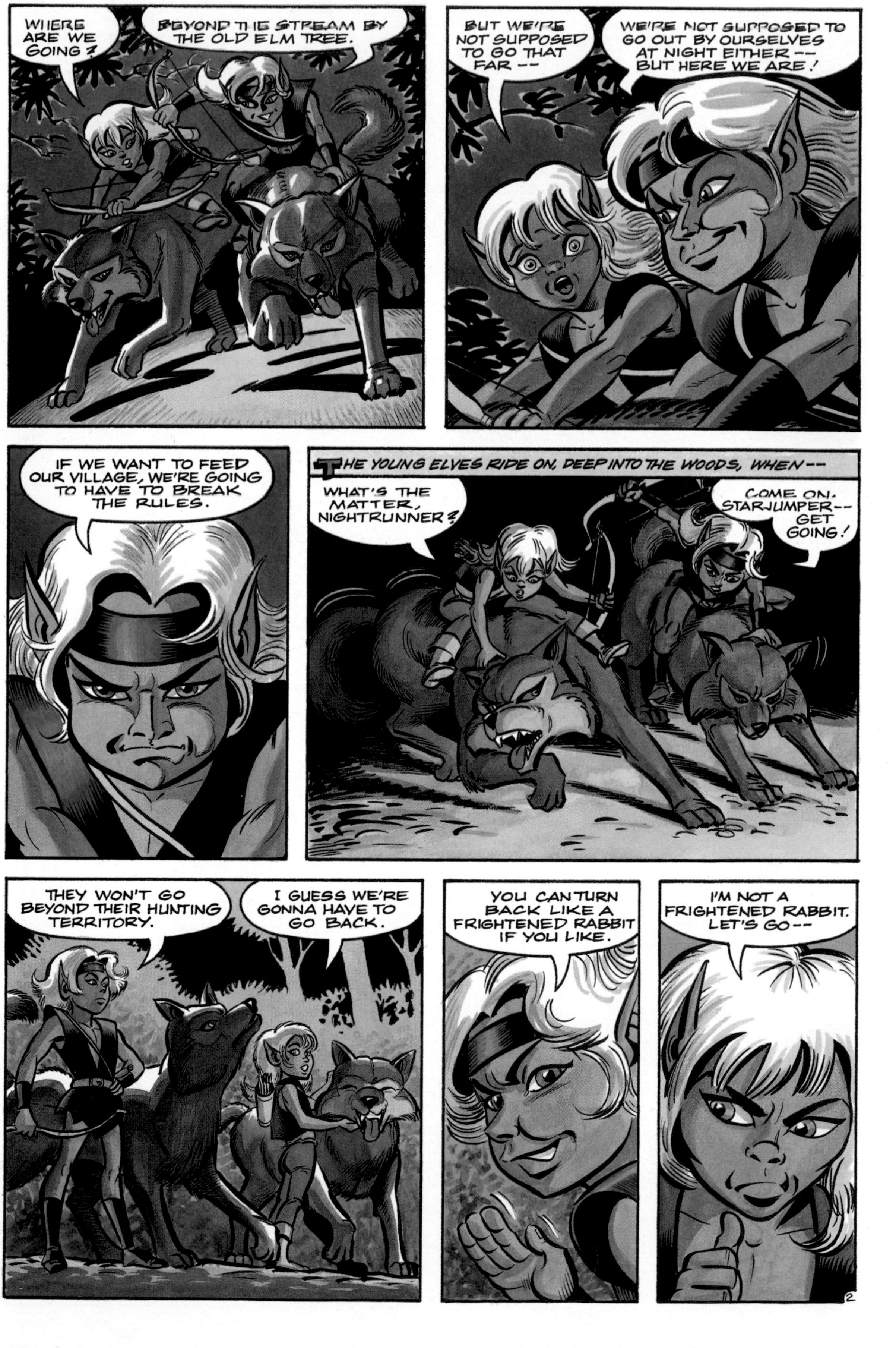

WHERE ARE WE GOING?
BEYOND THE STREAM BY THE OLD ELM TREE.
BUT WE'RE NOT SUPPOSED TO GO THAT FAR --
WE'RE NOT SUPPOSED TO GO OUT BY OURSELVES AT NIGHT EITHER -- BUT HERE WE ARE!
IF WE WANT TO FEED OUR VILLAGE, WE'RE GOING TO HAVE TO BREAK THE RULES.
THE YOUNG ELVES RIDE ON, DEEP INTO THE WOODS, WHEN --
WHAT'S THE MATTER, NIGHTRUNNER?
COME ON, STARJUMPER -- GET GOING!
THEY WON'T GO BEYOND THEIR HUNTING TERRITORY.
I GUESS WE'RE GONNA HAVE TO GO BACK.
YOU CAN TURN BACK LIKE A FRIGHTENED RABBIT IF YOU LIKE.
I'M NOT A FRIGHTENED RABBIT. LET'S GO --

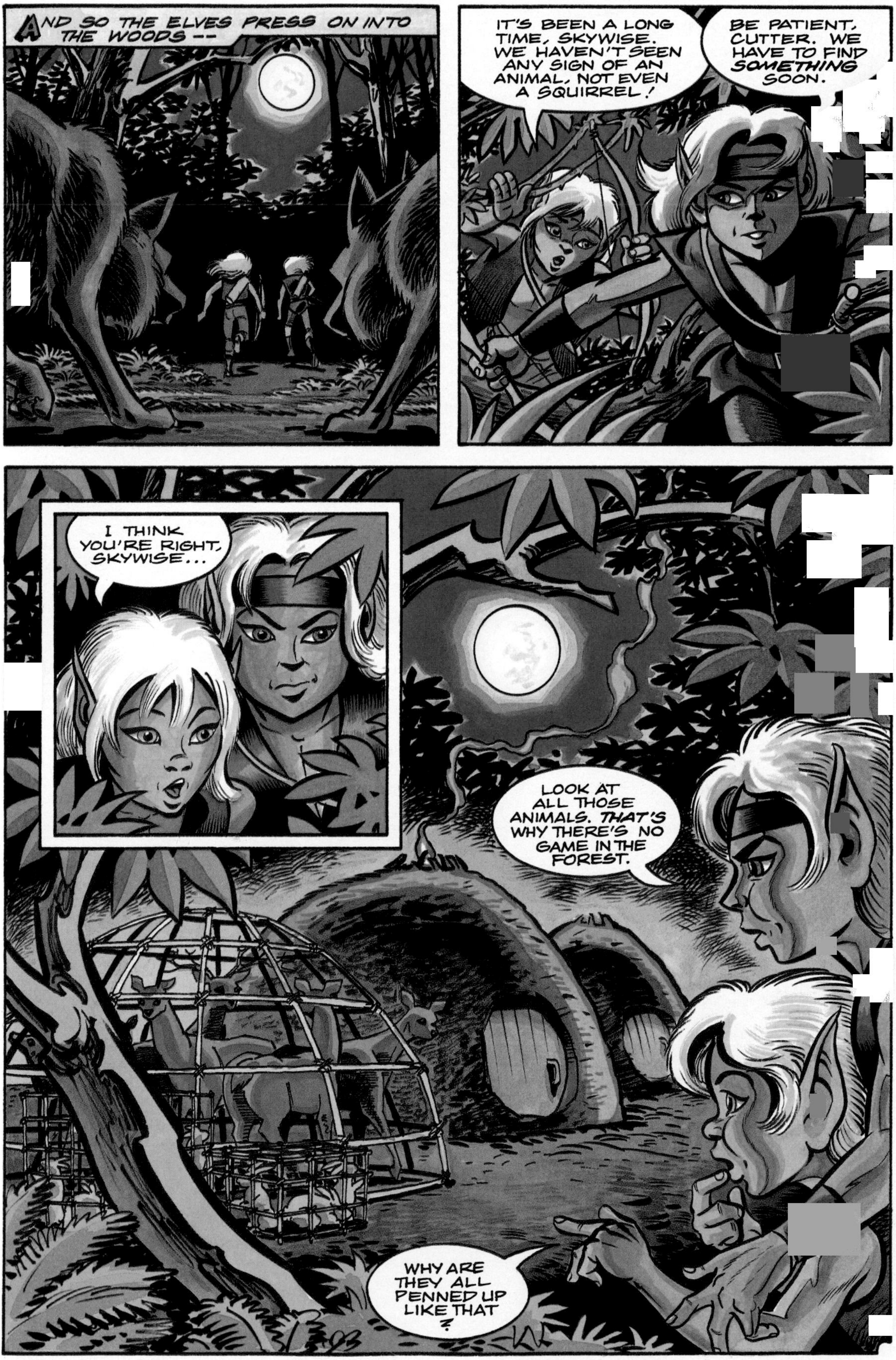
AND SO THE ELVES PRESS ON INTO THE WOODS --
IT'S BEEN A LONG TIME, SKYWISE. WE HAVEN'T SEEN ANY SIGN OF AN ANIMAL, NOT EVEN A SQUIRREL!
BE PATIENT, CUTTER. WE HAVE TO FIND SOMETHING SOON.
I THINK YOU'RE RIGHT, SKYWISE...
LOOK AT ALL THOSE ANIMALS. THAT'S WHY THERE'S NO GAME IN THE FOREST.
WHY ARE THEY ALL PENNED UP LIKE THAT?

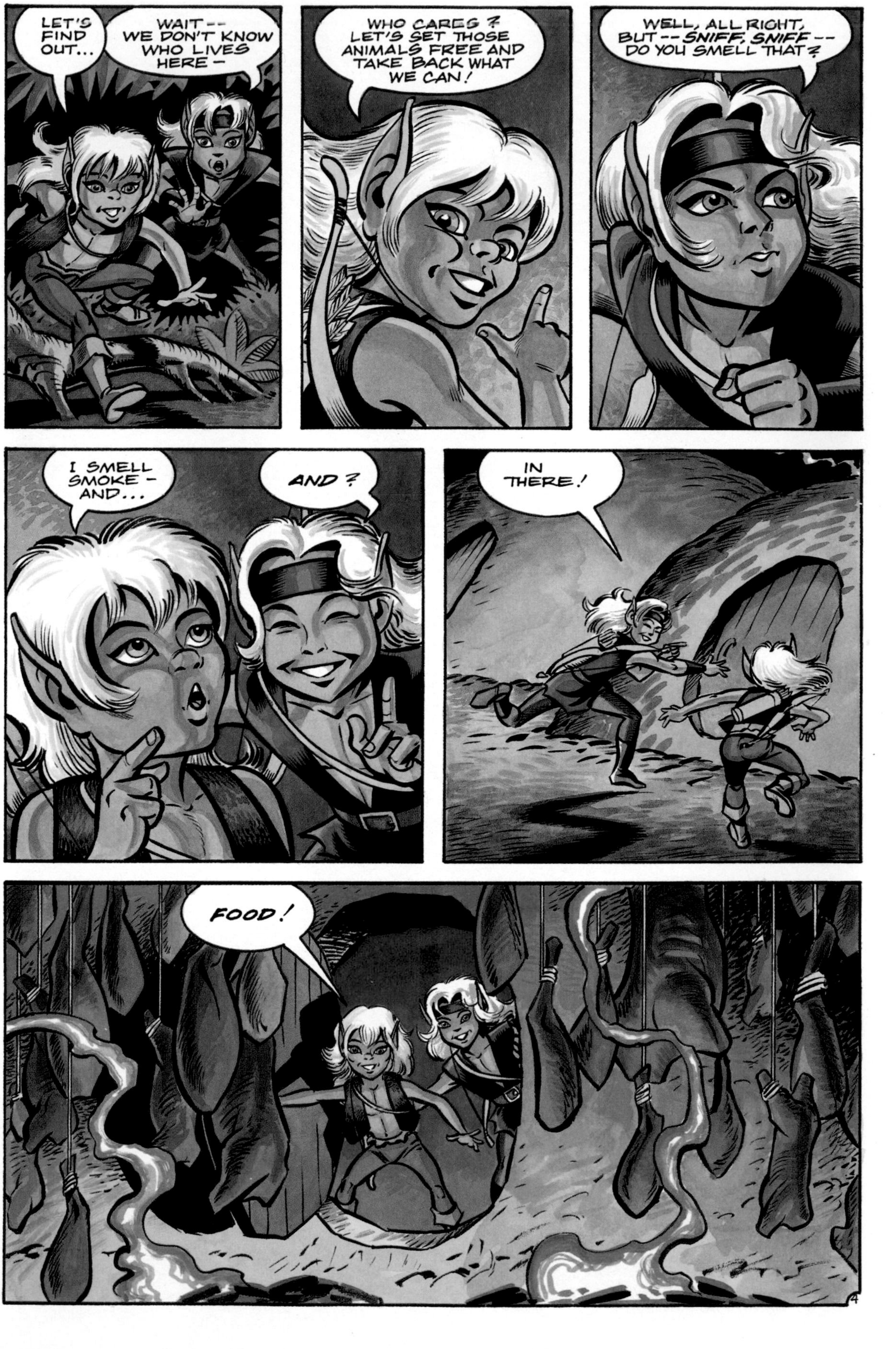
LET'S FIND OUT...
WAIT -- WE DON'T KNOW WHO LIVES HERE -
WHO CARES ? LET'S SET THOSE ANIMALS FREE AND TAKE BACK WHAT WE CAN!
WELL, ALL RIGHT, BUT -- SNIFF, SNIFF -- DO YOU SMELL THAT ?
I SMELL SMOKE - AND...
AND ?
IN THERE!
FOOD!

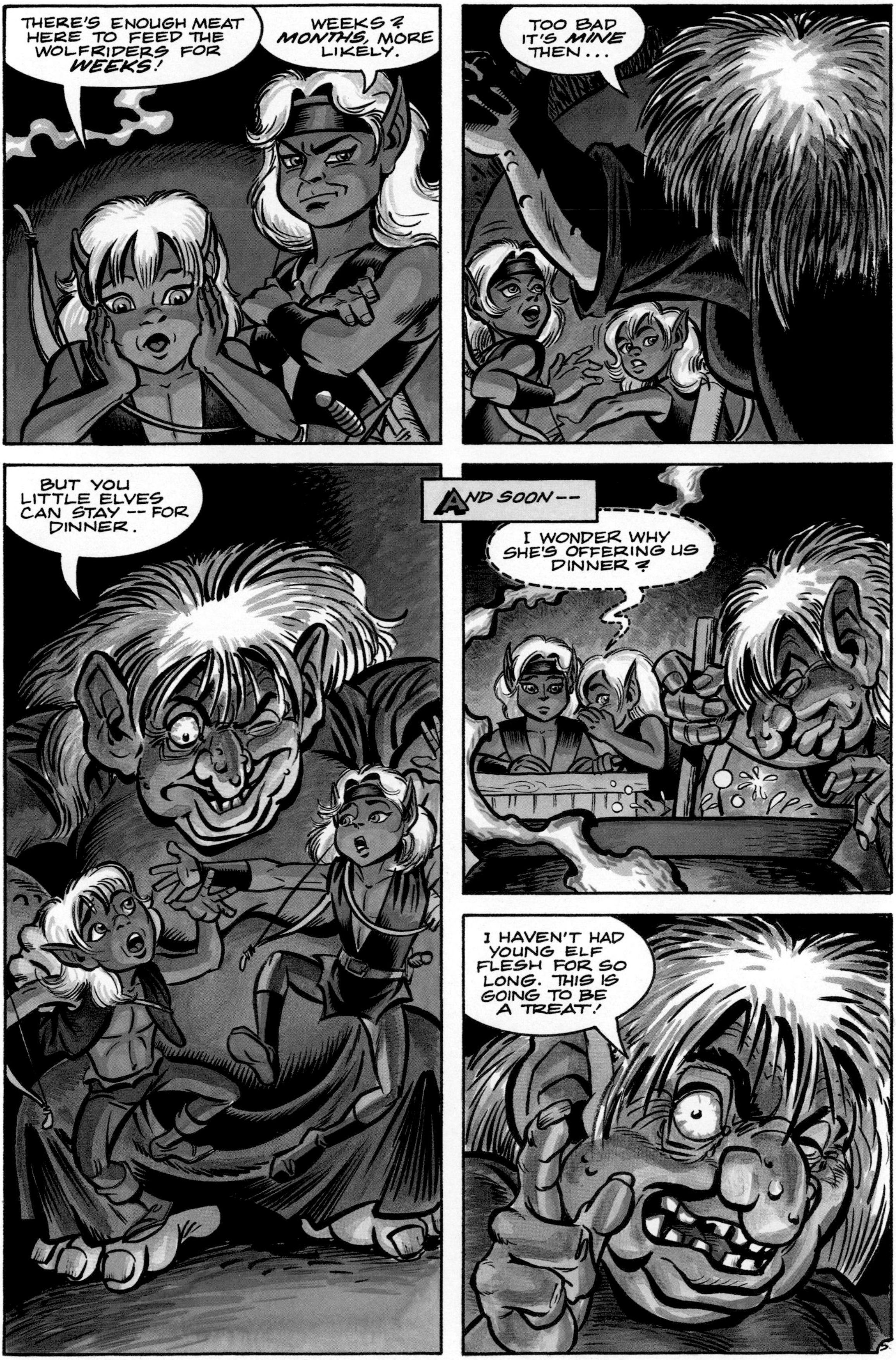
THERE'S ENOUGH MEAT HERE TO FEED THE WOLFRIDERS FOR WEEKS!
WEEKS? MONTHS, MORE LIKELY.
TOO BAD IT'S MINE THEN...
BUT YOU LITTLE ELVES CAN STAY -- FOR DINNER.
AND SOON --
I WONDER WHY SHE'S OFFERING US DINNER?
I HAVEN'T HAD YOUNG ELF FLESH FOR SO LONG. THIS IS GOING TO BE A TREAT!

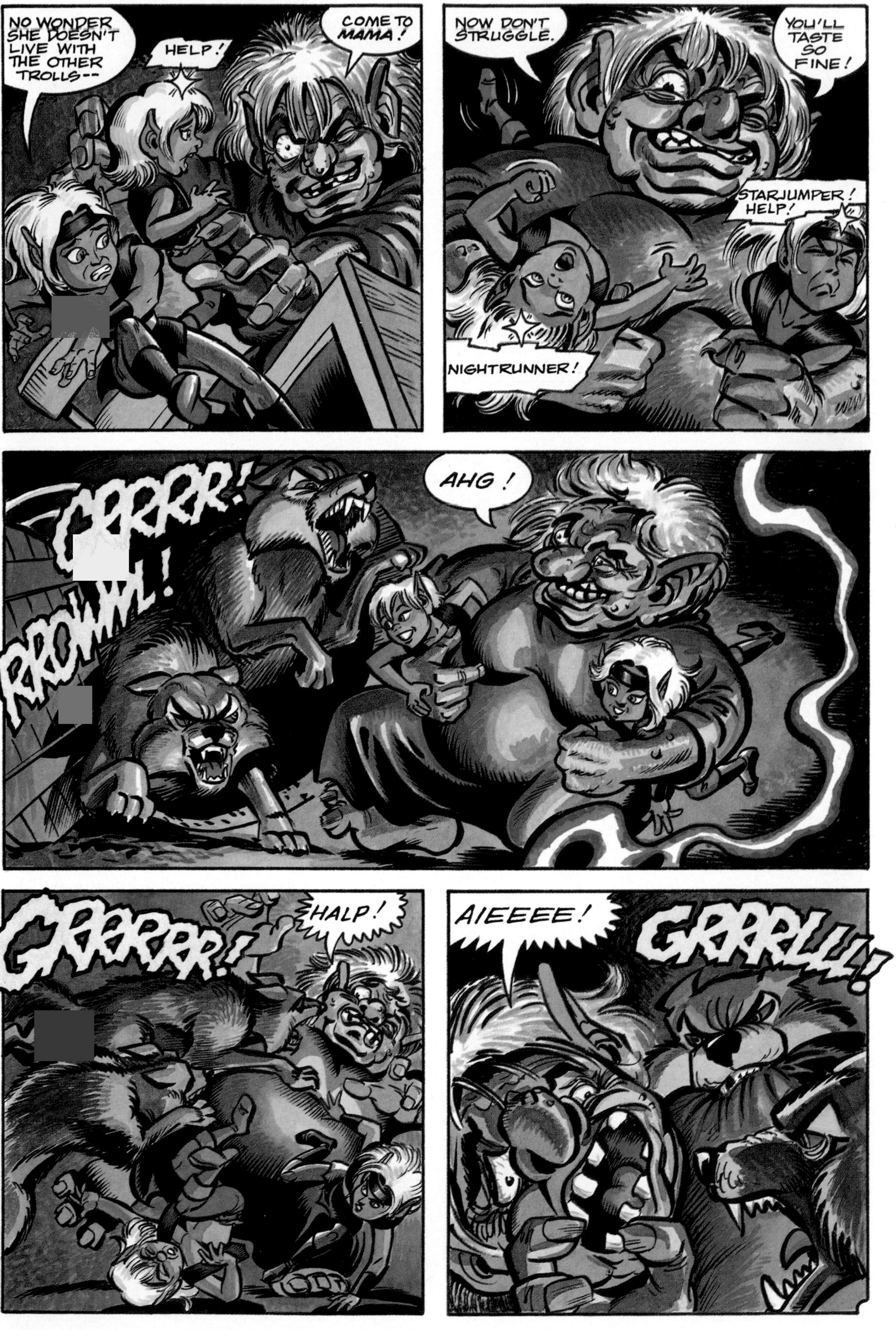
NO WONDER SHE DOESN'T LIVE WITH THE OTHER TROLLS--
HELP!
COME TO MAMA!
NOW DON'T STRUGGLE.
YOU'LL TASTE SO FINE!
STARJUMPER! HELP!
NIGHTRUNNER!
GRRRR!
RROWWL!
AHG!
GRRRRR!
HALP!
AIEEEE!
GRRRLL!

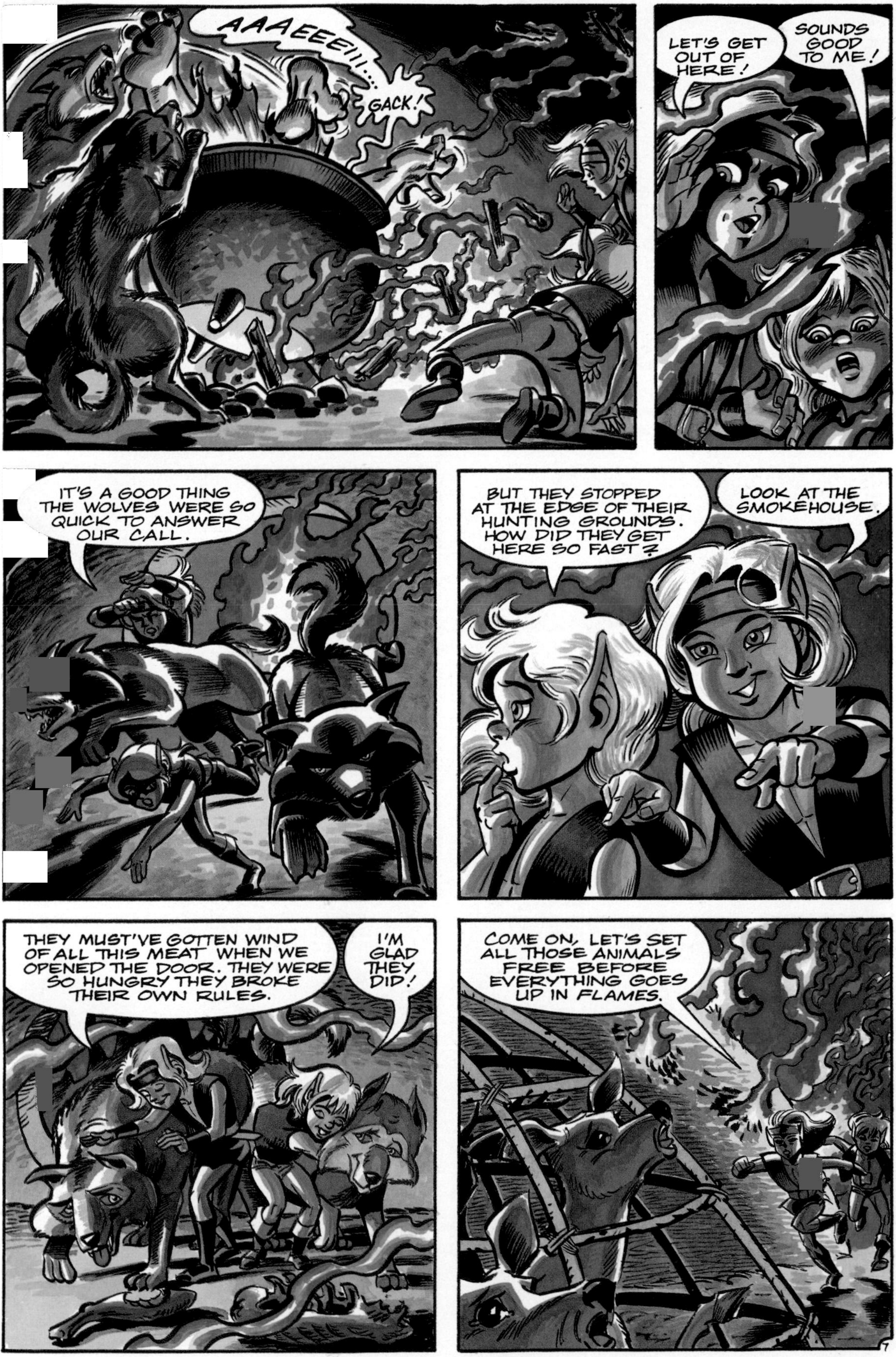
AAAEEE!!!...
GACK!
LET'S GET OUT OF HERE!
SOUNDS GOOD TO ME!
IT'S A GOOD THING THE WOLVES WERE SO QUICK TO ANSWER OUR CALL.
BUT THEY STOPPED AT THE EDGE OF THEIR HUNTING GROUNDS. HOW DID THEY GET HERE SO FAST?
LOOK AT THE SMOKEHOUSE.
THEY MUST'VE GOTTEN WIND OF ALL THIS MEAT WHEN WE OPENED THE DOOR. THEY WERE SO HUNGRY THEY BROKE THEIR OWN RULES.
I'M GLAD THEY DID!
COME ON, LET'S SET ALL THOSE ANIMALS FREE BEFORE EVERYTHING GOES UP IN FLAMES.

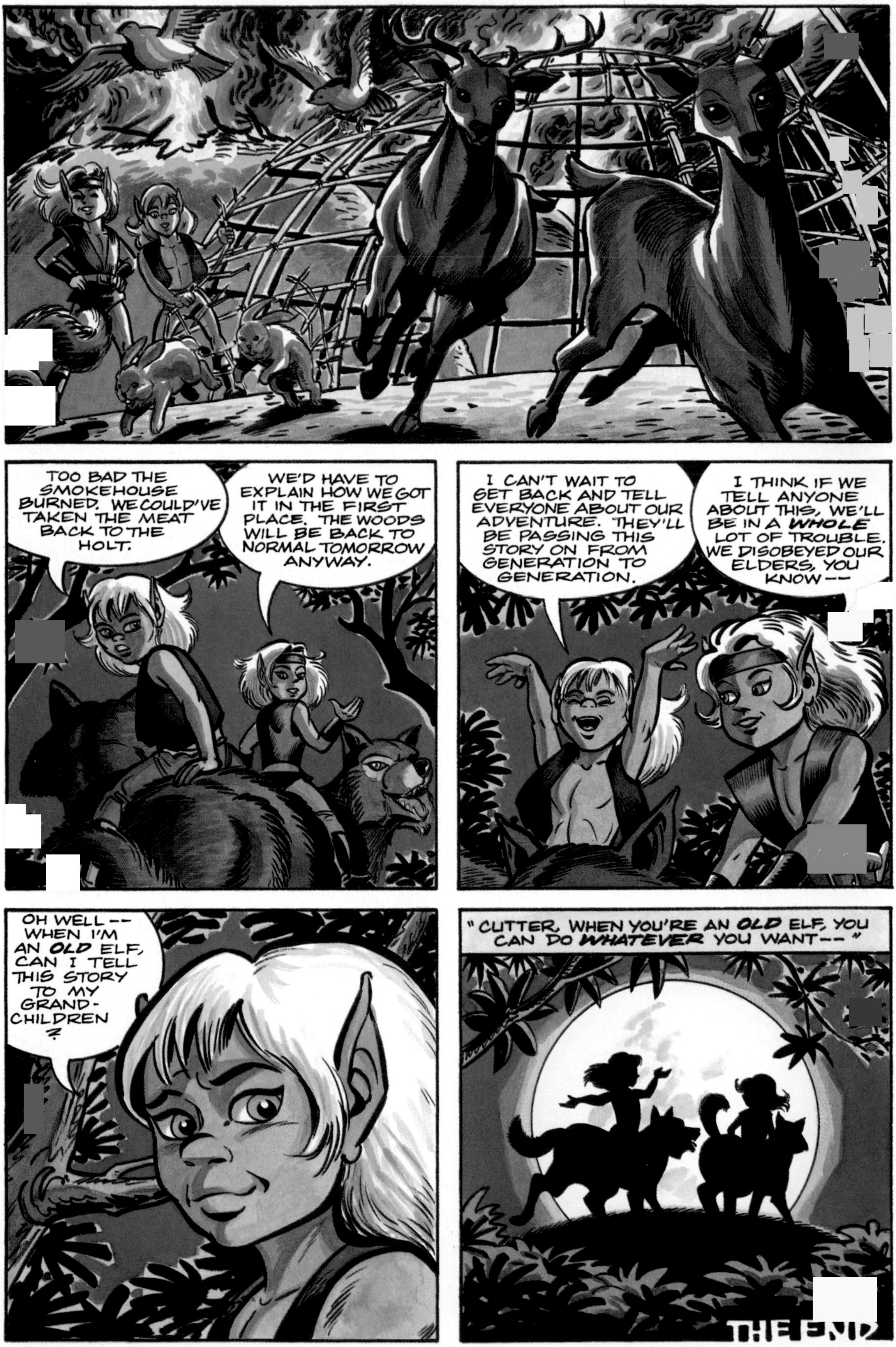
TOO BAD THE SMOKEHOUSE BURNED. WE COULD'VE TAKEN THE MEAT BACK TO THE HOLT.
WE'D HAVE TO EXPLAIN HOW WE GOT IT IN THE FIRST PLACE. THE WOODS WILL BE BACK TO NORMAL TOMORROW ANYWAY.
I CAN'T WAIT TO GET BACK AND TELL EVERYONE ABOUT OUR ADVENTURE. THEY'LL BE PASSING THIS STORY ON FROM GENERATION TO GENERATION.
I THINK IF WE TELL ANYONE ABOUT THIS, WE'LL BE IN A WHOLE LOT OF TROUBLE. WE DISOBEYED OUR ELDERS, YOU KNOW--
OH WELL -- WHEN I'M AN OLD ELF, CAN I TELL THIS STORY TO MY GRAND-CHILDREN ?
"CUTTER, WHEN YOU'RE AN OLD ELF, YOU CAN DO WHATEVER YOU WANT--"
THE END

DARKNESS RISING

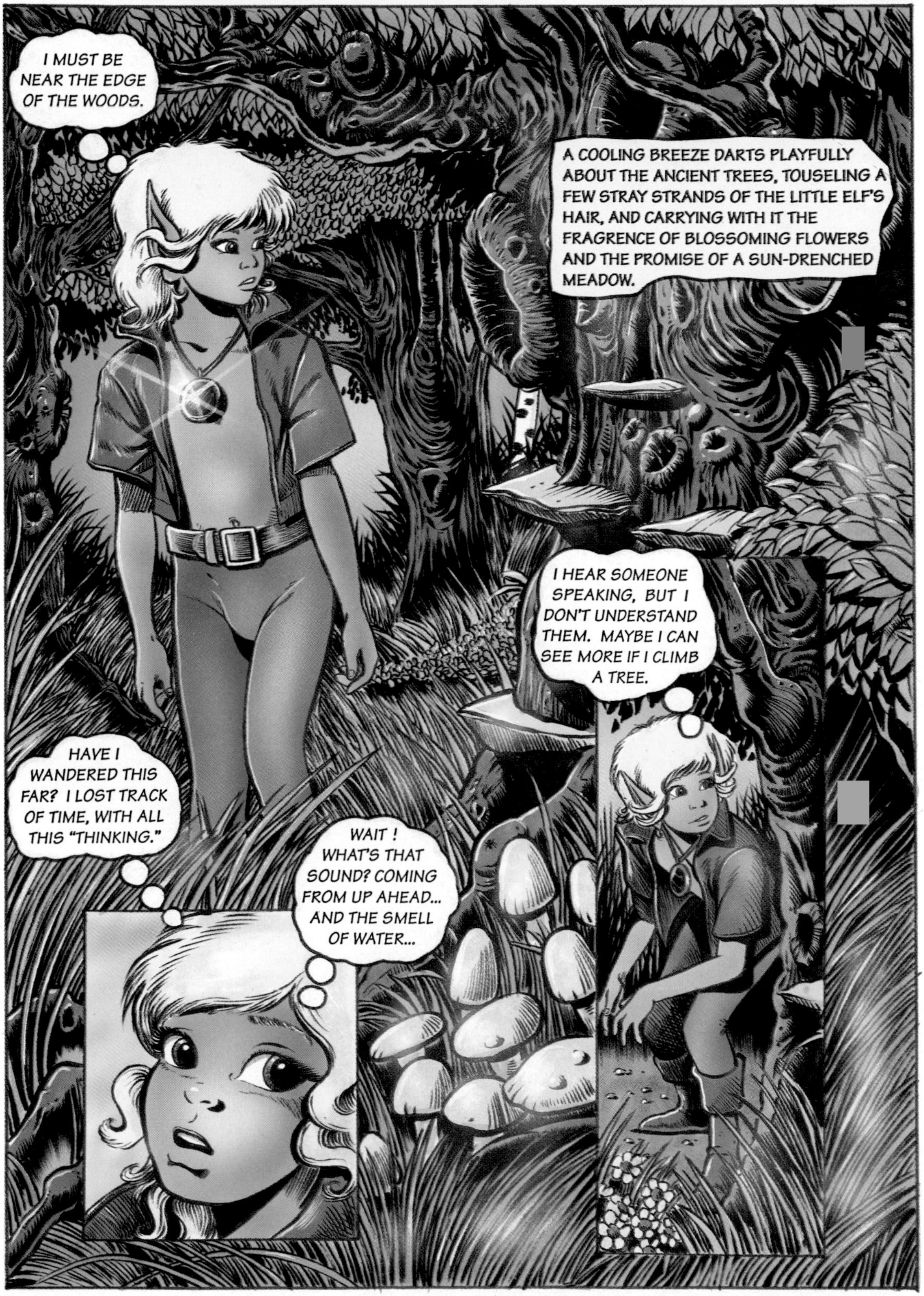
I MUST BE NEAR THE EDGE OF THE WOODS.
A COOLING BREEZE DARTS PLAYFULLY ABOUT THE ANCIENT TREES, TOUSELING A FEW STRAY STRANDS OF THE LITTLE ELF'S HAIR, AND CARRYING WITH IT THE FRAGRENCE OF BLOSSOMING FLOWERS AND THE PROMISE OF A SUN-DRENCHED MEADOW.
HAVE I WANDERED THIS FAR? I LOST TRACK OF TIME, WITH ALL THIS "THINKING."
WAIT ! WHAT'S THAT SOUND? COMING FROM UP AHEAD... AND THE SMELL OF WATER...
I HEAR SOMEONE SPEAKING, BUT I DON'T UNDERSTAND THEM. MAYBE I CAN SEE MORE IF I CLIMB A TREE.

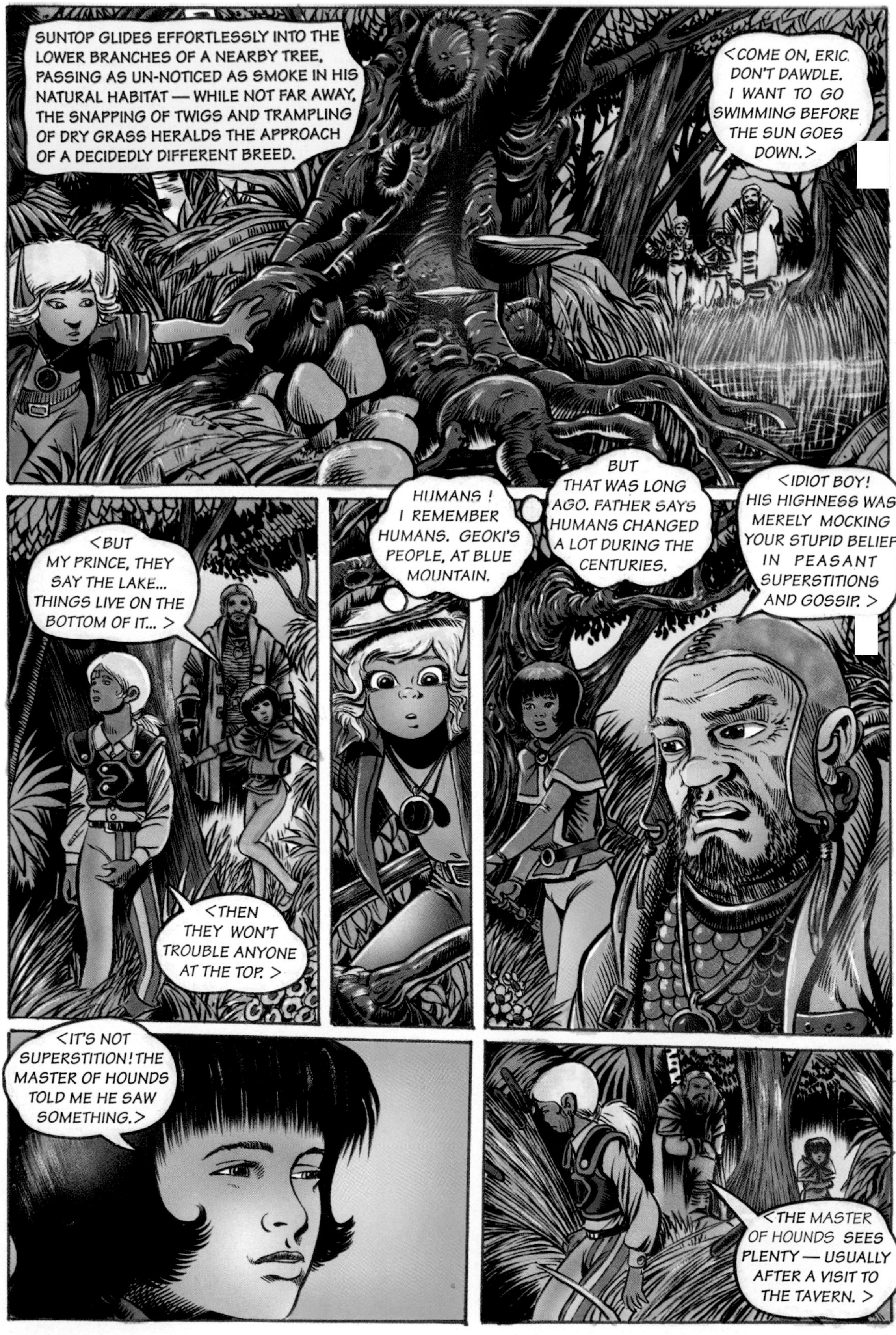
SUNTOP GLIDES EFFORTLESSLY INTO THE LOWER BRANCHES OF A NEARBY TREE, PASSING AS UN-NOTICED AS SMOKE IN HIS NATURAL HABITAT — WHILE NOT FAR AWAY, THE SNAPPING OF TWIGS AND TRAMPLING OF DRY GRASS HERALDS THE APPROACH OF A DECIDEDLY DIFFERENT BREED.
<COME ON, ERIC. DON'T DAWDLE. I WANT TO GO SWIMMING BEFORE THE SUN GOES DOWN.>
<BUT MY PRINCE, THEY SAY THE LAKE... THINGS LIVE ON THE BOTTOM OF IT... >
<THEN THEY WON'T TROUBLE ANYONE AT THE TOP. >
HUMANS ! I REMEMBER HUMANS. GEOKI'S PEOPLE, AT BLUE MOUNTAIN.
BUT THAT WAS LONG AGO. FATHER SAYS HUMANS CHANGED A LOT DURING THE CENTURIES.
<IDIOT BOY! HIS HIGHNESS WAS MERELY MOCKING YOUR STUPID BELIEF IN PEASANT SUPERSTITIONS AND GOSSIP. >
<IT'S NOT SUPERSTITION! THE MASTER OF HOUNDS TOLD ME HE SAW SOMETHING.>
<THE MASTER OF HOUNDS SEES PLENTY — USUALLY AFTER A VISIT TO THE TAVERN. >

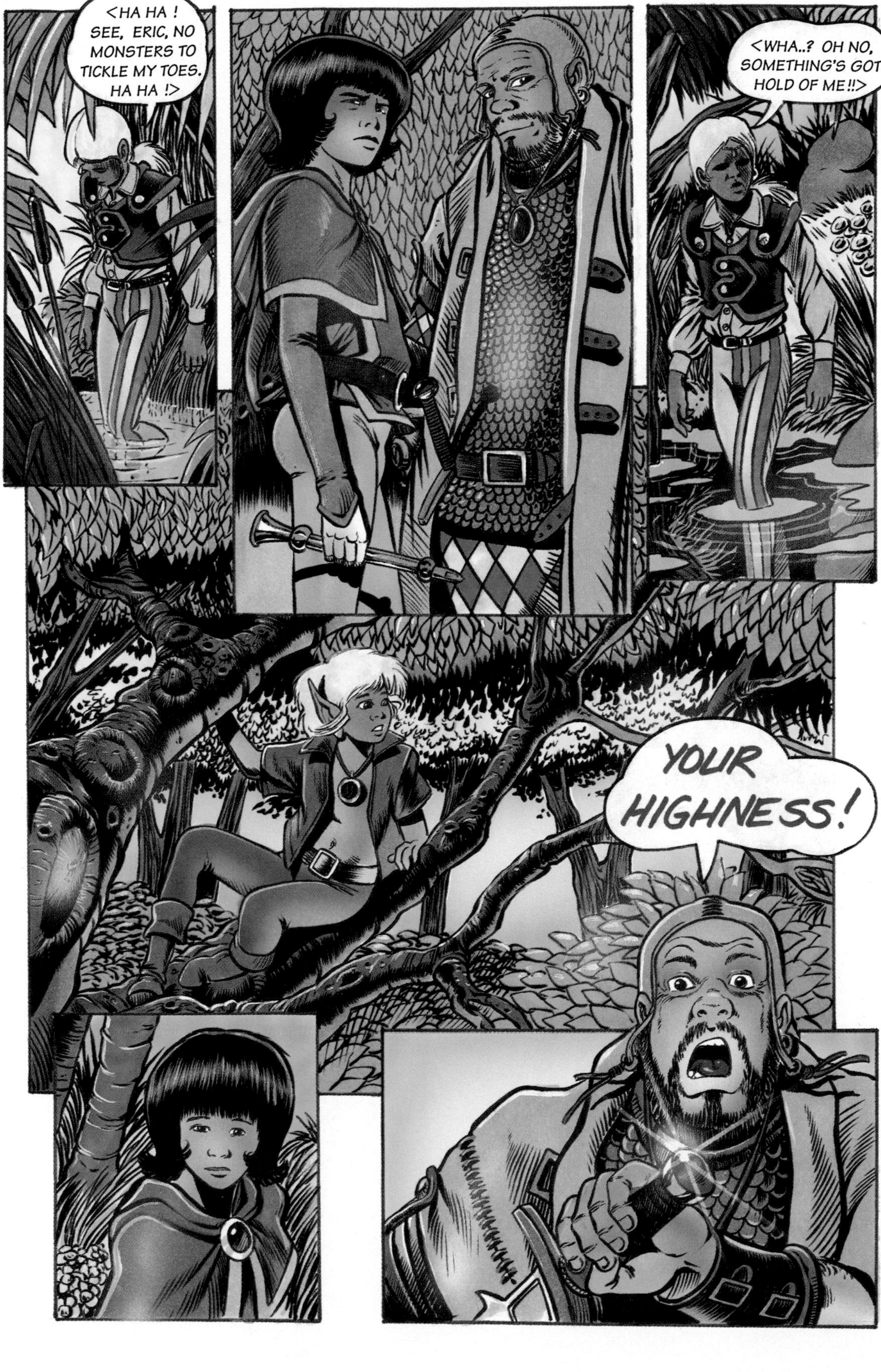
<HA HA ! SEE, ERIC, NO MONSTERS TO TICKLE MY TOES. HA HA !>
<WHA..? OH NO, SOMETHING'S GOT HOLD OF ME !!>
YOUR HIGHNESS!

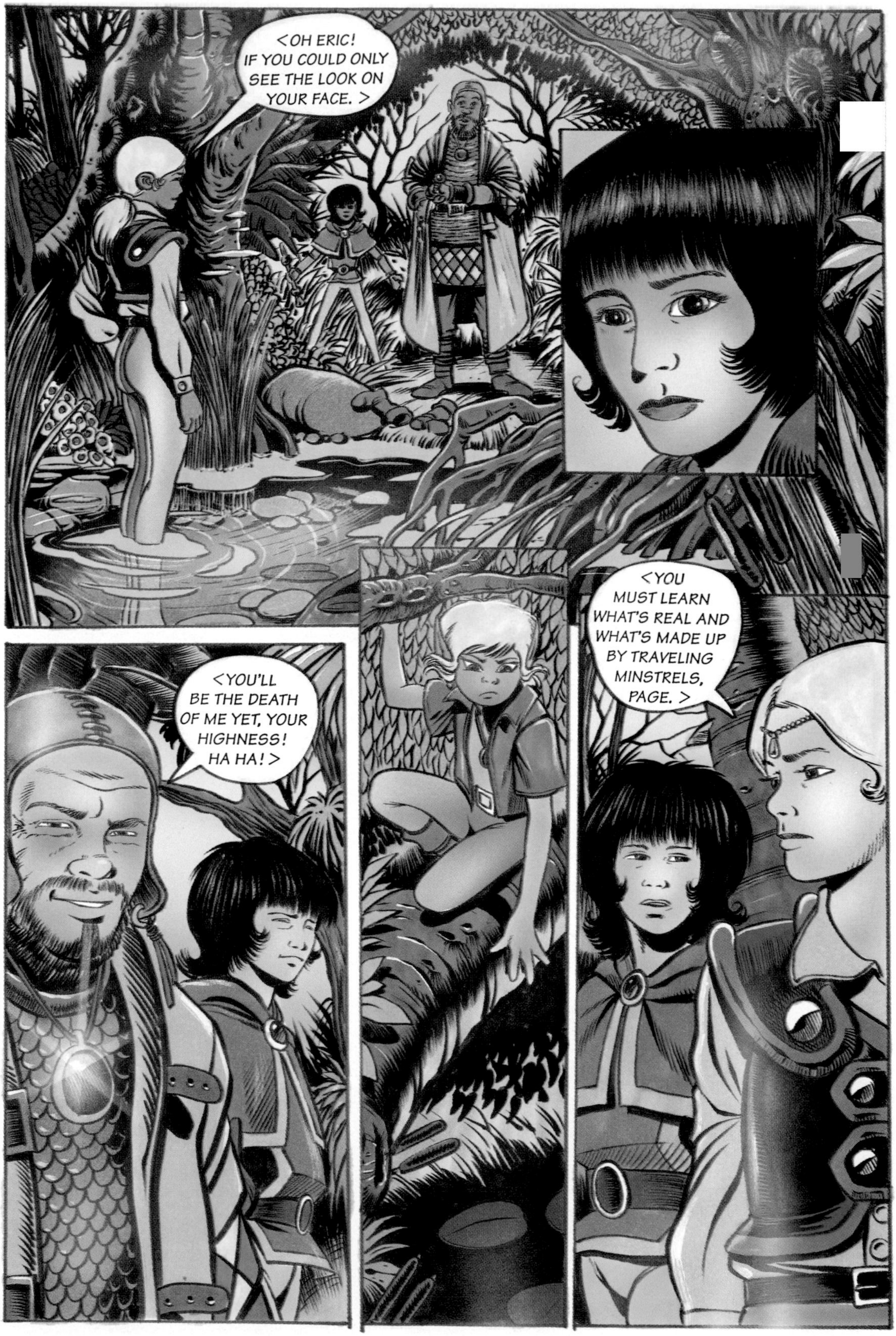
<OH ERIC! IF YOU COULD ONLY SEE THE LOOK ON YOUR FACE. >
<YOU'LL BE THE DEATH OF ME YET, YOUR HIGHNESS! HA HA! >
<YOU MUST LEARN WHAT'S REAL AND WHAT'S MADE UP BY TRAVELING MINSTRELS, PAGE. >

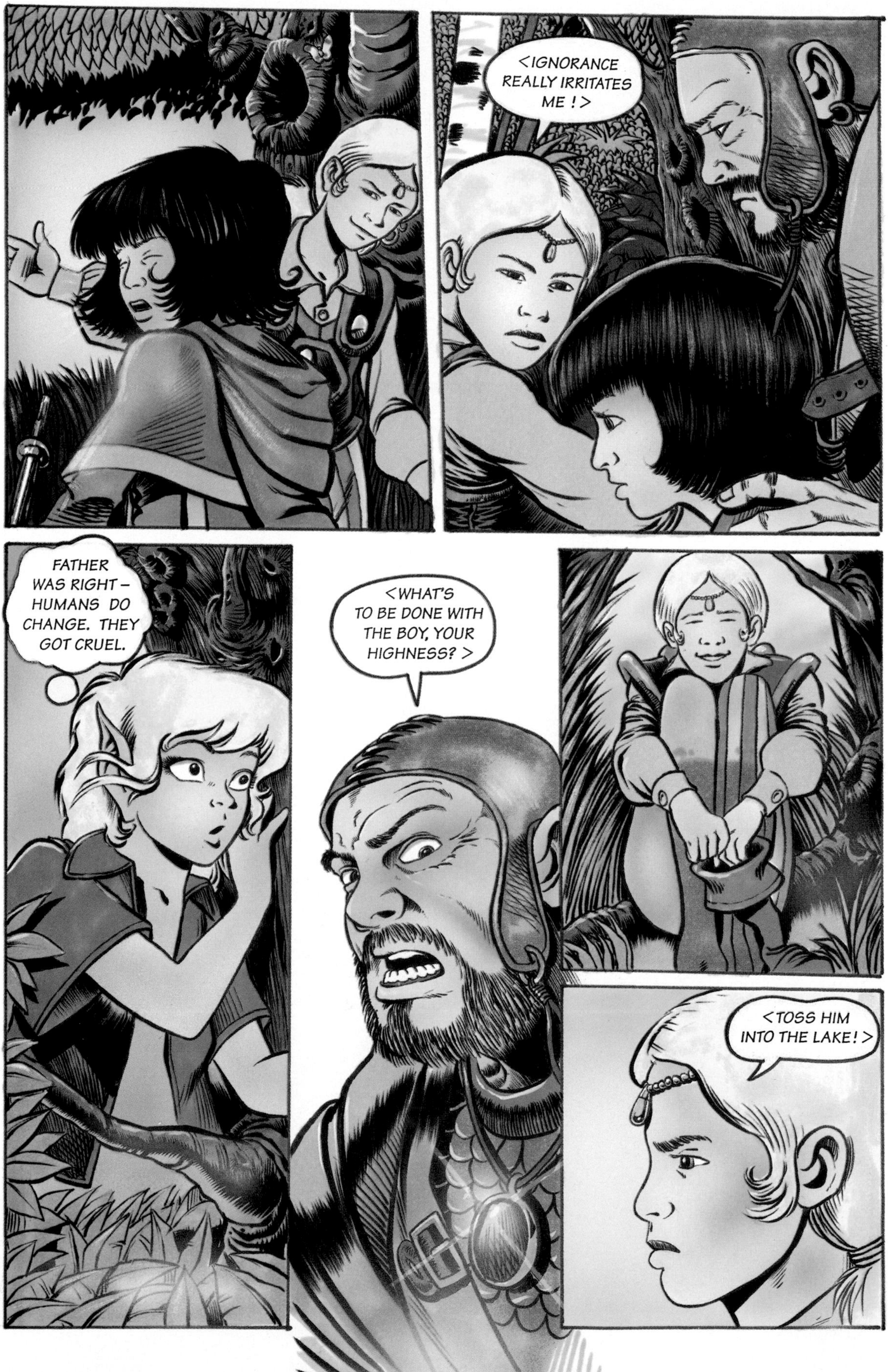

<IGNORANCE REALLY IRRITATES ME !>
FATHER WAS RIGHT – HUMANS DO CHANGE. THEY GOT CRUEL.
<WHAT'S TO BE DONE WITH THE BOY, YOUR HIGHNESS?>
<TOSS HIM INTO THE LAKE!>

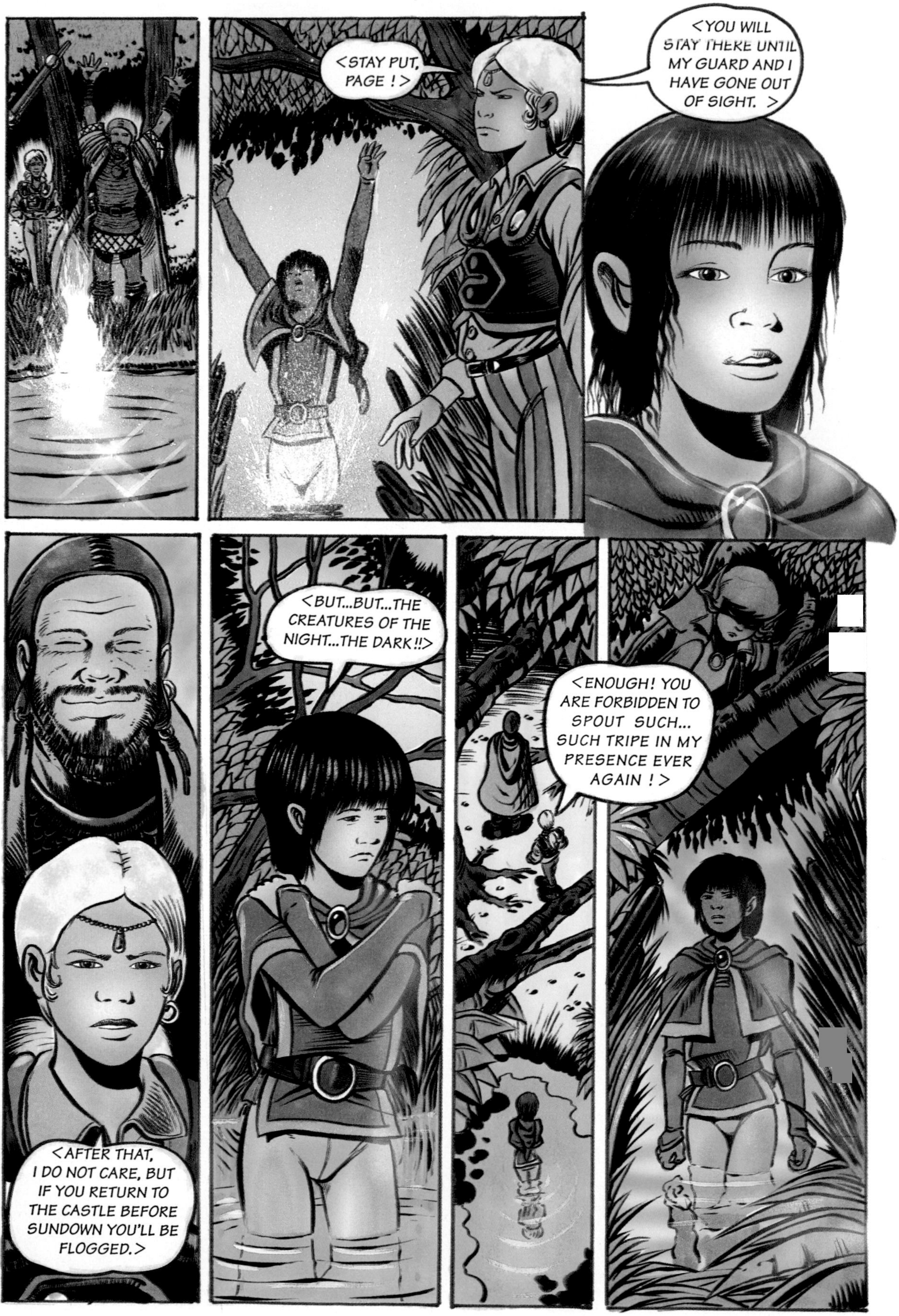
<STAY PUT, PAGE ! >
<YOU WILL STAY THERE UNTIL MY GUARD AND I HAVE GONE OUT OF SIGHT. >
<AFTER THAT, I DO NOT CARE, BUT IF YOU RETURN TO THE CASTLE BEFORE SUNDOWN YOU'LL BE FLOGGED.>
<BUT...BUT...THE CREATURES OF THE NIGHT...THE DARK!!>
<ENOUGH! YOU ARE FORBIDDEN TO SPOUT SUCH... SUCH TRIPE IN MY PRESENCE EVER AGAIN ! >

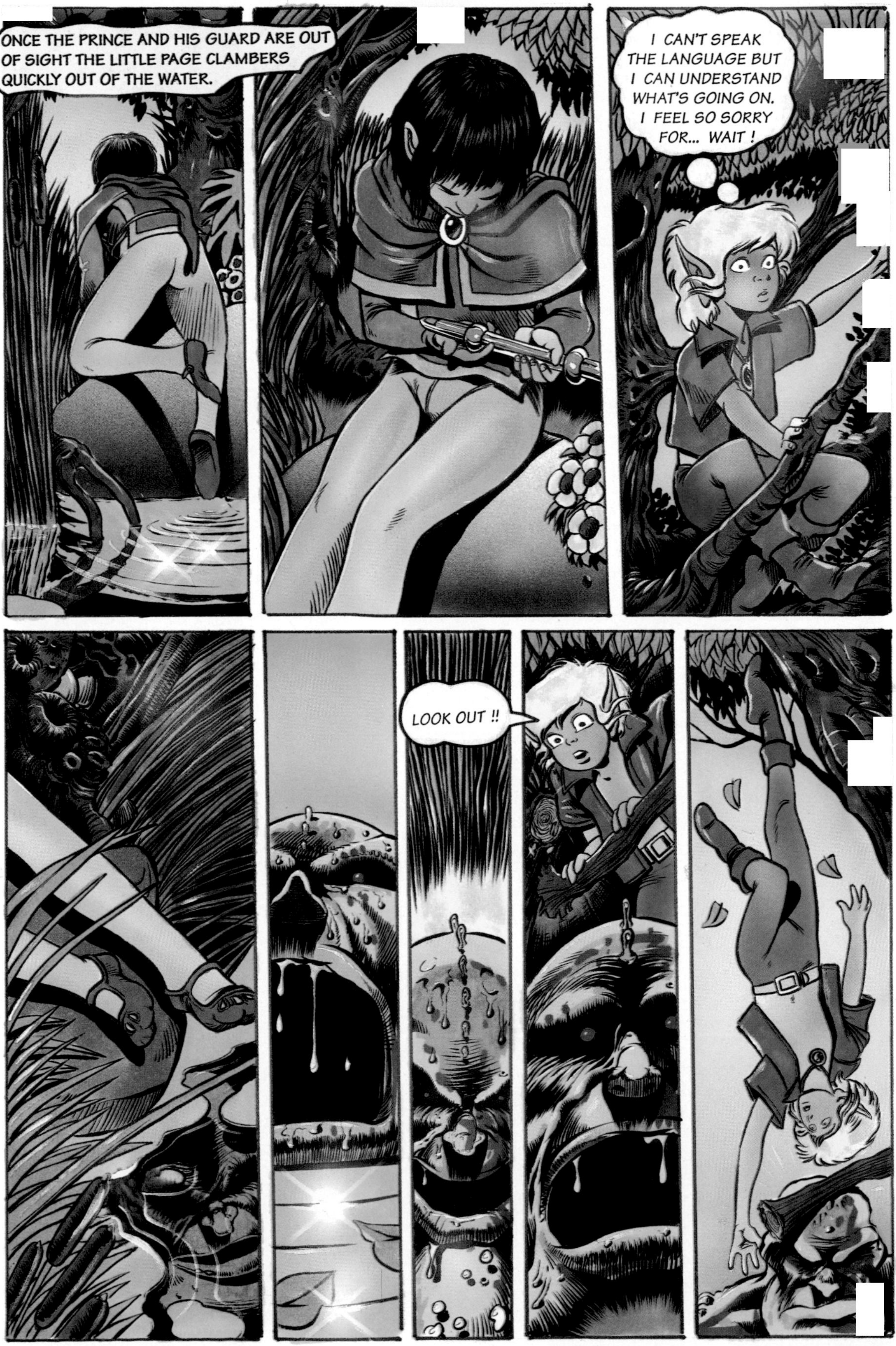
ONCE THE PRINCE AND HIS GUARD ARE OUT OF SIGHT THE LITTLE PAGE CLAMBERS QUICKLY OUT OF THE WATER.
I CAN'T SPEAK THE LANGUAGE BUT I CAN UNDERSTAND WHAT'S GOING ON. I FEEL SO SORRY FOR... WAIT !
LOOK OUT !!

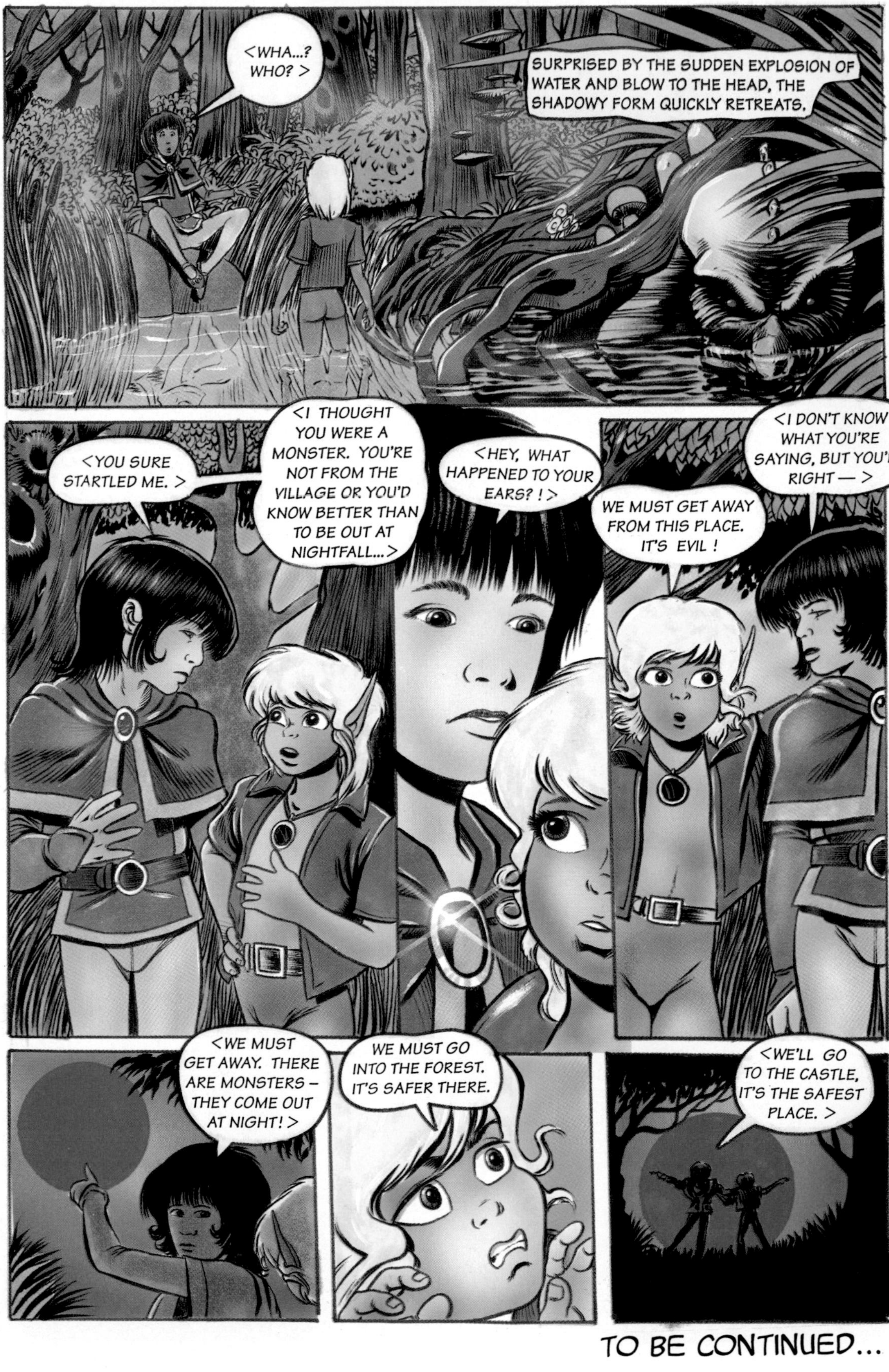
<WHA...? WHO? >
SURPRISED BY THE SUDDEN EXPLOSION OF WATER AND BLOW TO THE HEAD, THE SHADOWY FORM QUICKLY RETREATS.
<YOU SURE STARTLED ME. >
<I THOUGHT YOU WERE A MONSTER. YOU'RE NOT FROM THE VILLAGE OR YOU'D KNOW BETTER THAN TO BE OUT AT NIGHTFALL...>
<HEY, WHAT HAPPENED TO YOUR EARS? ! >
WE MUST GET AWAY FROM THIS PLACE. IT'S EVIL !
<I DON'T KNOW WHAT YOU'RE SAYING, BUT YOU'RE RIGHT — >
<WE MUST GET AWAY. THERE ARE MONSTERS – THEY COME OUT AT NIGHT! >
WE MUST GO INTO THE FOREST. IT'S SAFER THERE.
<WE'LL GO TO THE CASTLE, IT'S THE SAFEST PLACE. >

TO BE CONTINUED...

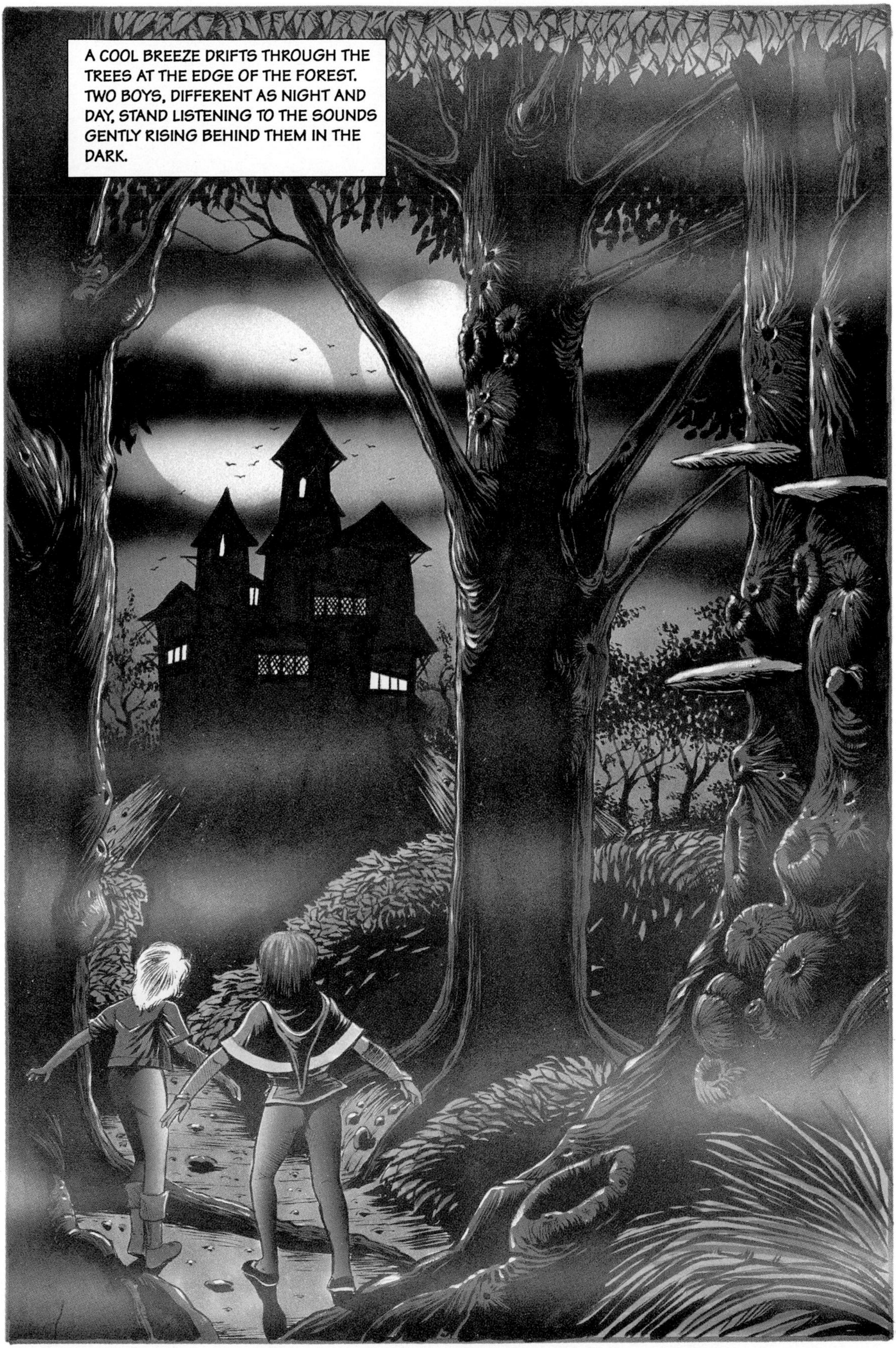
A COOL BREEZE DRIFTS THROUGH THE TREES AT THE EDGE OF THE FOREST. TWO BOYS, DIFFERENT AS NIGHT AND DAY, STAND LISTENING TO THE SOUNDS GENTLY RISING BEHIND THEM IN THE DARK.

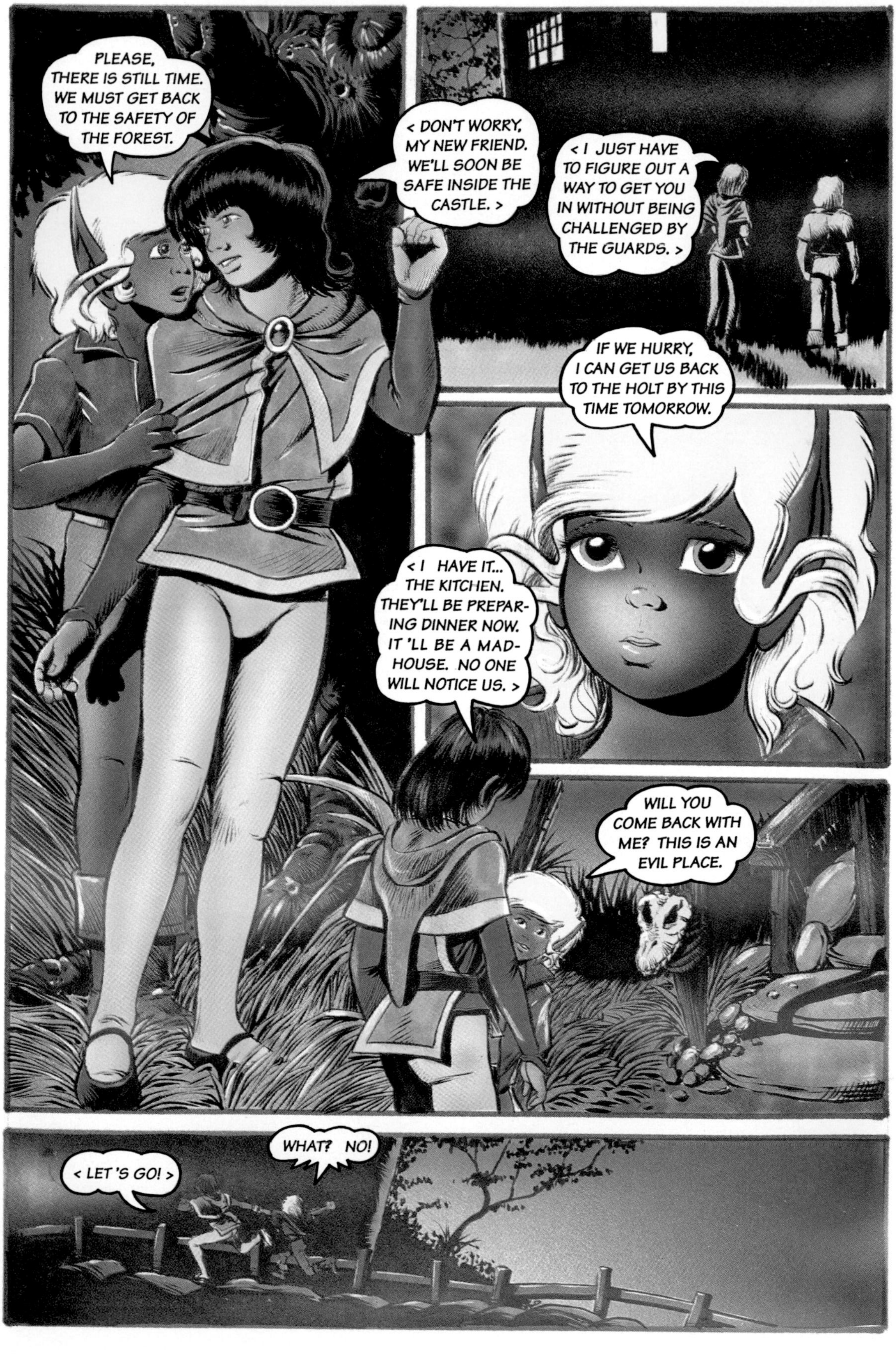
PLEASE, THERE IS STILL TIME. WE MUST GET BACK TO THE SAFETY OF THE FOREST.
< DON'T WORRY, MY NEW FRIEND. WE'LL SOON BE SAFE INSIDE THE CASTLE. >
< I JUST HAVE TO FIGURE OUT A WAY TO GET YOU IN WITHOUT BEING CHALLENGED BY THE GUARDS. >
IF WE HURRY, I CAN GET US BACK TO THE HOLT BY THIS TIME TOMORROW.
< I HAVE IT... THE KITCHEN. THEY'LL BE PREPARING DINNER NOW. IT 'LL BE A MAD-HOUSE. NO ONE WILL NOTICE US. >
WILL YOU COME BACK WITH ME? THIS IS AN EVIL PLACE.
< LET 'S GO! >
WHAT? NO!

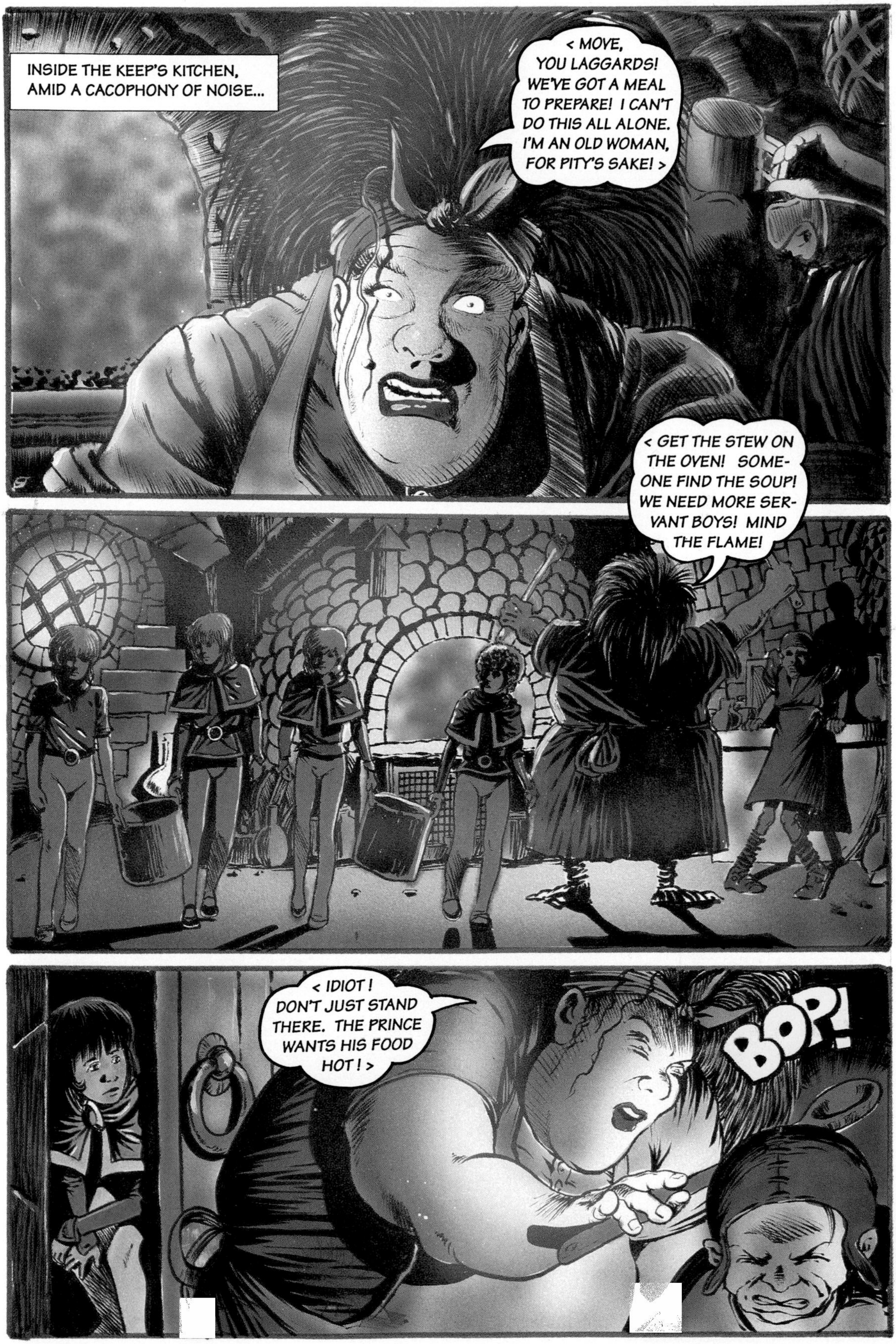
INSIDE THE KEEP'S KITCHEN, AMID A CACOPHONY OF NOISE...
< MOVE, YOU LAGGARDS! WE'VE GOT A MEAL TO PREPARE! I CAN'T DO THIS ALL ALONE. I'M AN OLD WOMAN, FOR PITY'S SAKE! >
< GET THE STEW ON THE OVEN! SOME-ONE FIND THE SOUP! WE NEED MORE SER-VANT BOYS! MIND THE FLAME!
< IDIOT! DON'T JUST STAND THERE. THE PRINCE WANTS HIS FOOD HOT! >
BOP!

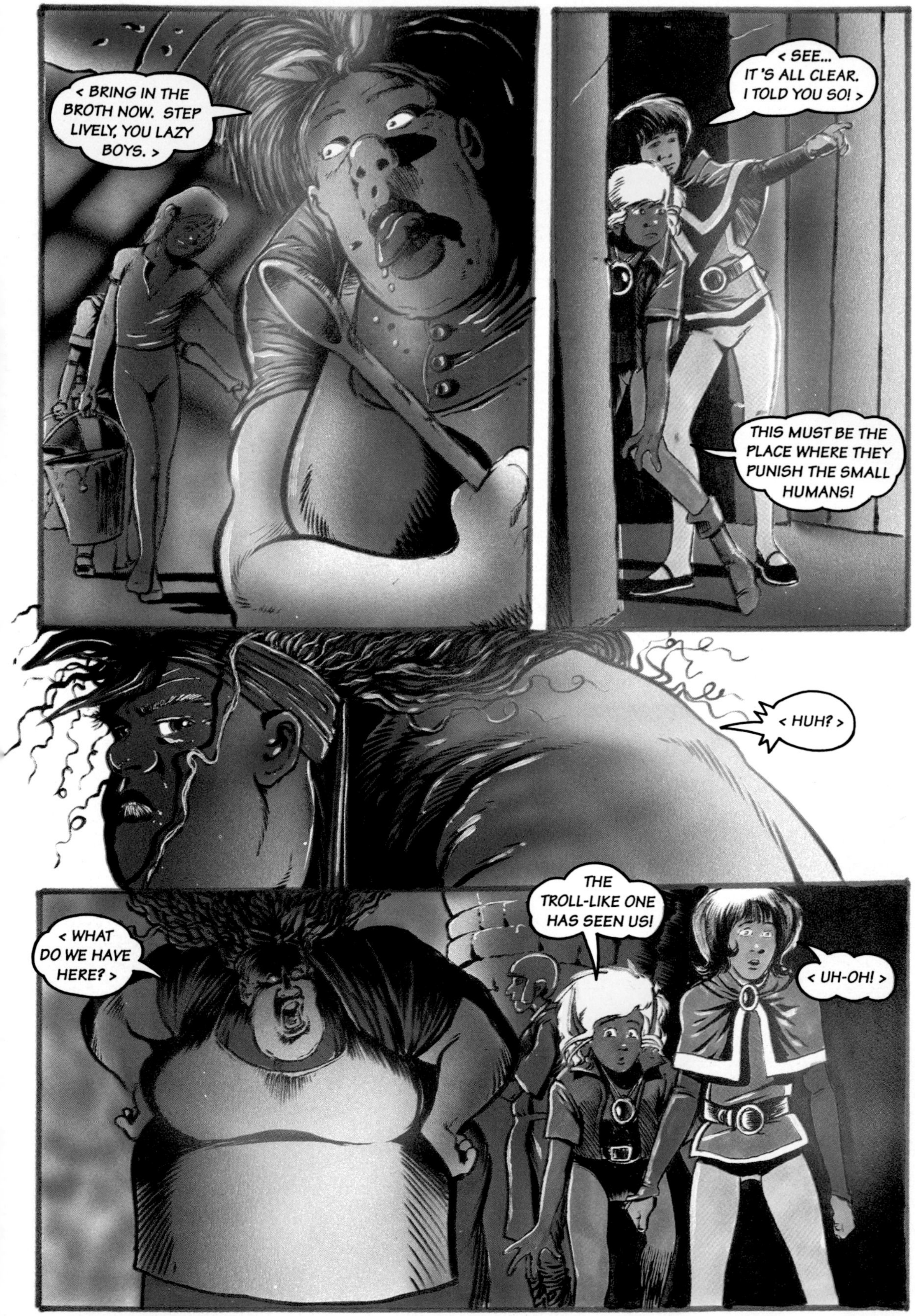

< BRING IN THE BROTH NOW. STEP LIVELY, YOU LAZY BOYS. >
< SEE... IT'S ALL CLEAR. I TOLD YOU SO! >
THIS MUST BE THE PLACE WHERE THEY PUNISH THE SMALL HUMANS!
< HUH? >
< WHAT DO WE HAVE HERE? >
THE TROLL-LIKE ONE HAS SEEN US!
< UH-OH! >

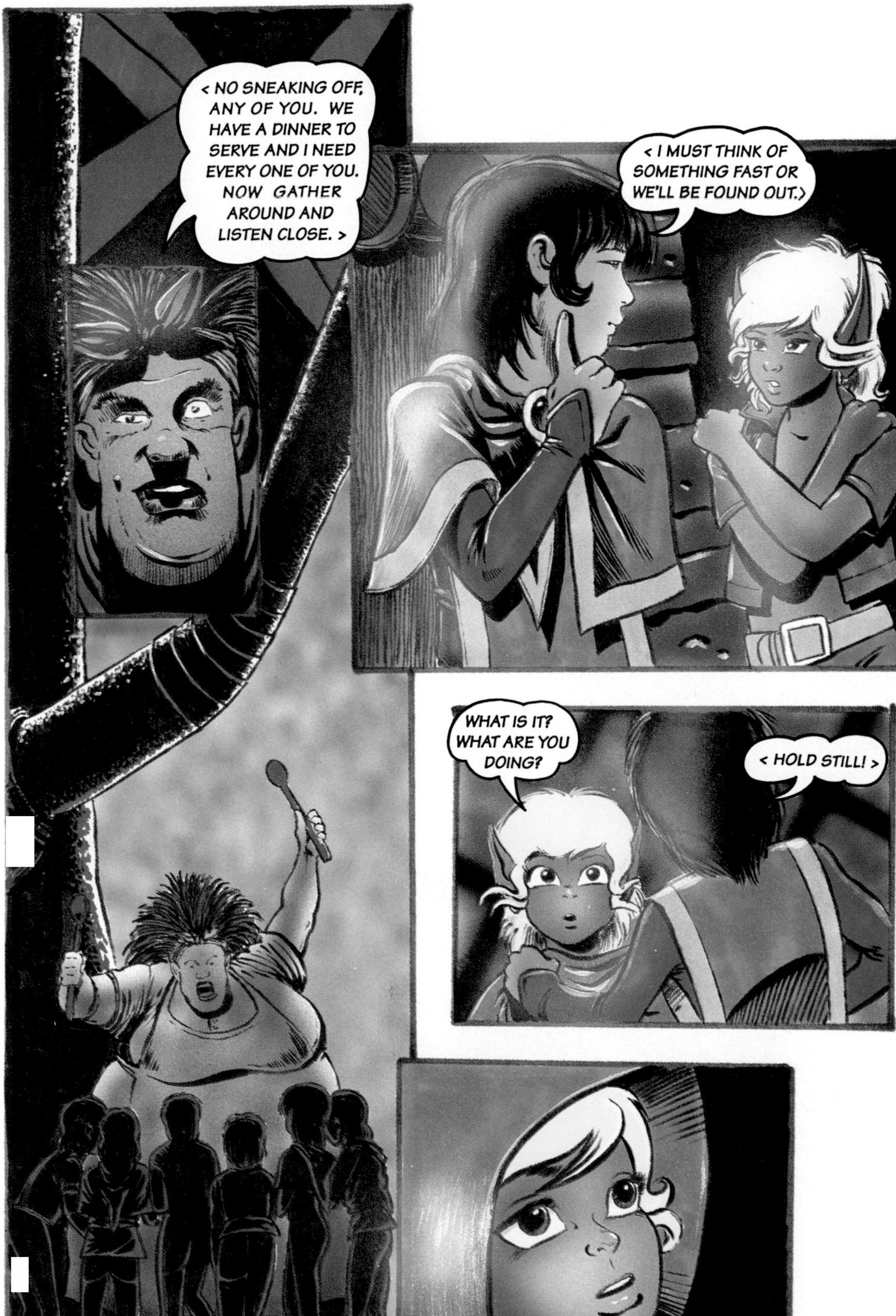
< NO SNEAKING OFF, ANY OF YOU. WE HAVE A DINNER TO SERVE AND I NEED EVERY ONE OF YOU. NOW GATHER AROUND AND LISTEN CLOSE. >
< I MUST THINK OF SOMETHING FAST OR WE'LL BE FOUND OUT.>
WHAT IS IT? WHAT ARE YOU DOING?
< HOLD STILL! >

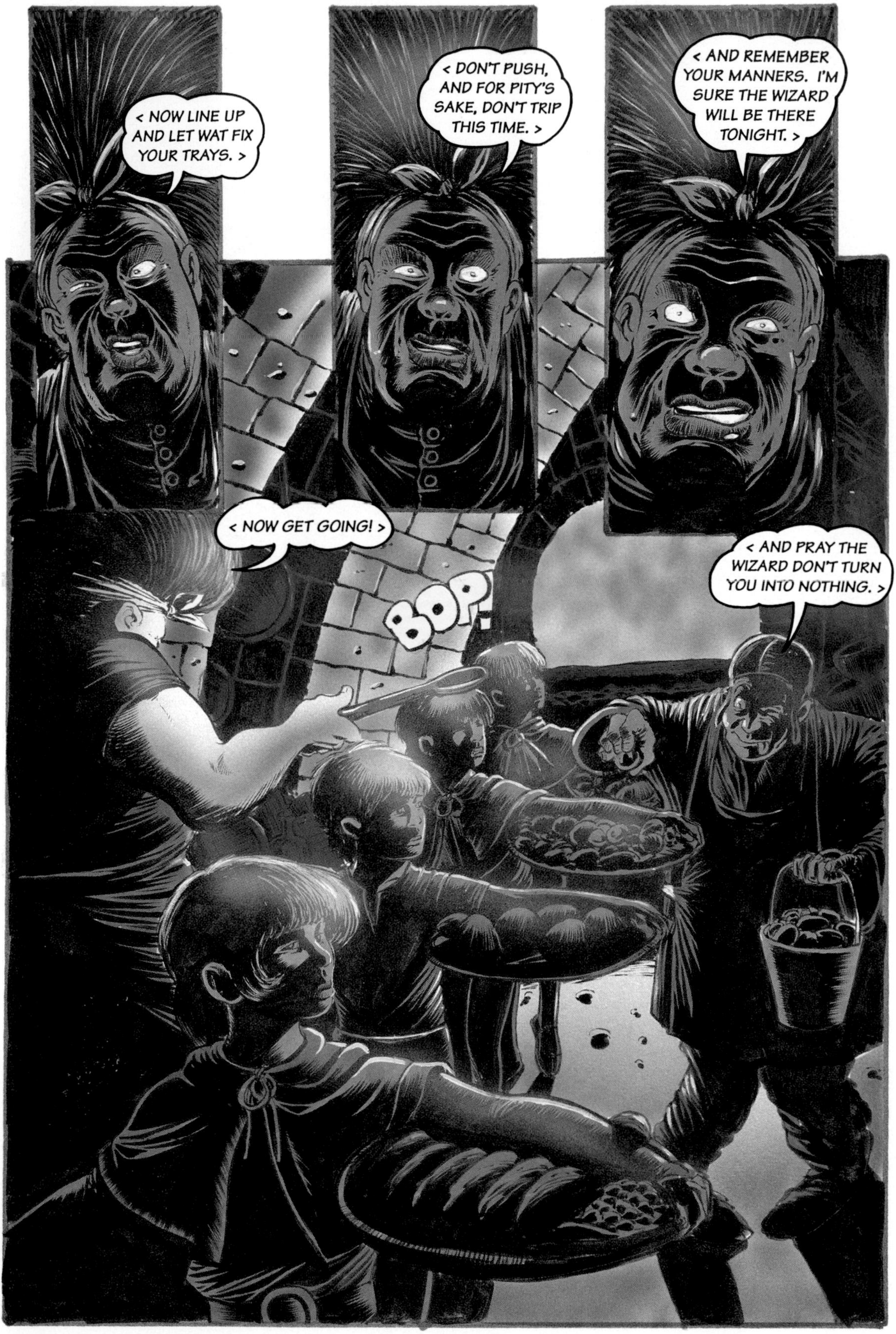
< NOW LINE UP AND LET WAT FIX YOUR TRAYS. >
< DON'T PUSH, AND FOR PITY'S SAKE, DON'T TRIP THIS TIME. >
< AND REMEMBER YOUR MANNERS. I'M SURE THE WIZARD WILL BE THERE TONIGHT. >
< NOW GET GOING! >
BOP!
< AND PRAY THE WIZARD DON'T TURN YOU INTO NOTHING. >

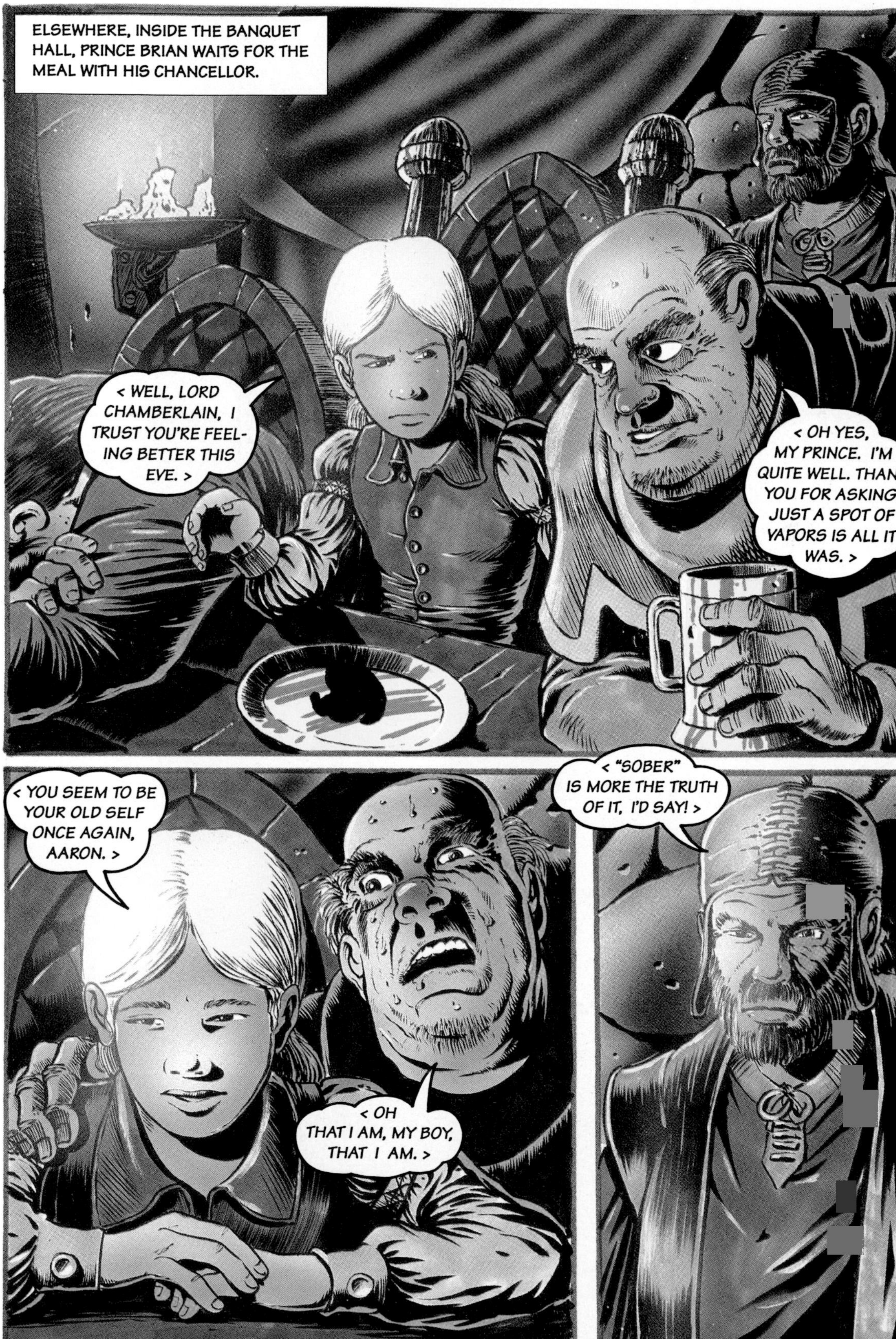
ELSEWHERE, INSIDE THE BANQUET HALL, PRINCE BRIAN WAITS FOR THE MEAL WITH HIS CHANCELLOR.
< WELL, LORD CHAMBERLAIN, I TRUST YOU'RE FEELING BETTER THIS EVE. >
< OH YES, MY PRINCE. I'M QUITE WELL. THANK YOU FOR ASKING. JUST A SPOT OF VAPORS IS ALL IT WAS. >
< YOU SEEM TO BE YOUR OLD SELF ONCE AGAIN, AARON. >
< OH THAT I AM, MY BOY, THAT I AM. >
< "SOBER" IS MORE THE TRUTH OF IT, I'D SAY! >

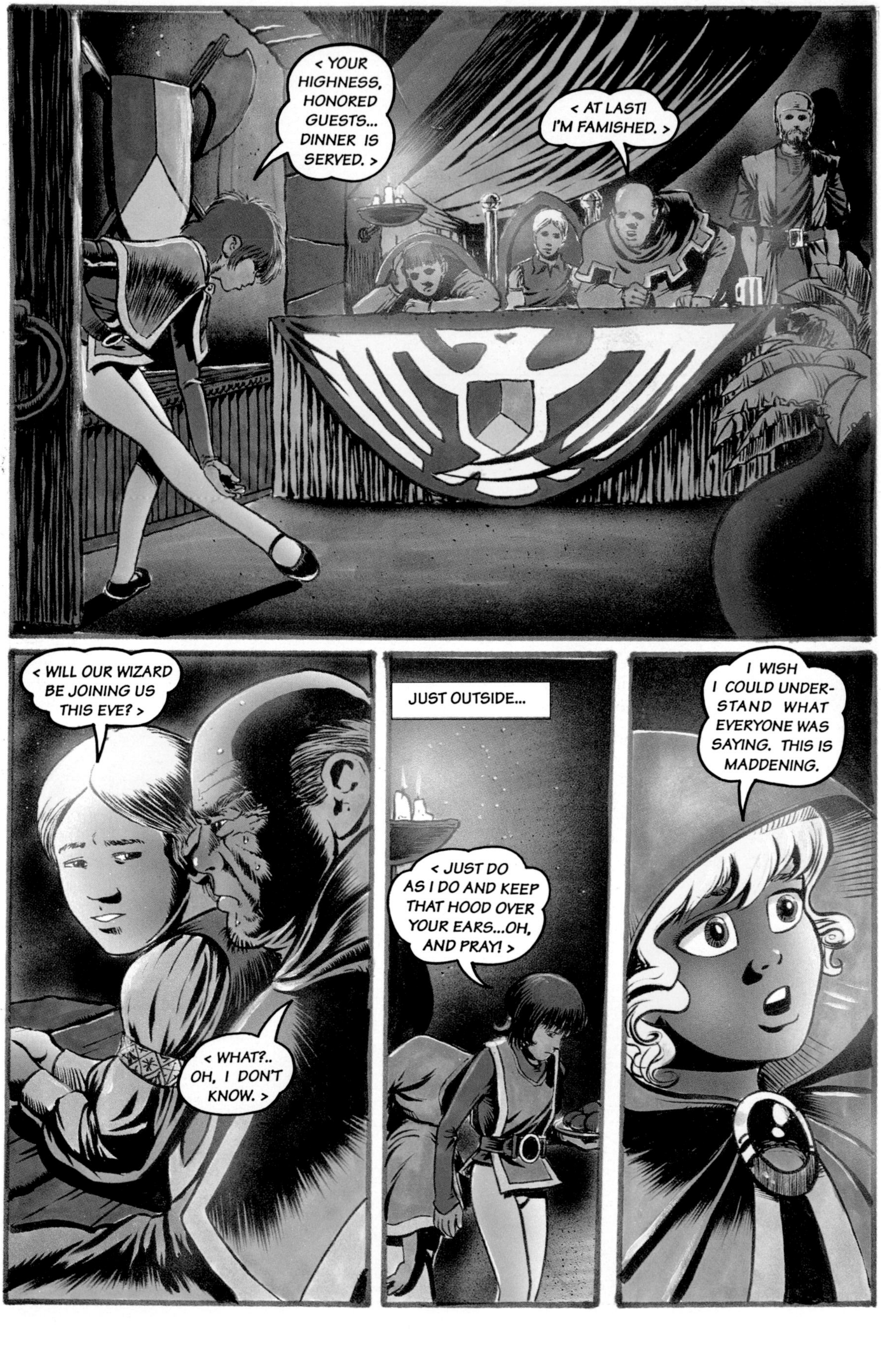
< YOUR HIGHNESS, HONORED GUESTS... DINNER IS SERVED. >
< AT LAST! I'M FAMISHED. >
< WILL OUR WIZARD BE JOINING US THIS EVE? >
< WHAT?.. OH, I DON'T KNOW. >
JUST OUTSIDE...
< JUST DO AS I DO AND KEEP THAT HOOD OVER YOUR EARS...OH, AND PRAY! >
I WISH I COULD UNDER-STAND WHAT EVERYONE WAS SAYING. THIS IS MADDENING.

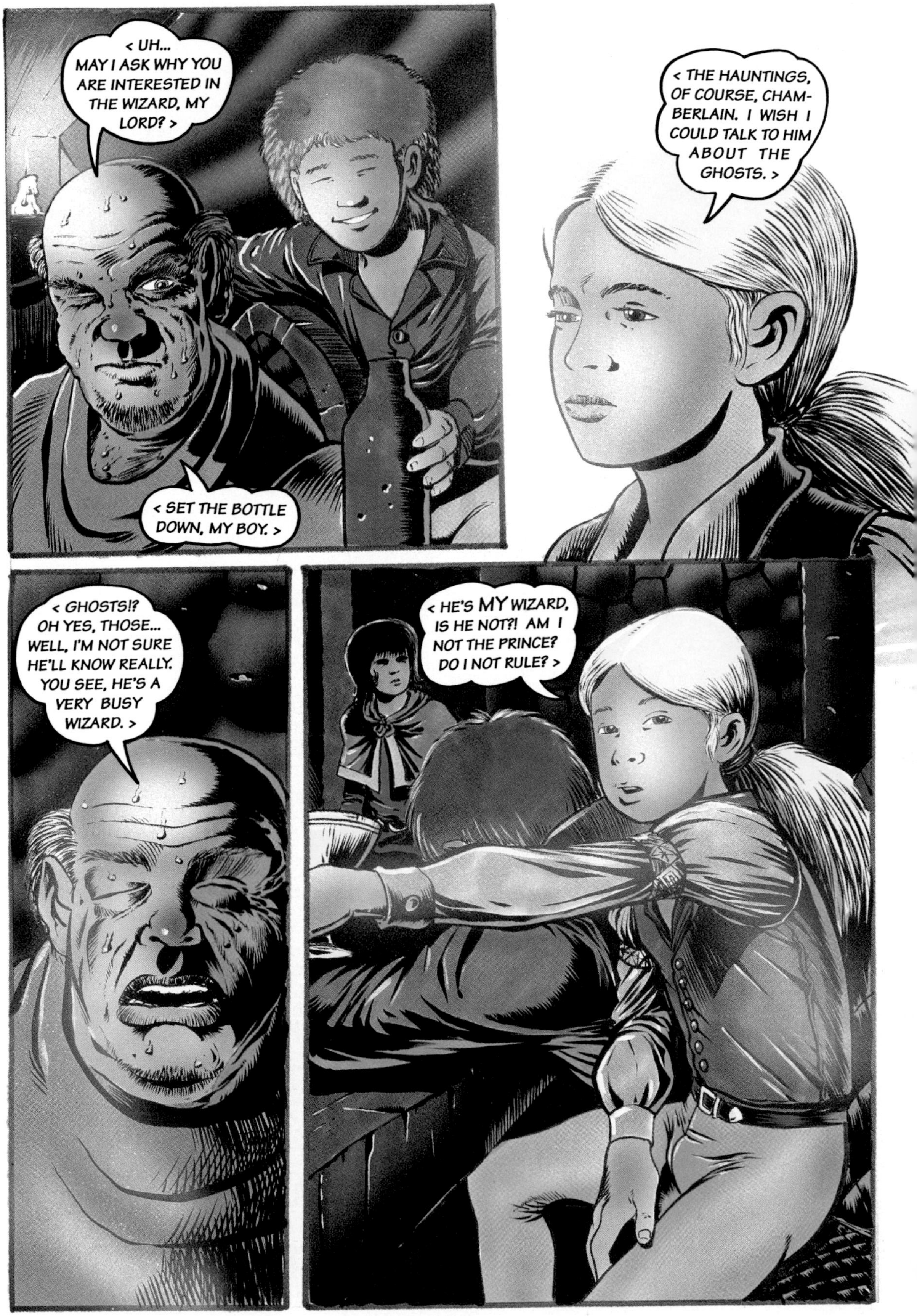
< UH... MAY I ASK WHY YOU ARE INTERESTED IN THE WIZARD, MY LORD? >
< SET THE BOTTLE DOWN, MY BOY. >
< THE HAUNTINGS, OF COURSE, CHAMBERLAIN. I WISH I COULD TALK TO HIM ABOUT THE GHOSTS. >
< GHOSTS!? OH YES, THOSE... WELL, I'M NOT SURE HE'LL KNOW REALLY. YOU SEE, HE'S A VERY BUSY WIZARD. >
< HE'S MY WIZARD, IS HE NOT?! AM I NOT THE PRINCE? DO I NOT RULE? >

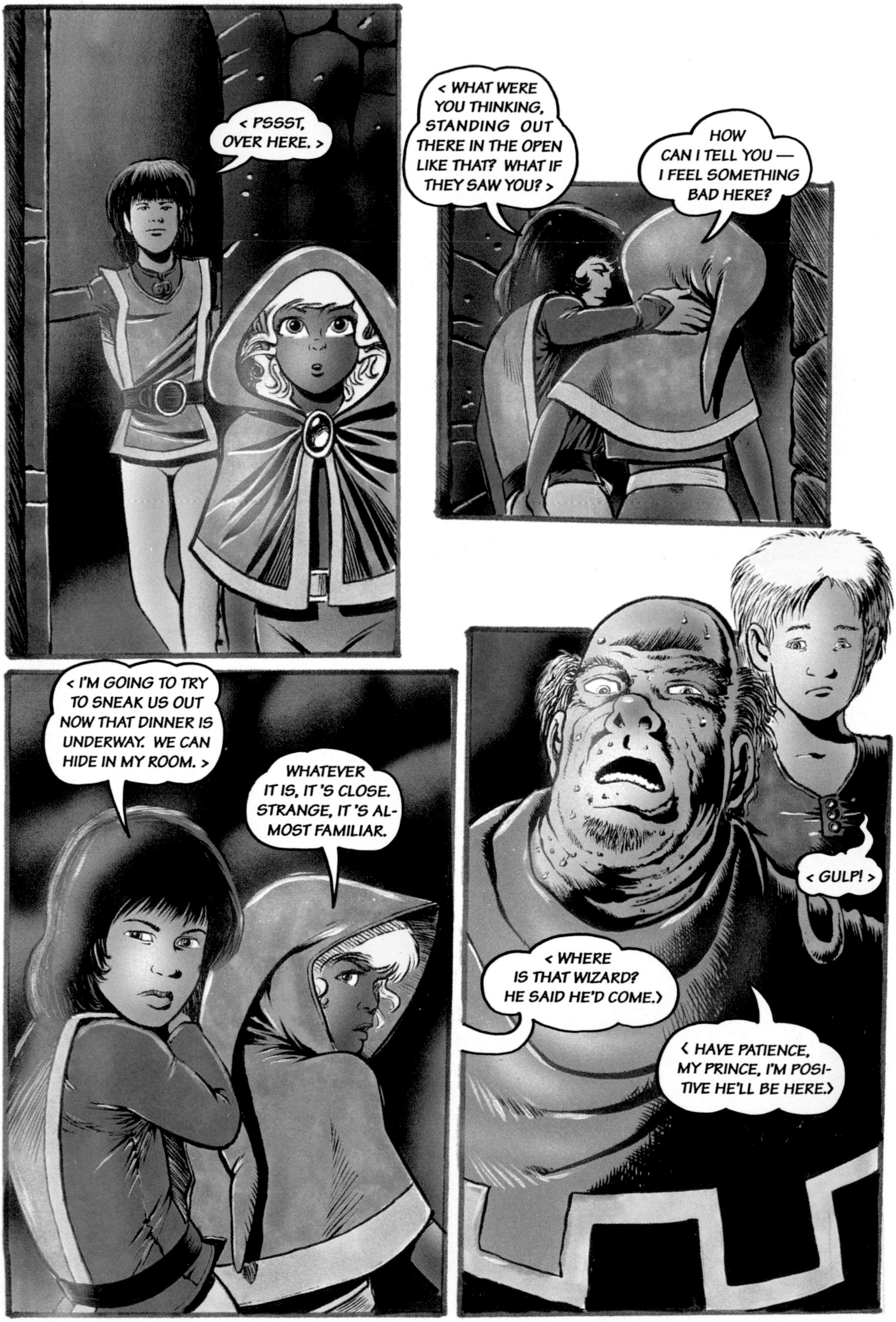
< PSSST, OVER HERE. >
< WHAT WERE YOU THINKING, STANDING OUT THERE IN THE OPEN LIKE THAT? WHAT IF THEY SAW YOU? >
HOW CAN I TELL YOU — I FEEL SOMETHING BAD HERE?
< I'M GOING TO TRY TO SNEAK US OUT NOW THAT DINNER IS UNDERWAY. WE CAN HIDE IN MY ROOM. >
WHATEVER IT IS, IT 'S CLOSE. STRANGE, IT 'S AL-MOST FAMILIAR.
< GULP! >
< WHERE IS THAT WIZARD? HE SAID HE'D COME.>
< HAVE PATIENCE, MY PRINCE, I'M POSI-TIVE HE'LL BE HERE.>

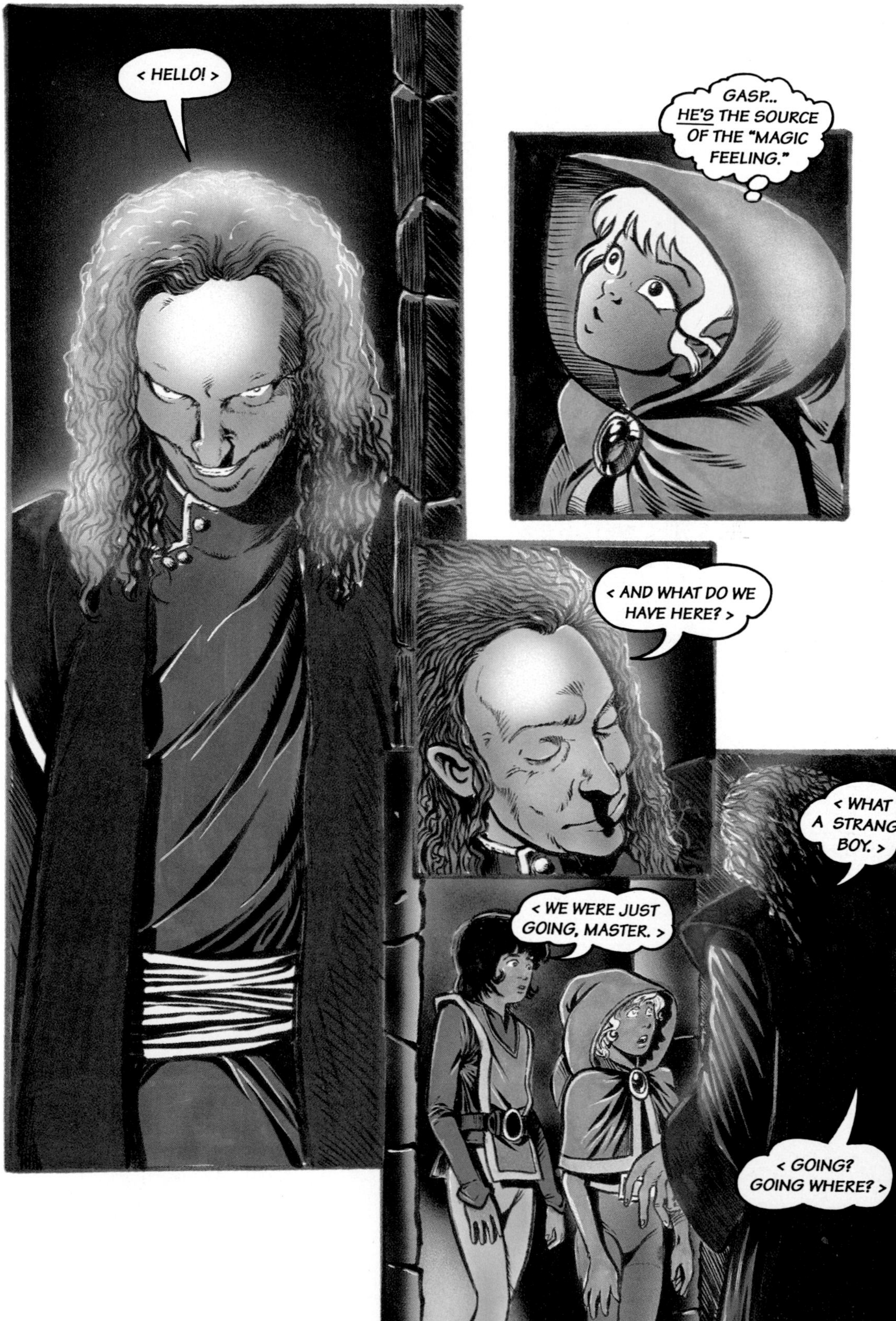

< HELLO! >
GASP... HE'S THE SOURCE OF THE "MAGIC FEELING."
< AND WHAT DO WE HAVE HERE? >
< WHAT A STRANGE BOY. >
< WE WERE JUST GOING, MASTER. >
< GOING? GOING WHERE? >

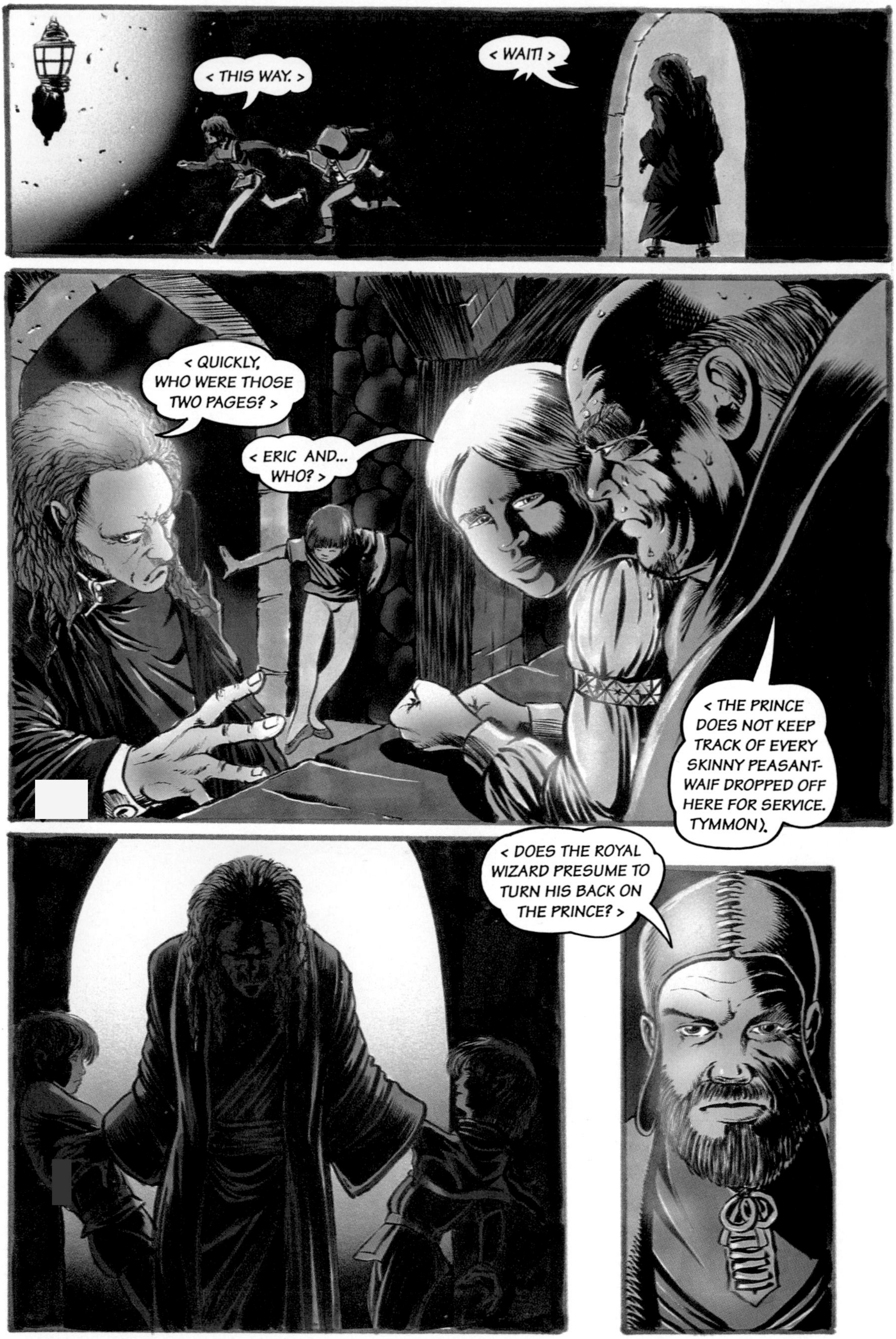
< THIS WAY. >
< WAIT! >
< QUICKLY, WHO WERE THOSE TWO PAGES? >
< ERIC AND... WHO? >
< THE PRINCE DOES NOT KEEP TRACK OF EVERY SKINNY PEASANT-WAIF DROPPED OFF HERE FOR SERVICE. TYMMON >.
< DOES THE ROYAL WIZARD PRESUME TO TURN HIS BACK ON THE PRINCE? >

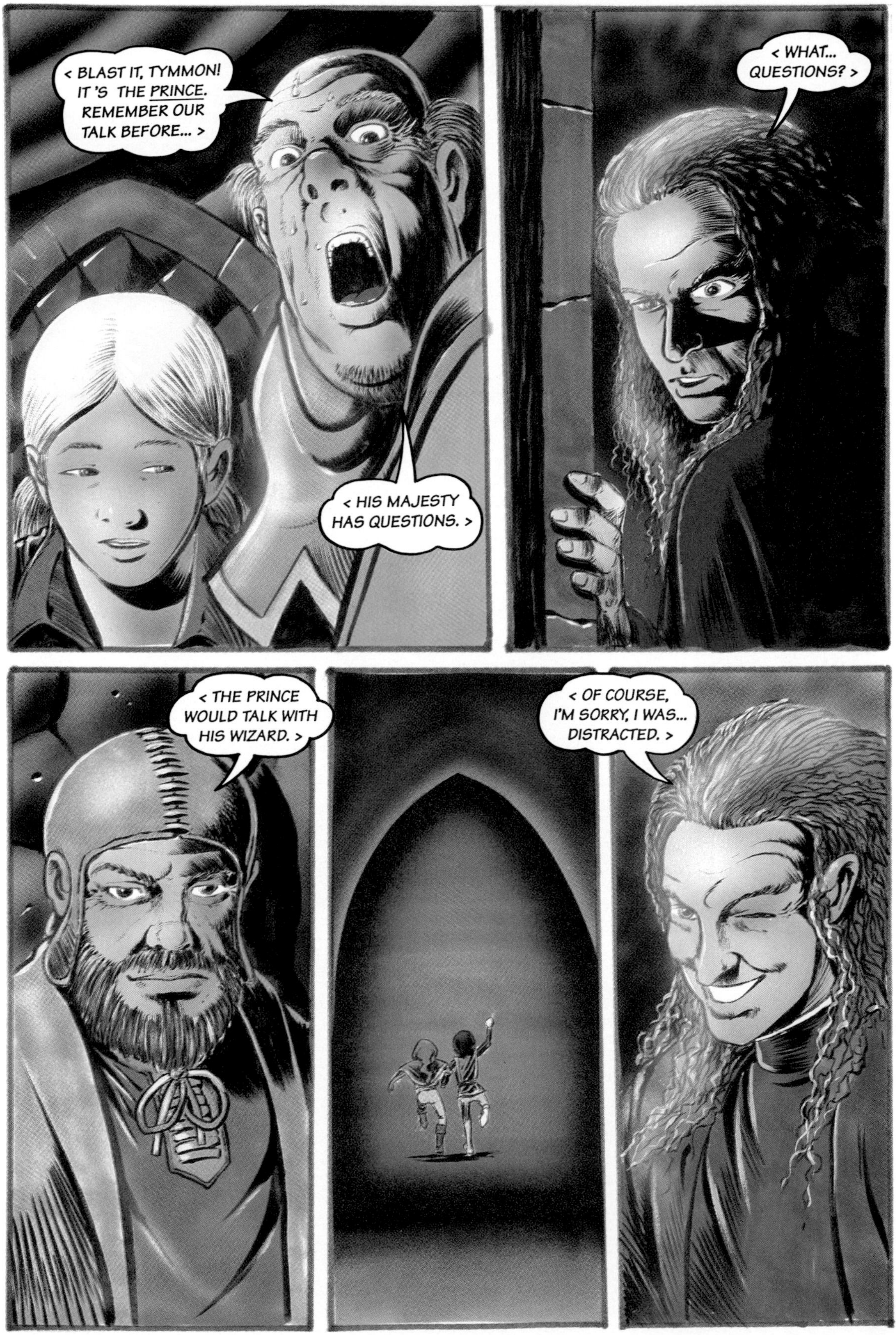
< BLAST IT, TYMMON! IT'S THE PRINCE. REMEMBER OUR TALK BEFORE... >
< HIS MAJESTY HAS QUESTIONS. >
< WHAT... QUESTIONS? >
< THE PRINCE WOULD TALK WITH HIS WIZARD. >
< OF COURSE, I'M SORRY, I WAS... DISTRACTED. >

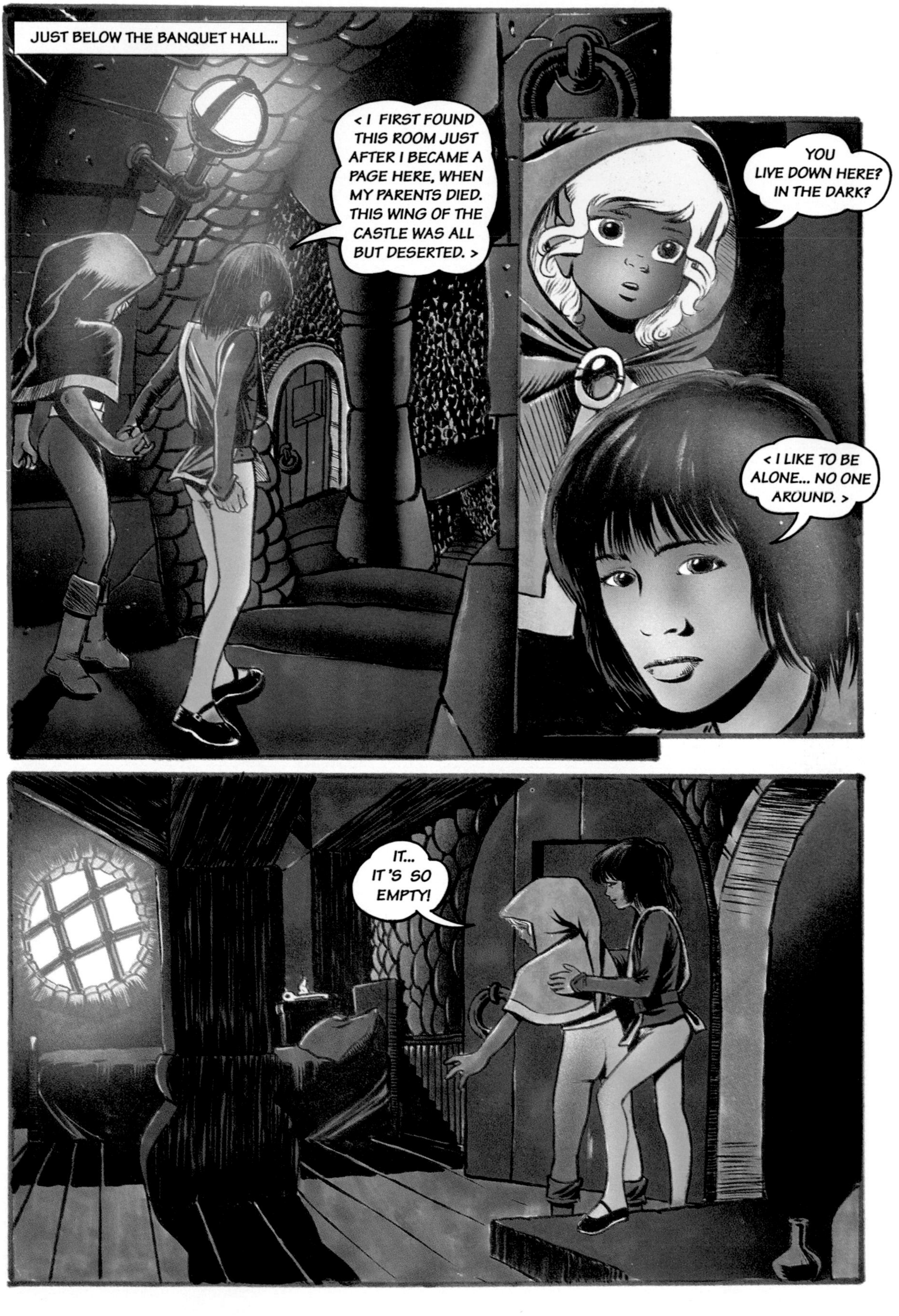
JUST BELOW THE BANQUET HALL...
< I FIRST FOUND THIS ROOM JUST AFTER I BECAME A PAGE HERE, WHEN MY PARENTS DIED. THIS WING OF THE CASTLE WAS ALL BUT DESERTED. >
YOU LIVE DOWN HERE? IN THE DARK?
< I LIKE TO BE ALONE... NO ONE AROUND. >
IT... IT'S SO EMPTY!

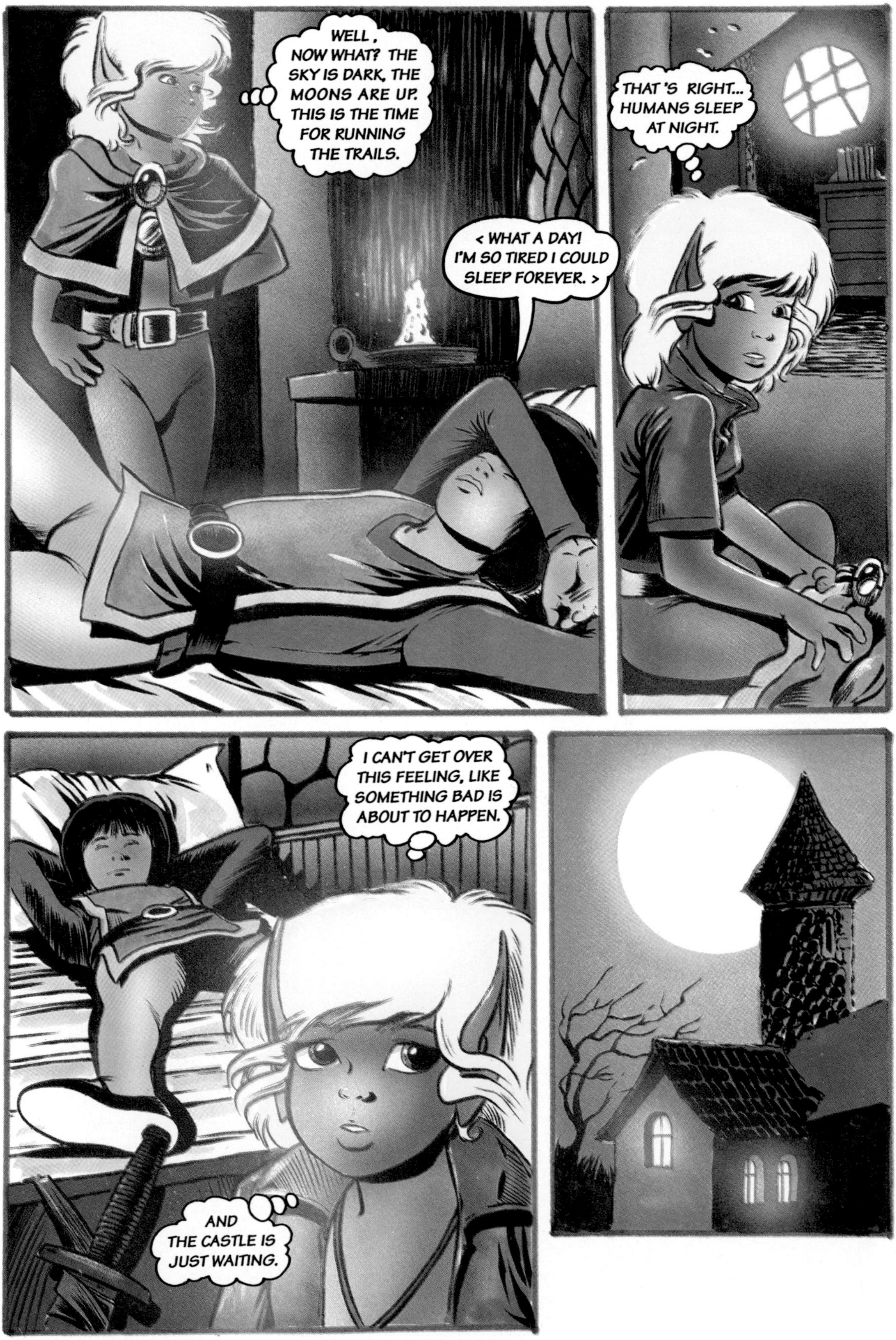
WELL, NOW WHAT? THE SKY IS DARK, THE MOONS ARE UP. THIS IS THE TIME FOR RUNNING THE TRAILS.
< WHAT A DAY! I'M SO TIRED I COULD SLEEP FOREVER. >
THAT'S RIGHT... HUMANS SLEEP AT NIGHT.
I CAN'T GET OVER THIS FEELING, LIKE SOMETHING BAD IS ABOUT TO HAPPEN.
AND THE CASTLE IS JUST WAITING.

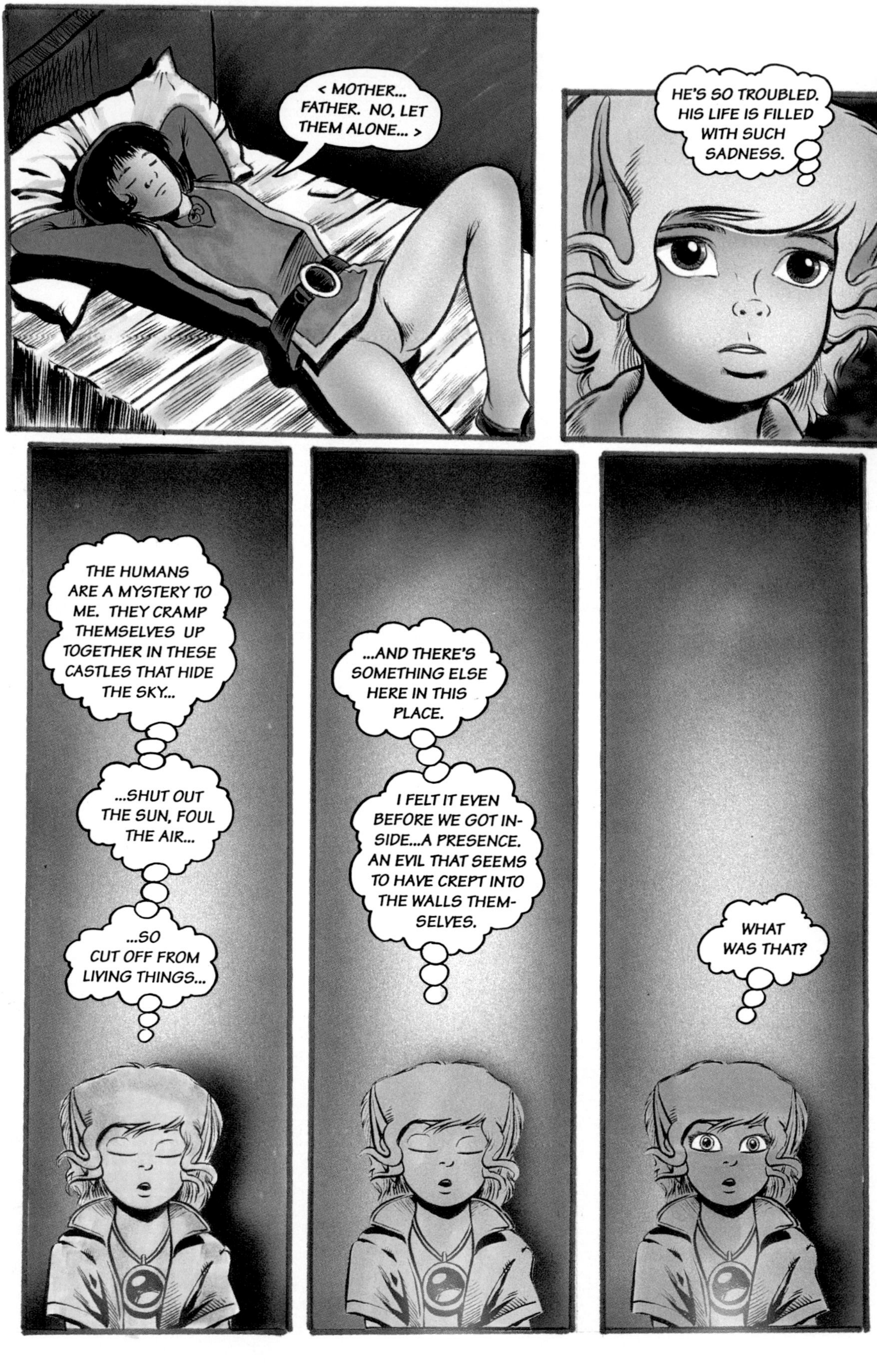
< MOTHER... FATHER. NO, LET THEM ALONE... >
HE'S SO TROUBLED. HIS LIFE IS FILLED WITH SUCH SADNESS.
THE HUMANS ARE A MYSTERY TO ME. THEY CRAMP THEMSELVES UP TOGETHER IN THESE CASTLES THAT HIDE THE SKY...
...SHUT OUT THE SUN, FOUL THE AIR...
...SO CUT OFF FROM LIVING THINGS...
...AND THERE'S SOMETHING ELSE HERE IN THIS PLACE.
I FELT IT EVEN BEFORE WE GOT IN-SIDE...A PRESENCE. AN EVIL THAT SEEMS TO HAVE CREPT INTO THE WALLS THEM-SELVES.
WHAT WAS THAT?

< ERIC, WHERE ARE YOU? >

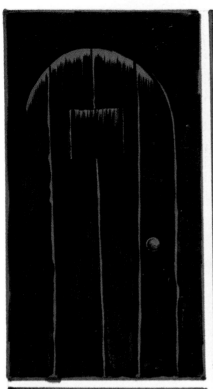

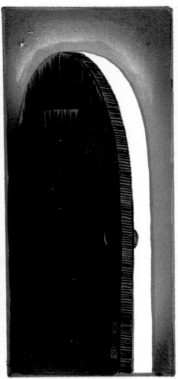

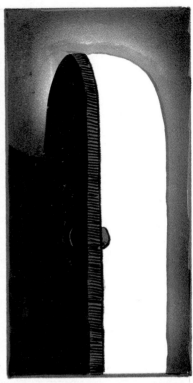

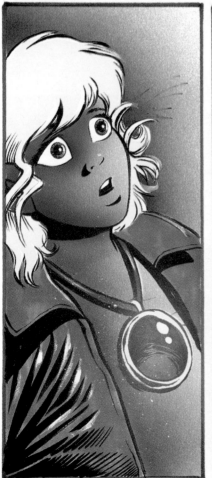

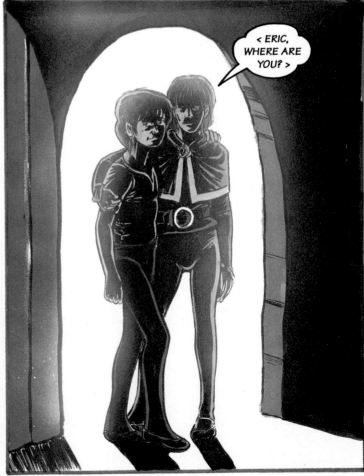

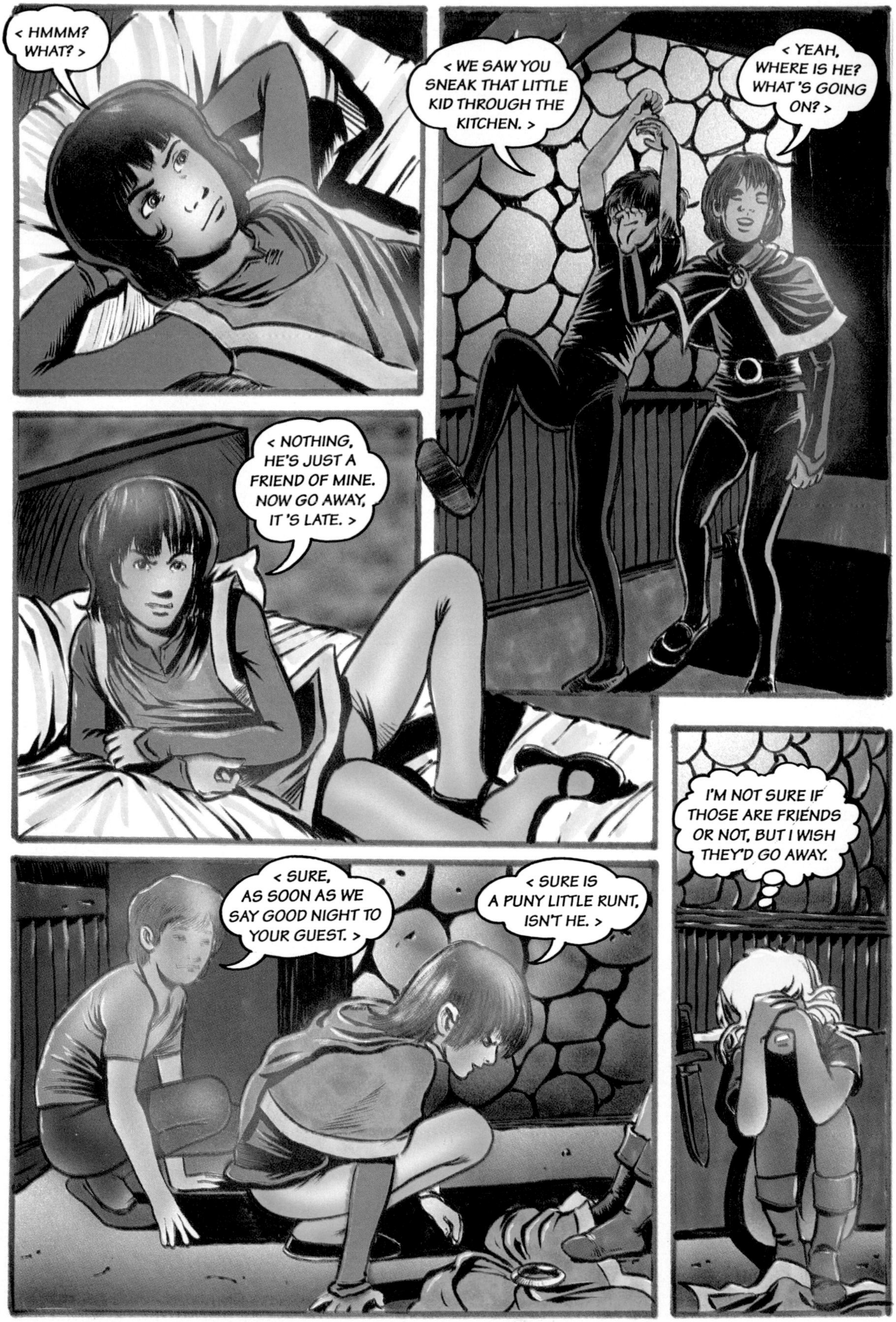
< HMMM? WHAT? >
< WE SAW YOU SNEAK THAT LITTLE KID THROUGH THE KITCHEN. >
< YEAH, WHERE IS HE? WHAT'S GOING ON? >
< NOTHING, HE'S JUST A FRIEND OF MINE. NOW GO AWAY, IT'S LATE. >
I'M NOT SURE IF THOSE ARE FRIENDS OR NOT, BUT I WISH THEY'D GO AWAY.
< SURE, AS SOON AS WE SAY GOOD NIGHT TO YOUR GUEST. >
< SURE IS A PUNY LITTLE RUNT, ISN'T HE. >

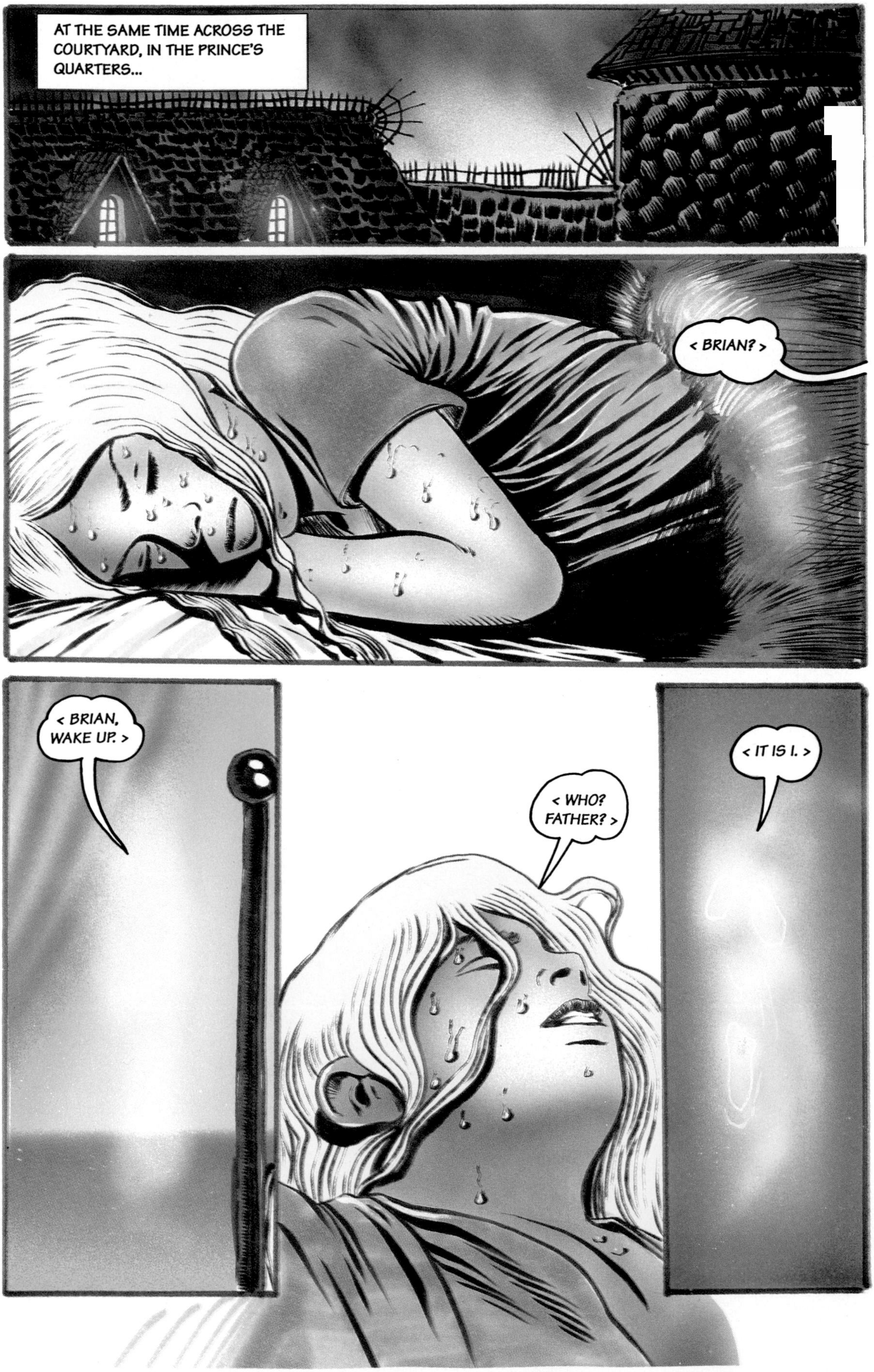
AT THE SAME TIME ACROSS THE COURTYARD, IN THE PRINCE'S QUARTERS...
< BRIAN? >
< BRIAN, WAKE UP. >
< WHO? FATHER? >
< IT IS I. >

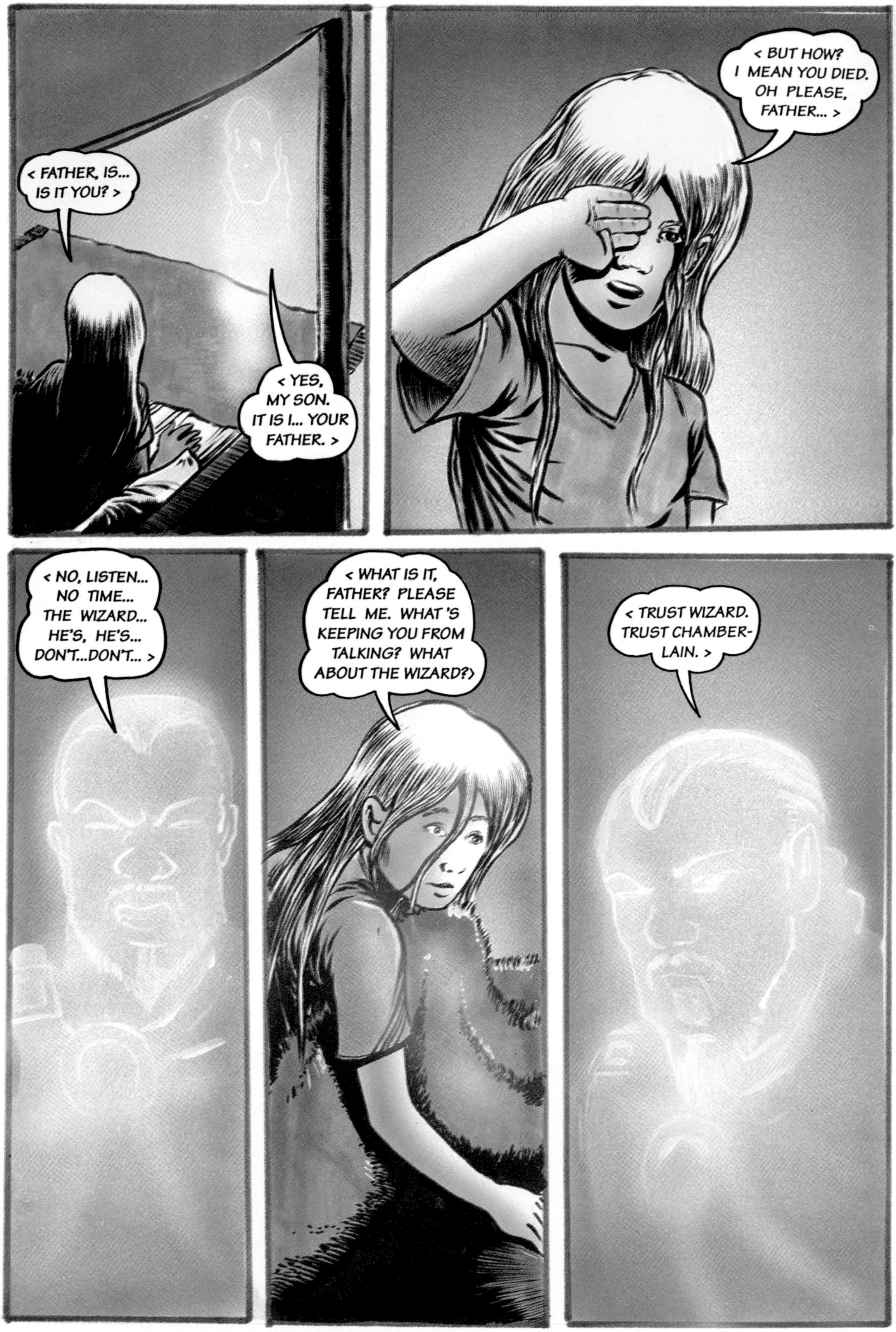

< FATHER, IS... IS IT YOU? >
< YES, MY SON. IT IS I... YOUR FATHER. >
< BUT HOW? I MEAN YOU DIED. OH PLEASE, FATHER... >
< NO, LISTEN... NO TIME... THE WIZARD... HE'S, HE'S... DON'T...DON'T... >
< WHAT IS IT, FATHER? PLEASE TELL ME. WHAT'S KEEPING YOU FROM TALKING? WHAT ABOUT THE WIZARD?>
< TRUST WIZARD. TRUST CHAMBER-LAIN. >

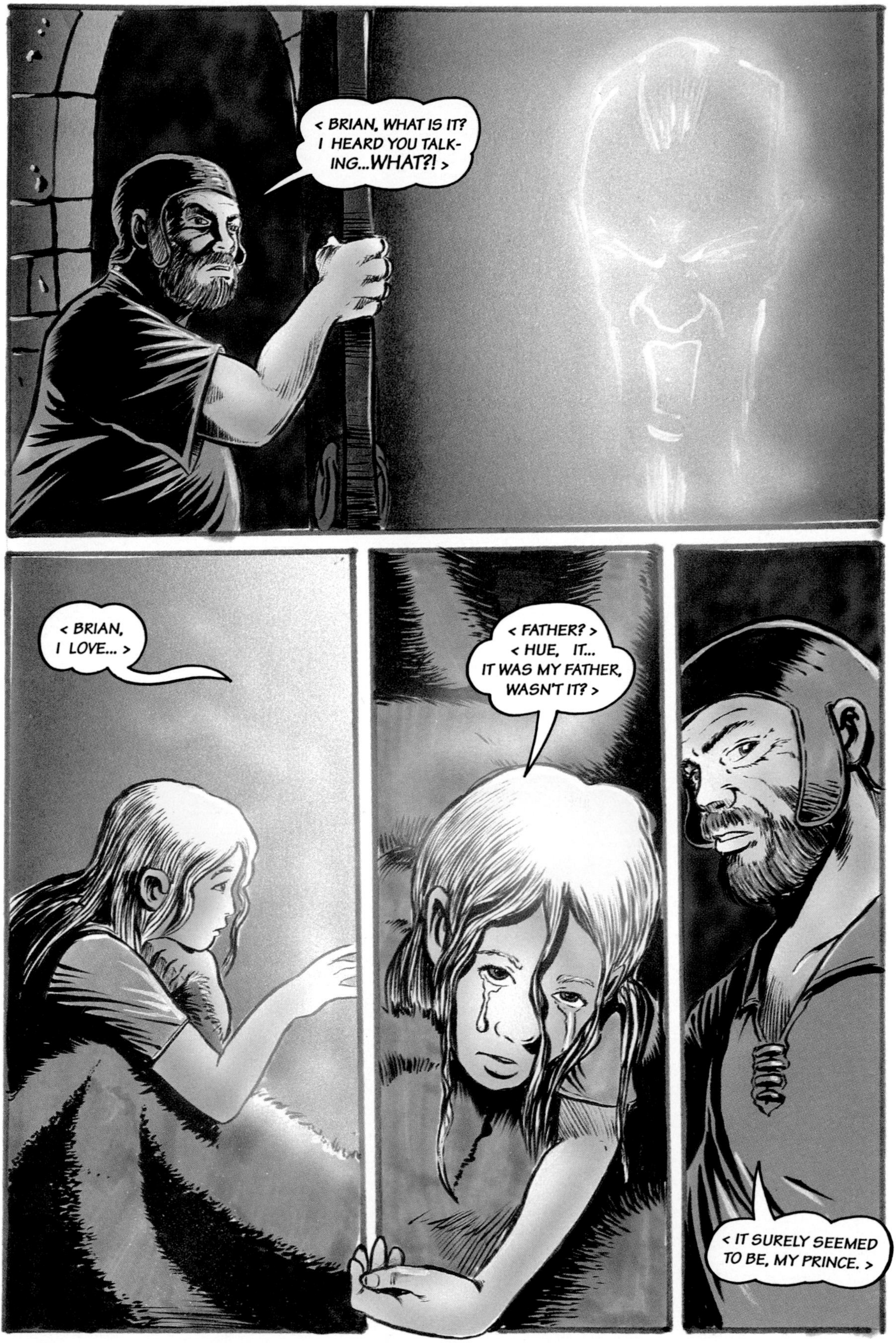
< BRIAN, WHAT IS IT? I HEARD YOU TALK-ING...WHAT?! >
< BRIAN, I LOVE... >
< FATHER? >
< HUE, IT... IT WAS MY FATHER, WASN'T IT? >
< IT SURELY SEEMED TO BE, MY PRINCE. >

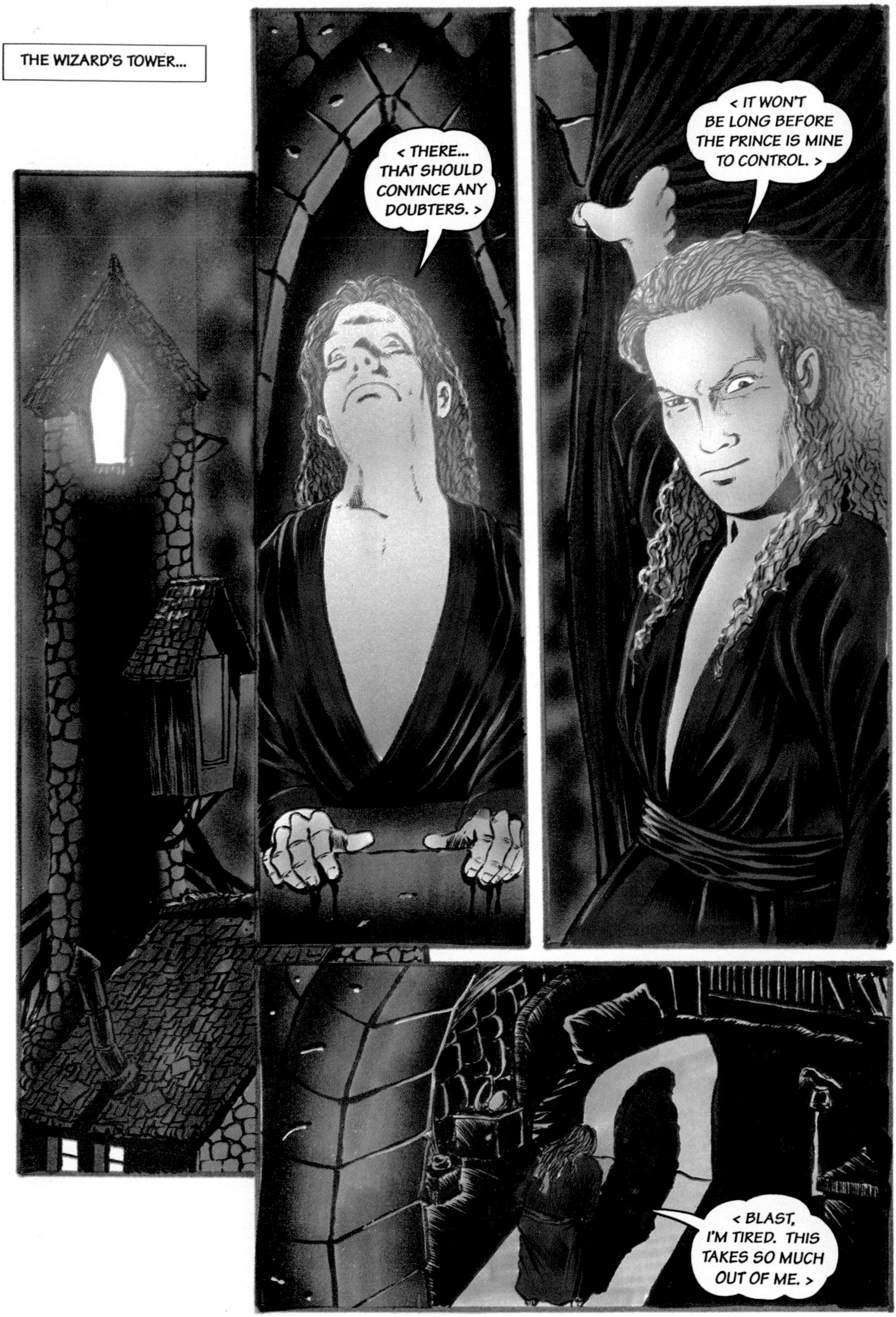
THE WIZARD'S TOWER...
< THERE... THAT SHOULD CONVINCE ANY DOUBTERS. >
< IT WON'T BE LONG BEFORE THE PRINCE IS MINE TO CONTROL. >
< BLAST, I'M TIRED. THIS TAKES SO MUCH OUT OF ME. >

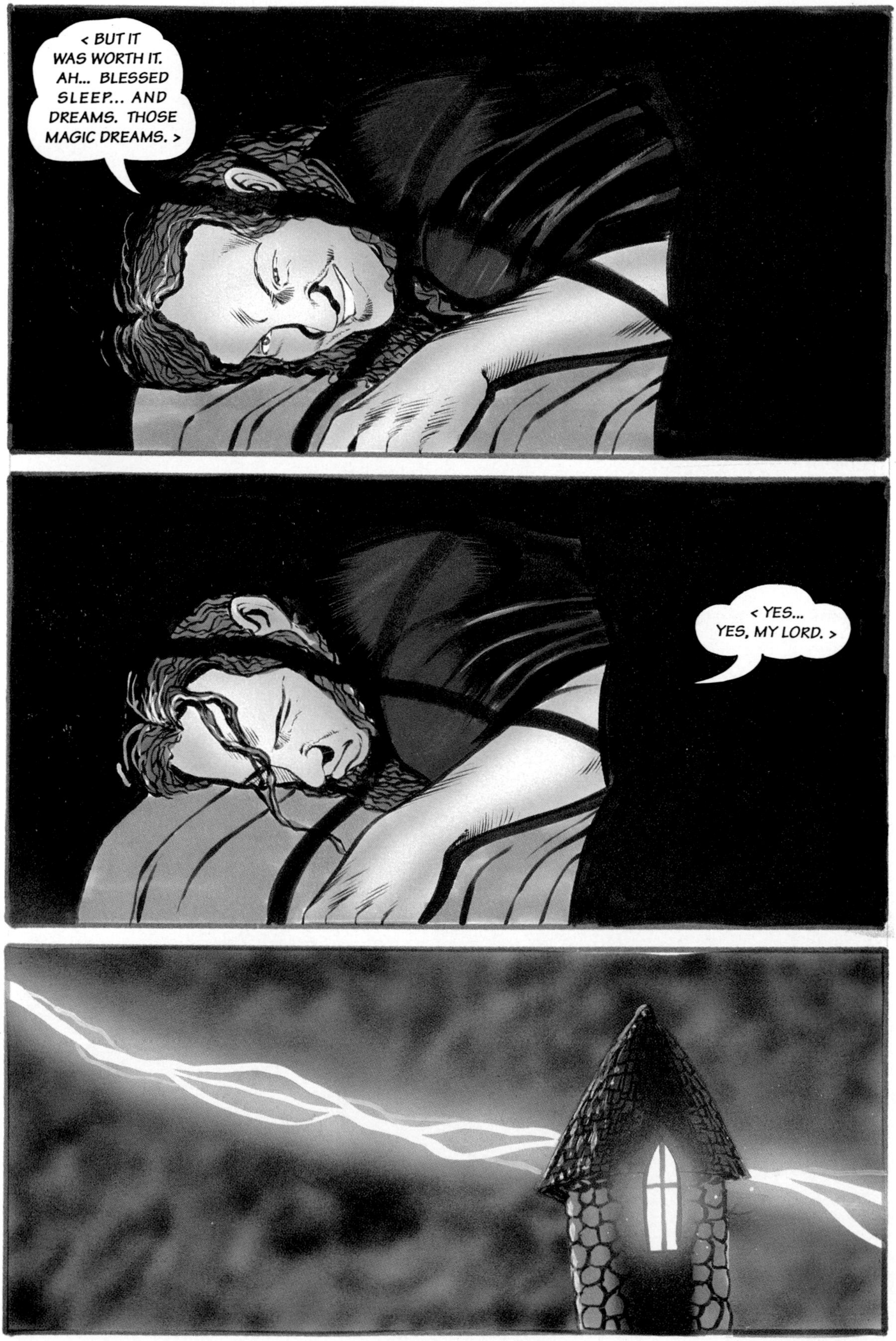
< BUT IT WAS WORTH IT. AH... BLESSED SLEEP... AND DREAMS. THOSE MAGIC DREAMS. >
< YES... YES, MY LORD. >

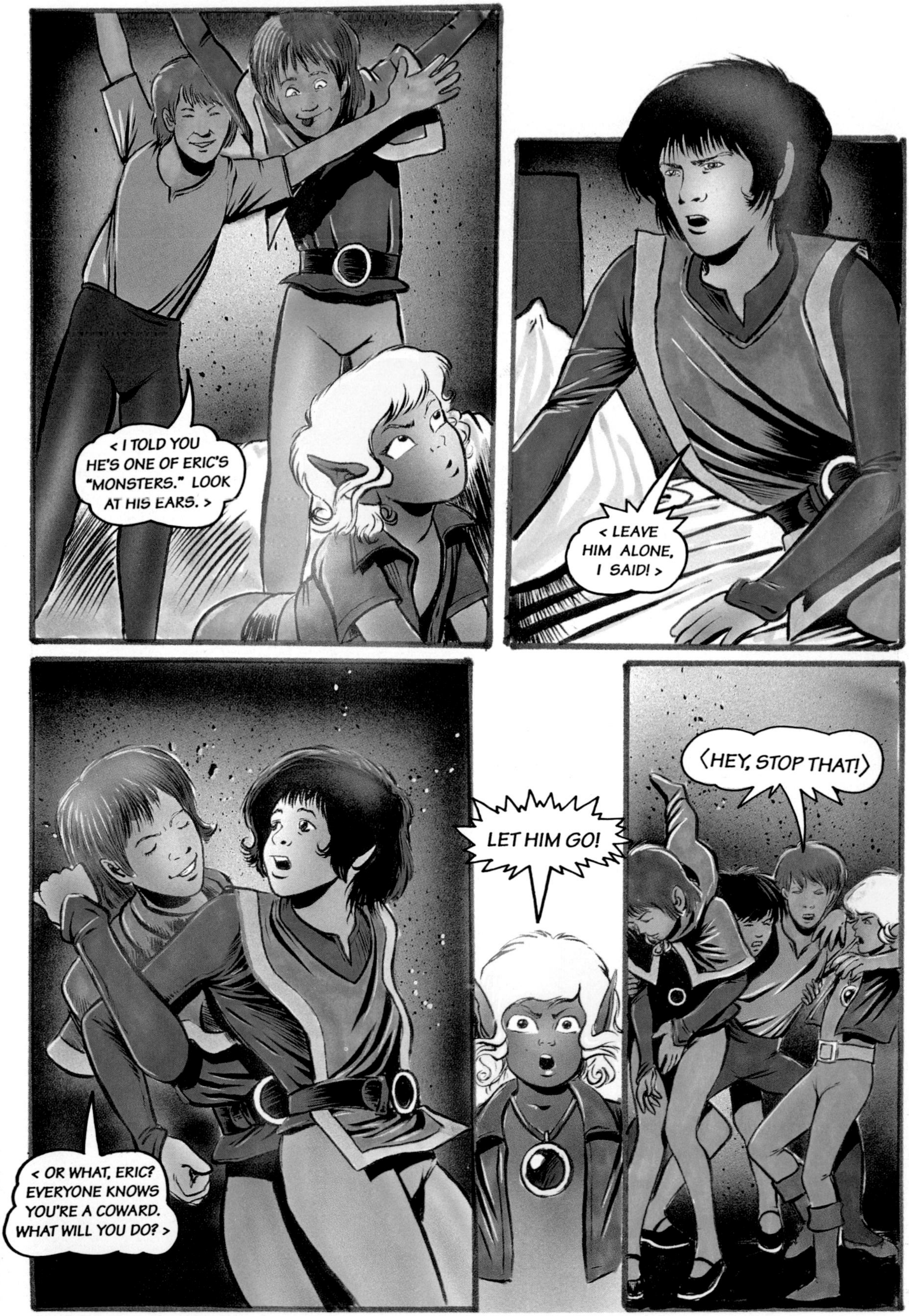
< I TOLD YOU HE'S ONE OF ERIC'S "MONSTERS." LOOK AT HIS EARS. >
< LEAVE HIM ALONE, I SAID! >
< OR WHAT, ERIC? EVERYONE KNOWS YOU'RE A COWARD. WHAT WILL YOU DO? >
LET HIM GO!
〈HEY, STOP THAT!〉

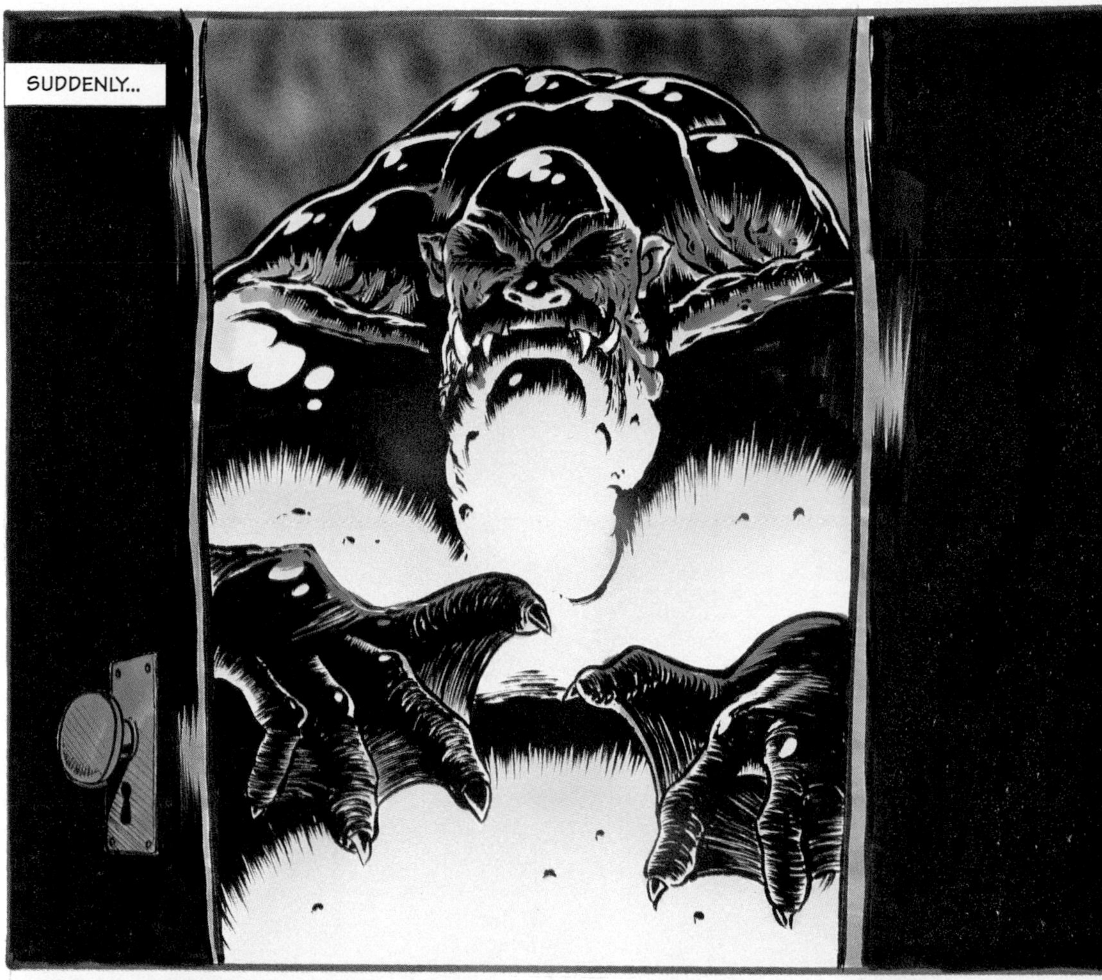
SUDDENLY...

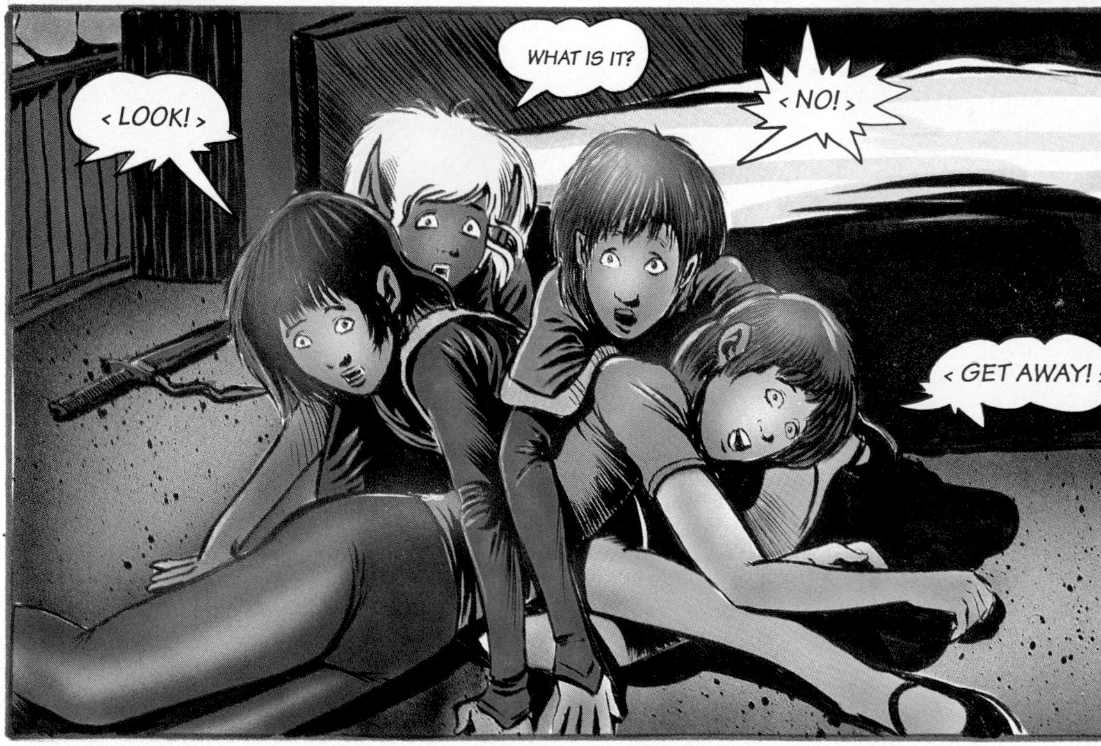
< LOOK! >
WHAT IS IT?
< NO! >
< GET AWAY! >

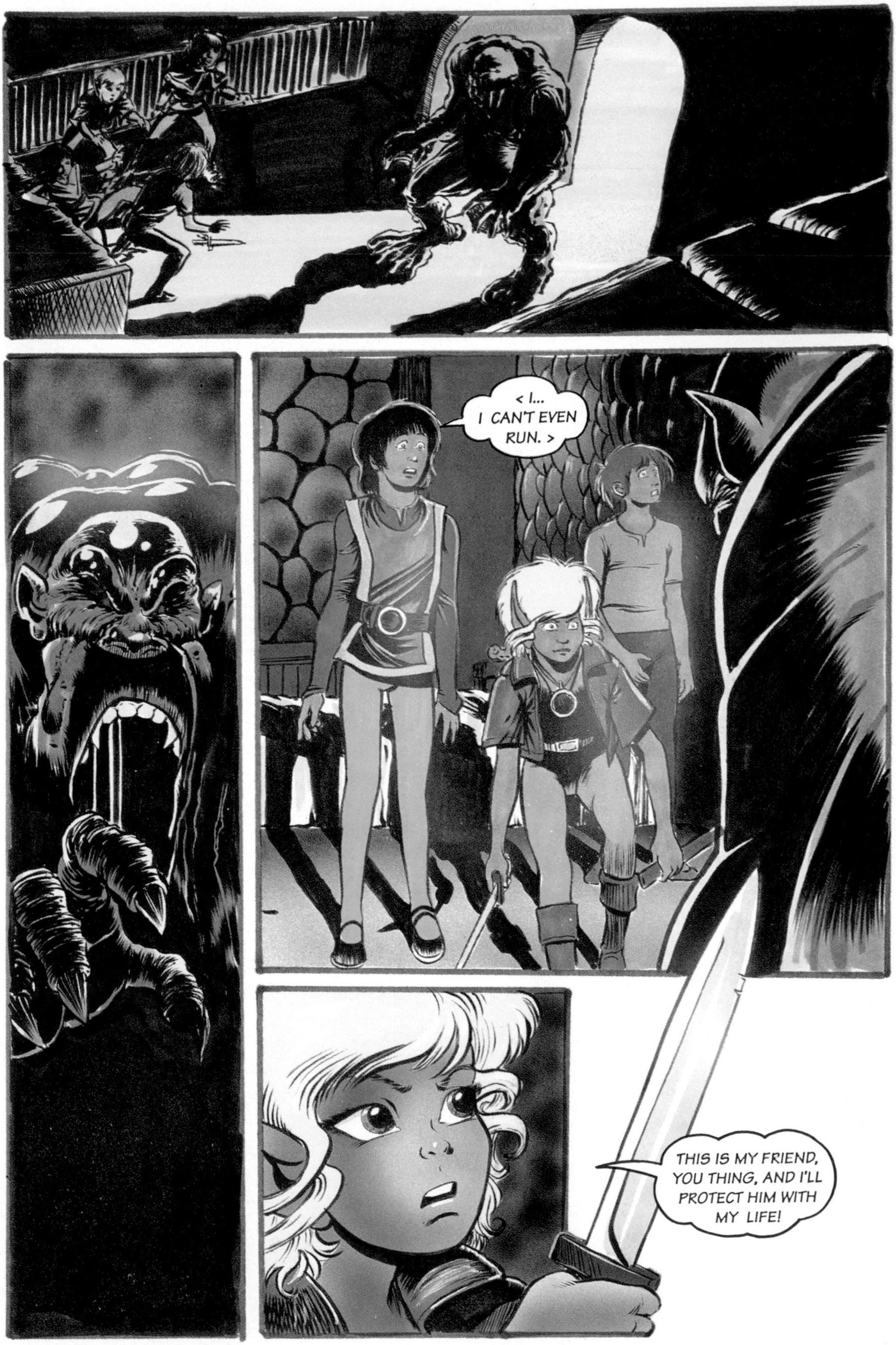
< I... I CAN'T EVEN RUN. >
THIS IS MY FRIEND, YOU THING, AND I'LL PROTECT HIM WITH MY LIFE!

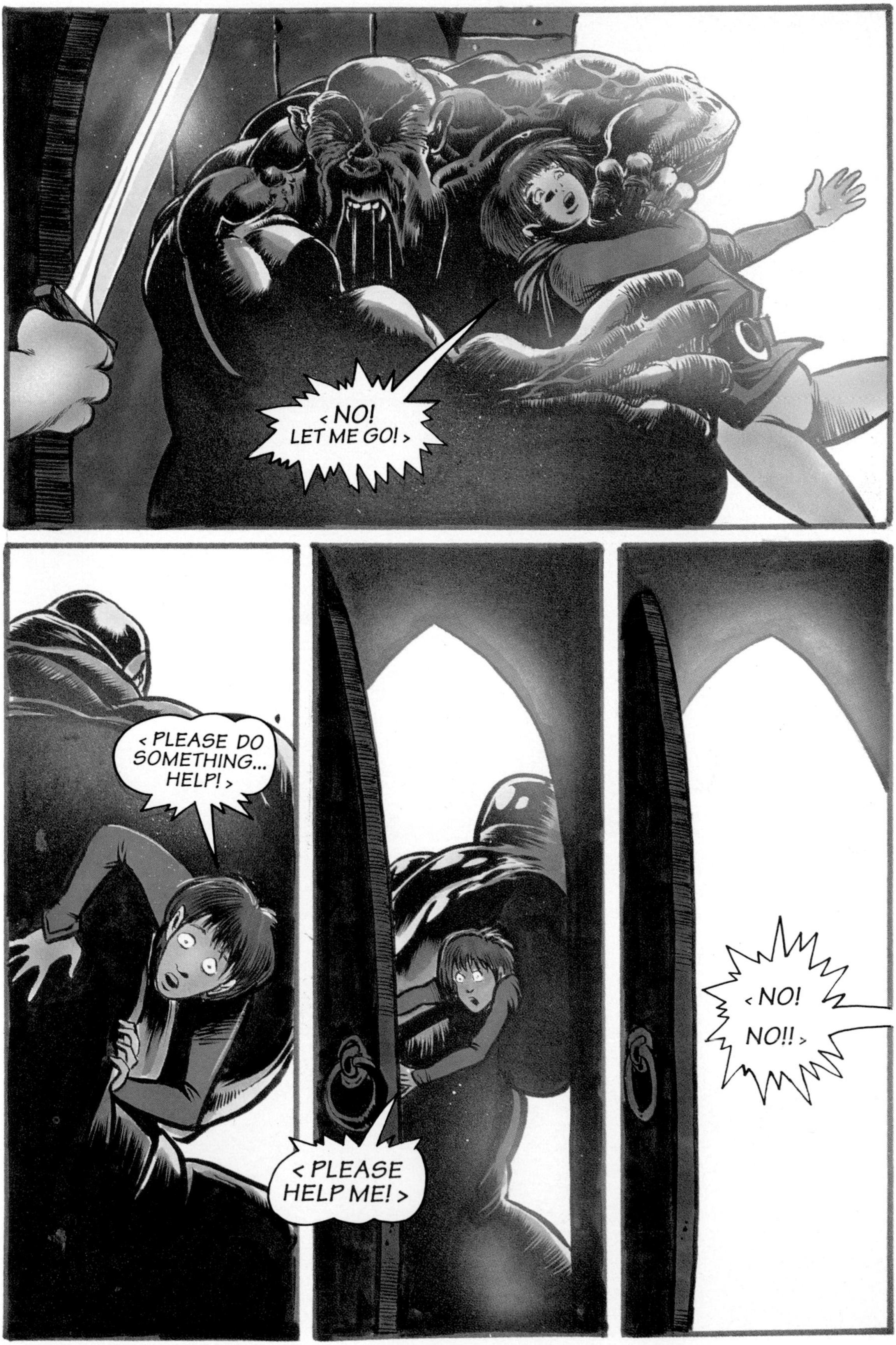
< NO! LET ME GO! >
< PLEASE DO SOMETHING... HELP! >
< PLEASE HELP ME! >
< NO! NO!! >

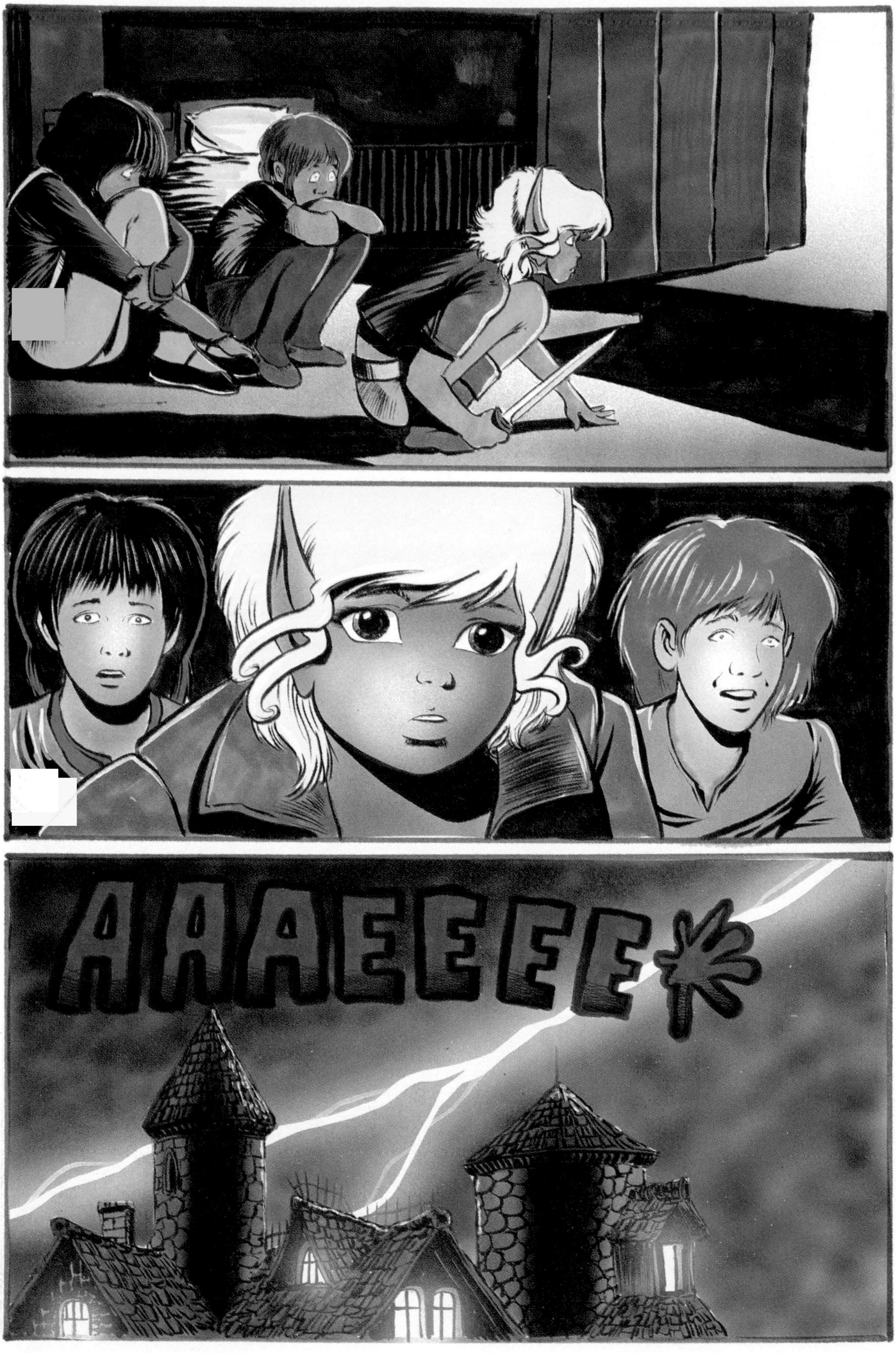
AAAEEEE

TO BE CONCLUDED...

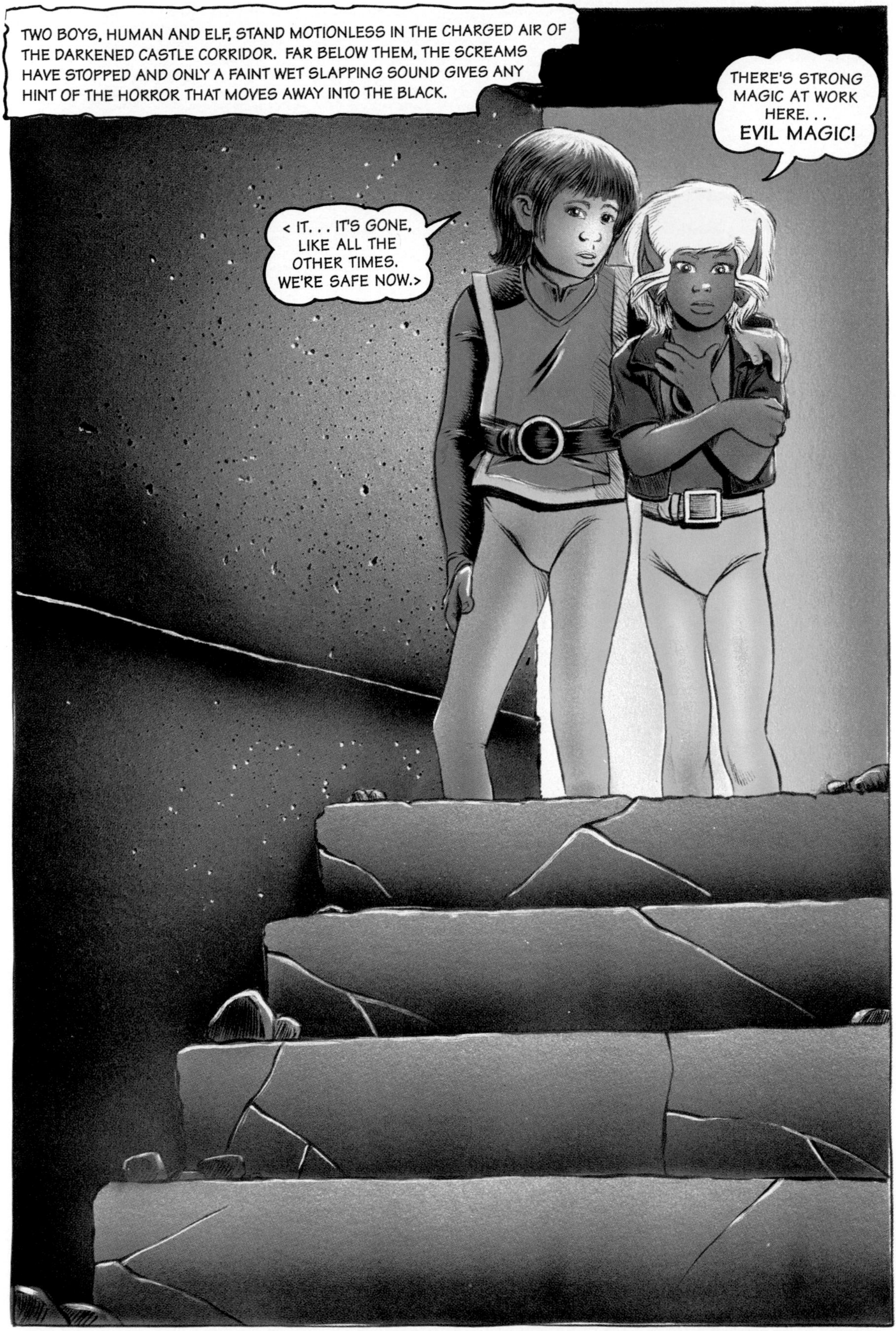
TWO BOYS, HUMAN AND ELF, STAND MOTIONLESS IN THE CHARGED AIR OF THE DARKENED CASTLE CORRIDOR. FAR BELOW THEM, THE SCREAMS HAVE STOPPED AND ONLY A FAINT WET SLAPPING SOUND GIVES ANY HINT OF THE HORROR THAT MOVES AWAY INTO THE BLACK.
THERE'S STRONG MAGIC AT WORK HERE. . . EVIL MAGIC!
< IT. . . IT'S GONE, LIKE ALL THE OTHER TIMES. WE'RE SAFE NOW.>

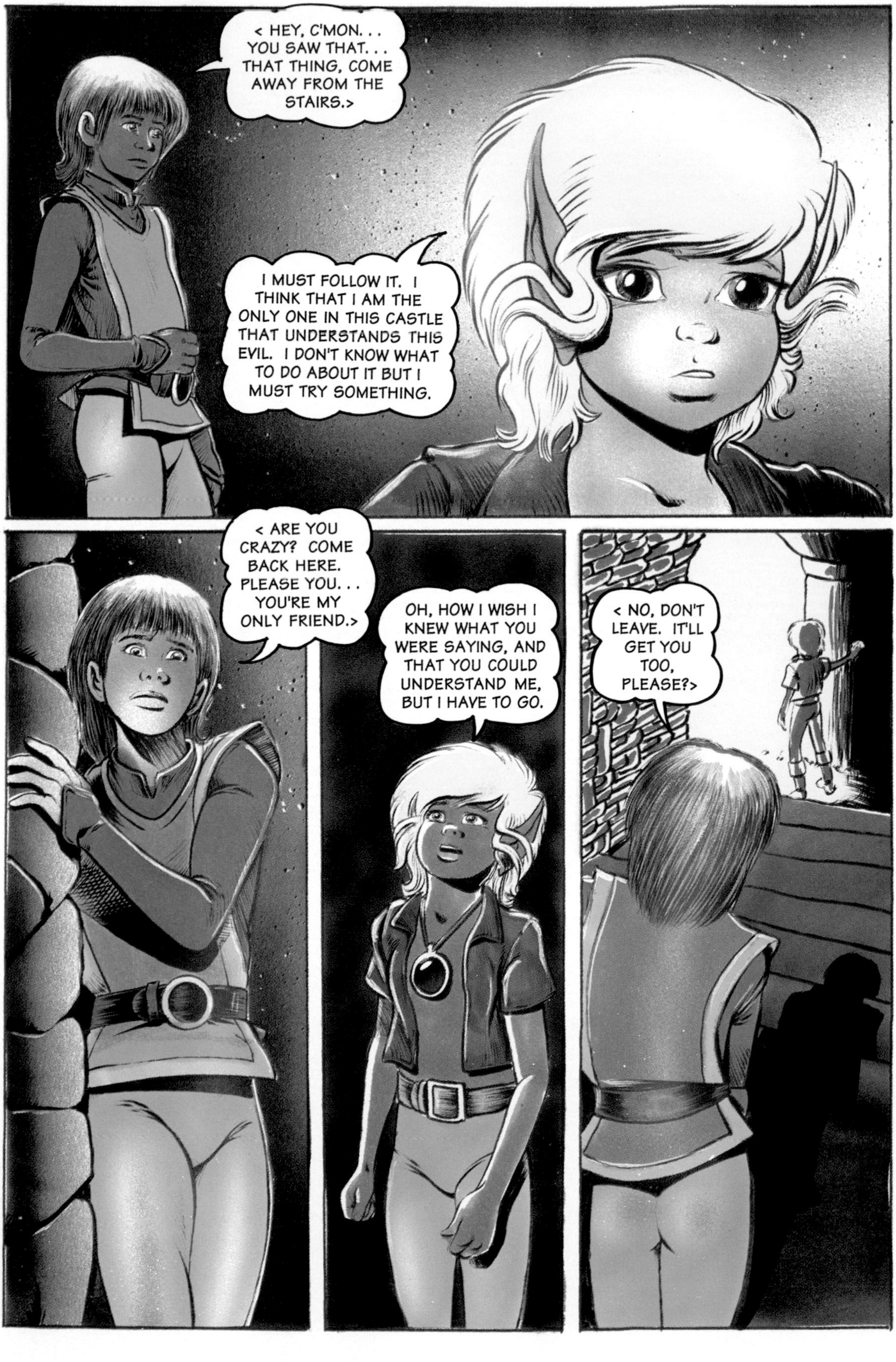
< HEY, C'MON. . . YOU SAW THAT. . . THAT THING, COME AWAY FROM THE STAIRS.>
I MUST FOLLOW IT. I THINK THAT I AM THE ONLY ONE IN THIS CASTLE THAT UNDERSTANDS THIS EVIL. I DON'T KNOW WHAT TO DO ABOUT IT BUT I MUST TRY SOMETHING.
< ARE YOU CRAZY? COME BACK HERE. PLEASE YOU. . . YOU'RE MY ONLY FRIEND.>
OH, HOW I WISH I KNEW WHAT YOU WERE SAYING, AND THAT YOU COULD UNDERSTAND ME, BUT I HAVE TO GO.
< NO, DON'T LEAVE. IT'LL GET YOU TOO, PLEASE?>

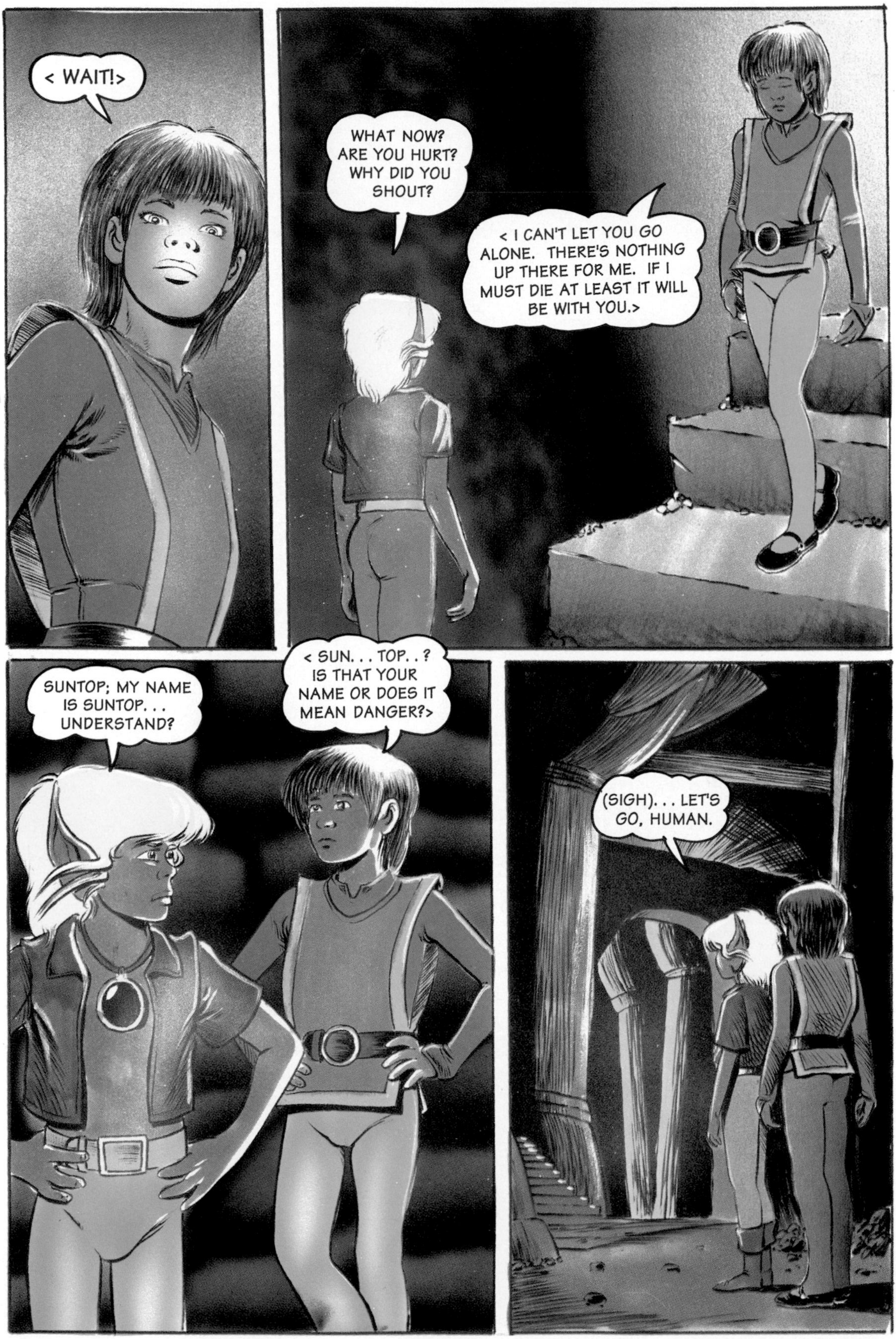

< WAIT!>
WHAT NOW? ARE YOU HURT? WHY DID YOU SHOUT?
< I CAN'T LET YOU GO ALONE. THERE'S NOTHING UP THERE FOR ME. IF I MUST DIE AT LEAST IT WILL BE WITH YOU.>
SUNTOP; MY NAME IS SUNTOP. . . UNDERSTAND?
< SUN. . . TOP. . ? IS THAT YOUR NAME OR DOES IT MEAN DANGER?>
(SIGH). . . LET'S GO, HUMAN.

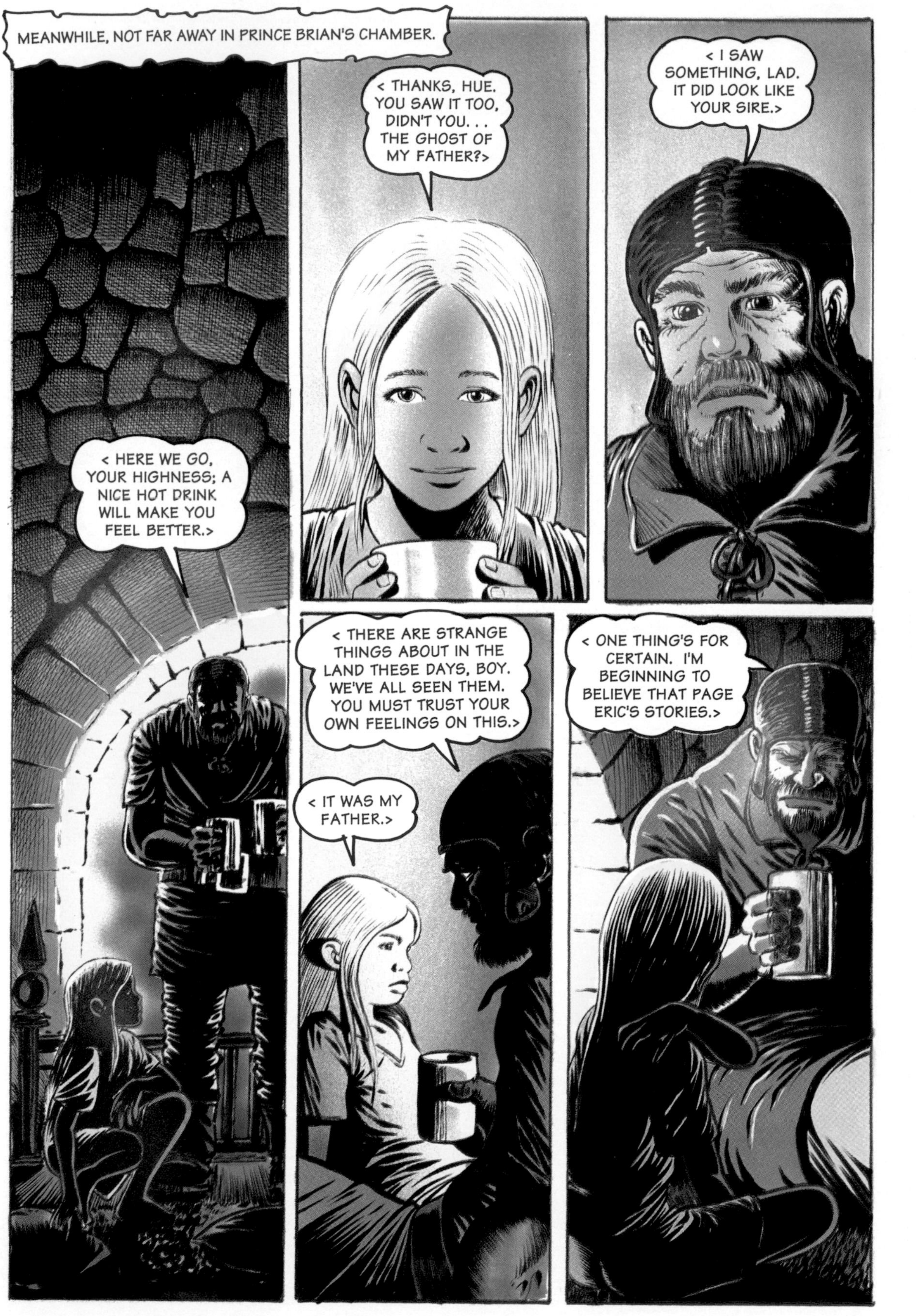
MEANWHILE, NOT FAR AWAY IN PRINCE BRIAN'S CHAMBER.
< HERE WE GO, YOUR HIGHNESS; A NICE HOT DRINK WILL MAKE YOU FEEL BETTER.>
< THANKS, HUE. YOU SAW IT TOO, DIDN'T YOU. . . THE GHOST OF MY FATHER?>
< I SAW SOMETHING, LAD. IT DID LOOK LIKE YOUR SIRE.>
< THERE ARE STRANGE THINGS ABOUT IN THE LAND THESE DAYS, BOY. WE'VE ALL SEEN THEM. YOU MUST TRUST YOUR OWN FEELINGS ON THIS.>
< IT WAS MY FATHER.>
< ONE THING'S FOR CERTAIN. I'M BEGINNING TO BELIEVE THAT PAGE ERIC'S STORIES.>

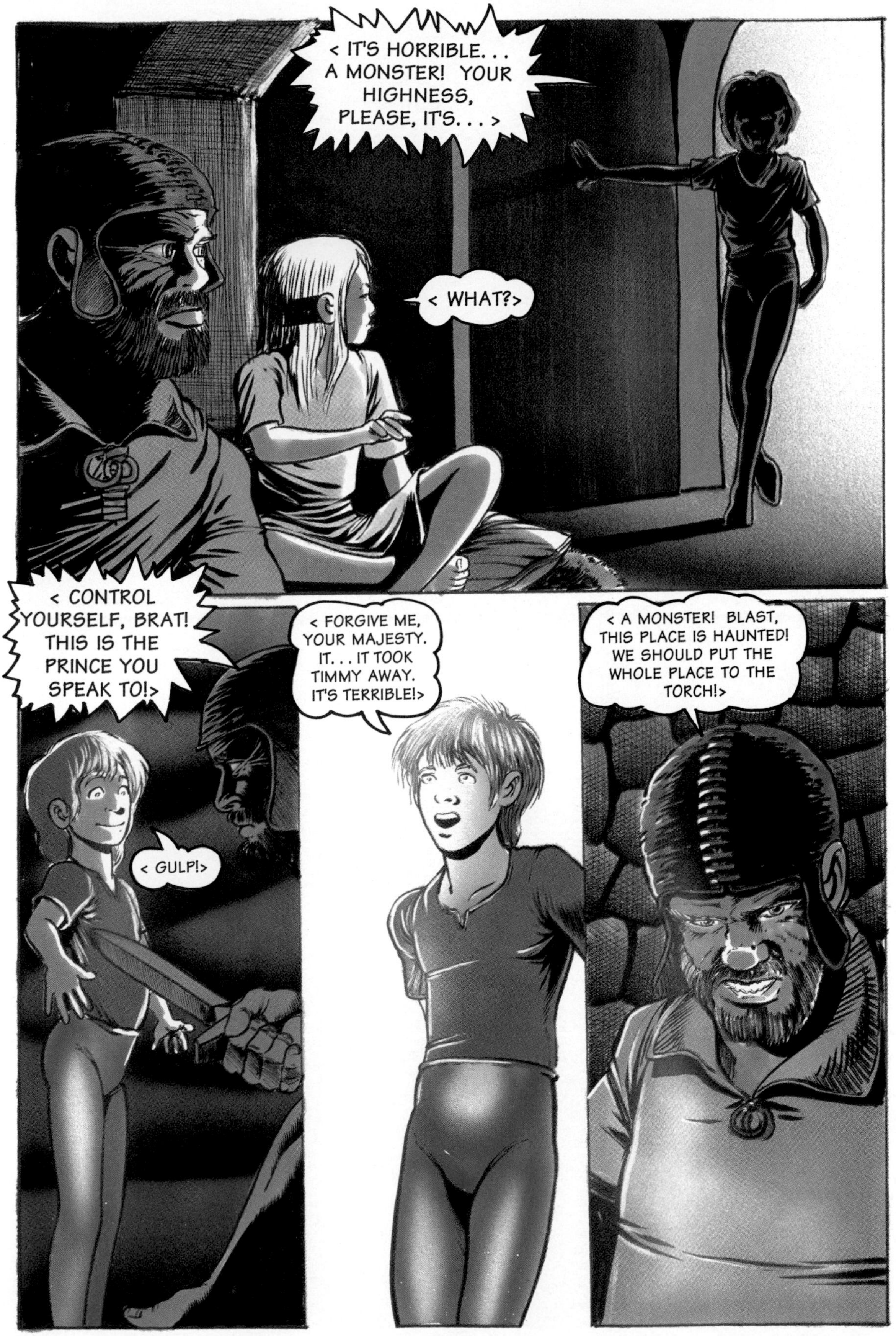

< IT'S HORRIBLE. . . A MONSTER! YOUR HIGHNESS, PLEASE, IT'S. . . >
< WHAT?>
< CONTROL YOURSELF, BRAT! THIS IS THE PRINCE YOU SPEAK TO!>
< GULP!>
< FORGIVE ME, YOUR MAJESTY. IT. . . IT TOOK TIMMY AWAY. IT'S TERRIBLE!>
< A MONSTER! BLAST, THIS PLACE IS HAUNTED! WE SHOULD PUT THE WHOLE PLACE TO THE TORCH!>

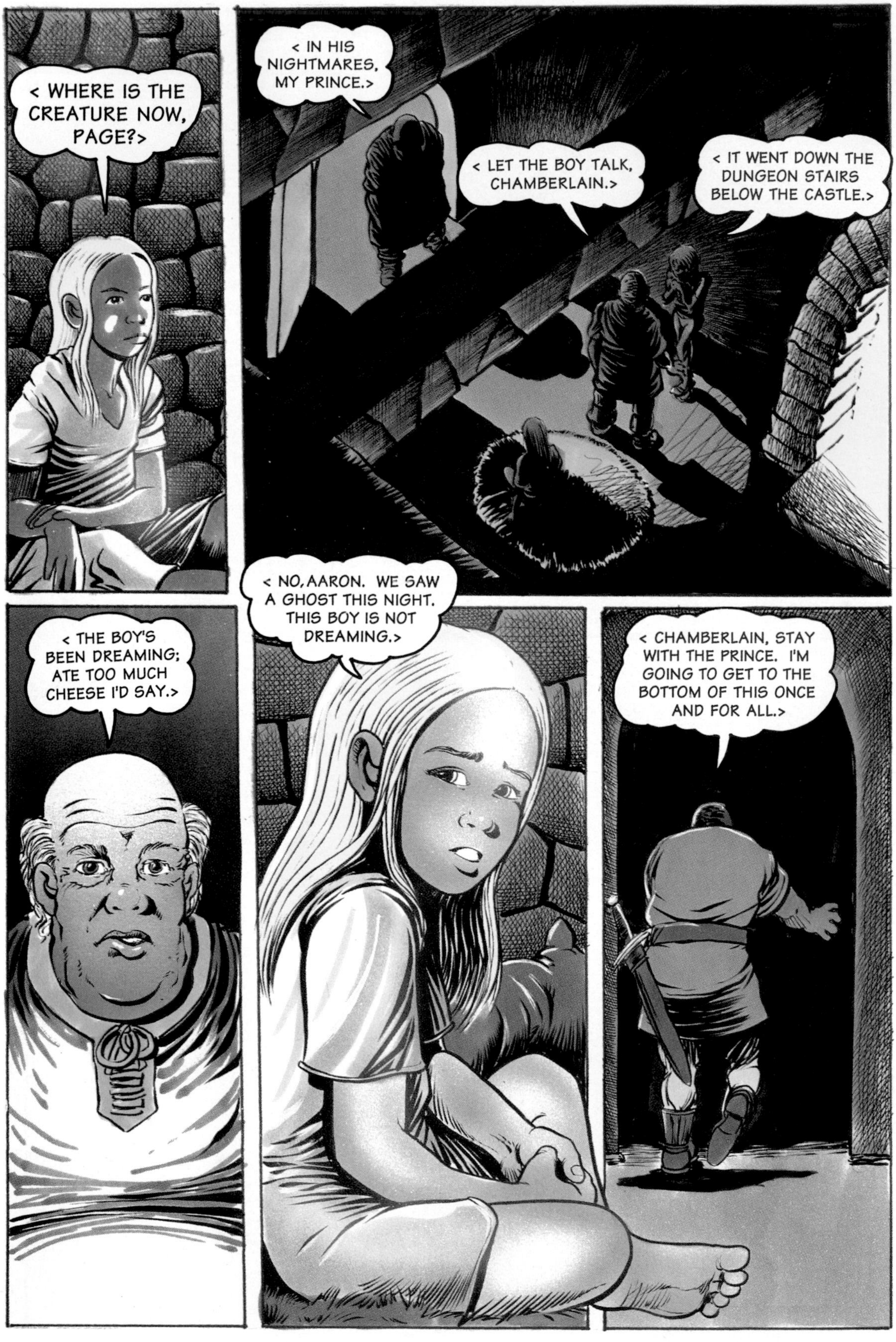
< WHERE IS THE CREATURE NOW, PAGE?>
< IN HIS NIGHTMARES, MY PRINCE.>
< LET THE BOY TALK, CHAMBERLAIN.>
< IT WENT DOWN THE DUNGEON STAIRS BELOW THE CASTLE.>
< THE BOY'S BEEN DREAMING; ATE TOO MUCH CHEESE I'D SAY.>
< NO, AARON. WE SAW A GHOST THIS NIGHT. THIS BOY IS NOT DREAMING.>
< CHAMBERLAIN, STAY WITH THE PRINCE. I'M GOING TO GET TO THE BOTTOM OF THIS ONCE AND FOR ALL.>

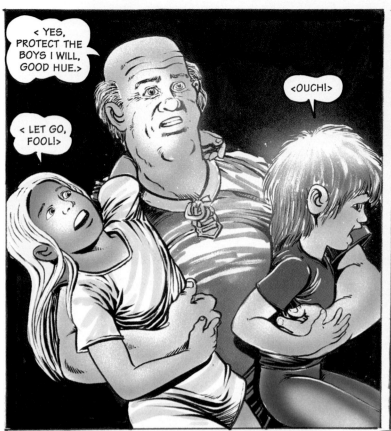

< YES, PROTECT THE BOYS I WILL, GOOD HUE. >

< LET GO, FOOL! >

<OUCH!>

< FORGIVE ME, MY PRINCE. I ONLY WANT YOU TO BE SAFE. WE CAN'T ALLOW ANY "MONSTERS" TO ATTACK YOU. >

< I THOUGHT YOU SCOFFED AT THE VERY IDEA. WHAT'S GOTTEN INTO YOU, CHAMBERLAIN? >

< JUST YOUR SAFETY, MY PRINCE. IN FACT, I THINK THE ROYAL WIZARD SHOULD BE NOTIFIED RIGHT AWAY. YES, THAT'S JUST WHAT I'LL DO. PAGE, GUARD THE PRINCE. >

< (GULP), I'LL TRY! >

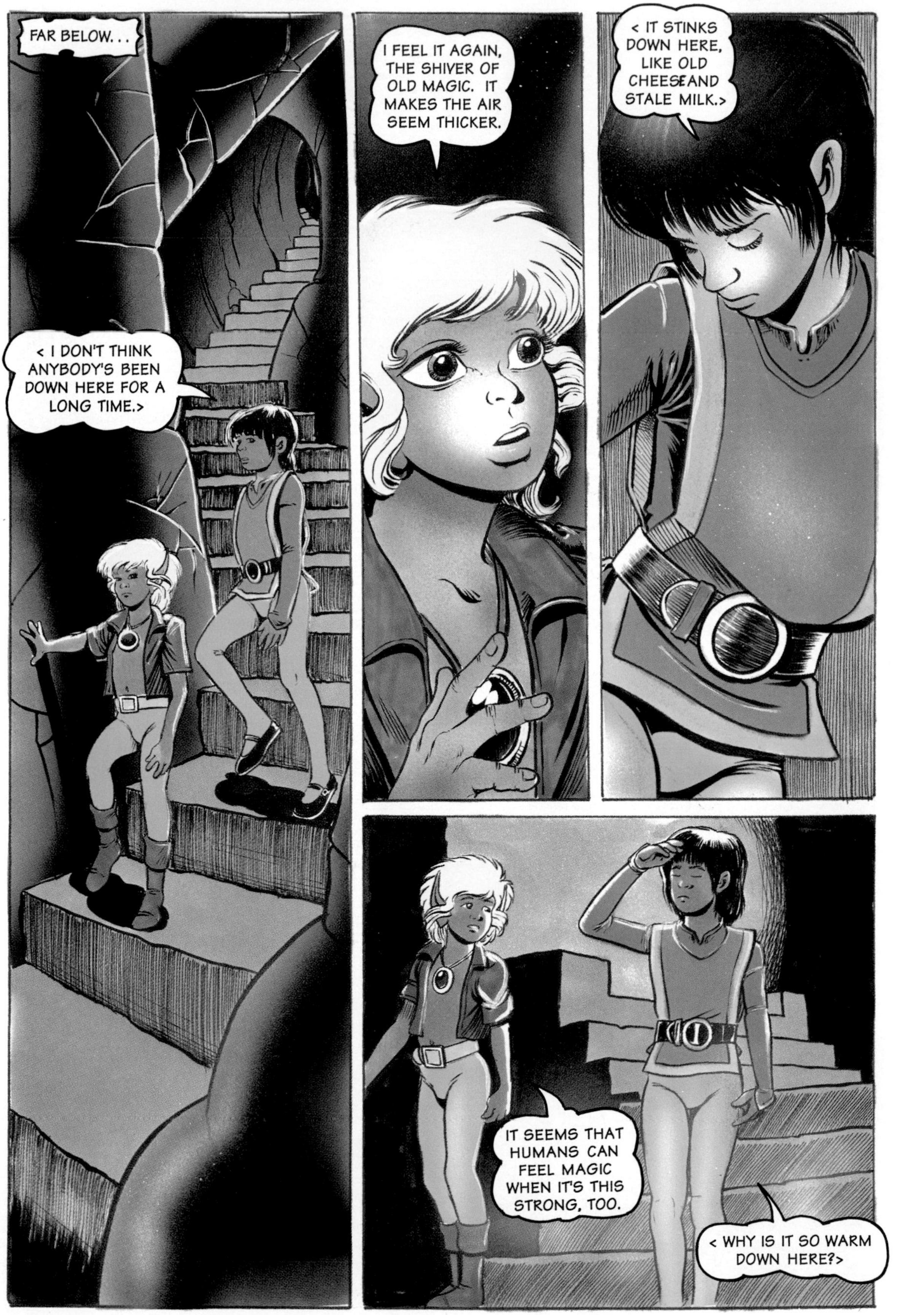
FAR BELOW. . .
< I DON'T THINK ANYBODY'S BEEN DOWN HERE FOR A LONG TIME.>
I FEEL IT AGAIN, THE SHIVER OF OLD MAGIC. IT MAKES THE AIR SEEM THICKER.
< IT STINKS DOWN HERE, LIKE OLD CHEESE AND STALE MILK.>
IT SEEMS THAT HUMANS CAN FEEL MAGIC WHEN IT'S THIS STRONG, TOO.
< WHY IS IT SO WARM DOWN HERE?>

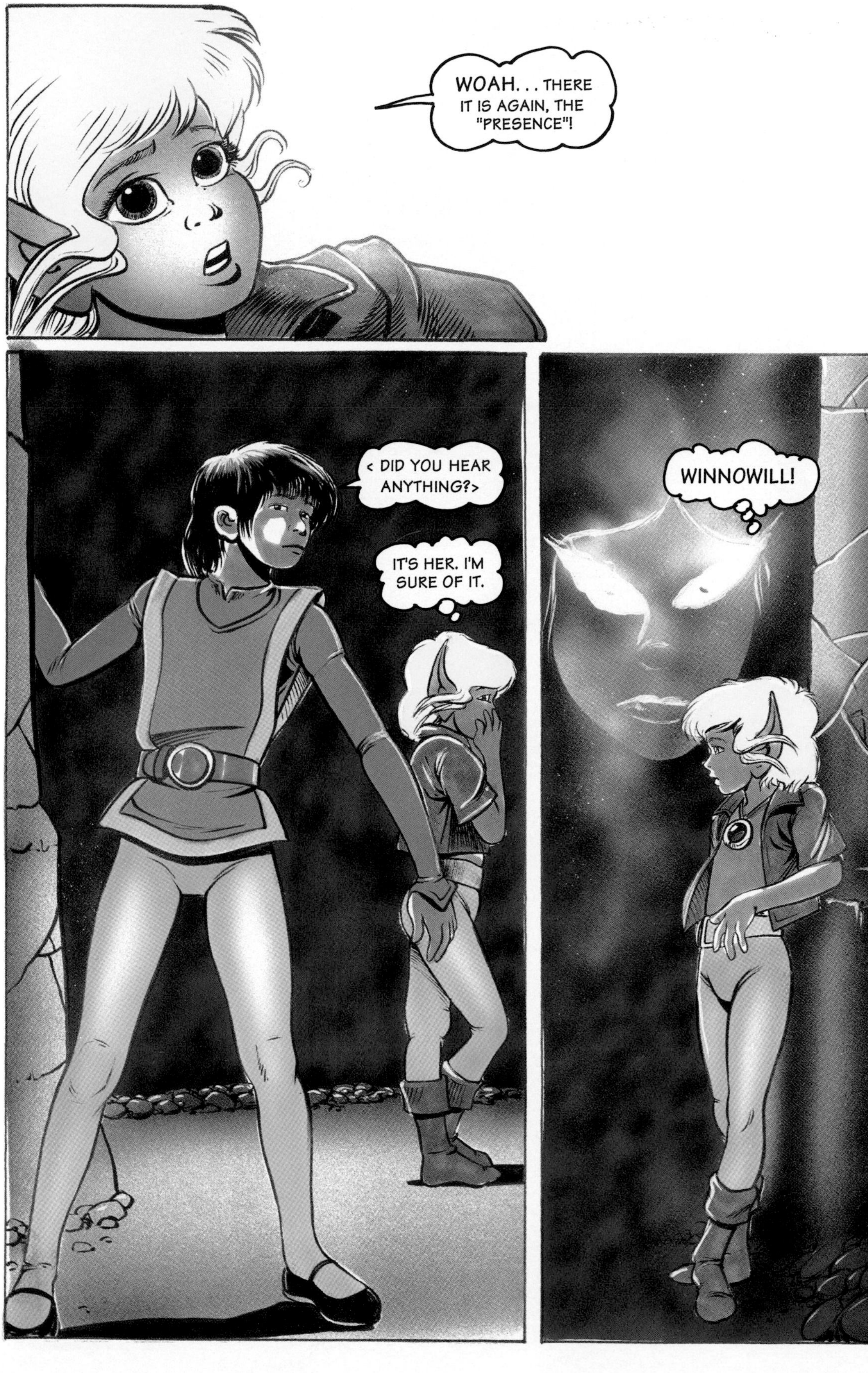
WOAH. . . THERE IT IS AGAIN, THE "PRESENCE"!
< DID YOU HEAR ANYTHING?>
IT'S HER. I'M SURE OF IT.
WINNOWILL!

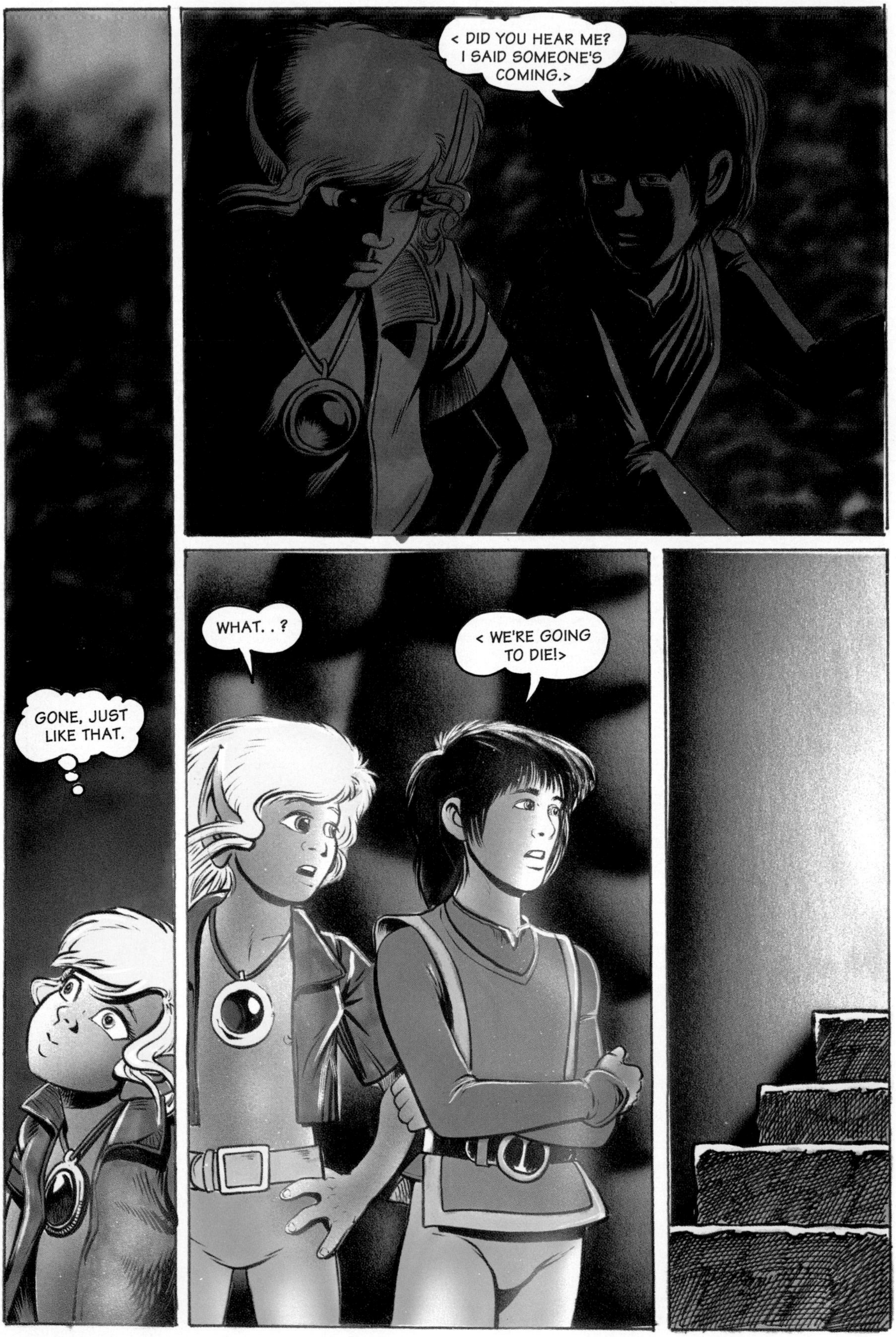

< DID YOU HEAR ME? I SAID SOMEONE'S COMING.>
GONE, JUST LIKE THAT.
WHAT. . ?
< WE'RE GOING TO DIE!>

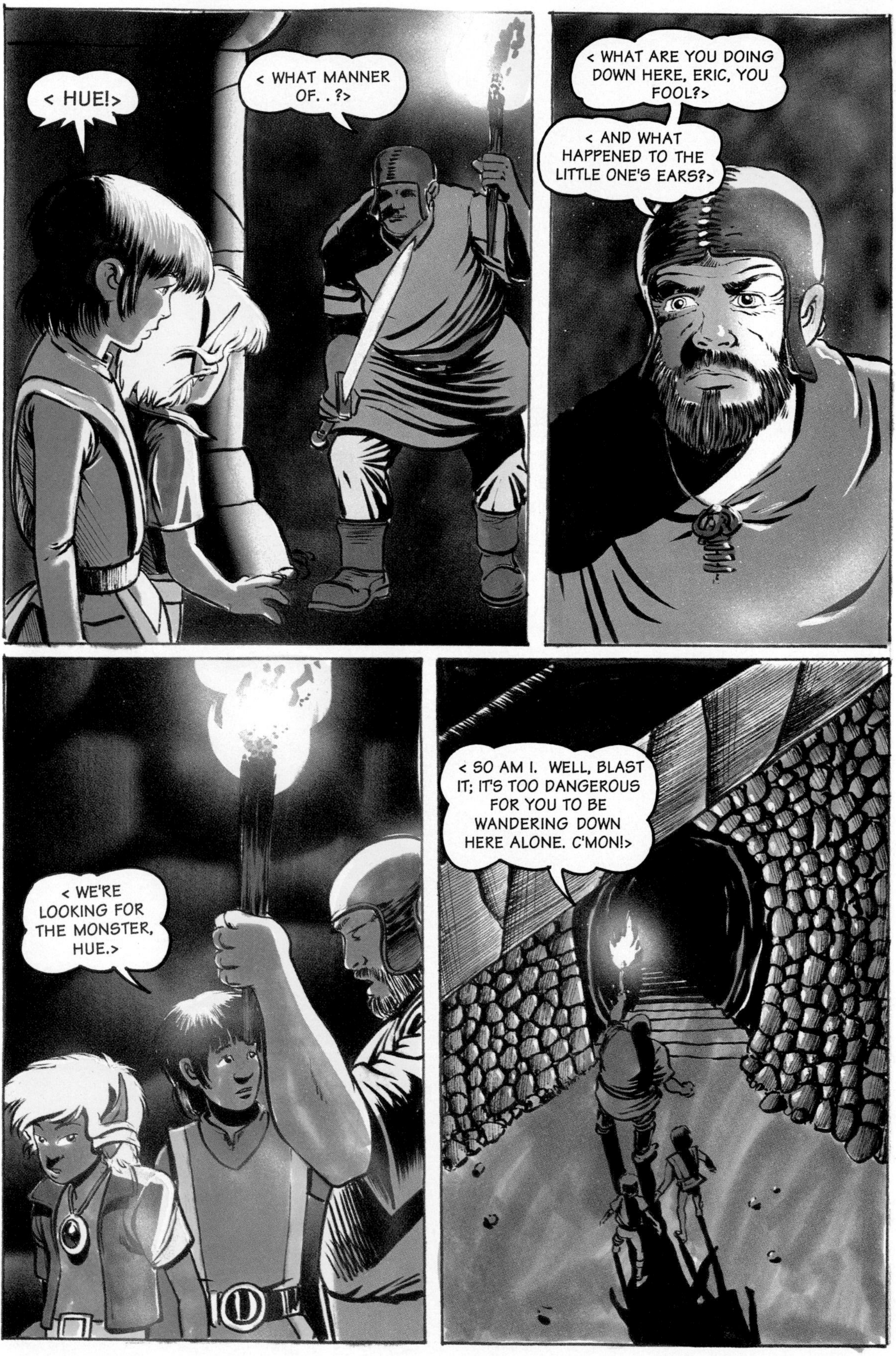
< HUE!>
< WHAT MANNER OF. . ?>
< WHAT ARE YOU DOING DOWN HERE, ERIC, YOU FOOL?>
< AND WHAT HAPPENED TO THE LITTLE ONE'S EARS?>
< WE'RE LOOKING FOR THE MONSTER, HUE.>
< SO AM I. WELL, BLAST IT; IT'S TOO DANGEROUS FOR YOU TO BE WANDERING DOWN HERE ALONE. C'MON!>

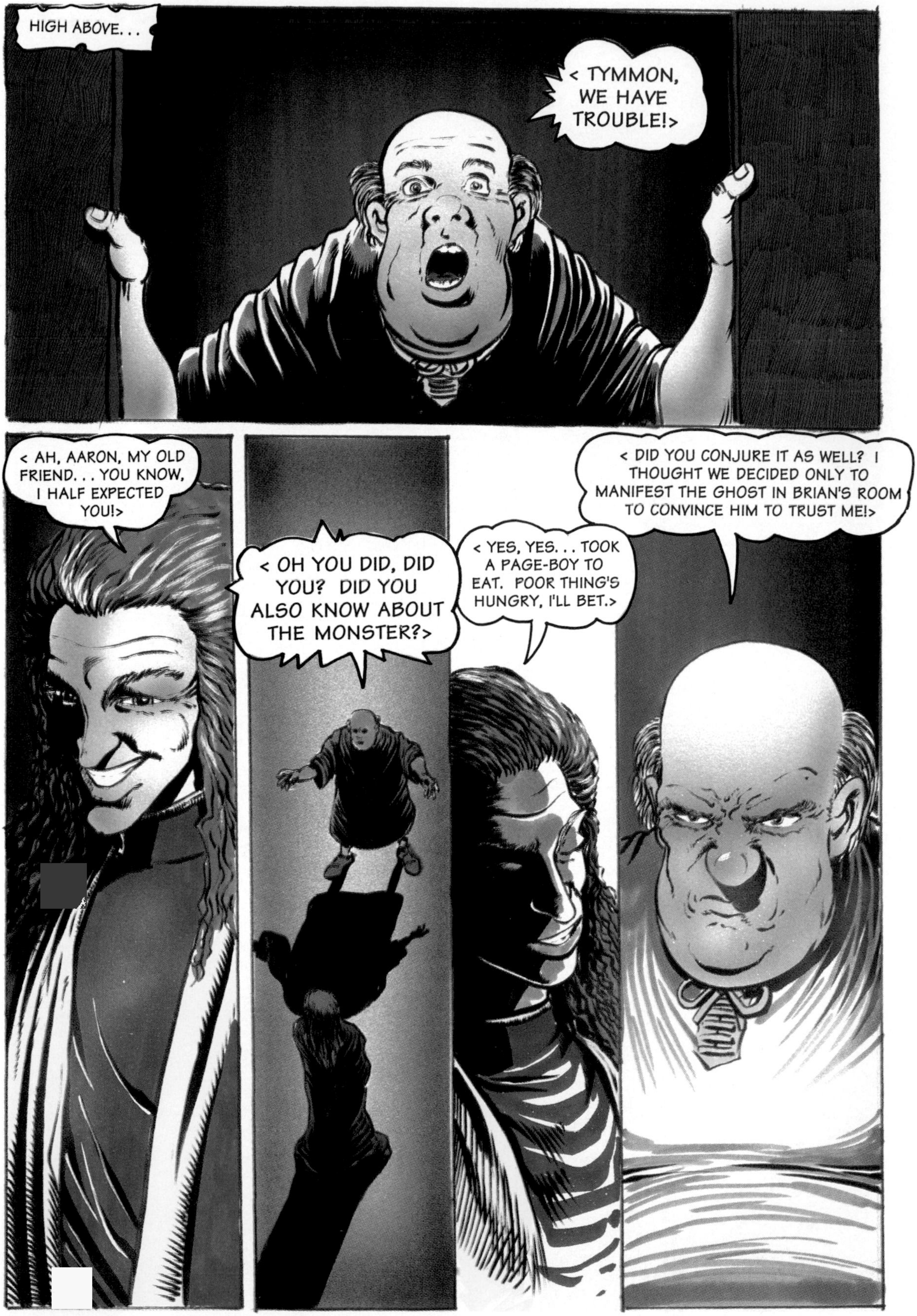
HIGH ABOVE. . .
< TYMMON, WE HAVE TROUBLE!>
< AH, AARON, MY OLD FRIEND. . . YOU KNOW, I HALF EXPECTED YOU!>
< OH YOU DID, DID YOU? DID YOU ALSO KNOW ABOUT THE MONSTER?>
< YES, YES. . . TOOK A PAGE-BOY TO EAT. POOR THING'S HUNGRY, I'LL BET.>
< DID YOU CONJURE IT AS WELL? I THOUGHT WE DECIDED ONLY TO MANIFEST THE GHOST IN BRIAN'S ROOM TO CONVINCE HIM TO TRUST ME!>

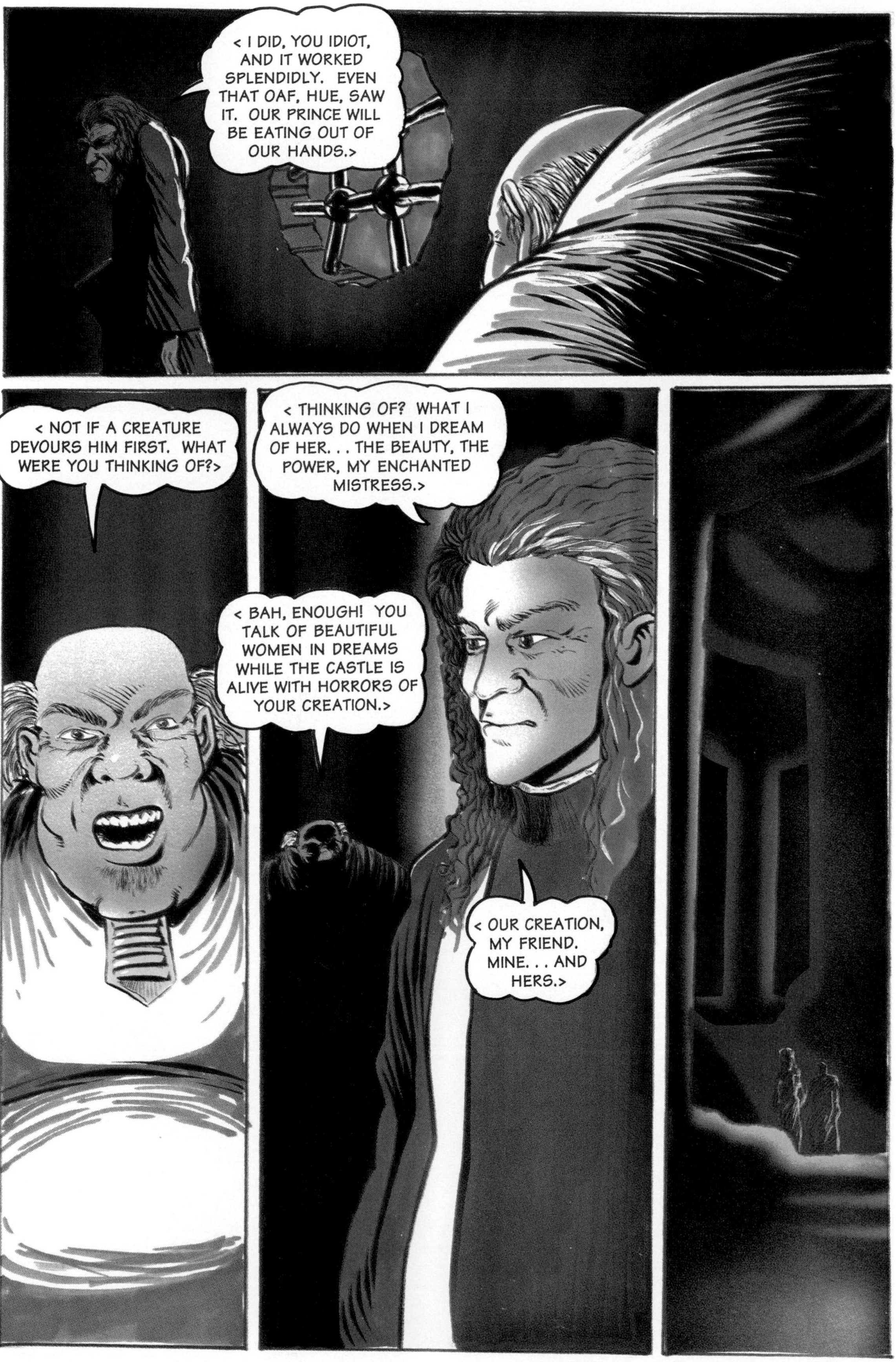
< I DID, YOU IDIOT, AND IT WORKED SPLENDIDLY. EVEN THAT OAF, HUE, SAW IT. OUR PRINCE WILL BE EATING OUT OF OUR HANDS.>
< NOT IF A CREATURE DEVOURS HIM FIRST. WHAT WERE YOU THINKING OF?>
< THINKING OF? WHAT I ALWAYS DO WHEN I DREAM OF HER. . . THE BEAUTY, THE POWER, MY ENCHANTED MISTRESS.>
< BAH, ENOUGH! YOU TALK OF BEAUTIFUL WOMEN IN DREAMS WHILE THE CASTLE IS ALIVE WITH HORRORS OF YOUR CREATION.>
< OUR CREATION, MY FRIEND. MINE. . . AND HERS.>

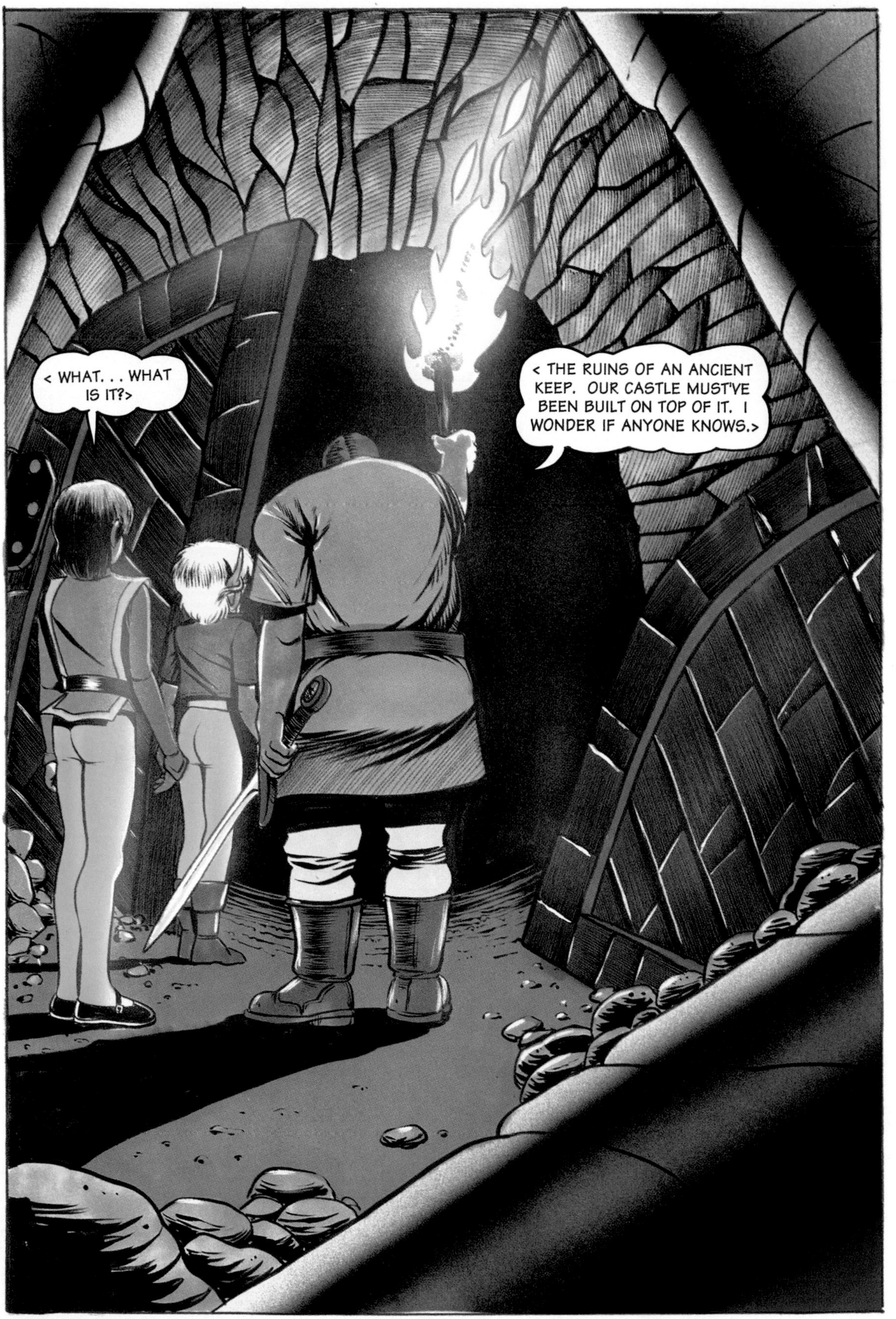
< WHAT. . . WHAT IS IT?>
< THE RUINS OF AN ANCIENT KEEP. OUR CASTLE MUST'VE BEEN BUILT ON TOP OF IT. I WONDER IF ANYONE KNOWS.>

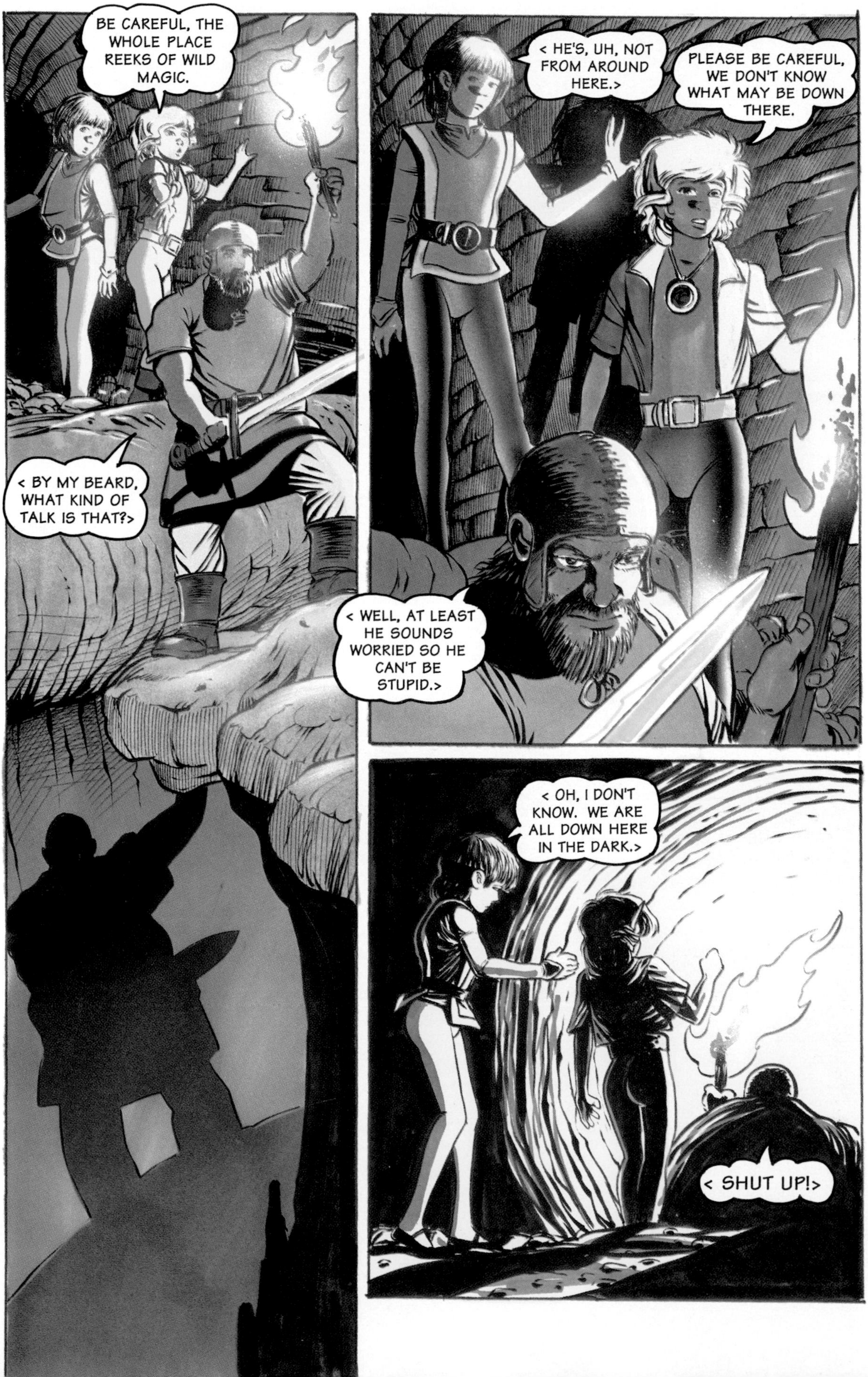
BE CAREFUL, THE WHOLE PLACE REEKS OF WILD MAGIC.
< BY MY BEARD, WHAT KIND OF TALK IS THAT?>
< HE'S, UH, NOT FROM AROUND HERE.>
PLEASE BE CAREFUL, WE DON'T KNOW WHAT MAY BE DOWN THERE.
< WELL, AT LEAST HE SOUNDS WORRIED SO HE CAN'T BE STUPID.>
< OH, I DON'T KNOW. WE ARE ALL DOWN HERE IN THE DARK.>
< SHUT UP!>

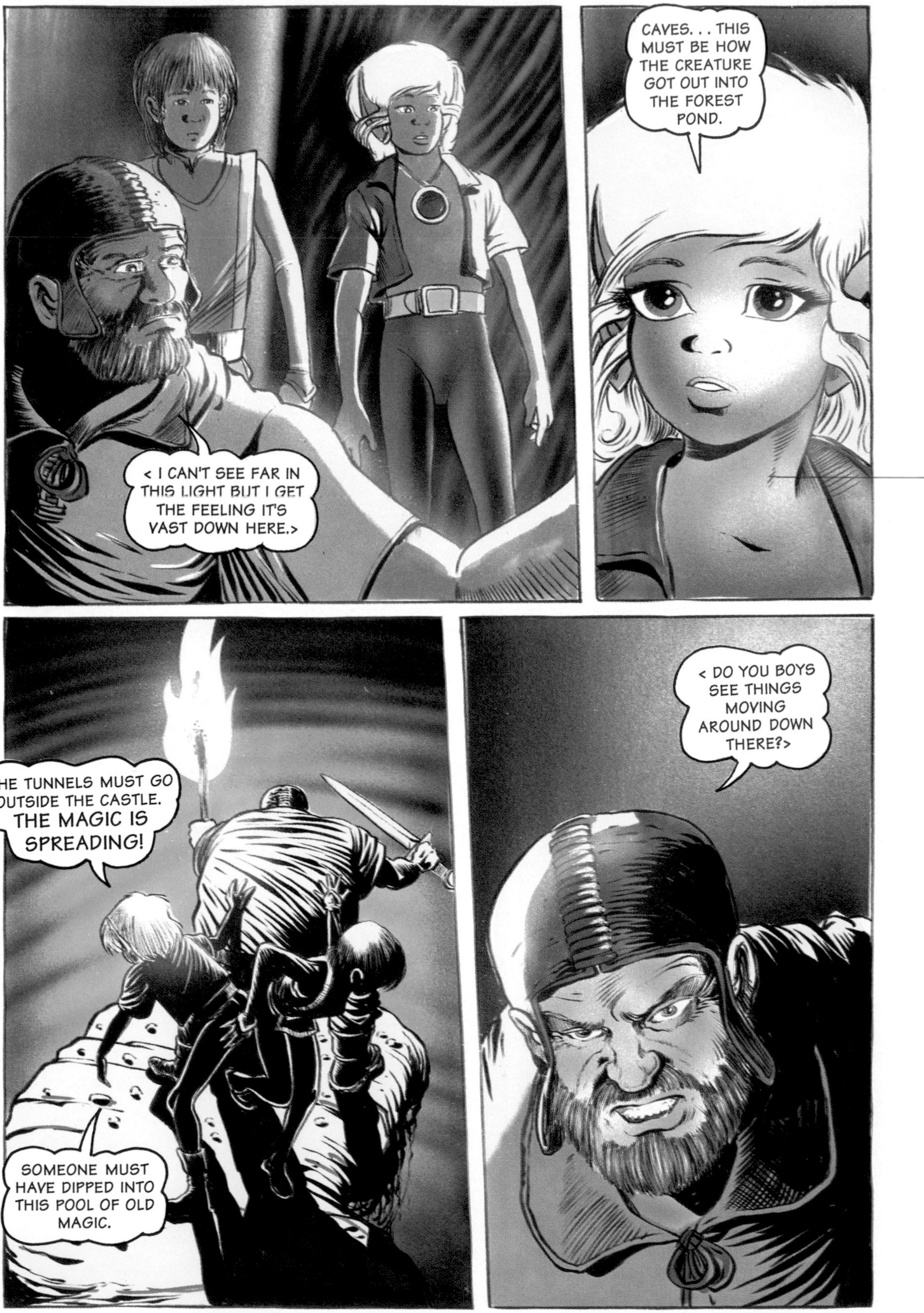

< I CAN'T SEE FAR IN THIS LIGHT BUT I GET THE FEELING IT'S VAST DOWN HERE.>
CAVES. . . THIS MUST BE HOW THE CREATURE GOT OUT INTO THE FOREST POND.
THE TUNNELS MUST GO OUTSIDE THE CASTLE. THE MAGIC IS SPREADING!
SOMEONE MUST HAVE DIPPED INTO THIS POOL OF OLD MAGIC.
< DO YOU BOYS SEE THINGS MOVING AROUND DOWN THERE?>

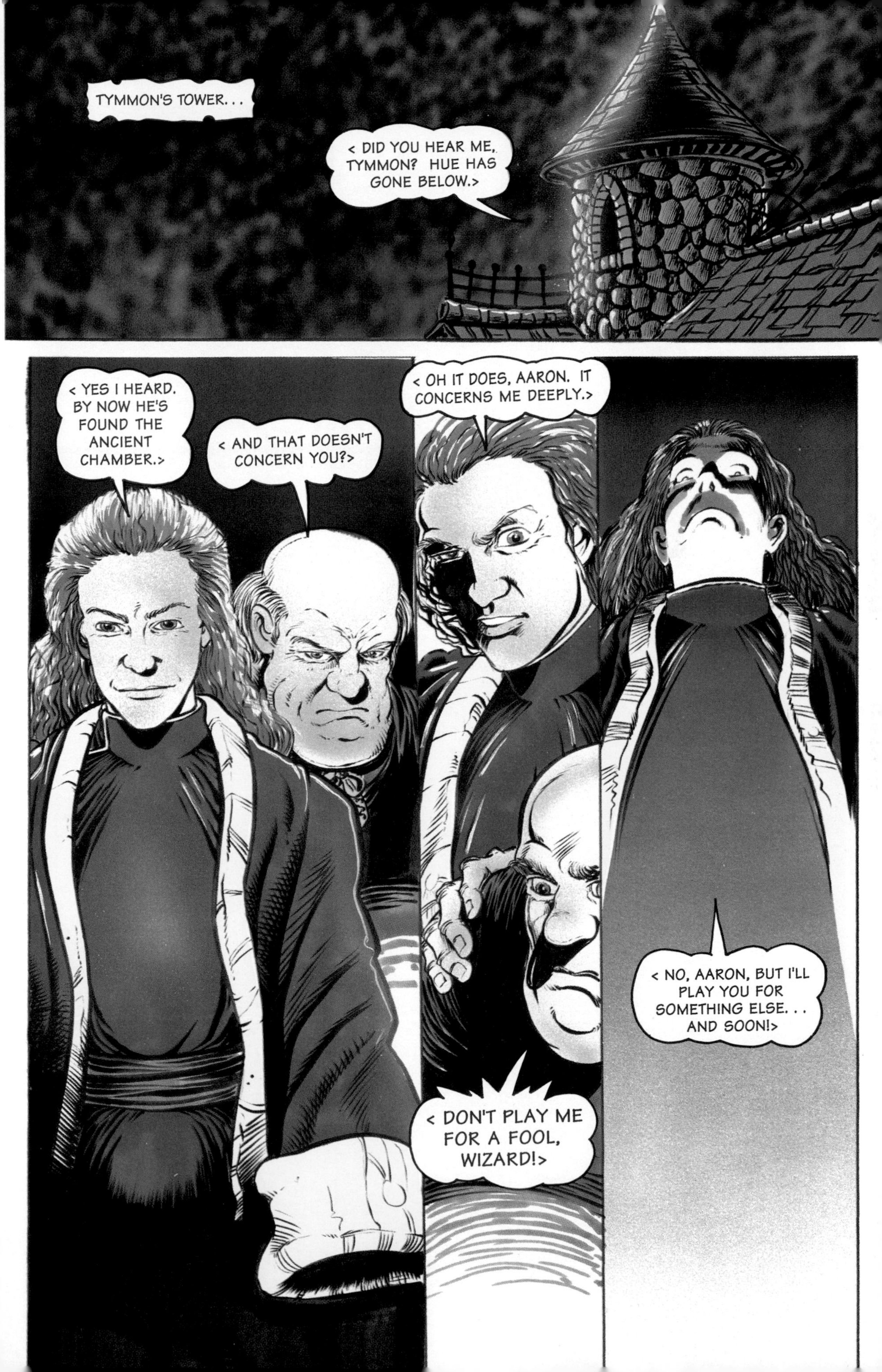
TYMMON'S TOWER...
< DID YOU HEAR ME, TYMMON? HUE HAS GONE BELOW.>
< YES I HEARD. BY NOW HE'S FOUND THE ANCIENT CHAMBER.>
< AND THAT DOESN'T CONCERN YOU?>
< OH IT DOES, AARON. IT CONCERNS ME DEEPLY.>
< DON'T PLAY ME FOR A FOOL, WIZARD!>
< NO, AARON, BUT I'LL PLAY YOU FOR SOMETHING ELSE... AND SOON!>

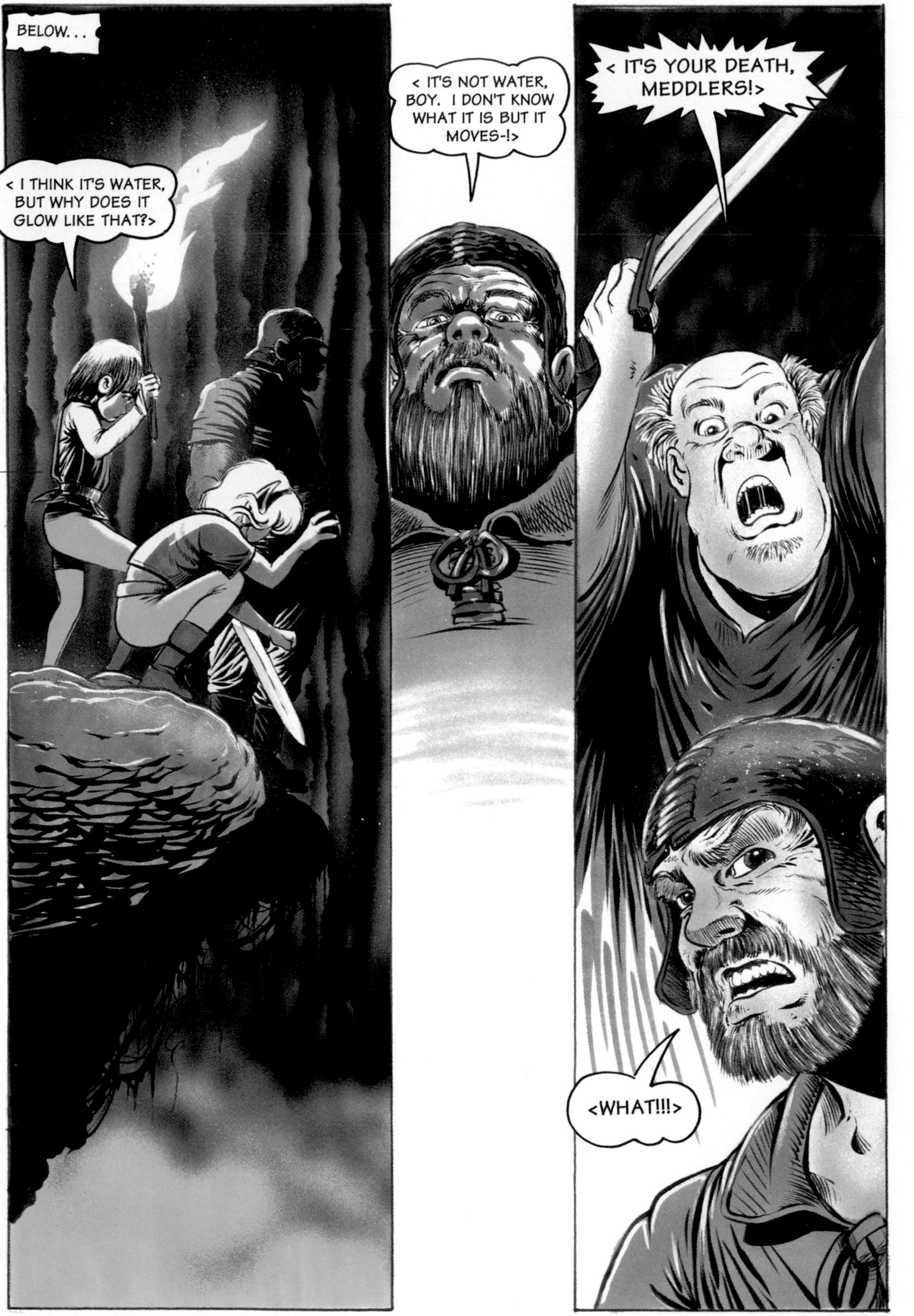
BELOW. . .
< I THINK IT'S WATER, BUT WHY DOES IT GLOW LIKE THAT?>
< IT'S NOT WATER, BOY. I DON'T KNOW WHAT IT IS BUT IT MOVES-!>
< IT'S YOUR DEATH, MEDDLERS!>
<WHAT!!!>

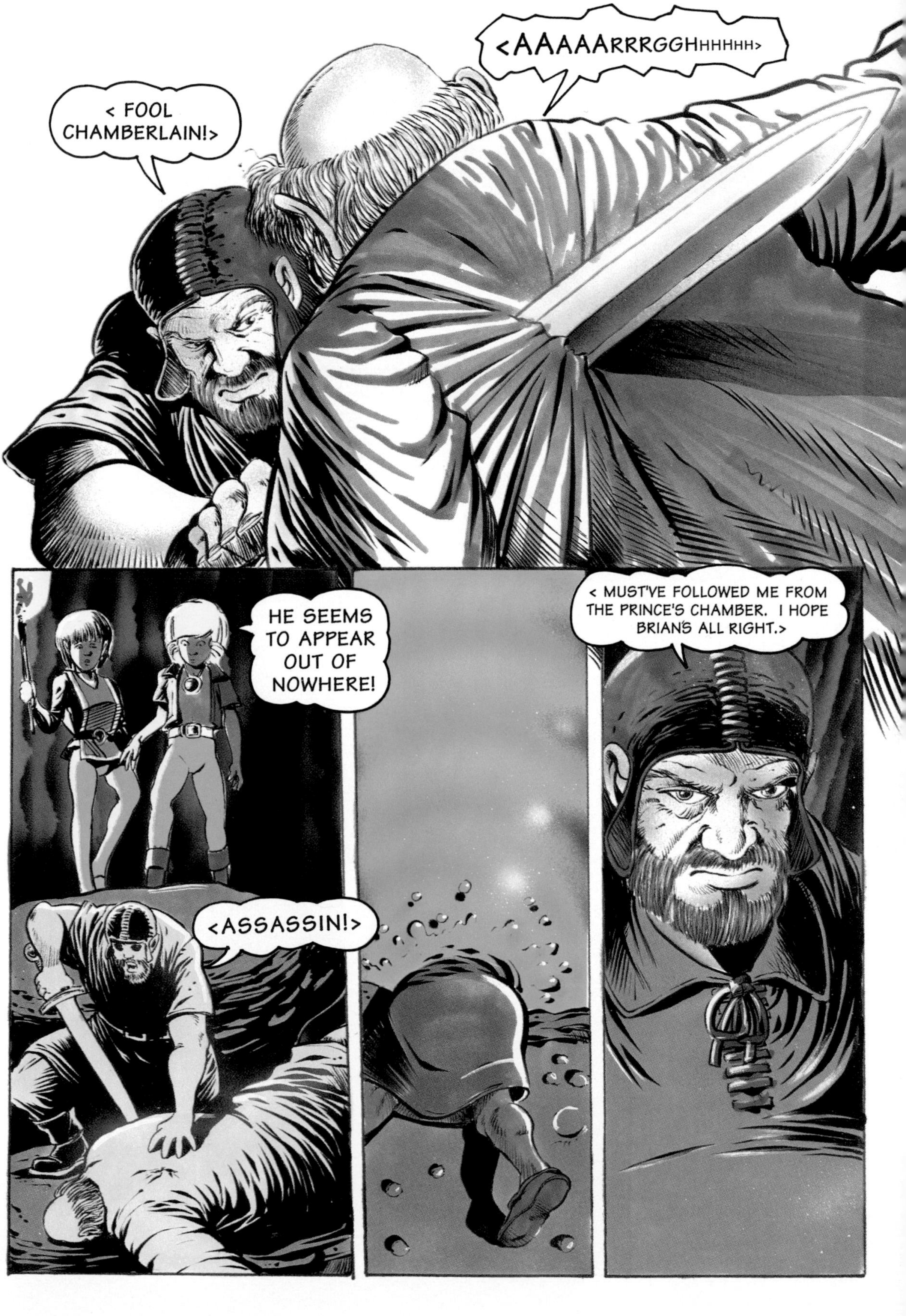
<AAAAARRRGGHHHHHH>
< FOOL CHAMBERLAIN!>
HE SEEMS TO APPEAR OUT OF NOWHERE!
<ASSASSIN!>
< MUST'VE FOLLOWED ME FROM THE PRINCE'S CHAMBER. I HOPE BRIAN'S ALL RIGHT.>

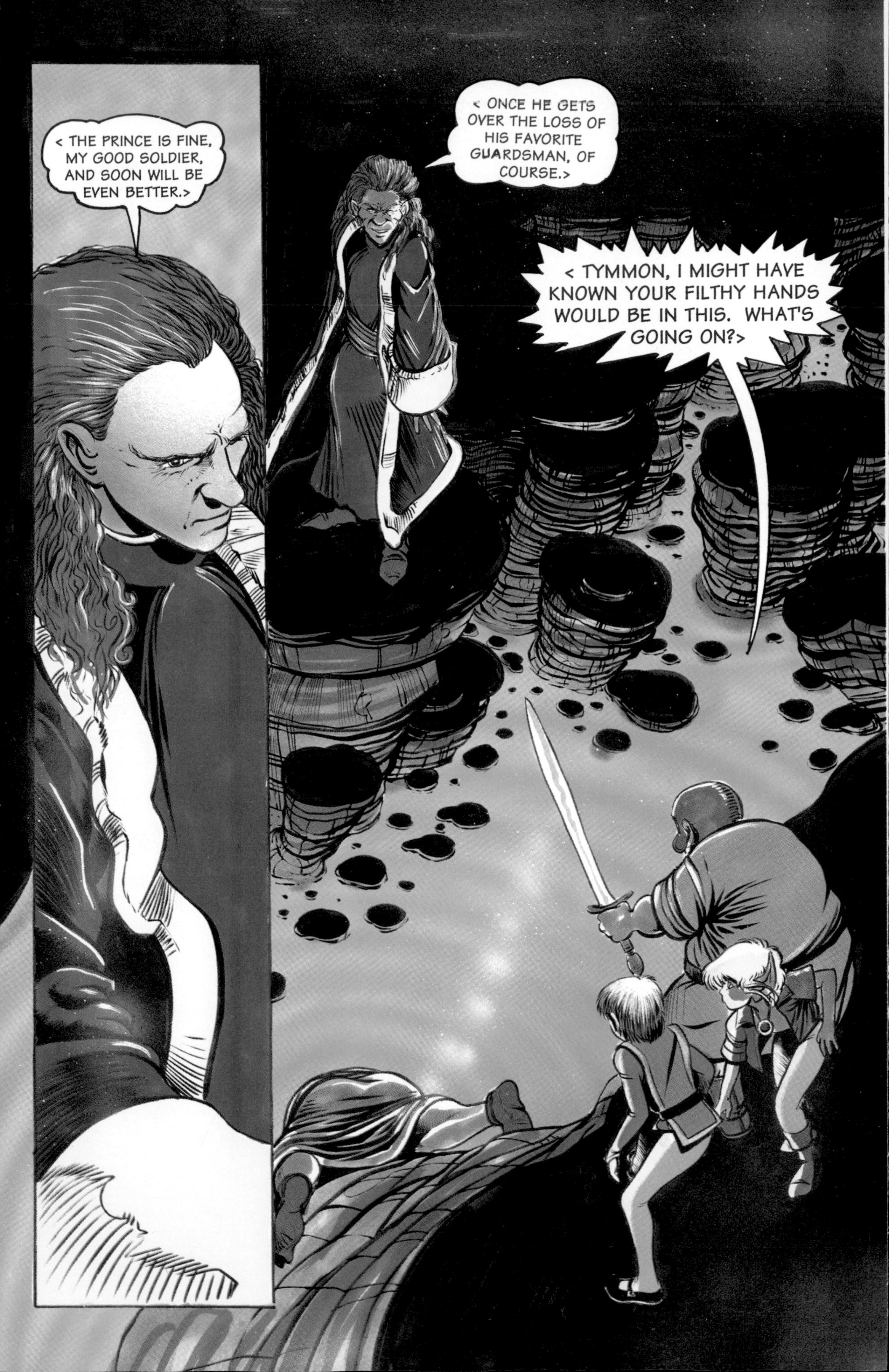
< THE PRINCE IS FINE, MY GOOD SOLDIER, AND SOON WILL BE EVEN BETTER.>
< ONCE HE GETS OVER THE LOSS OF HIS FAVORITE GUARDSMAN, OF COURSE.>
< TYMMON, I MIGHT HAVE KNOWN YOUR FILTHY HANDS WOULD BE IN THIS. WHAT'S GOING ON?>

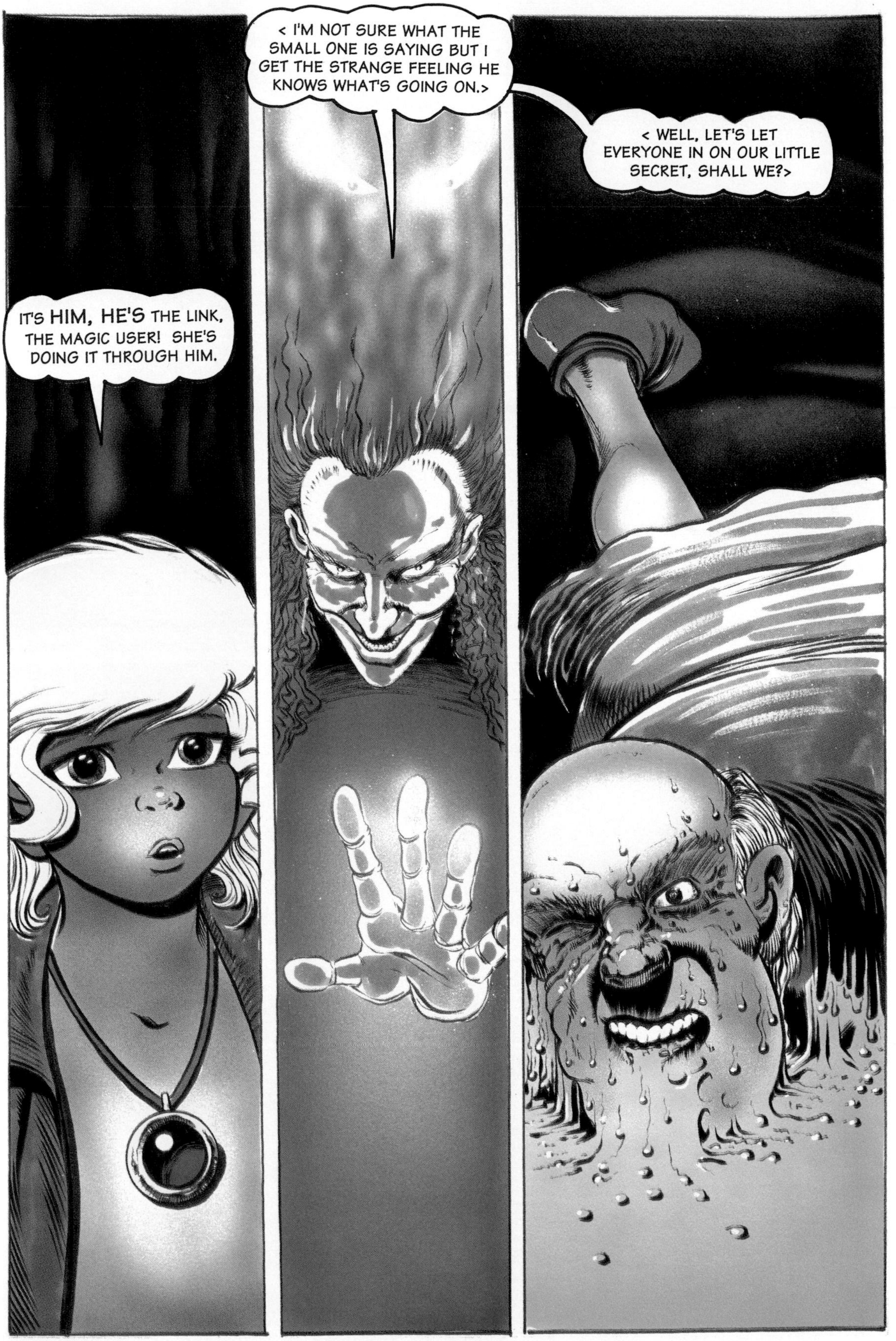
< I'M NOT SURE WHAT THE SMALL ONE IS SAYING BUT I GET THE STRANGE FEELING HE KNOWS WHAT'S GOING ON.>
< WELL, LET'S LET EVERYONE IN ON OUR LITTLE SECRET, SHALL WE?>
IT'S HIM, HE'S THE LINK, THE MAGIC USER! SHE'S DOING IT THROUGH HIM.

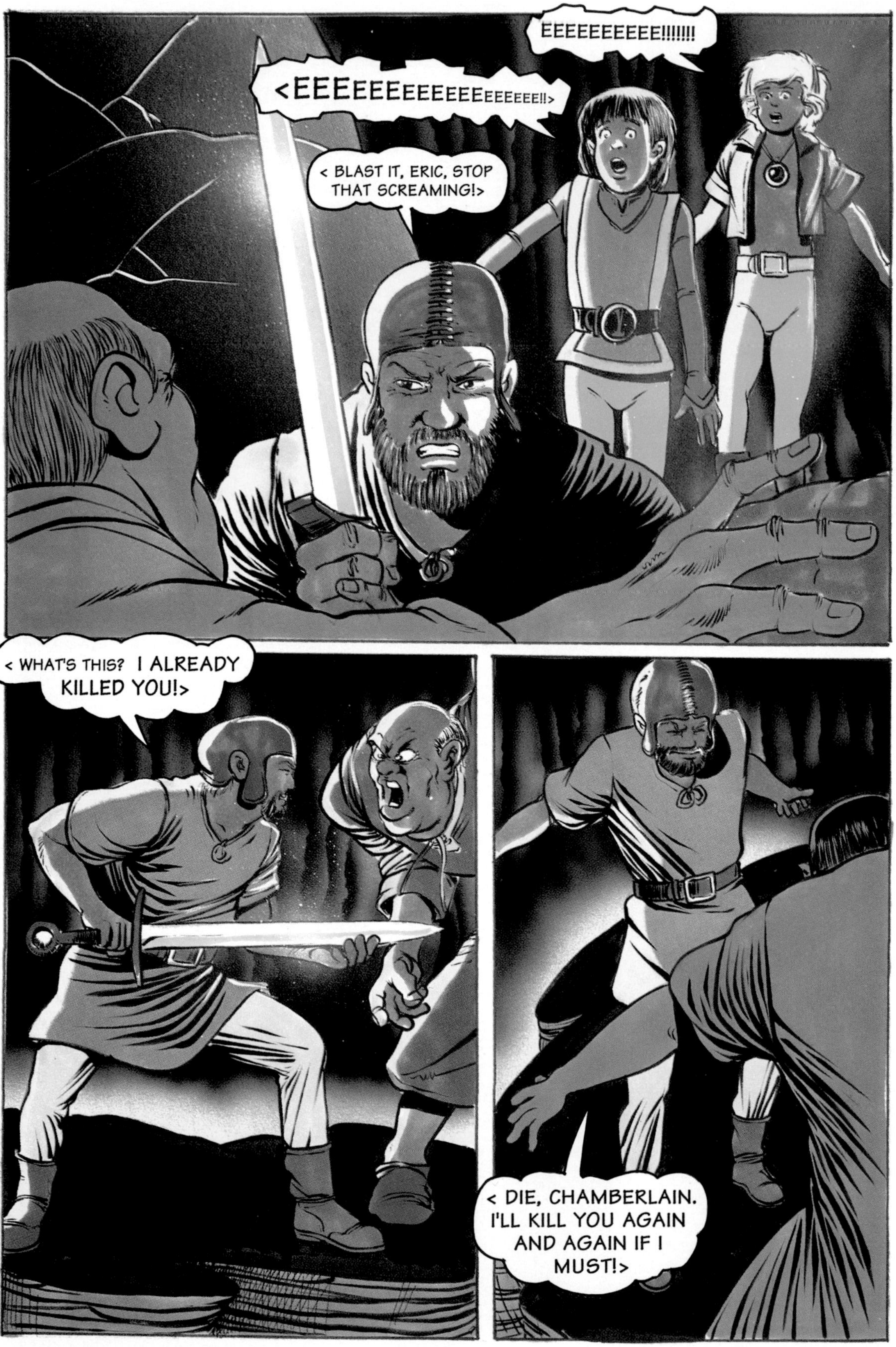
EEEEEEEEEE!!!!!!!
<EEEEEEEEEEEEEEEEEE!!>
< BLAST IT, ERIC, STOP THAT SCREAMING!>
< WHAT'S THIS? I ALREADY KILLED YOU!>
< DIE, CHAMBERLAIN. I'LL KILL YOU AGAIN AND AGAIN IF I MUST!>

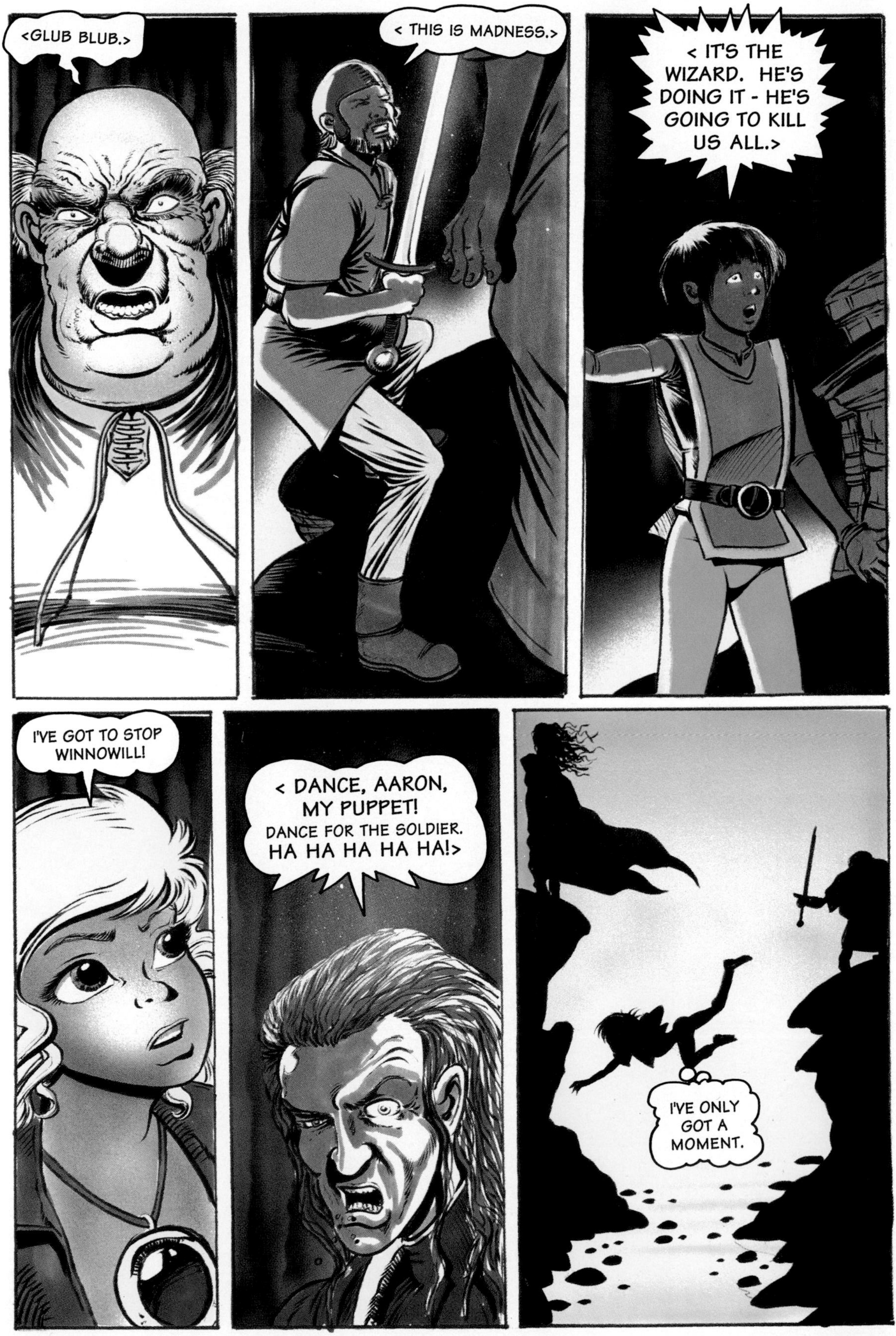
<GLUB BLUB.>
< THIS IS MADNESS.>
< IT'S THE WIZARD. HE'S DOING IT - HE'S GOING TO KILL US ALL.>
I'VE GOT TO STOP WINNOWILL!
< DANCE, AARON, MY PUPPET! DANCE FOR THE SOLDIER. HA HA HA HA HA!>
I'VE ONLY GOT A MOMENT.

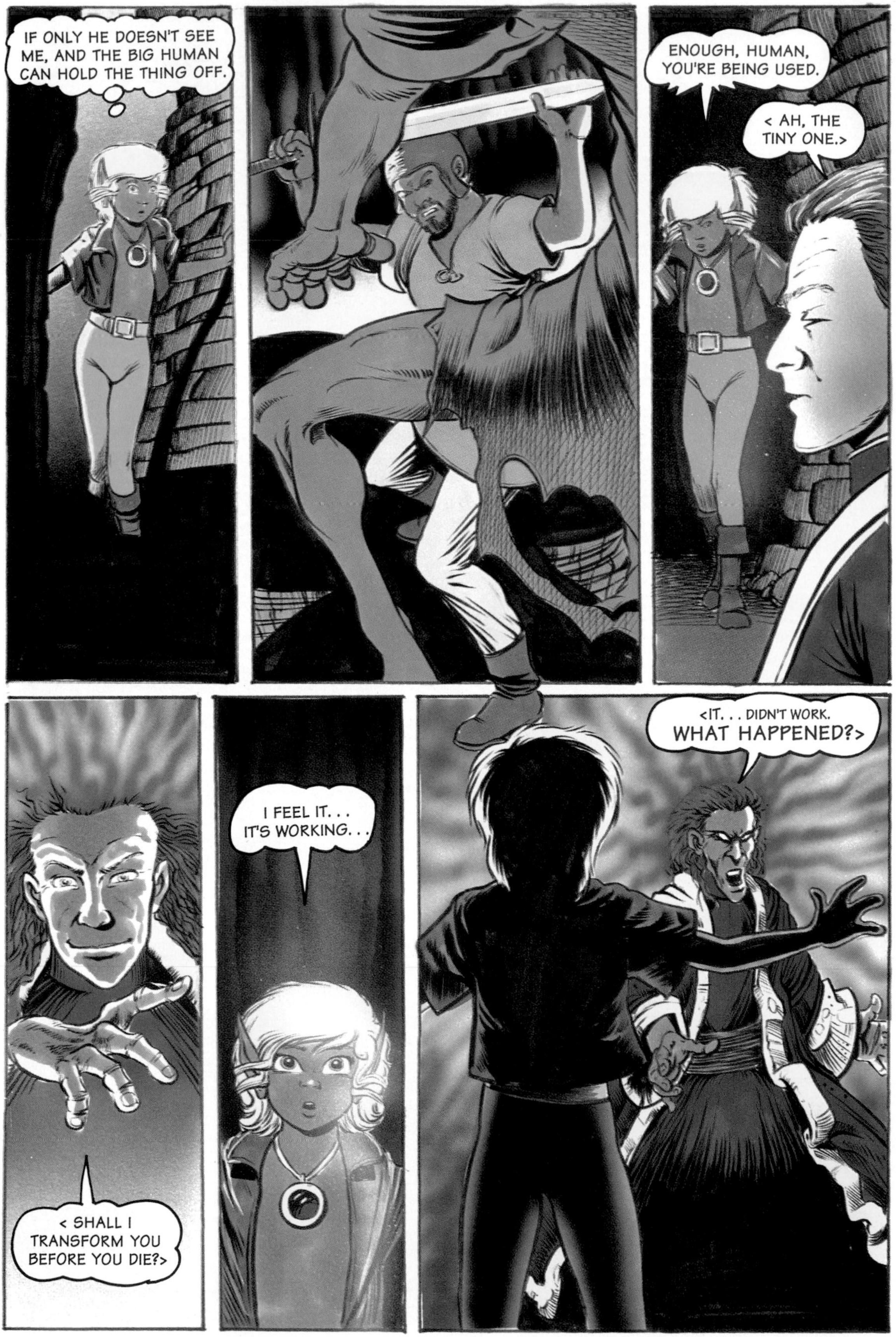
IF ONLY HE DOESN'T SEE ME, AND THE BIG HUMAN CAN HOLD THE THING OFF.
ENOUGH, HUMAN, YOU'RE BEING USED.
< AH, THE TINY ONE.>
< SHALL I TRANSFORM YOU BEFORE YOU DIE?>
I FEEL IT. . . IT'S WORKING. . .
<IT. . . DIDN'T WORK. WHAT HAPPENED?>

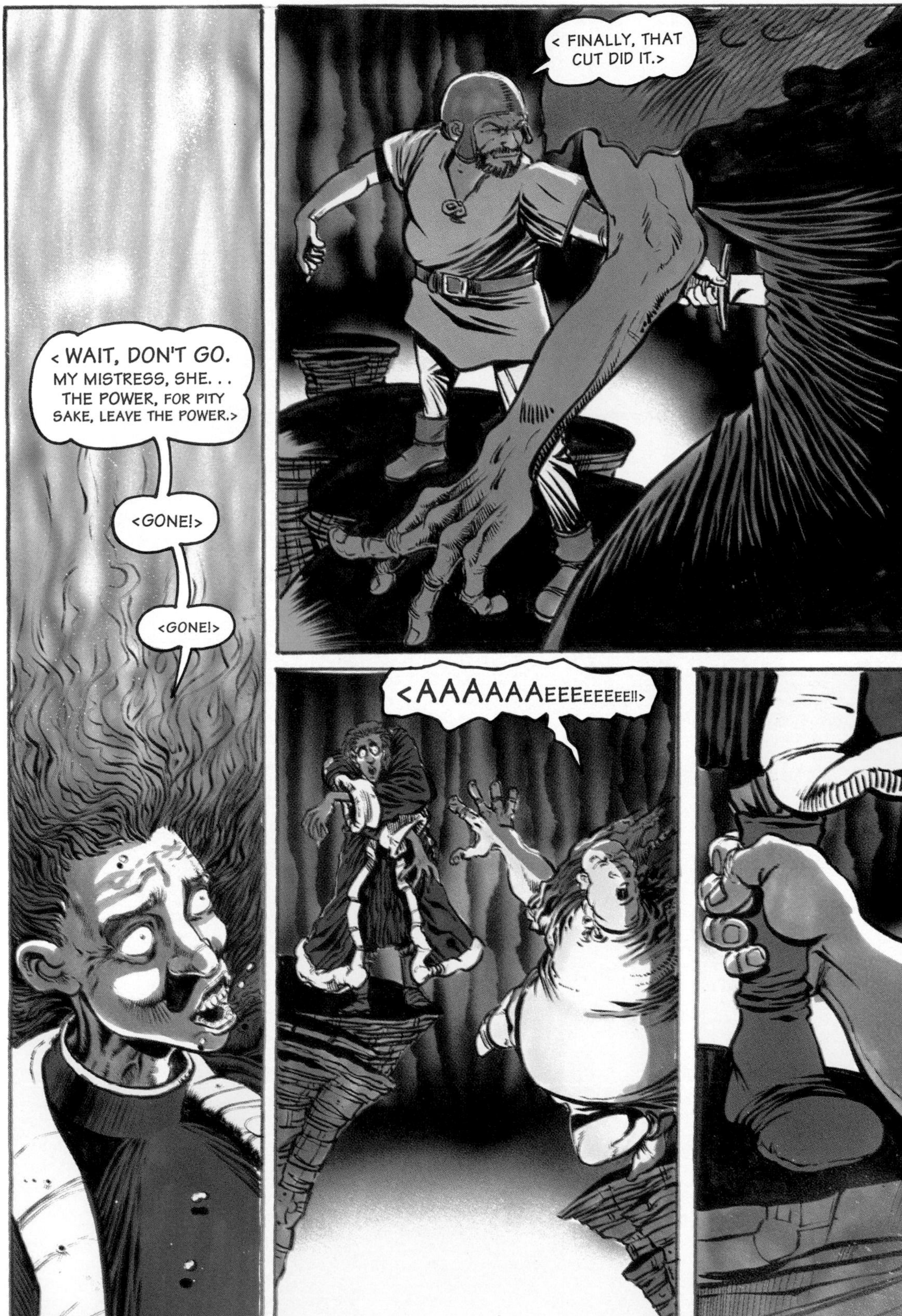
< WAIT, DON'T GO. MY MISTRESS, SHE. . . THE POWER, FOR PITY SAKE, LEAVE THE POWER.>
<GONE!>
<GONE!>
< FINALLY, THAT CUT DID IT.>
<AAAAAAEEEEEEEE!!>

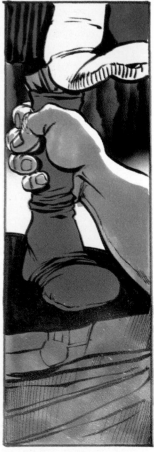

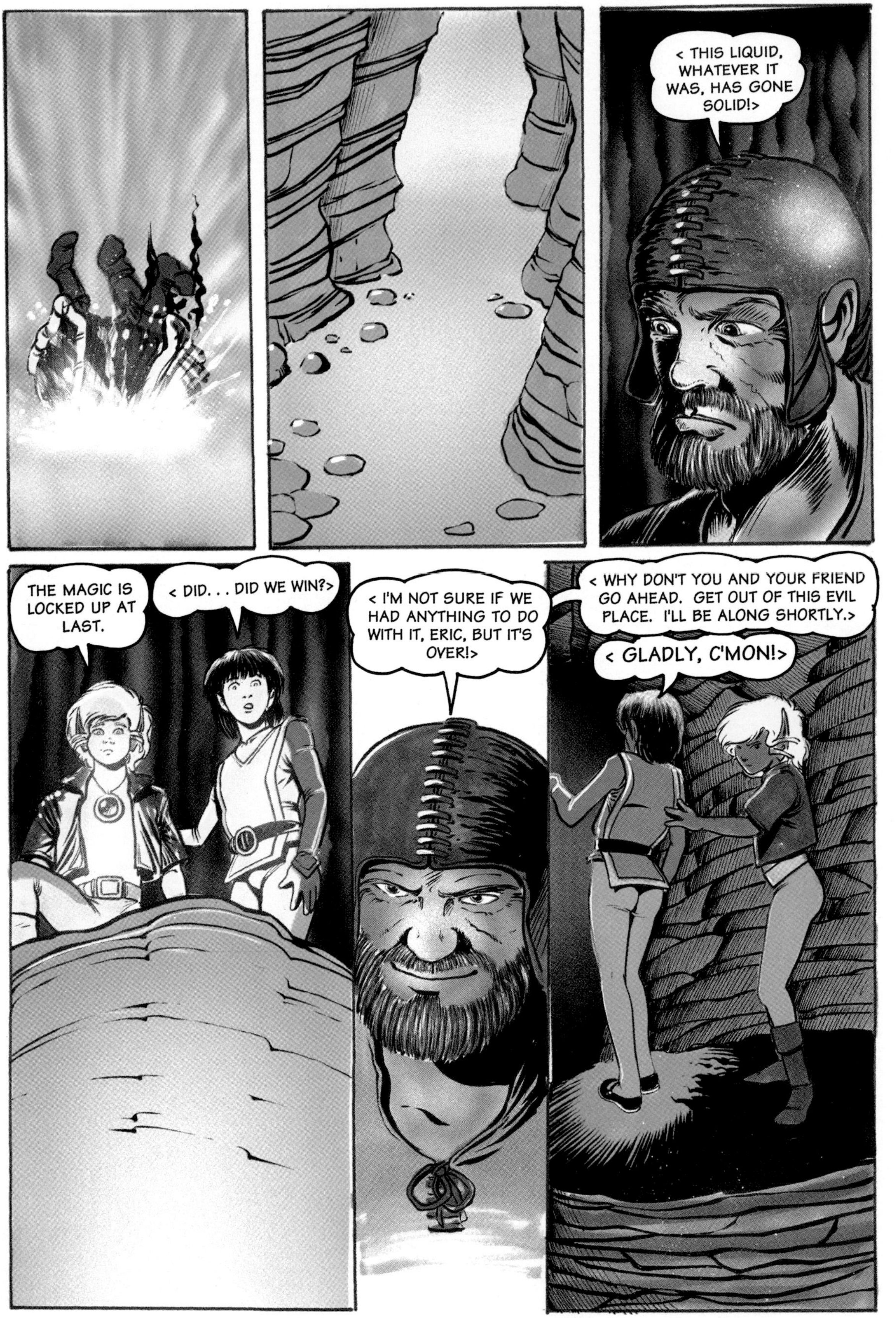
< THIS LIQUID, WHATEVER IT WAS, HAS GONE SOLID!>
THE MAGIC IS LOCKED UP AT LAST.
< DID. . . DID WE WIN?>
< I'M NOT SURE IF WE HAD ANYTHING TO DO WITH IT, ERIC, BUT IT'S OVER!>
< WHY DON'T YOU AND YOUR FRIEND GO AHEAD. GET OUT OF THIS EVIL PLACE. I'LL BE ALONG SHORTLY.>
< GLADLY, C'MON!>

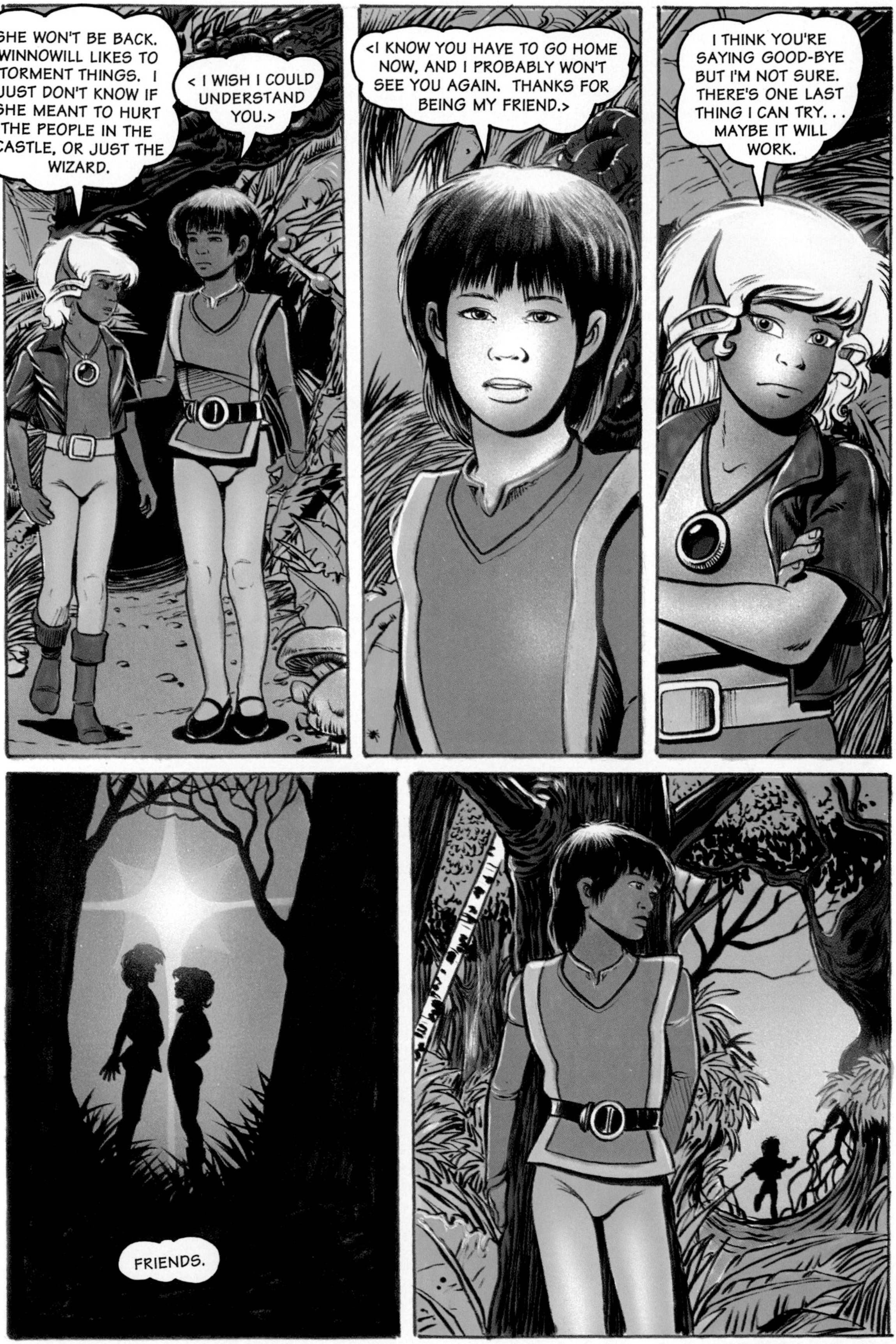
SHE WON'T BE BACK. WINNOWILL LIKES TO TORMENT THINGS. I JUST DON'T KNOW IF SHE MEANT TO HURT THE PEOPLE IN THE CASTLE, OR JUST THE WIZARD.
< I WISH I COULD UNDERSTAND YOU.>
<I KNOW YOU HAVE TO GO HOME NOW, AND I PROBABLY WON'T SEE YOU AGAIN. THANKS FOR BEING MY FRIEND.>
I THINK YOU'RE SAYING GOOD-BYE BUT I'M NOT SURE. THERE'S ONE LAST THING I CAN TRY. . . MAYBE IT WILL WORK.
FRIENDS.

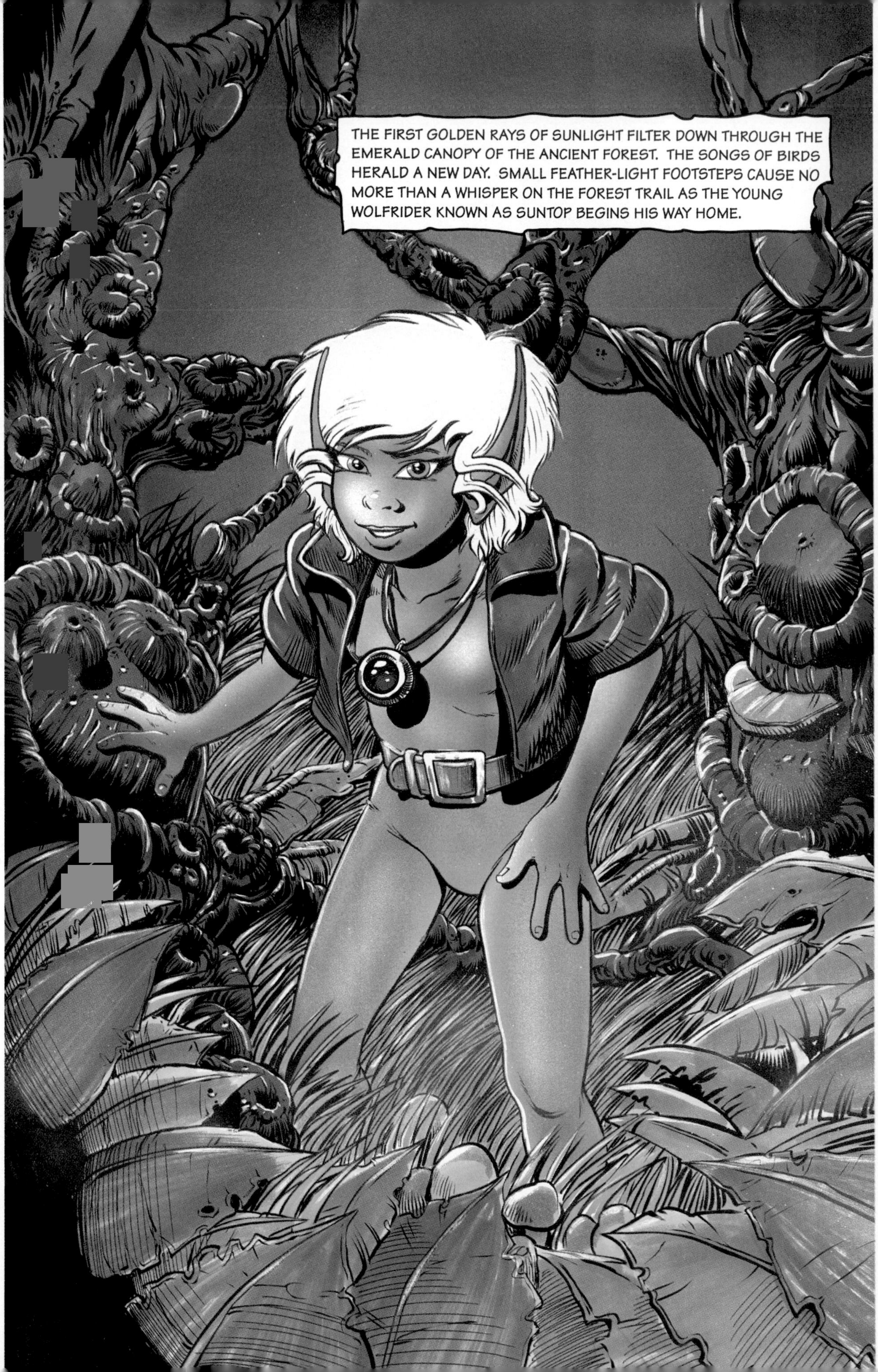
THE FIRST GOLDEN RAYS OF SUNLIGHT FILTER DOWN THROUGH THE EMERALD CANOPY OF THE ANCIENT FOREST. THE SONGS OF BIRDS HERALD A NEW DAY. SMALL FEATHER-LIGHT FOOTSTEPS CAUSE NO MORE THAN A WHISPER ON THE FOREST TRAIL AS THE YOUNG WOLFRIDER KNOWN AS SUNTOP BEGINS HIS WAY HOME.

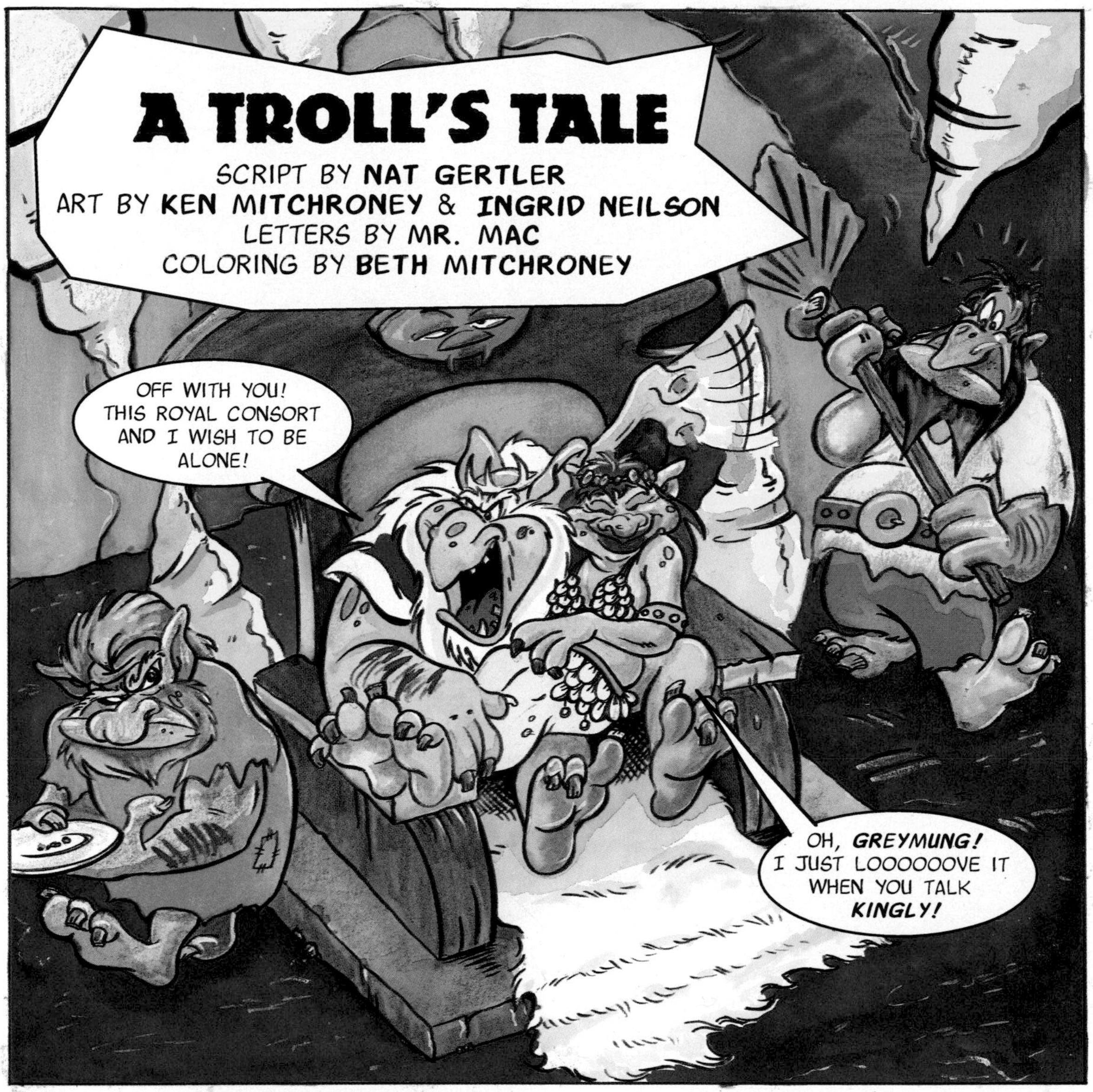
A TROLL'S TALE
SCRIPT BY NAT GERTLER
ART BY KEN MITCHRONEY & INGRID NEILSON
LETTERS BY MR. MAC
COLORING BY BETH MITCHRONEY
OFF WITH YOU! THIS ROYAL CONSORT AND I WISH TO BE ALONE!
OH, GREYMUNG! I JUST LOOOOOOVE IT WHEN YOU TALK KINGLY!

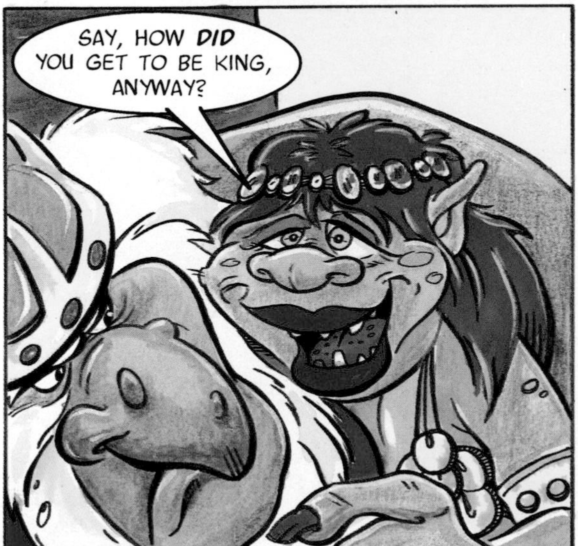
SAY, HOW DID YOU GET TO BE KING, ANYWAY?

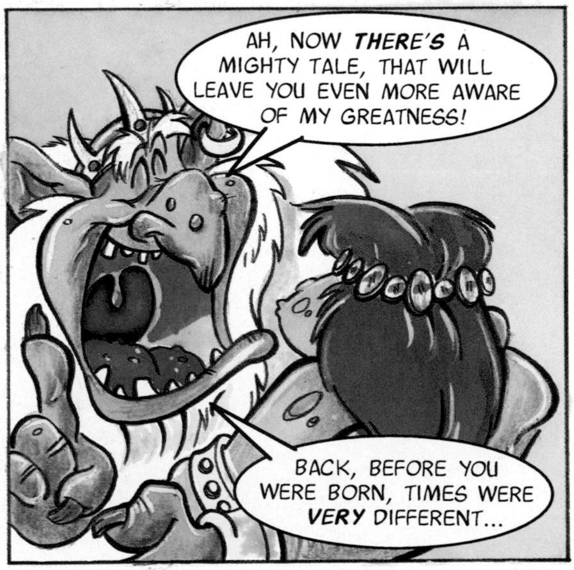
AH, NOW THERE'S A MIGHTY TALE, THAT WILL LEAVE YOU EVEN MORE AWARE OF MY GREATNESS!
BACK, BEFORE YOU WERE BORN, TIMES WERE VERY DIFFERENT...

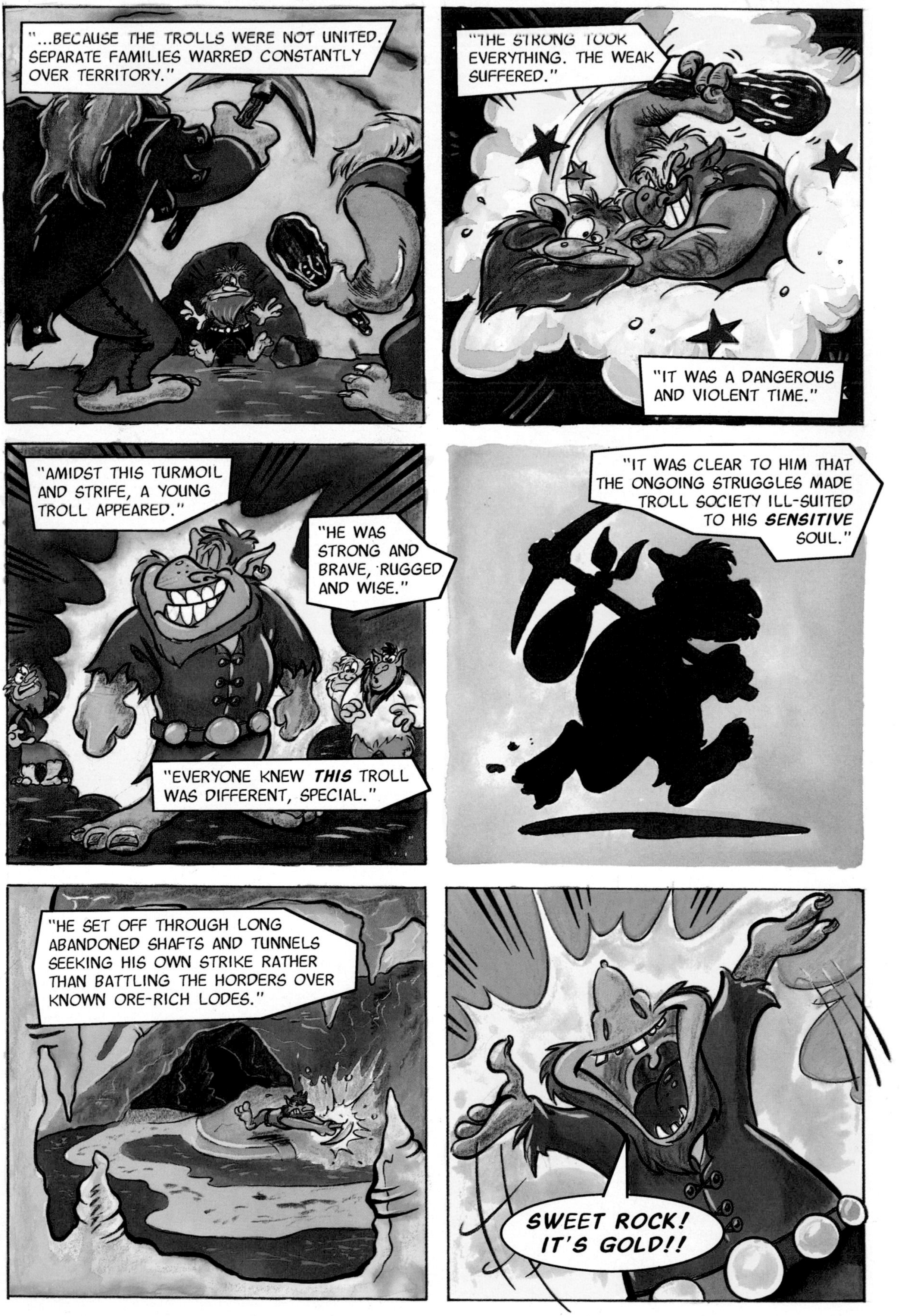
"...BECAUSE THE TROLLS WERE NOT UNITED. SEPARATE FAMILIES WARRED CONSTANTLY OVER TERRITORY."
"THE STRONG TOOK EVERYTHING. THE WEAK SUFFERED."
"IT WAS A DANGEROUS AND VIOLENT TIME."
"AMIDST THIS TURMOIL AND STRIFE, A YOUNG TROLL APPEARED."
"HE WAS STRONG AND BRAVE, RUGGED AND WISE."
"EVERYONE KNEW ***THIS*** TROLL WAS DIFFERENT, SPECIAL."
"IT WAS CLEAR TO HIM THAT THE ONGOING STRUGGLES MADE TROLL SOCIETY ILL-SUITED TO HIS ***SENSITIVE*** SOUL."
"HE SET OFF THROUGH LONG ABANDONED SHAFTS AND TUNNELS SEEKING HIS OWN STRIKE RATHER THAN BATTLING THE HORDERS OVER KNOWN ORE-RICH LODES."
SWEET ROCK! IT'S GOLD!!

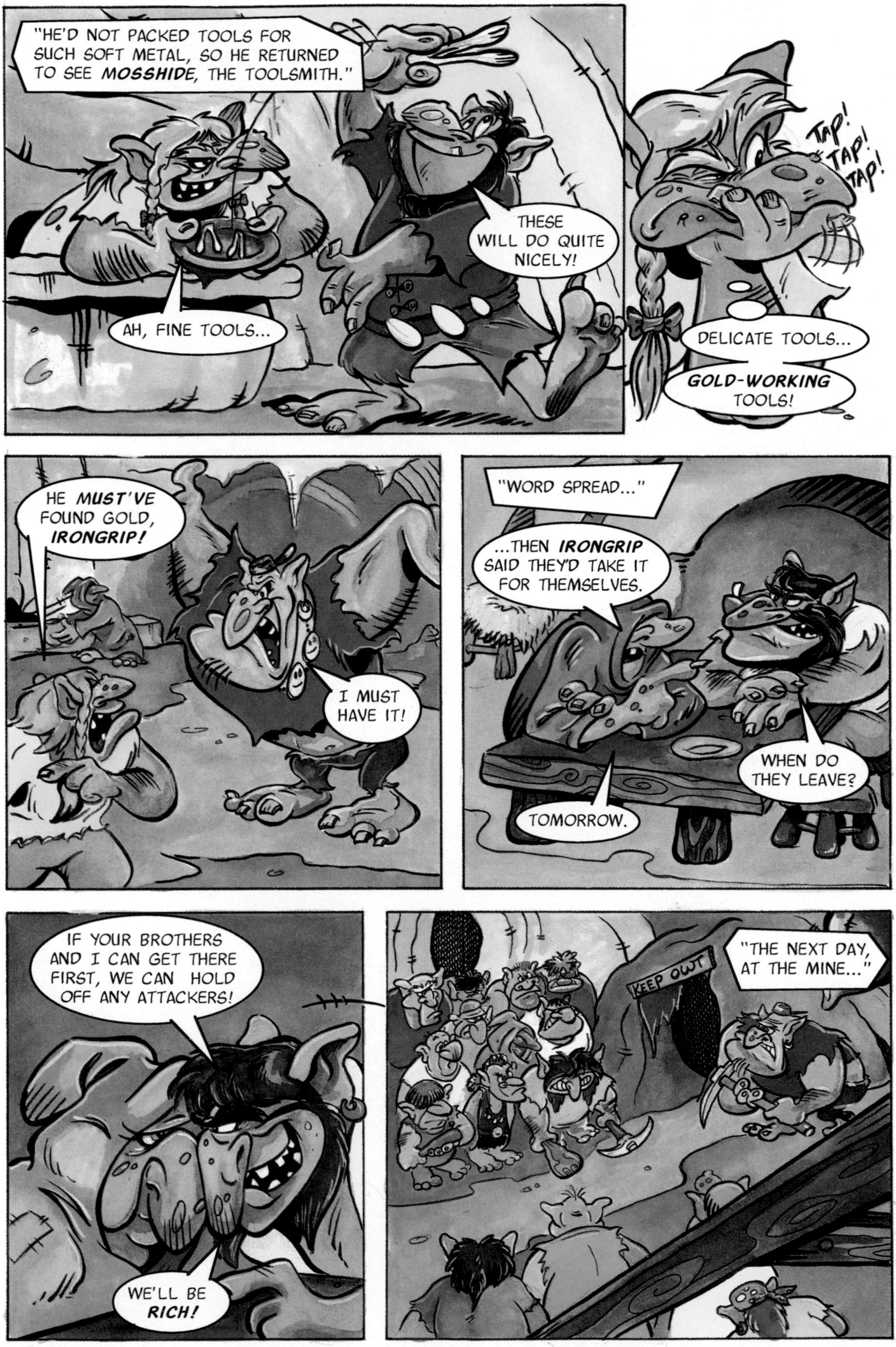
"HE'D NOT PACKED TOOLS FOR SUCH SOFT METAL, SO HE RETURNED TO SEE MOSSHIDE, THE TOOLSMITH."
THESE WILL DO QUITE NICELY!
AH, FINE TOOLS...
TAP! TAP! TAP!
DELICATE TOOLS...
GOLD-WORKING TOOLS!
HE MUST'VE FOUND GOLD, IRONGRIP!
I MUST HAVE IT!
"WORD SPREAD..."
...THEN IRONGRIP SAID THEY'D TAKE IT FOR THEMSELVES.
WHEN DO THEY LEAVE?
TOMORROW.
IF YOUR BROTHERS AND I CAN GET THERE FIRST, WE CAN HOLD OFF ANY ATTACKERS!
WE'LL BE RICH!
KEEP OWT
"THE NEXT DAY, AT THE MINE..."

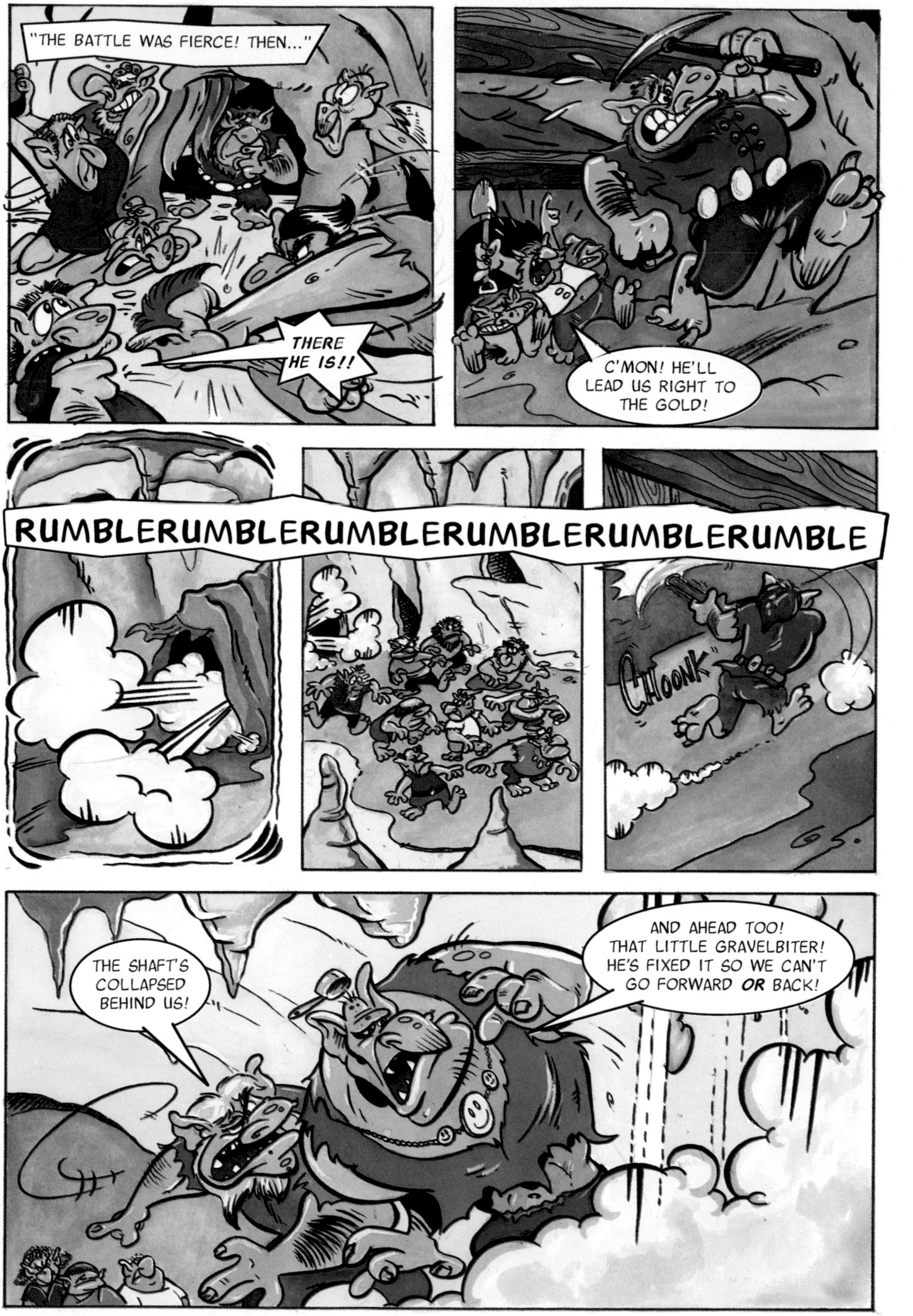
"THE BATTLE WAS FIERCE! THEN..."
THERE HE IS!!
C'MON! HE'LL LEAD US RIGHT TO THE GOLD!
RUMBLERUMBLERUMBLERUMBLERUMBLERUMBLE
CHOONK
THE SHAFT'S COLLAPSED BEHIND US!
AND AHEAD TOO! THAT LITTLE GRAVELBITER! HE'S FIXED IT SO WE CAN'T GO FORWARD **OR** BACK!

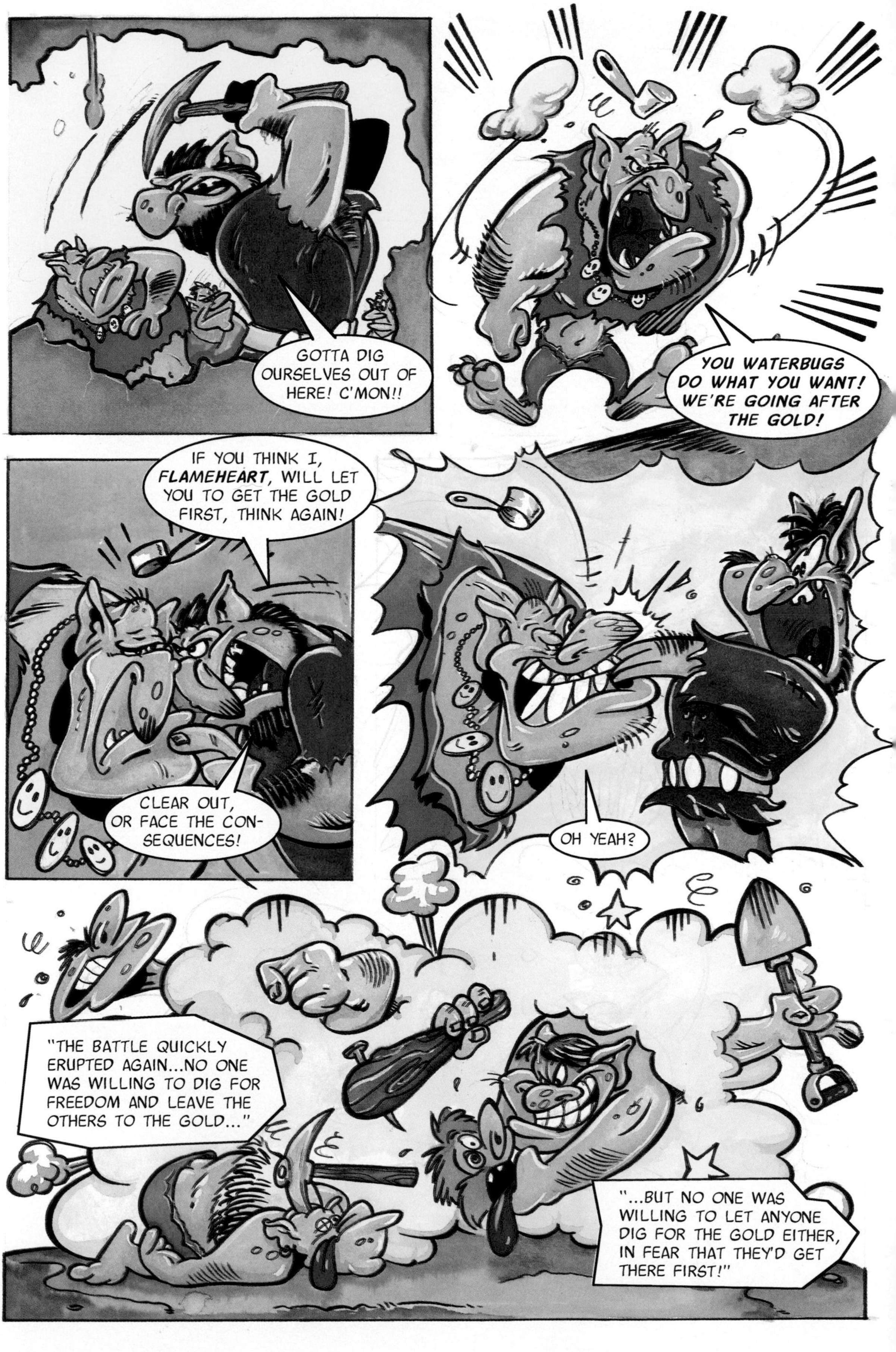
GOTTA DIG OURSELVES OUT OF HERE! C'MON!!
YOU WATERBUGS DO WHAT YOU WANT! WE'RE GOING AFTER THE GOLD!
IF YOU THINK I, FLAMEHEART, WILL LET YOU TO GET THE GOLD FIRST, THINK AGAIN!
CLEAR OUT, OR FACE THE CON-SEQUENCES!
OH YEAH?
"THE BATTLE QUICKLY ERUPTED AGAIN...NO ONE WAS WILLING TO DIG FOR FREEDOM AND LEAVE THE OTHERS TO THE GOLD..."
"...BUT NO ONE WAS WILLING TO LET ANYONE DIG FOR THE GOLD EITHER, IN FEAR THAT THEY'D GET THERE FIRST!"

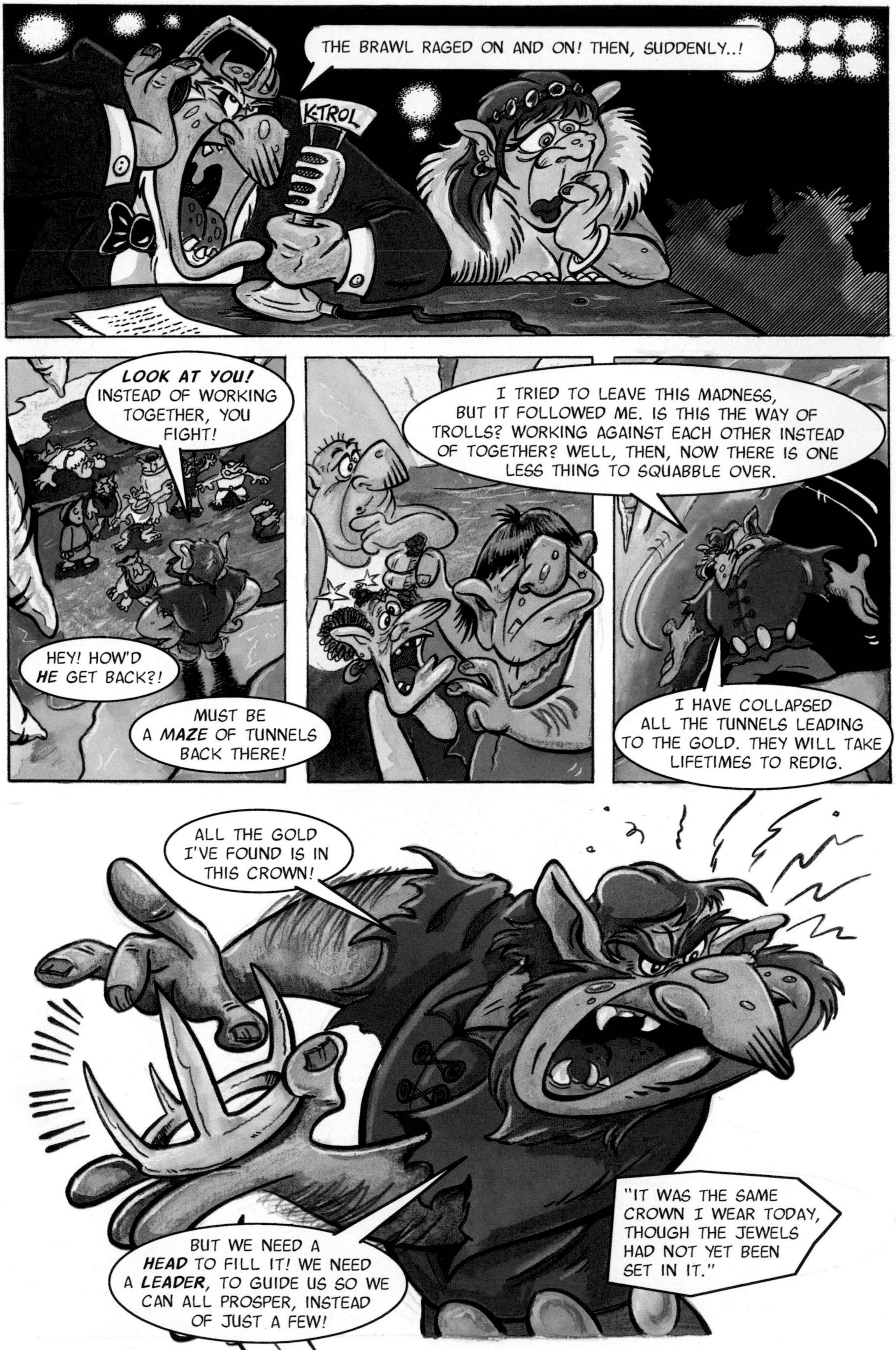
THE BRAWL RAGED ON AND ON! THEN, SUDDENLY..!
K-TROL
LOOK AT YOU! INSTEAD OF WORKING TOGETHER, YOU FIGHT!
HEY! HOW'D HE GET BACK?!
MUST BE A MAZE OF TUNNELS BACK THERE!
I TRIED TO LEAVE THIS MADNESS, BUT IT FOLLOWED ME. IS THIS THE WAY OF TROLLS? WORKING AGAINST EACH OTHER INSTEAD OF TOGETHER? WELL, THEN, NOW THERE IS ONE LESS THING TO SQUABBLE OVER.
I HAVE COLLAPSED ALL THE TUNNELS LEADING TO THE GOLD. THEY WILL TAKE LIFETIMES TO REDIG.
ALL THE GOLD I'VE FOUND IS IN THIS CROWN!
BUT WE NEED A HEAD TO FILL IT! WE NEED A LEADER, TO GUIDE US SO WE CAN ALL PROSPER, INSTEAD OF JUST A FEW!
"IT WAS THE SAME CROWN I WEAR TODAY, THOUGH THE JEWELS HAD NOT YET BEEN SET IN IT."

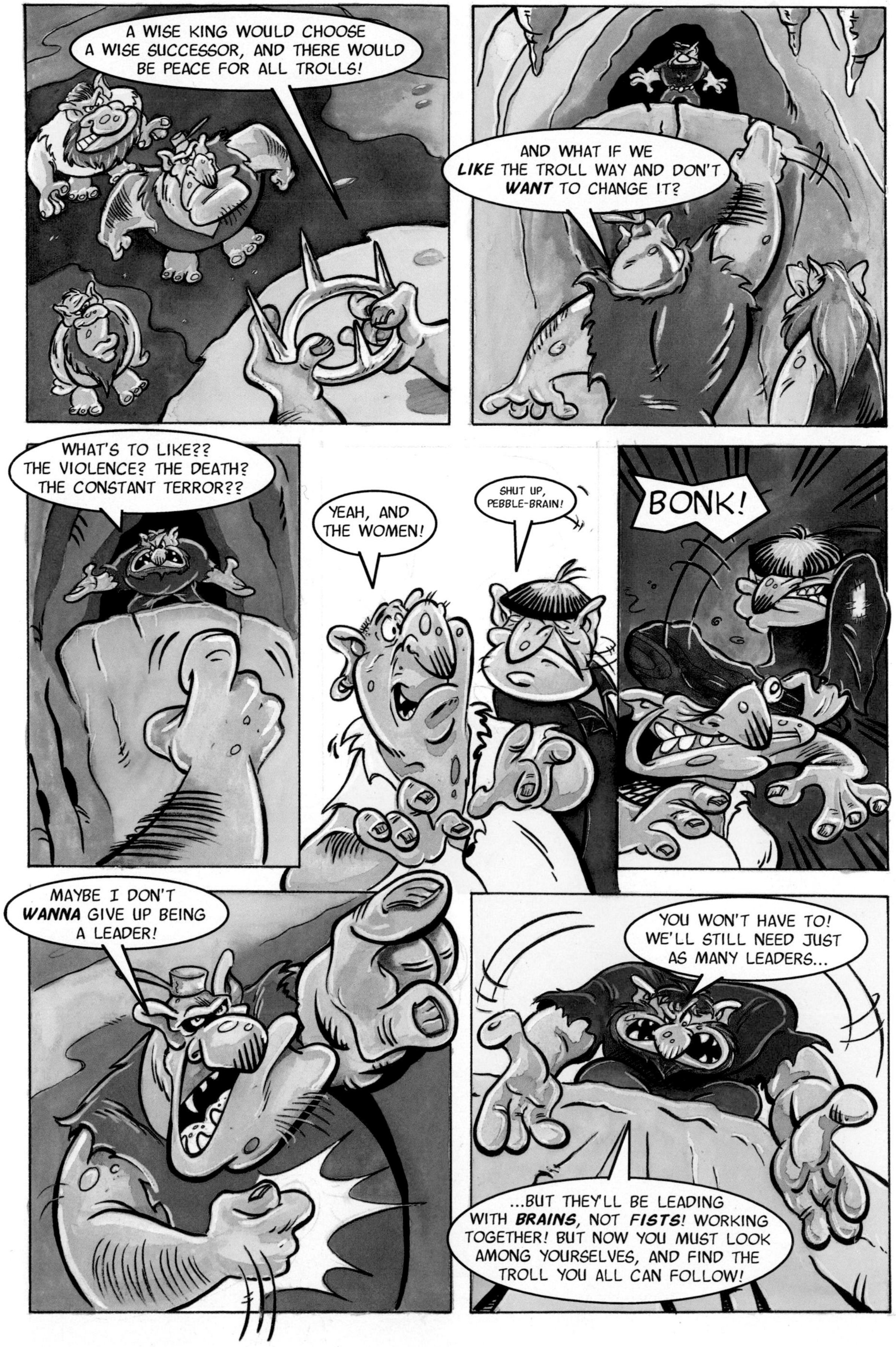
A WISE KING WOULD CHOOSE A WISE SUCCESSOR, AND THERE WOULD BE PEACE FOR ALL TROLLS!
AND WHAT IF WE LIKE THE TROLL WAY AND DON'T WANT TO CHANGE IT?
WHAT'S TO LIKE?? THE VIOLENCE? THE DEATH? THE CONSTANT TERROR??
YEAH, AND THE WOMEN!
SHUT UP, PEBBLE-BRAIN!
BONK!
MAYBE I DON'T WANNA GIVE UP BEING A LEADER!
YOU WON'T HAVE TO! WE'LL STILL NEED JUST AS MANY LEADERS...
...BUT THEY'LL BE LEADING WITH BRAINS, NOT FISTS! WORKING TOGETHER! BUT NOW YOU MUST LOOK AMONG YOURSELVES, AND FIND THE TROLL YOU ALL CAN FOLLOW!

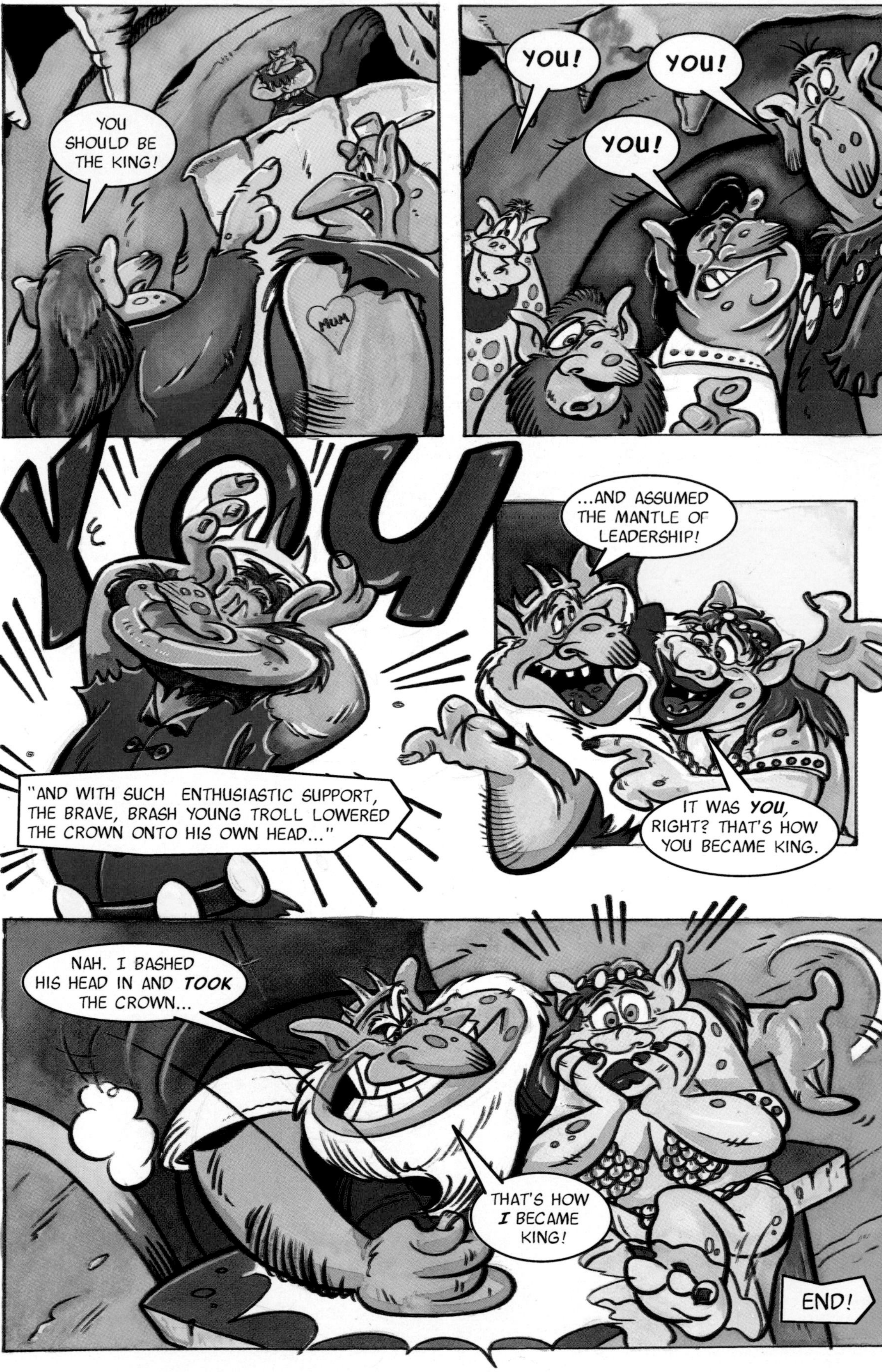

YOU SHOULD BE THE KING!
MUM
YOU!
YOU!
YOU!
YOU
...AND ASSUMED THE MANTLE OF LEADERSHIP!
"AND WITH SUCH ENTHUSIASTIC SUPPORT, THE BRAVE, BRASH YOUNG TROLL LOWERED THE CROWN ONTO HIS OWN HEAD..."
IT WAS *YOU*, RIGHT? THAT'S HOW YOU BECAME KING.
NAH. I BASHED HIS HEAD IN AND *TOOK* THE CROWN...
THAT'S HOW *I* BECAME KING!
END!

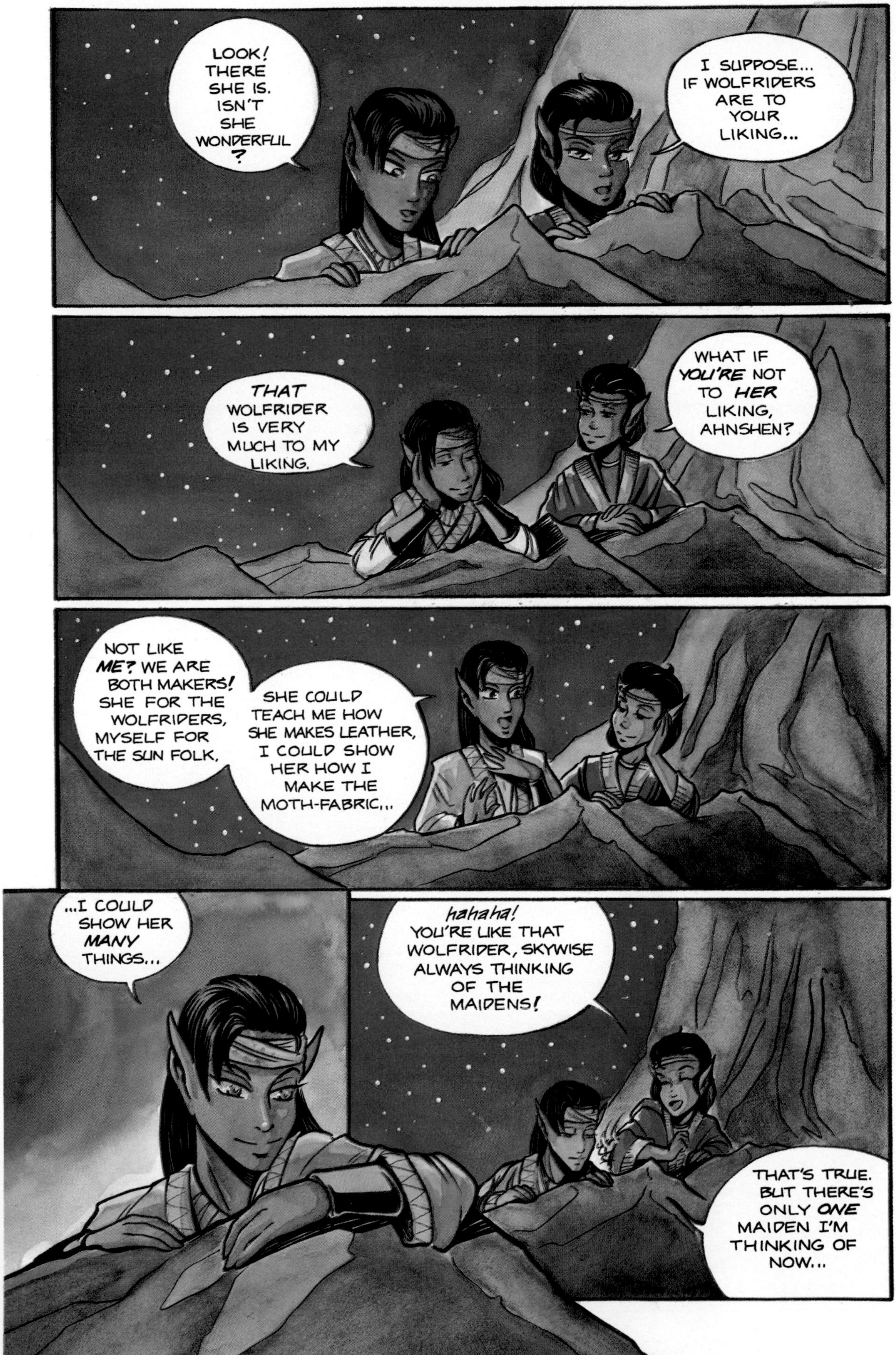
LOOK! THERE SHE IS. ISN'T SHE WONDERFUL?
I SUPPOSE... IF WOLFRIDERS ARE TO YOUR LIKING...
THAT WOLFRIDER IS VERY MUCH TO MY LIKING.
WHAT IF YOU'RE NOT TO HER LIKING, AHNSHEN?
NOT LIKE ME? WE ARE BOTH MAKERS! SHE FOR THE WOLFRIDERS, MYSELF FOR THE SUN FOLK.
SHE COULD TEACH ME HOW SHE MAKES LEATHER, I COULD SHOW HER HOW I MAKE THE MOTH-FABRIC...
...I COULD SHOW HER MANY THINGS...
hahaha! YOU'RE LIKE THAT WOLFRIDER, SKYWISE ALWAYS THINKING OF THE MAIDENS!
THAT'S TRUE. BUT THERE'S ONLY ONE MAIDEN I'M THINKING OF NOW...

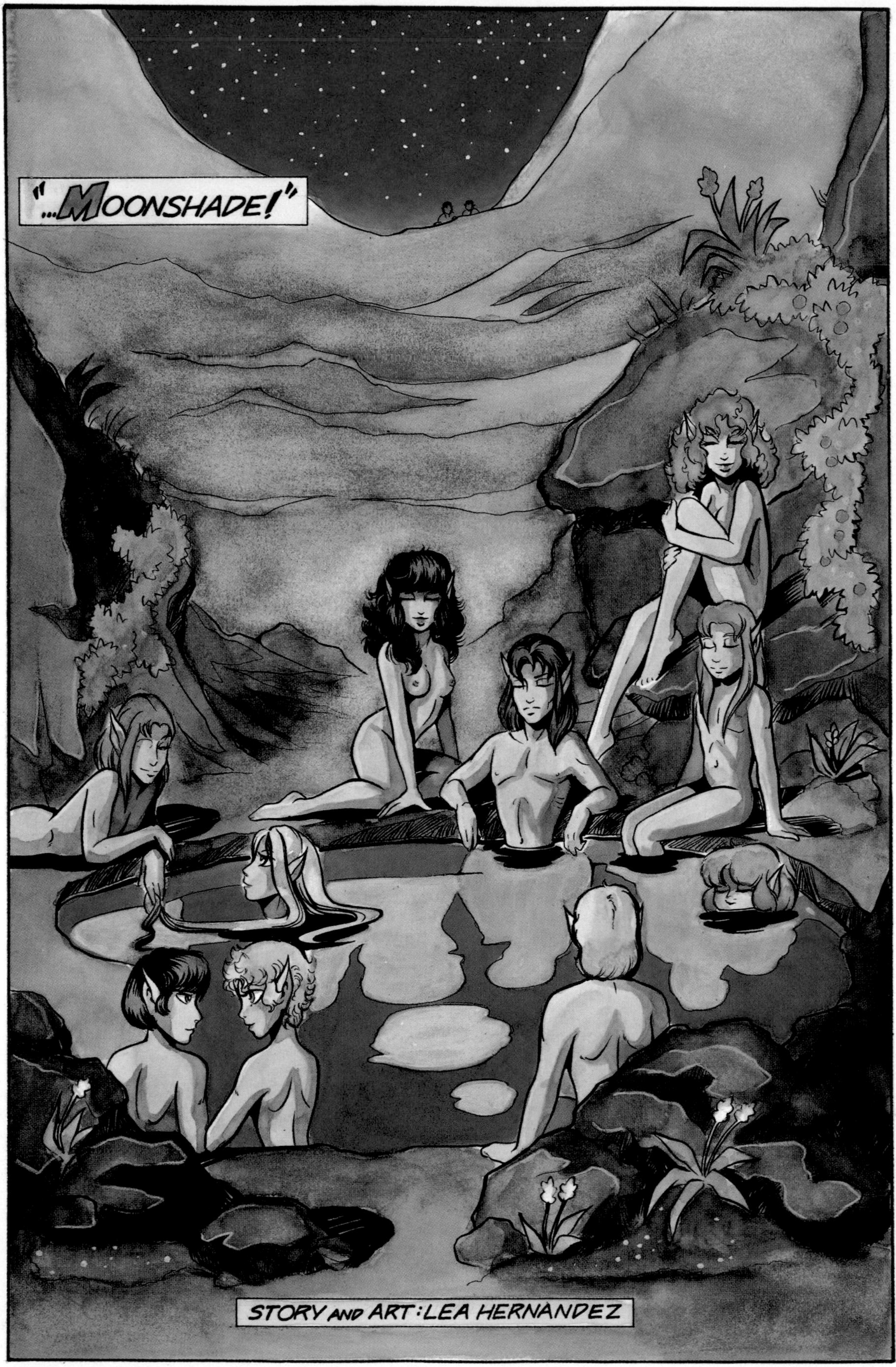
"...MOONSHADE!"
STORY AND ART: LEA HERNANDEZ

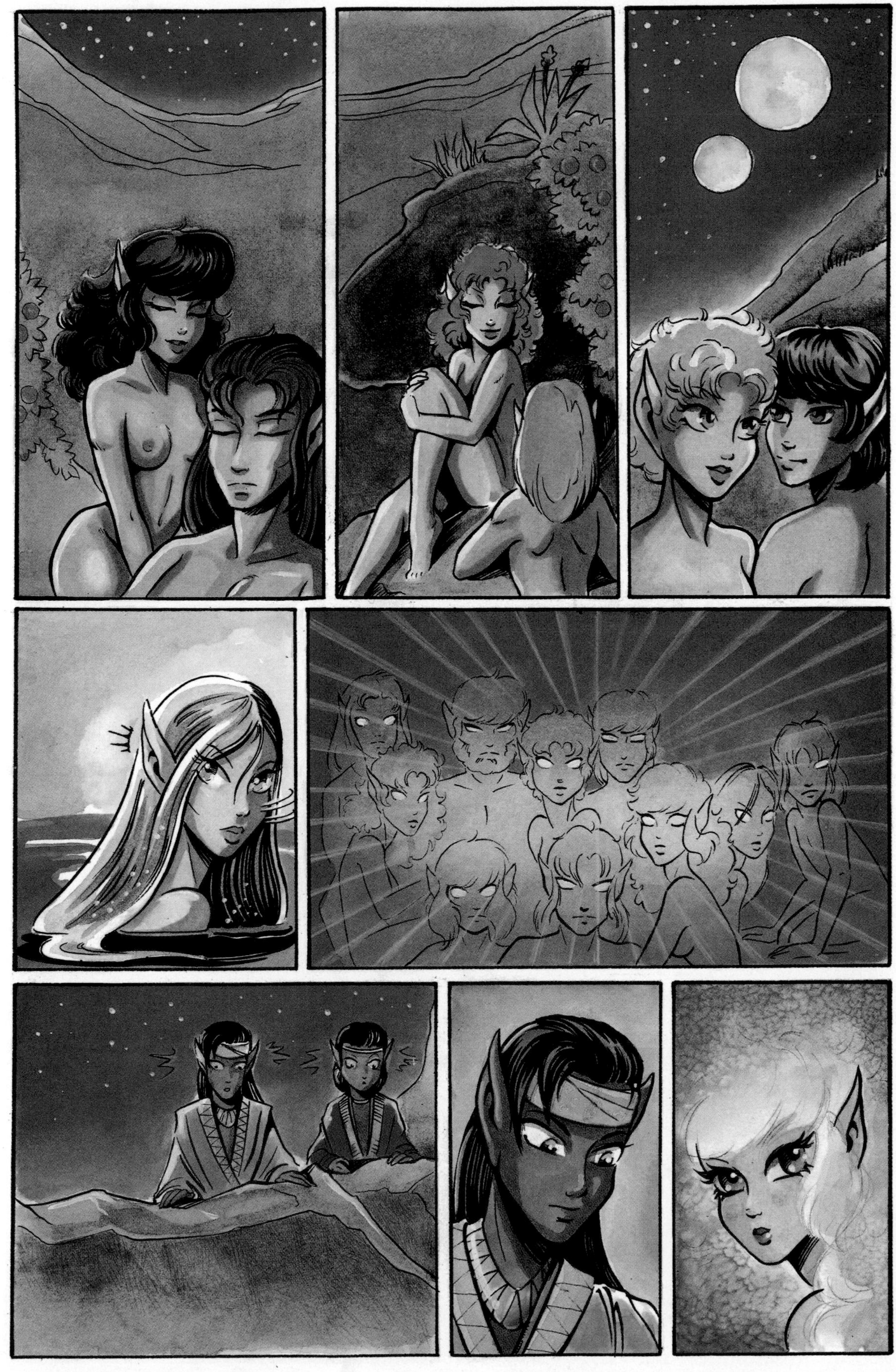

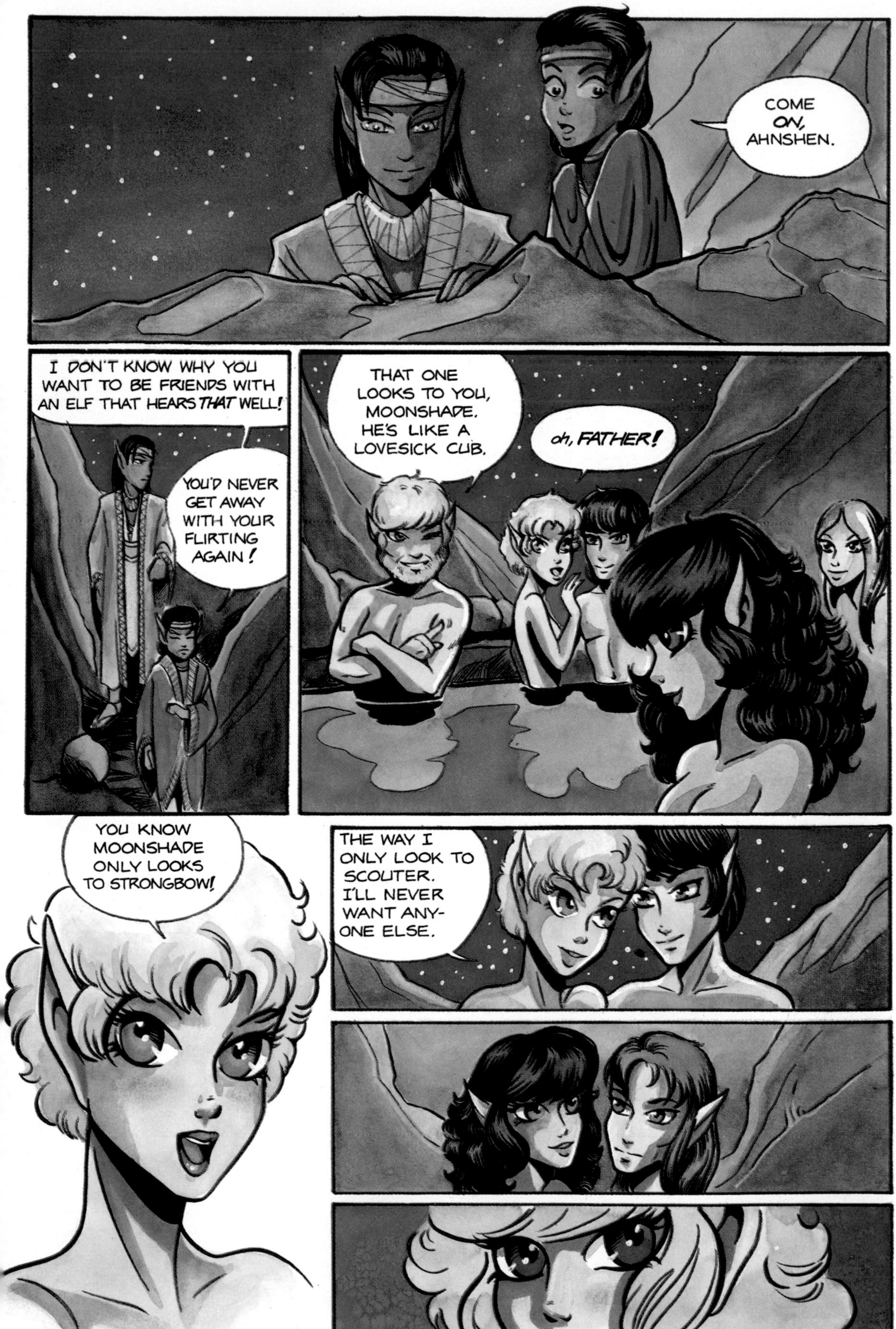
COME ON, AHNSHEN.
I DON'T KNOW WHY YOU WANT TO BE FRIENDS WITH AN ELF THAT HEARS THAT WELL!
YOU'D NEVER GET AWAY WITH YOUR FLIRTING AGAIN!
THAT ONE LOOKS TO YOU, MOONSHADE. HE'S LIKE A LOVESICK CUB.
oh, FATHER!
YOU KNOW MOONSHADE ONLY LOOKS TO STRONGBOW!
THE WAY I ONLY LOOK TO SCOUTER. I'LL NEVER WANT ANY-ONE ELSE.

TO BE CONTINUED...

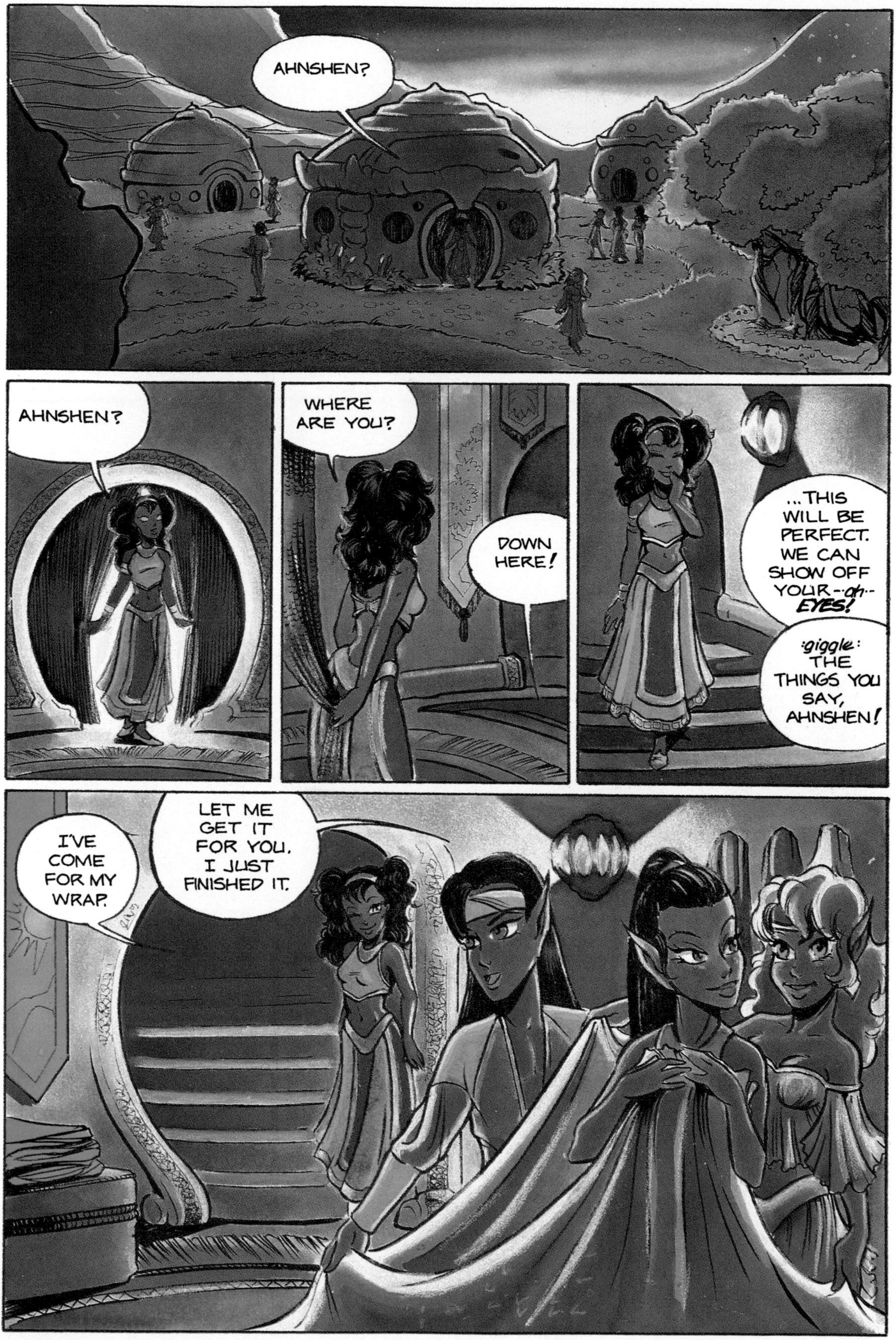
AHNSHEN?
AHNSHEN?
WHERE ARE YOU?
DOWN HERE!
...THIS WILL BE PERFECT. WE CAN SHOW OFF YOUR--oh--EYES!
:giggle: THE THINGS YOU SAY, AHNSHEN!
I'VE COME FOR MY WRAP.
LET ME GET IT FOR YOU. I JUST FINISHED IT.

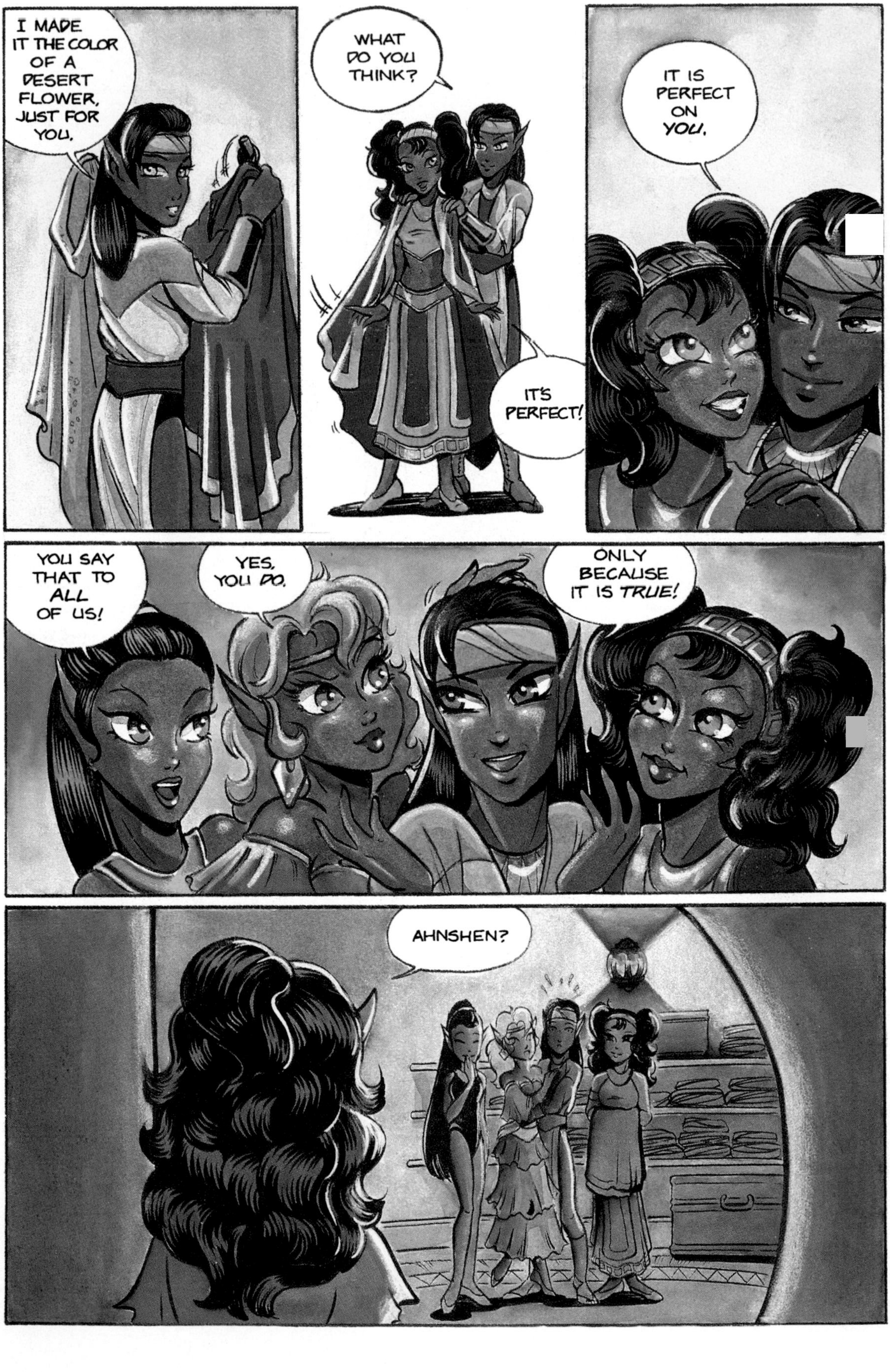
I MADE IT THE COLOR OF A DESERT FLOWER, JUST FOR YOU.
WHAT DO YOU THINK?
IT'S PERFECT!
IT IS PERFECT ON *YOU*.
YOU SAY THAT TO *ALL* OF US!
YES, YOU *DO*.
ONLY BECAUSE IT IS *TRUE*!
AHNSHEN?

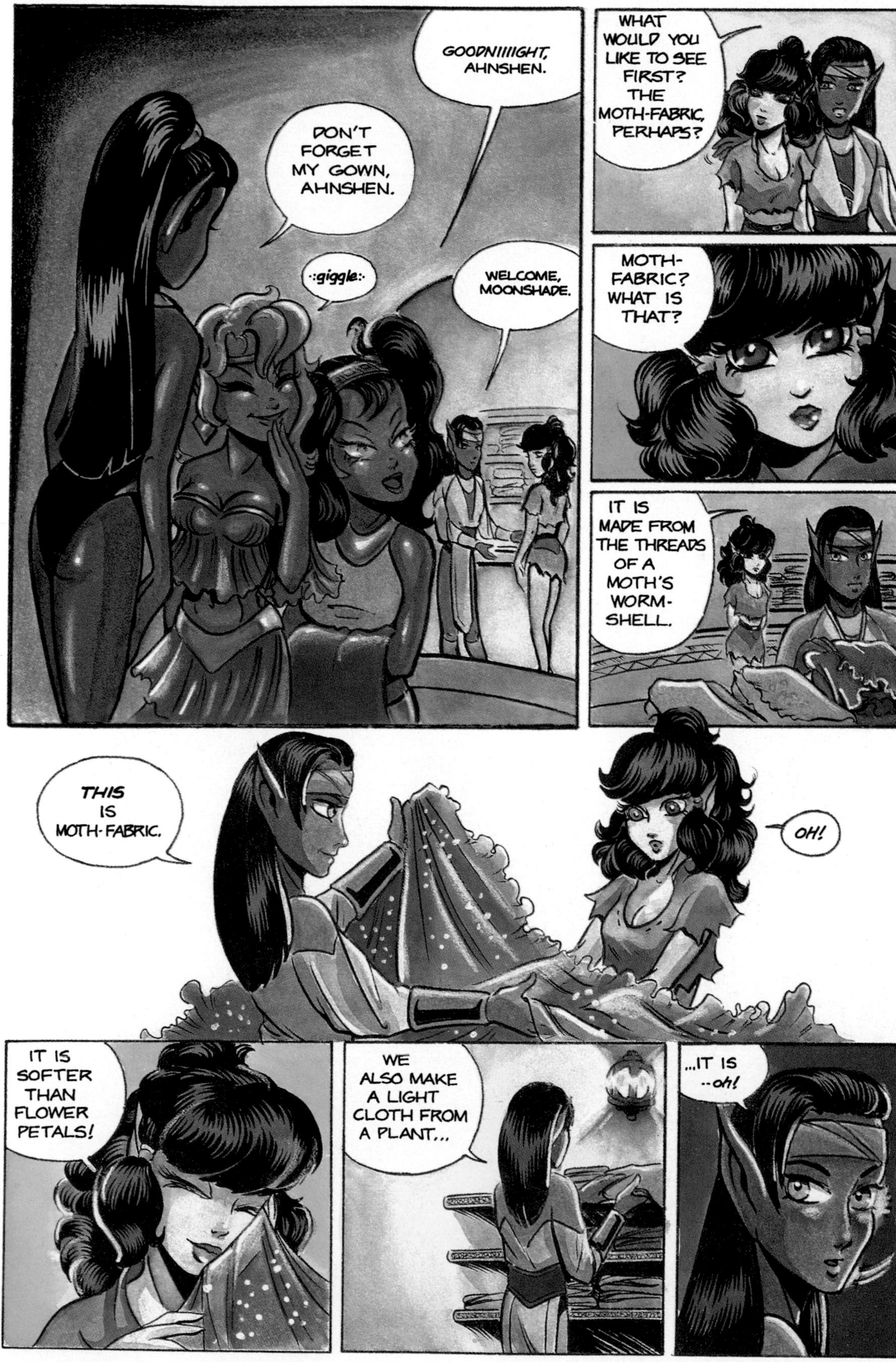
DON'T FORGET MY GOWN, AHNSHEN.
GOODNIIIIGHT, AHNSHEN.
::giggle::
WELCOME, MOONSHADE.
WHAT WOULD YOU LIKE TO SEE FIRST? THE MOTH-FABRIC, PERHAPS?
MOTH-FABRIC? WHAT IS THAT?
IT IS MADE FROM THE THREADS OF A MOTH'S WORM-SHELL.
THIS IS MOTH-FABRIC.
OH!
IT IS SOFTER THAN FLOWER PETALS!
WE ALSO MAKE A LIGHT CLOTH FROM A PLANT...
...IT IS --oh!

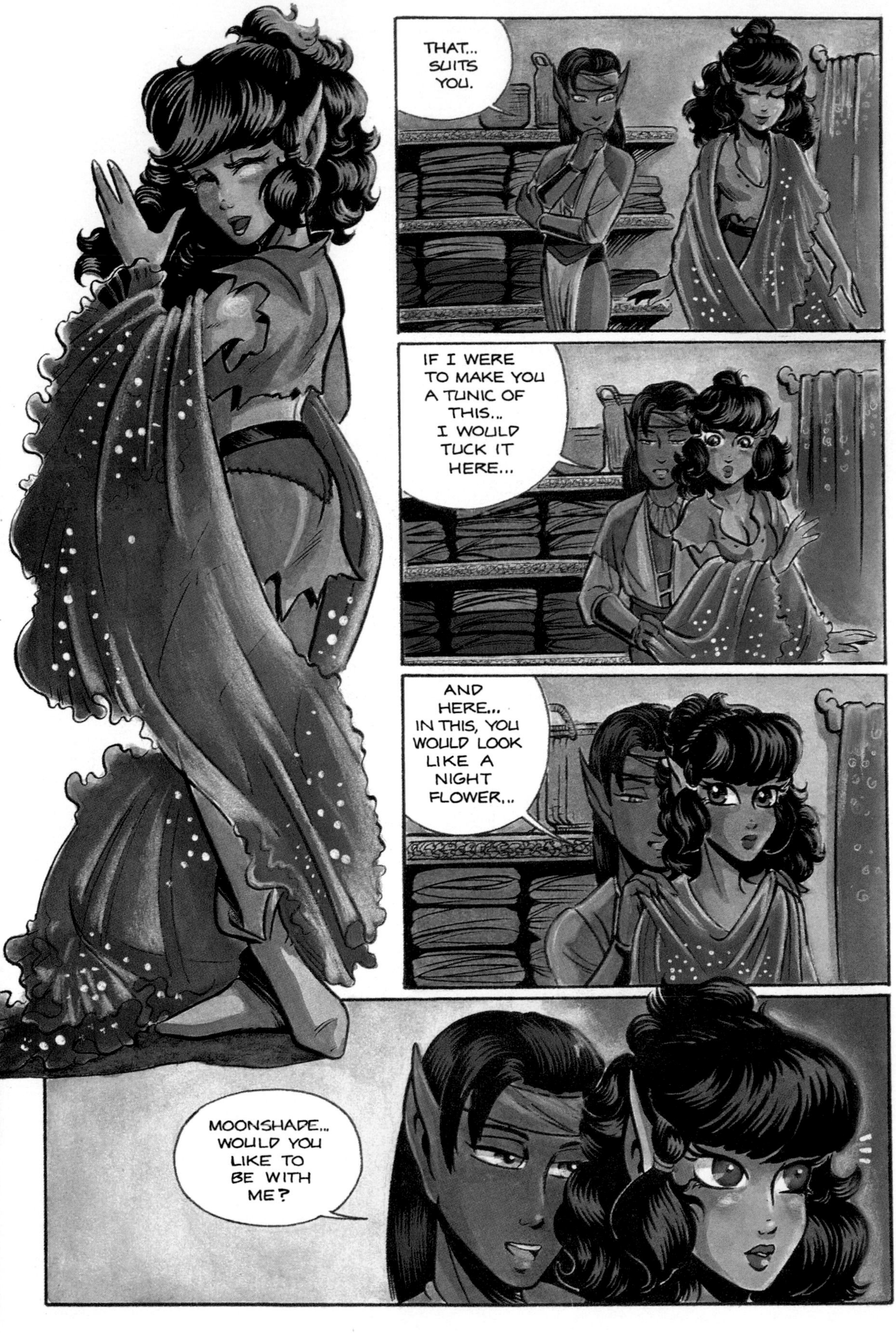
THAT... SUITS YOU.
IF I WERE TO MAKE YOU A TUNIC OF THIS... I WOULD TUCK IT HERE...
AND HERE... IN THIS, YOU WOULD LOOK LIKE A NIGHT FLOWER...
MOONSHADE... WOULD YOU LIKE TO BE WITH ME?

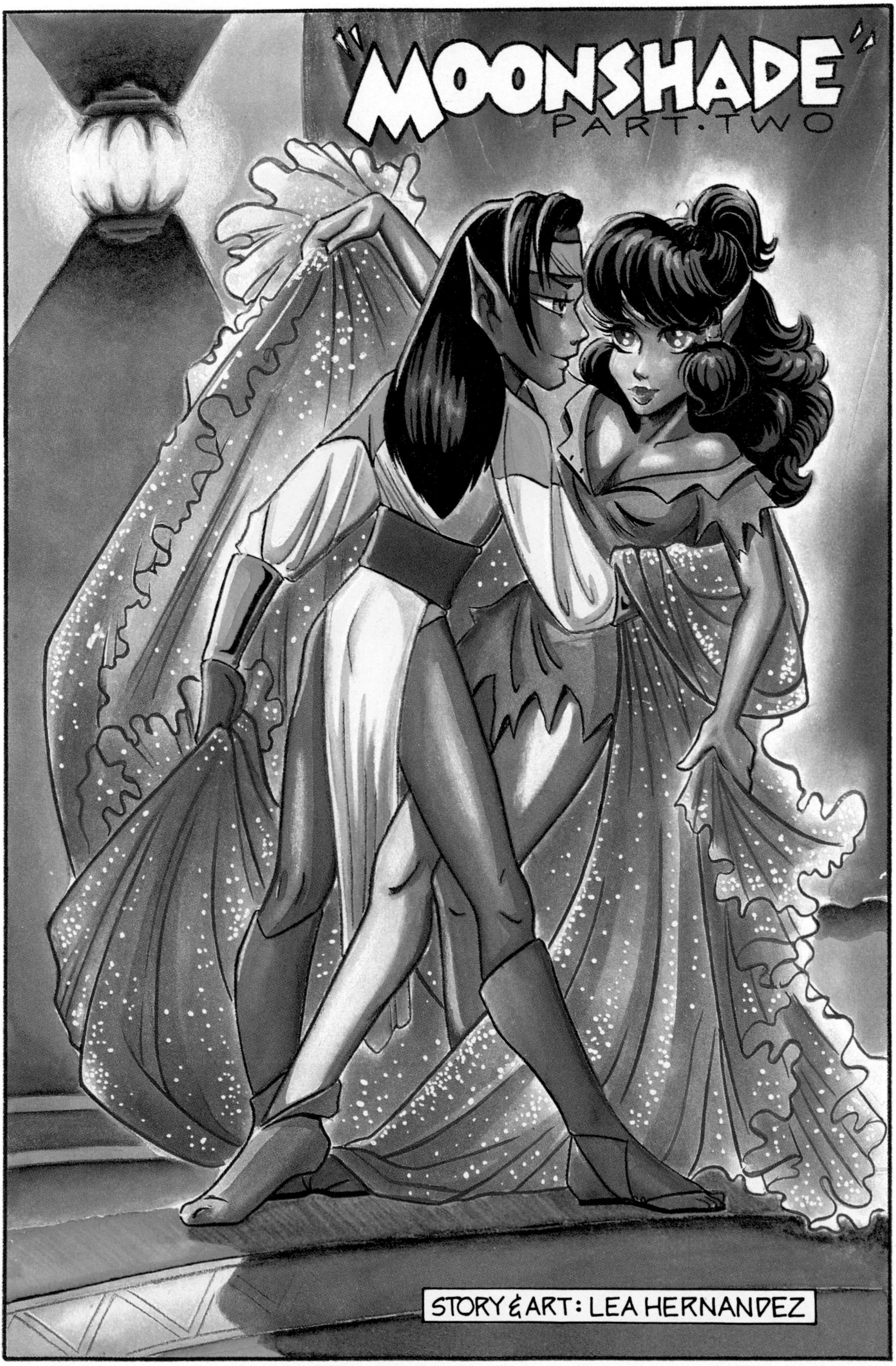
"MOONSHADE"
PART·TWO
STORY & ART: LEA HERNANDEZ

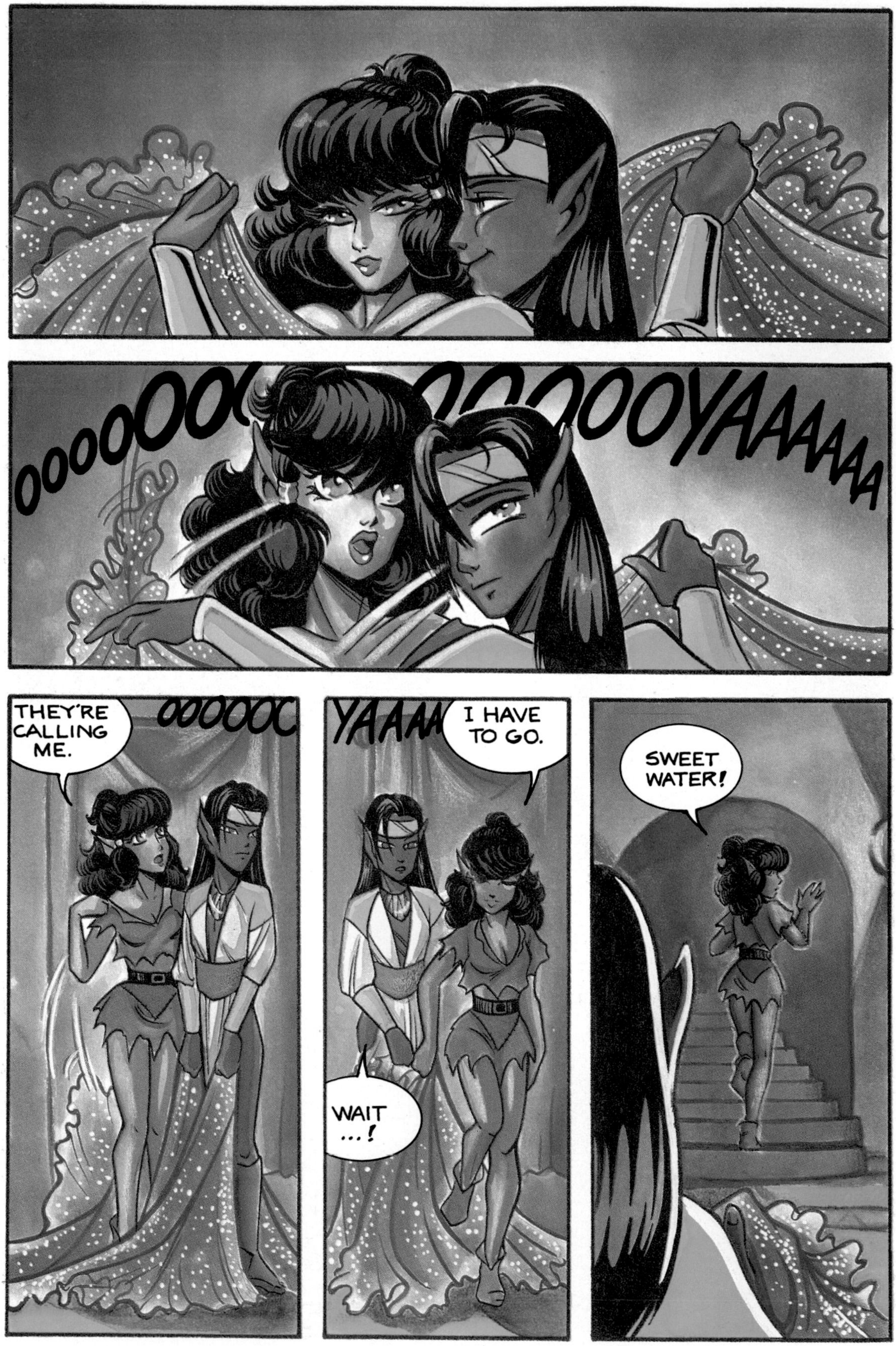
OOOOOOOOOOOOOOOOYAAAAAAA
THEY'RE CALLING ME.
OOOOOC
YAAAA
I HAVE TO GO.
WAIT ...!
SWEET WATER!

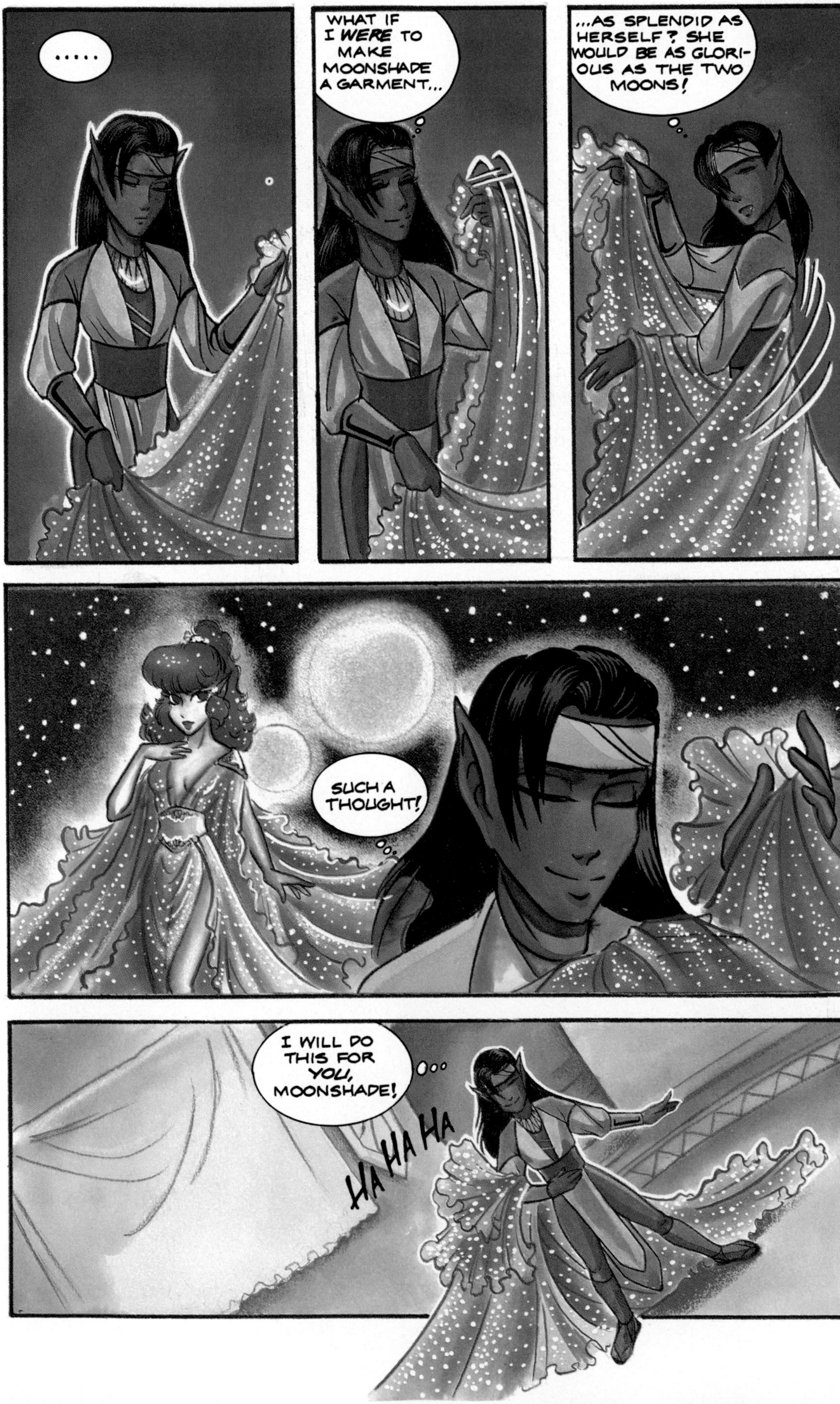
......
WHAT IF I WERE TO MAKE MOONSHADE A GARMENT...
...AS SPLENDID AS HERSELF? SHE WOULD BE AS GLORI-OUS AS THE TWO MOONS!
SUCH A THOUGHT!
I WILL DO THIS FOR YOU, MOONSHADE!
HA HA HA HA

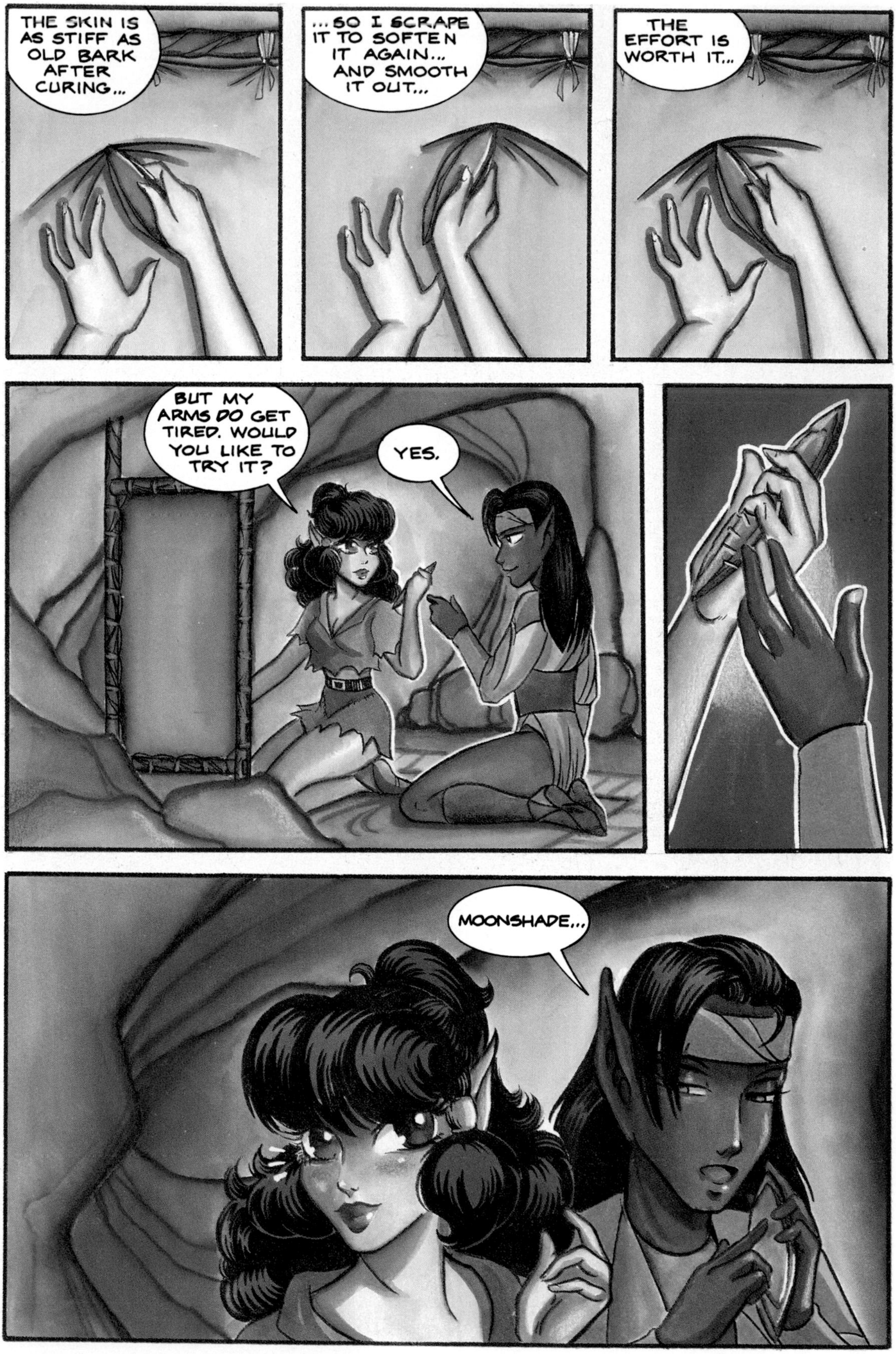
THE SKIN IS AS STIFF AS OLD BARK AFTER CURING...
...SO I SCRAPE IT TO SOFTEN IT AGAIN... AND SMOOTH IT OUT...
THE EFFORT IS WORTH IT...
BUT MY ARMS DO GET TIRED. WOULD YOU LIKE TO TRY IT?
YES.
MOONSHADE...

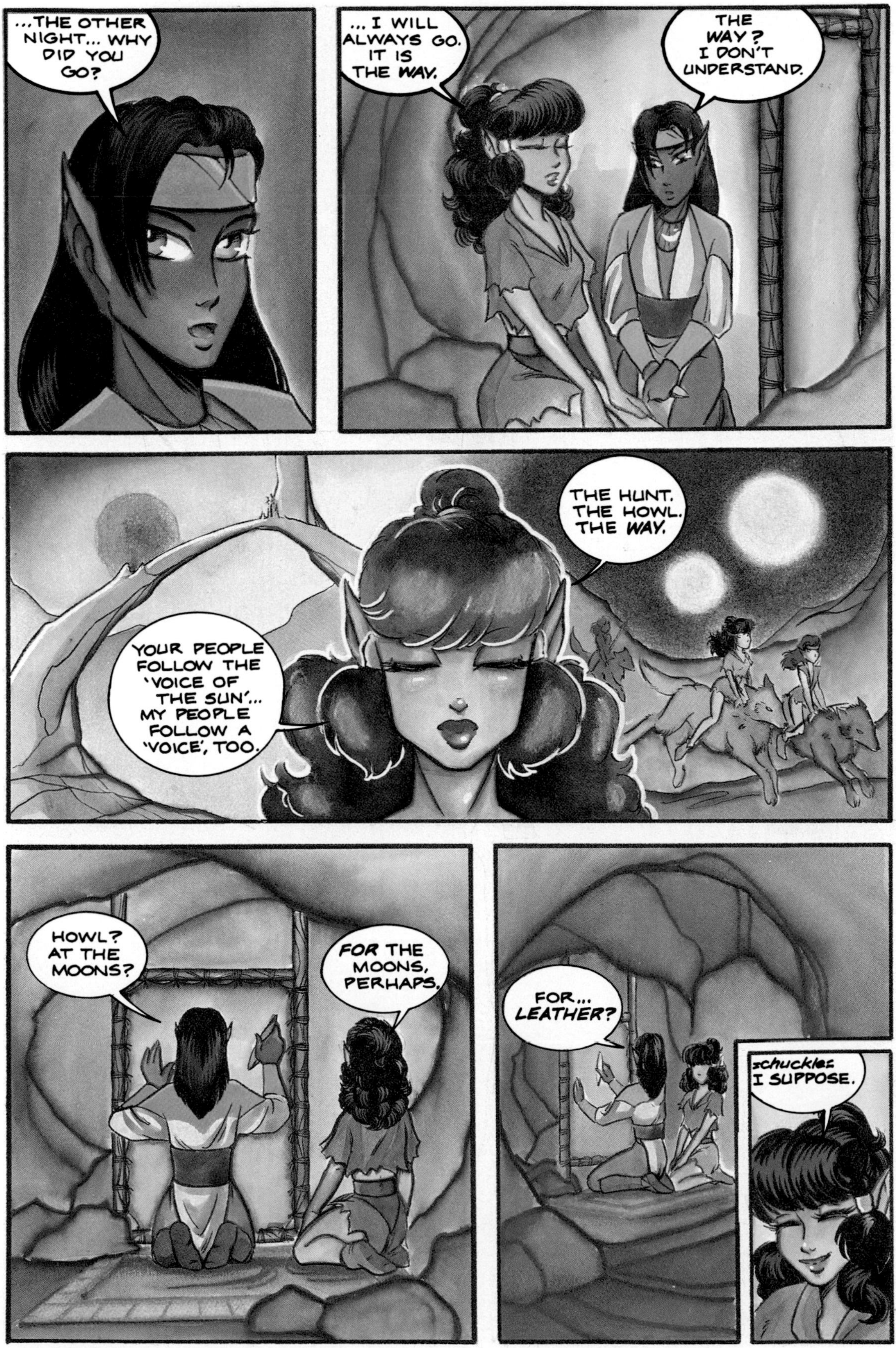
...THE OTHER NIGHT... WHY DID YOU GO?
...I WILL ALWAYS GO. IT IS THE WAY.
THE WAY? I DON'T UNDERSTAND.
THE HUNT. THE HOWL. THE WAY.
YOUR PEOPLE FOLLOW THE 'VOICE OF THE SUN'... MY PEOPLE FOLLOW A 'VOICE', TOO.
HOWL? AT THE MOONS?
FOR THE MOONS, PERHAPS.
FOR... LEATHER?
chuckle I SUPPOSE.

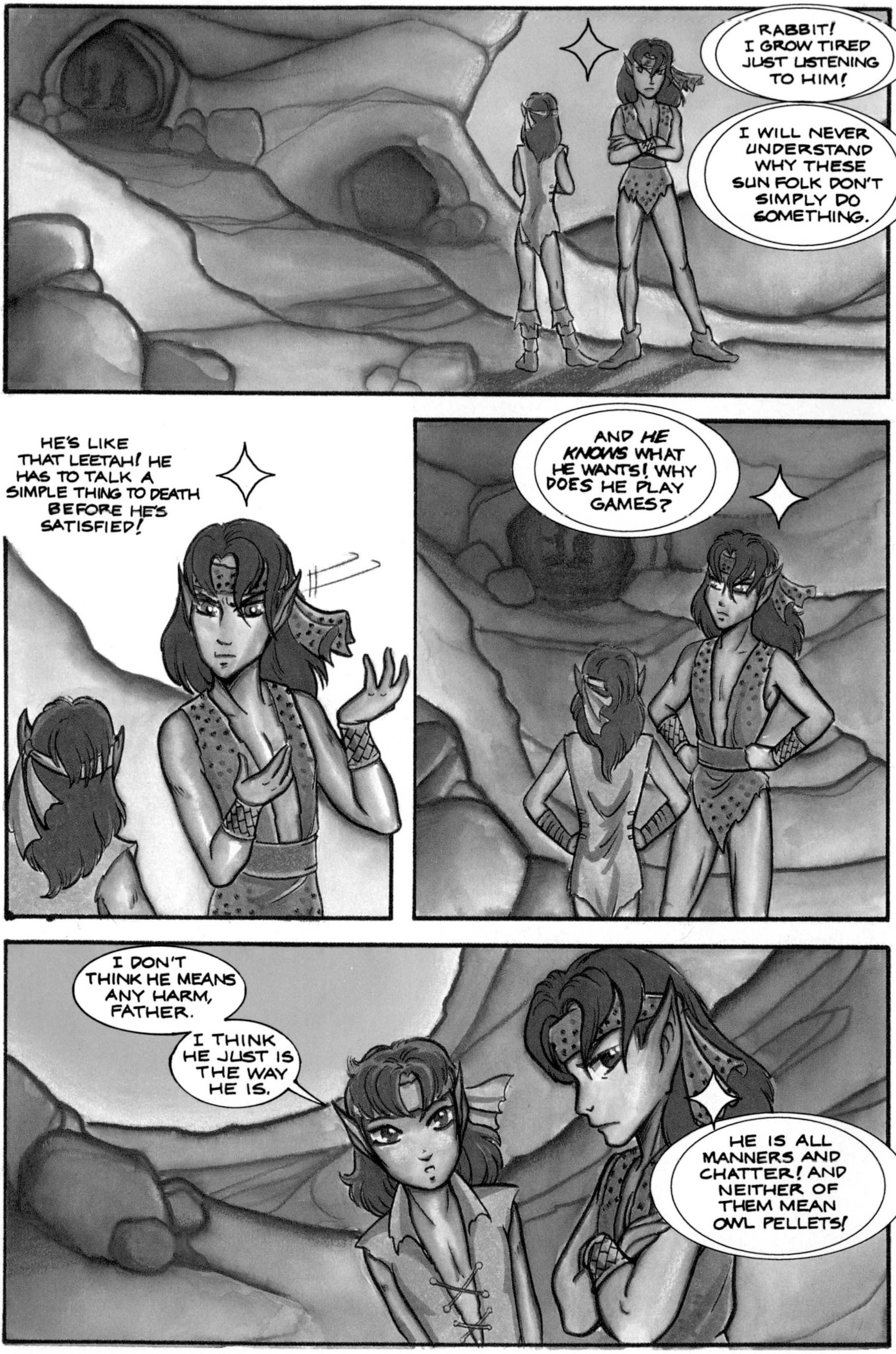

RABBIT! I GROW TIRED JUST LISTENING TO HIM!
I WILL NEVER UNDERSTAND WHY THESE SUN FOLK DON'T SIMPLY DO SOMETHING.
HE'S LIKE THAT LEETAH! HE HAS TO TALK A SIMPLE THING TO DEATH BEFORE HE'S SATISFIED!
AND HE KNOWS WHAT HE WANTS! WHY DOES HE PLAY GAMES?
I DON'T THINK HE MEANS ANY HARM, FATHER.
I THINK HE JUST IS THE WAY HE IS.
HE IS ALL MANNERS AND CHATTER! AND NEITHER OF THEM MEAN OWL PELLETS!

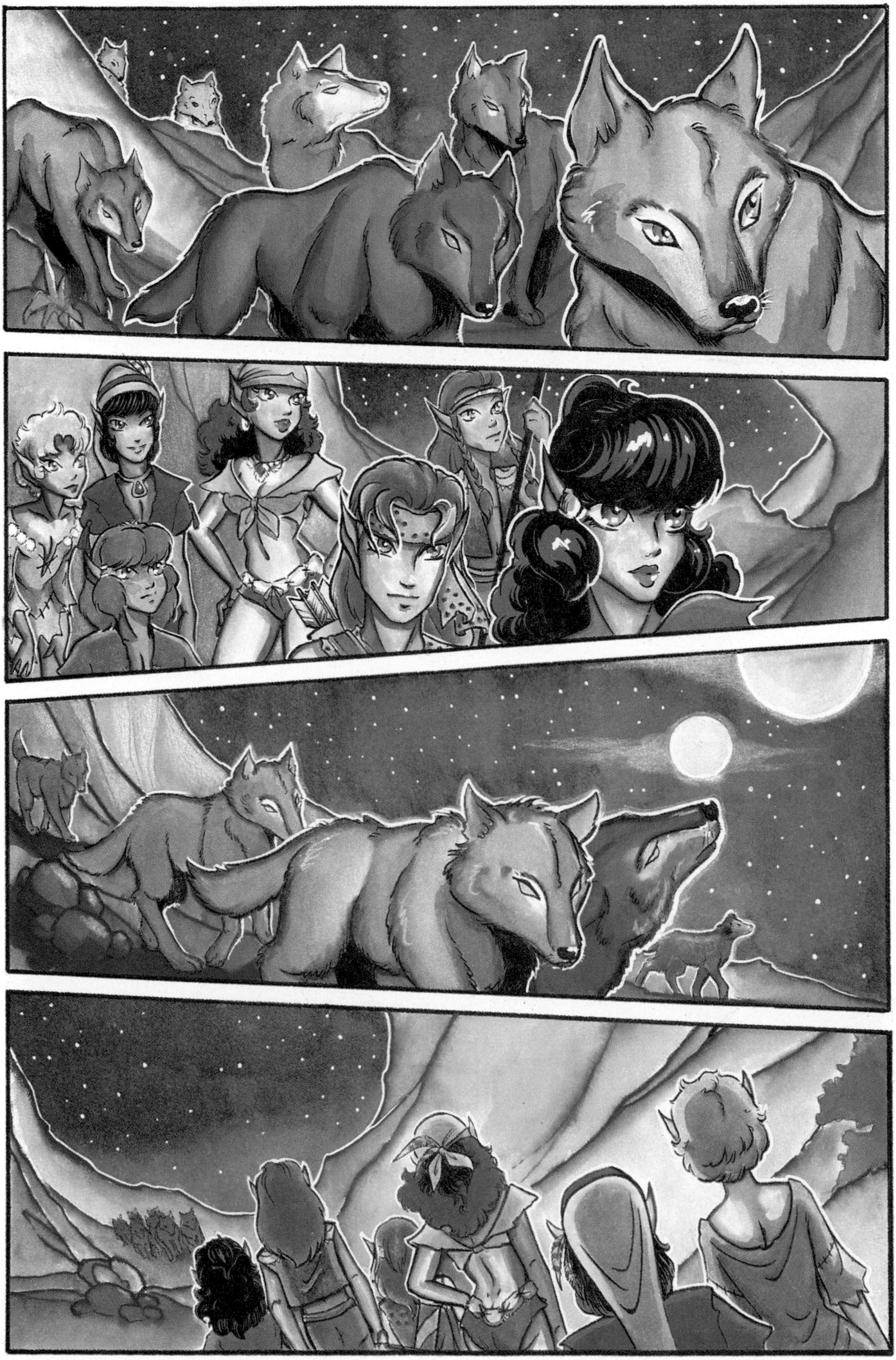

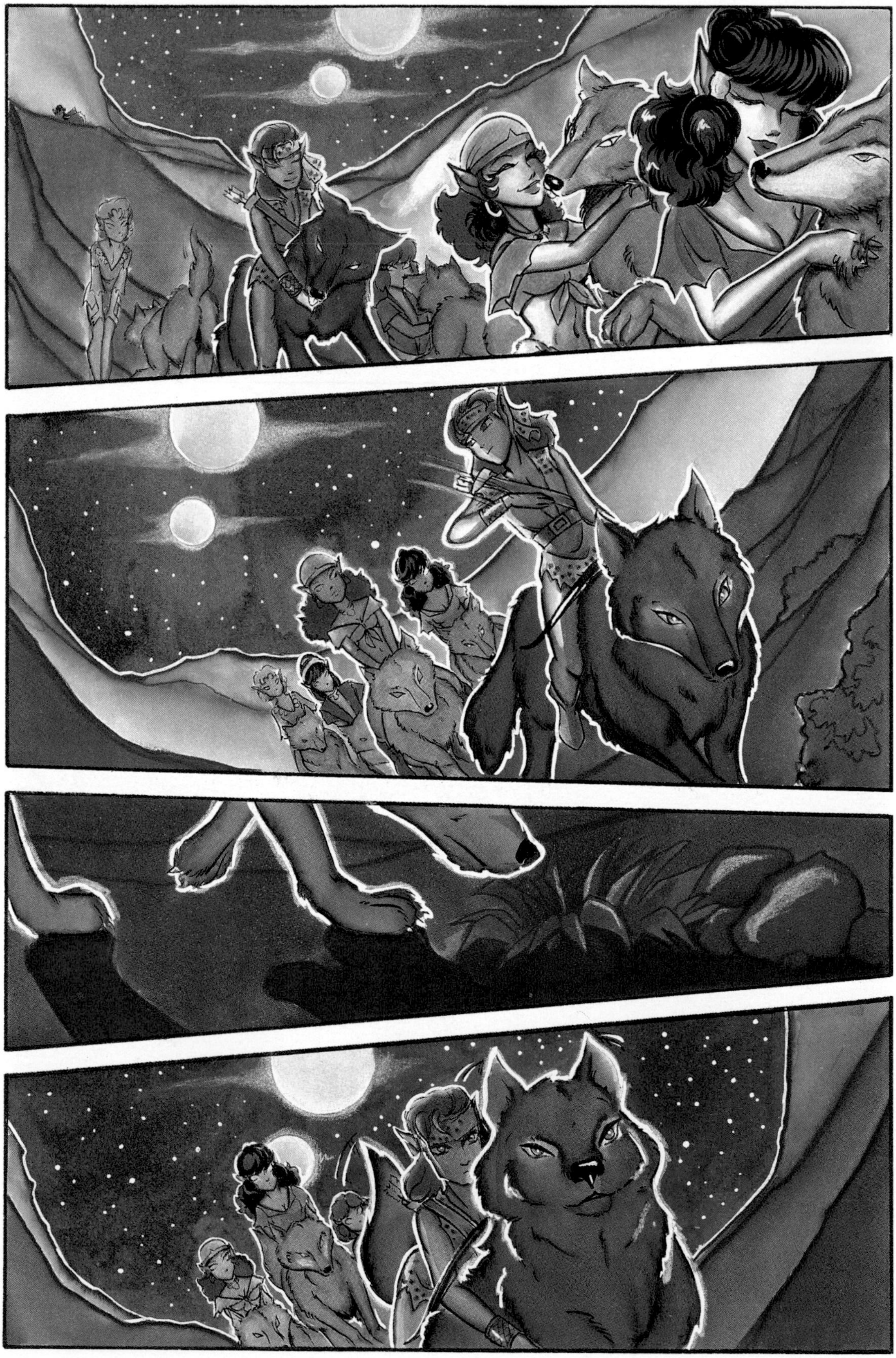

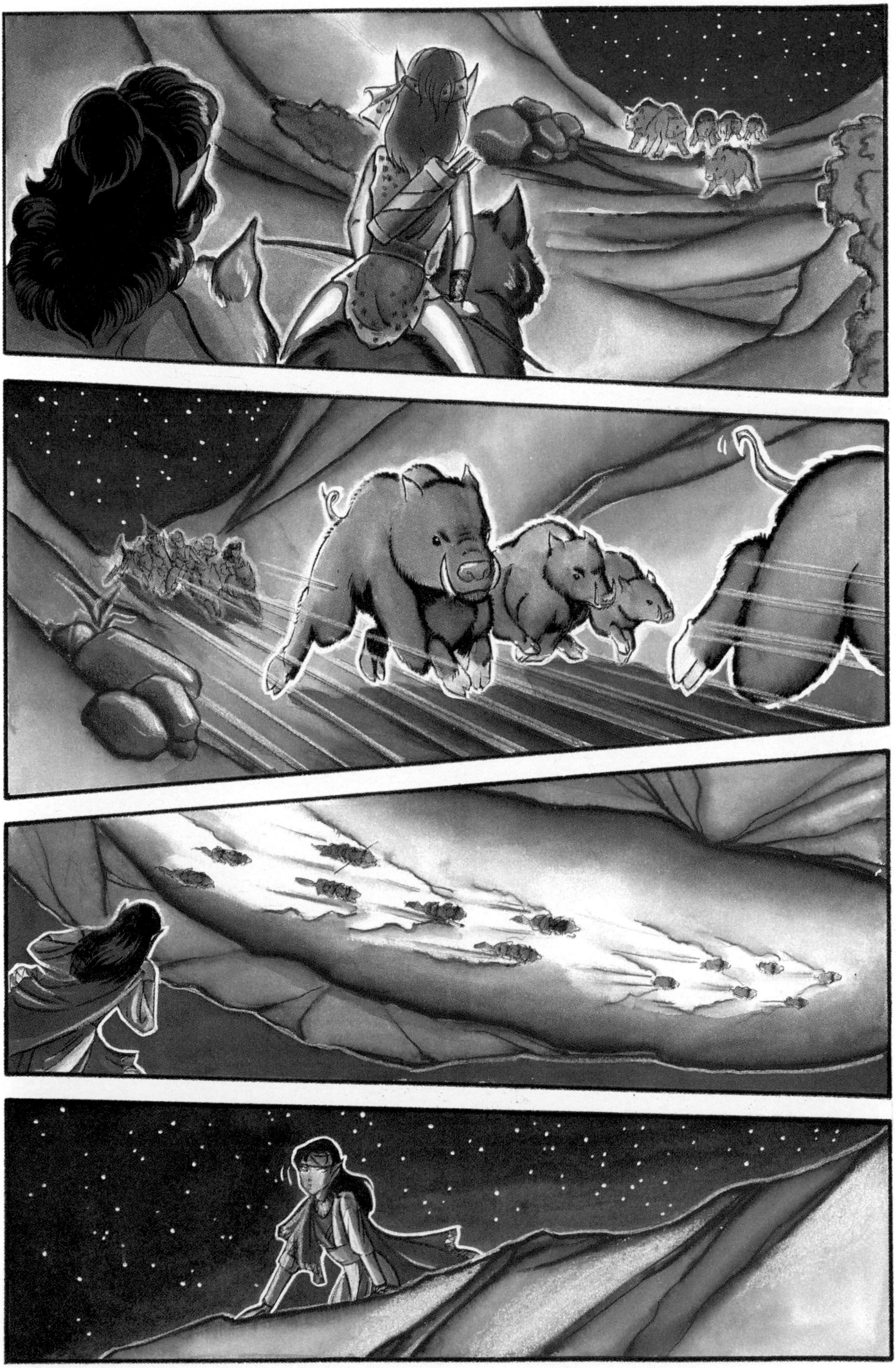

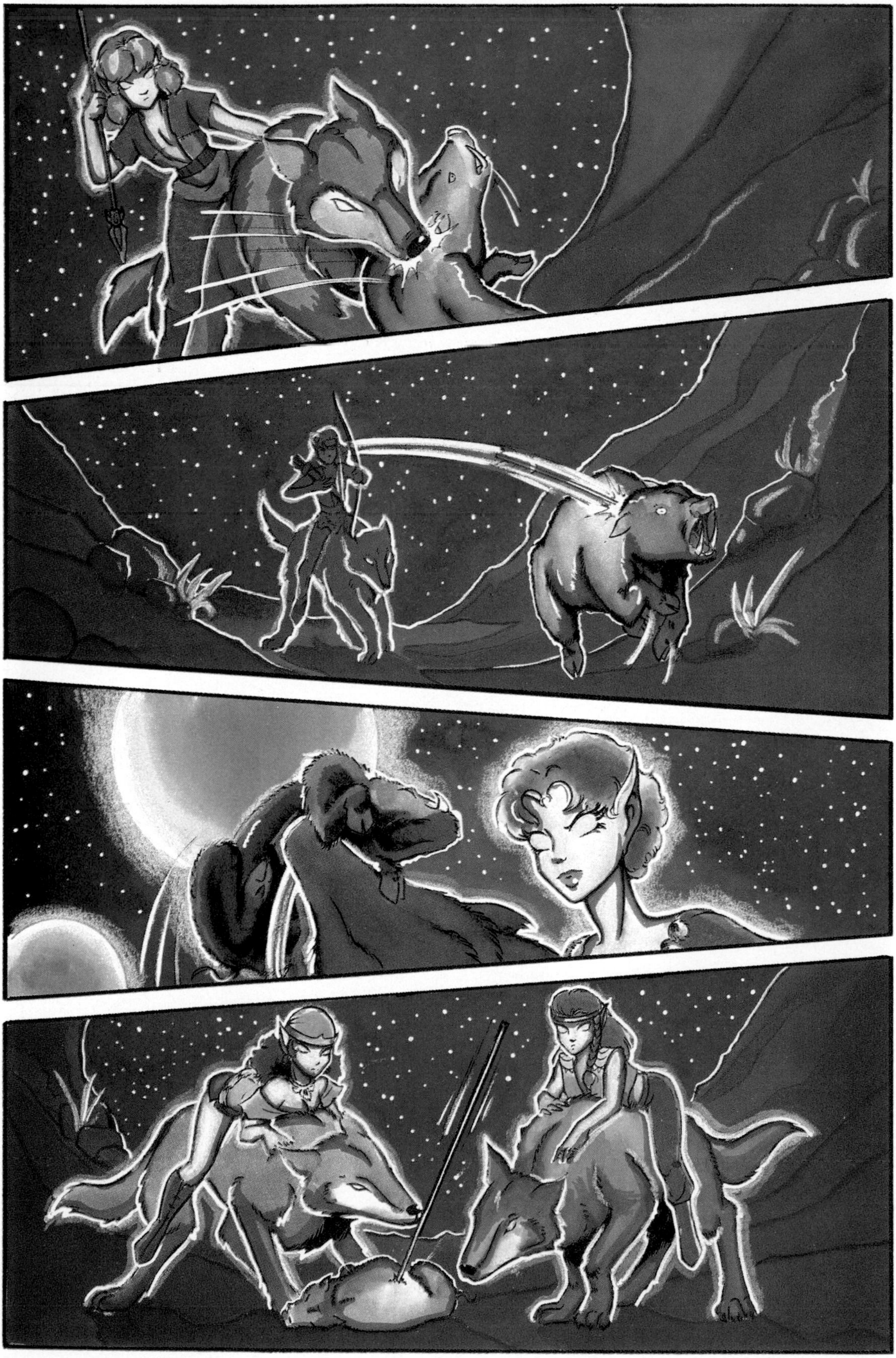

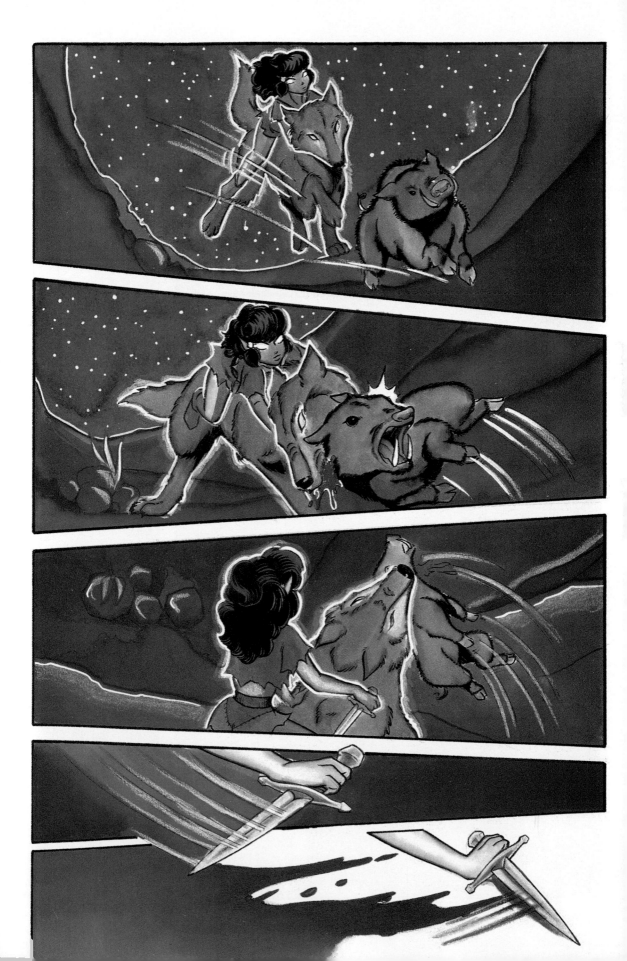

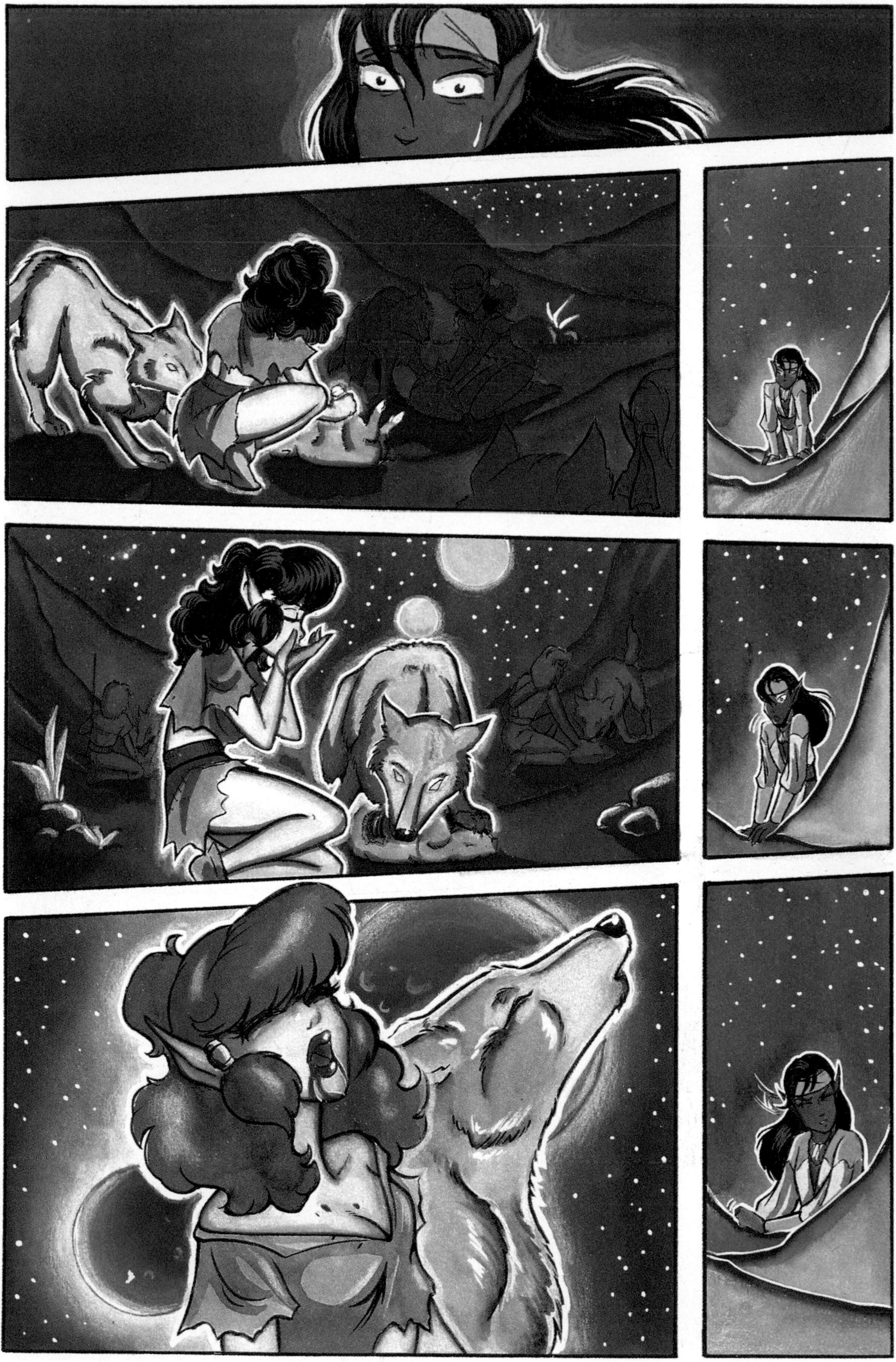

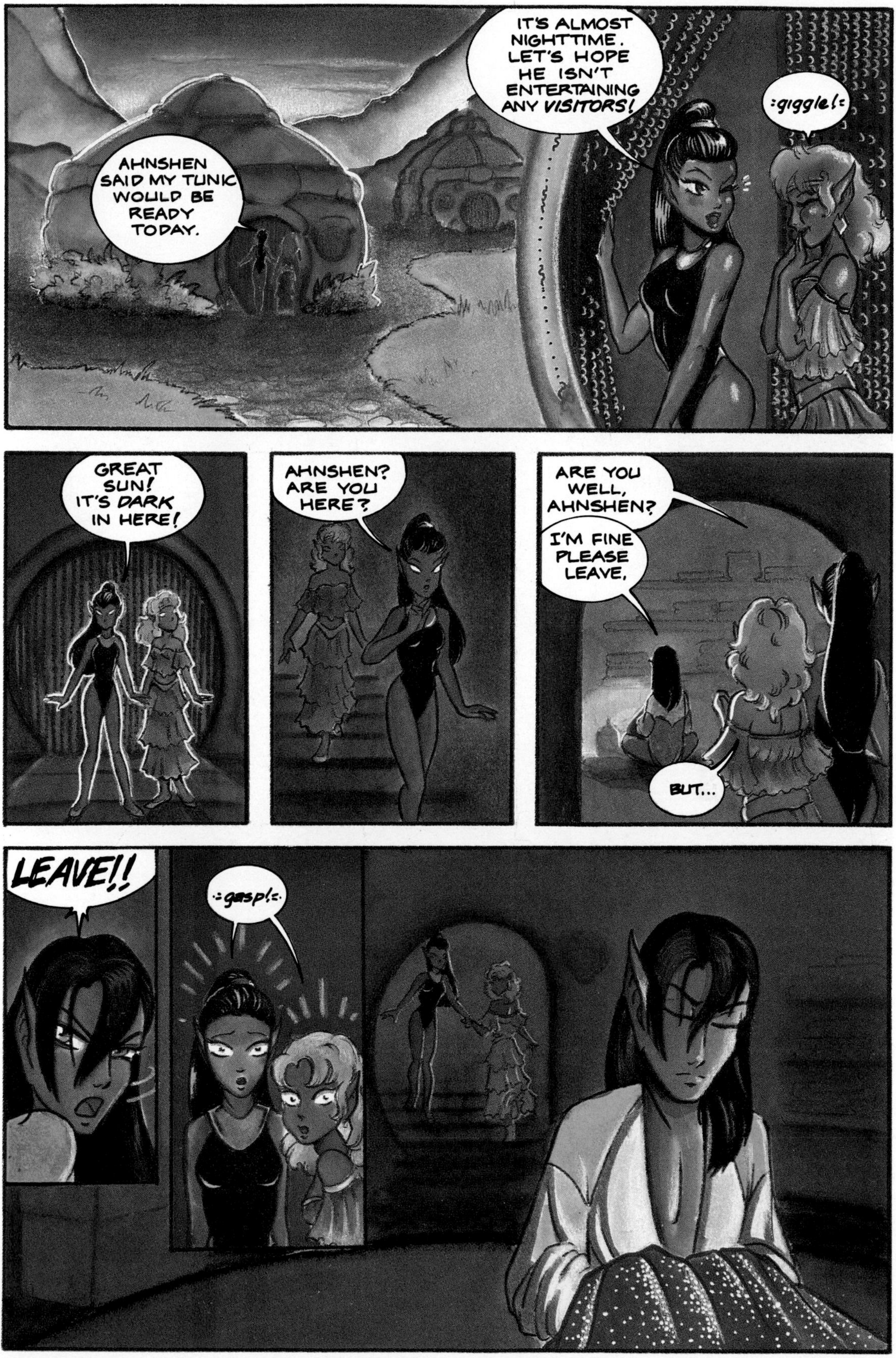
AHNSHEN SAID MY TUNIC WOULD BE READY TODAY.
IT'S ALMOST NIGHTTIME. LET'S HOPE HE ISN'T ENTERTAINING ANY VISITORS!
:giggle!:
GREAT SUN! IT'S DARK IN HERE!
AHNSHEN? ARE YOU HERE?
ARE YOU WELL, AHNSHEN?
I'M FINE PLEASE LEAVE.
BUT...
LEAVE!!
:gasp!:

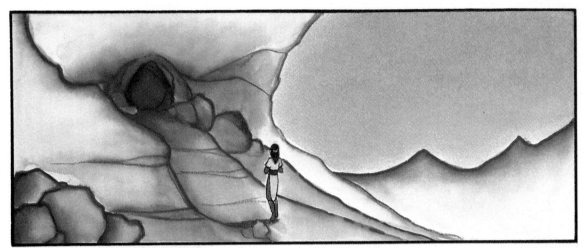

MOONSHADE...

I...I AM CONFUSED. I DON'T KNOW HOW YOU CAN BE WHAT YOU ARE...

...AND BE SOMETHING HORR--

RABBIT!!

STRONGBOW!

AAAH!

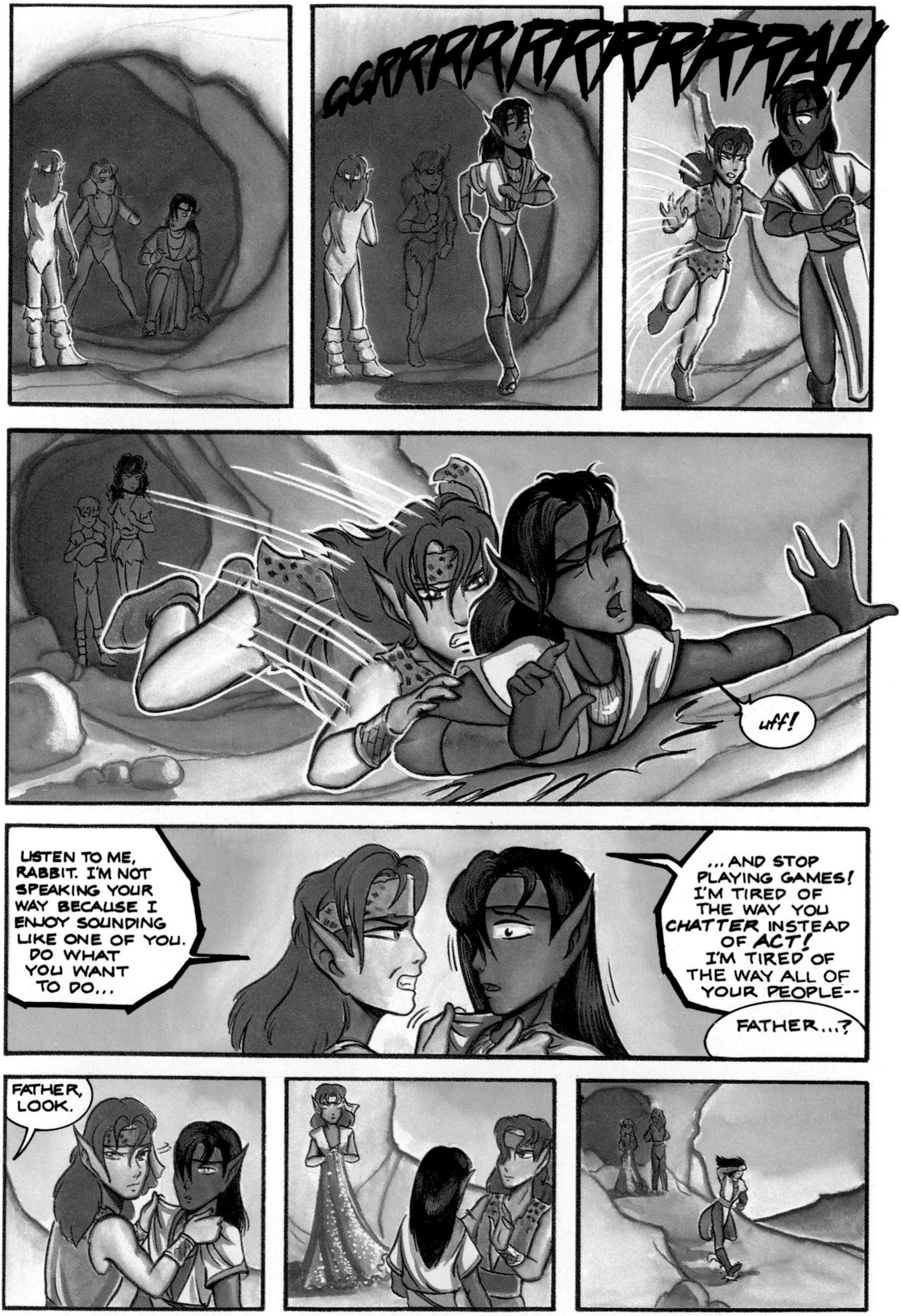
GGRRRRRRRRRRRRRRRRAH
uff!
LISTEN TO ME, RABBIT. I'M NOT SPEAKING YOUR WAY BECAUSE I ENJOY SOUNDING LIKE ONE OF YOU. DO WHAT YOU WANT TO DO...
...AND STOP PLAYING GAMES! I'M TIRED OF THE WAY YOU CHATTER INSTEAD OF ACT! I'M TIRED OF THE WAY ALL OF YOUR PEOPLE--
FATHER...?
FATHER, LOOK.

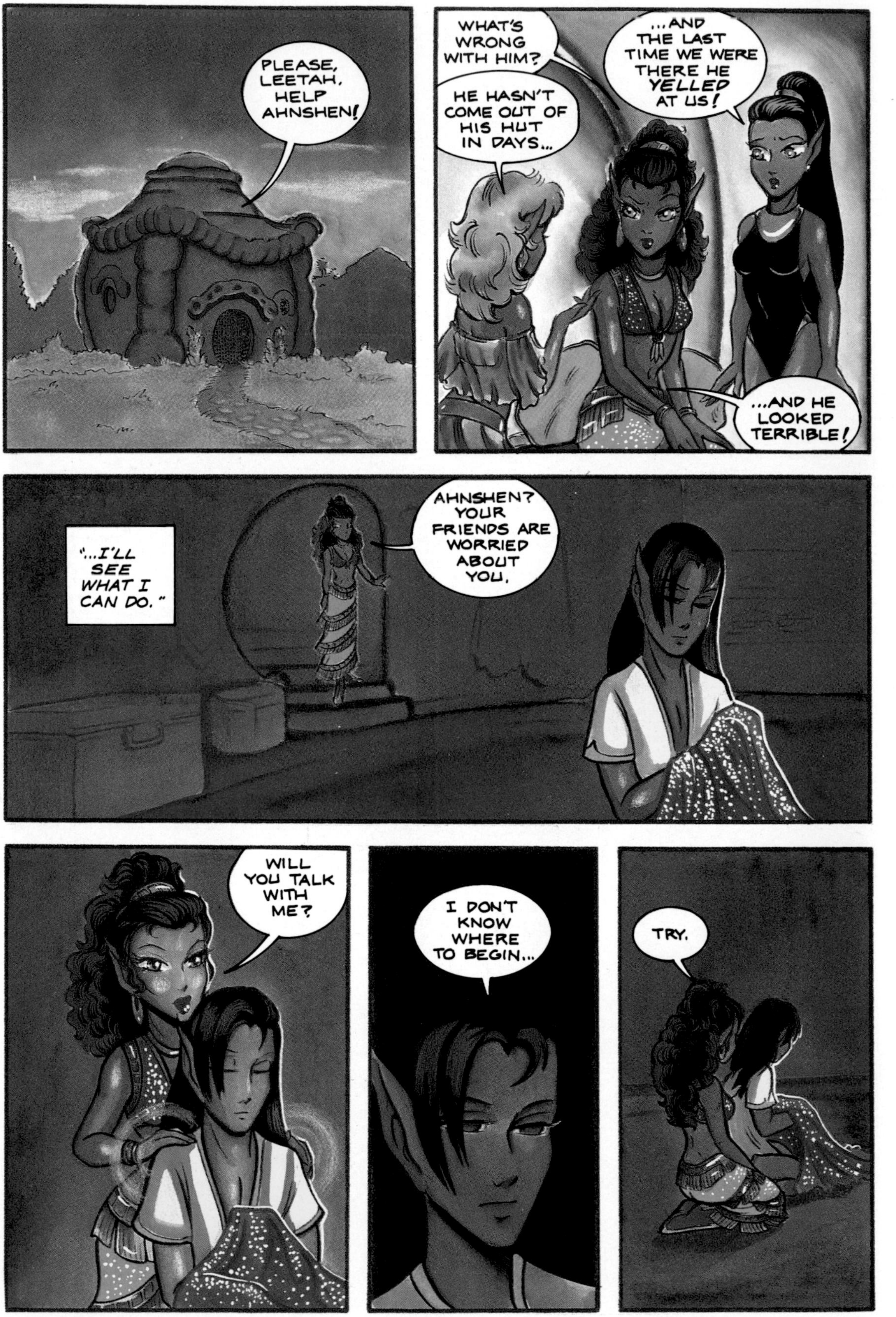
PLEASE, LEETAH, HELP AHNSHEN!
WHAT'S WRONG WITH HIM?
HE HASN'T COME OUT OF HIS HUT IN DAYS...
...AND THE LAST TIME WE WERE THERE HE YELLED AT US!
...AND HE LOOKED TERRIBLE!
"...I'LL SEE WHAT I CAN DO."
AHNSHEN? YOUR FRIENDS ARE WORRIED ABOUT YOU.
WILL YOU TALK WITH ME?
I DON'T KNOW WHERE TO BEGIN...
TRY.

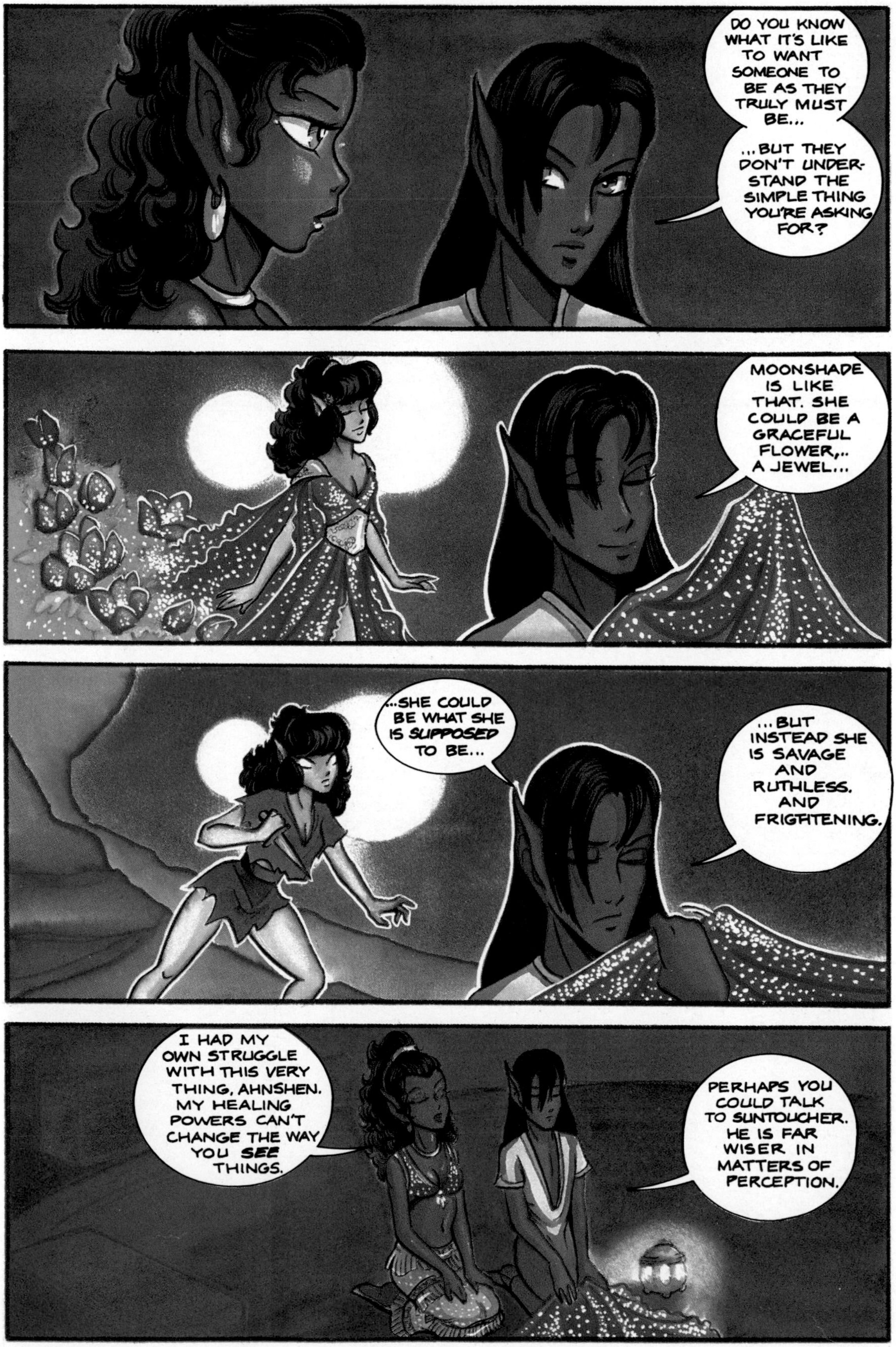
DO YOU KNOW WHAT IT'S LIKE TO WANT SOMEONE TO BE AS THEY TRULY MUST BE...
...BUT THEY DON'T UNDER-STAND THE SIMPLE THING YOU'RE ASKING FOR?
MOONSHADE IS LIKE THAT. SHE COULD BE A GRACEFUL FLOWER,.. A JEWEL...
..SHE COULD BE WHAT SHE IS SUPPOSED TO BE...
...BUT INSTEAD SHE IS SAVAGE AND RUTHLESS. AND FRIGHTENING.
I HAD MY OWN STRUGGLE WITH THIS VERY THING, AHNSHEN. MY HEALING POWERS CAN'T CHANGE THE WAY YOU SEE THINGS.
PERHAPS YOU COULD TALK TO SUNTOUCHER. HE IS FAR WISER IN MATTERS OF PERCEPTION.

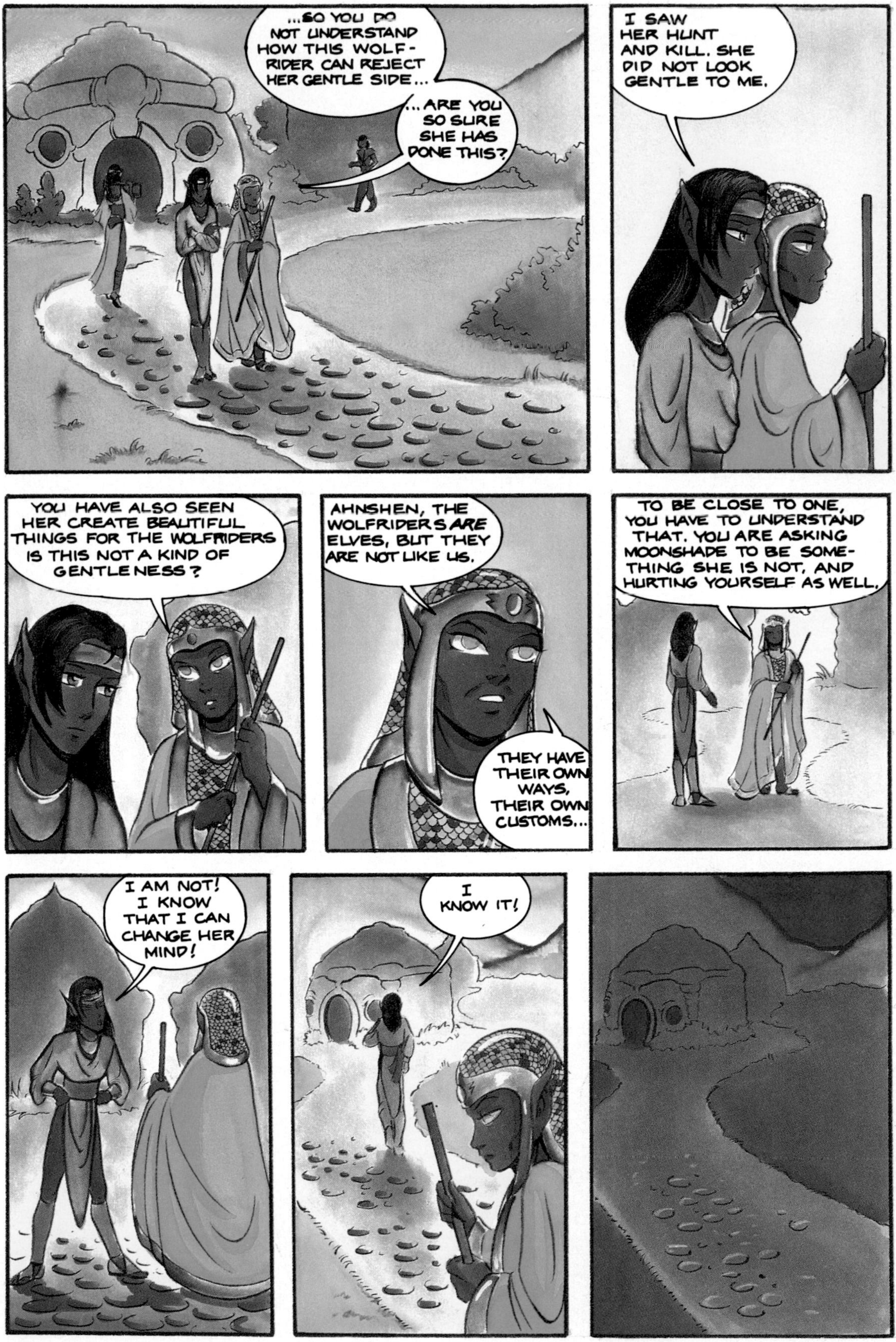
...SO YOU DO NOT UNDERSTAND HOW THIS WOLF-RIDER CAN REJECT HER GENTLE SIDE...
...ARE YOU SO SURE SHE HAS DONE THIS?
I SAW HER HUNT AND KILL. SHE DID NOT LOOK GENTLE TO ME.
YOU HAVE ALSO SEEN HER CREATE BEAUTIFUL THINGS FOR THE WOLFRIDERS IS THIS NOT A KIND OF GENTLENESS?
AHNSHEN, THE WOLFRIDERS ARE ELVES, BUT THEY ARE NOT LIKE US.
THEY HAVE THEIR OWN WAYS, THEIR OWN CUSTOMS...
TO BE CLOSE TO ONE, YOU HAVE TO UNDERSTAND THAT. YOU ARE ASKING MOONSHADE TO BE SOME-THING SHE IS NOT, AND HURTING YOURSELF AS WELL.
I AM NOT! I KNOW THAT I CAN CHANGE HER MIND!
I KNOW IT!

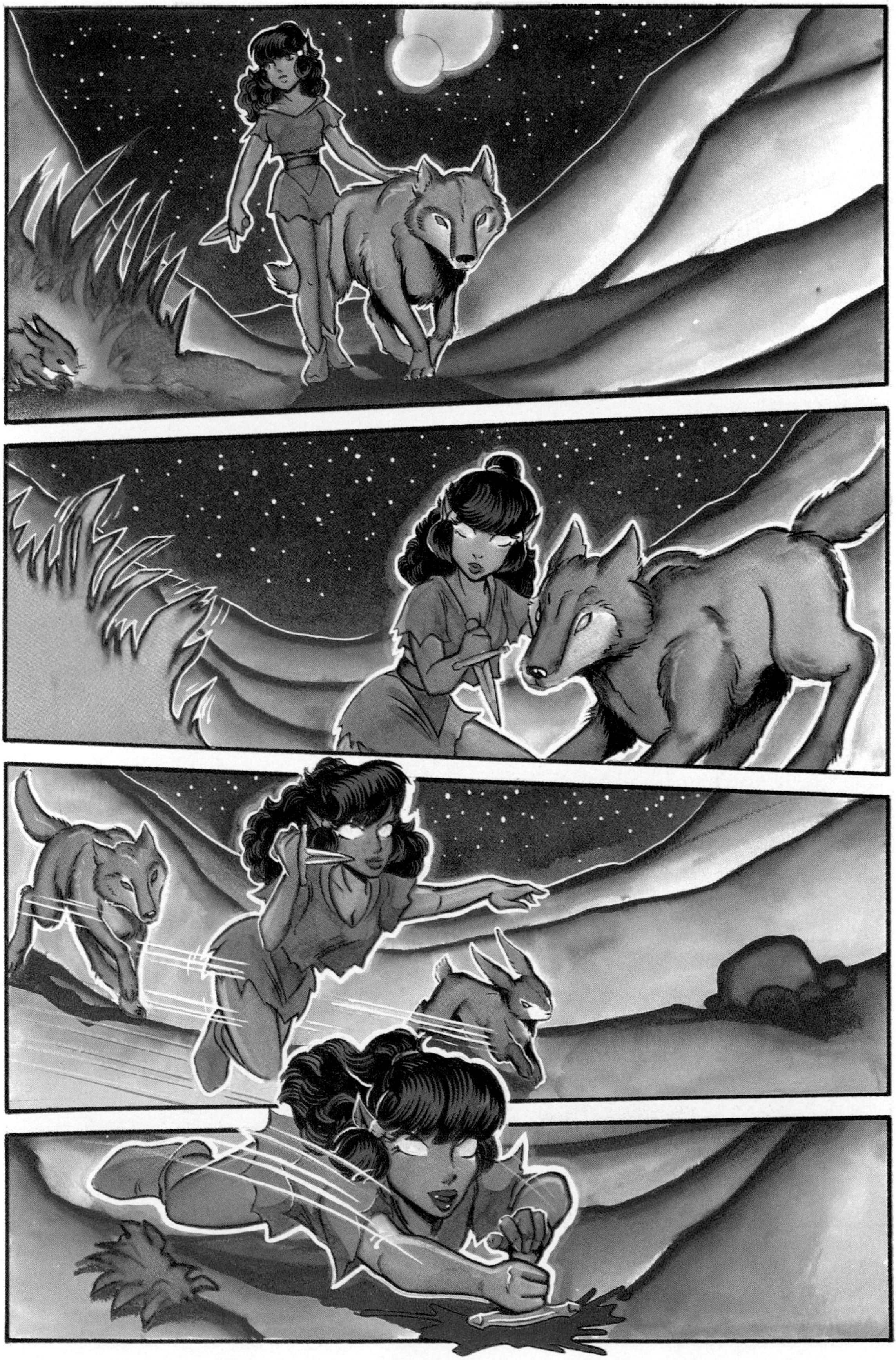

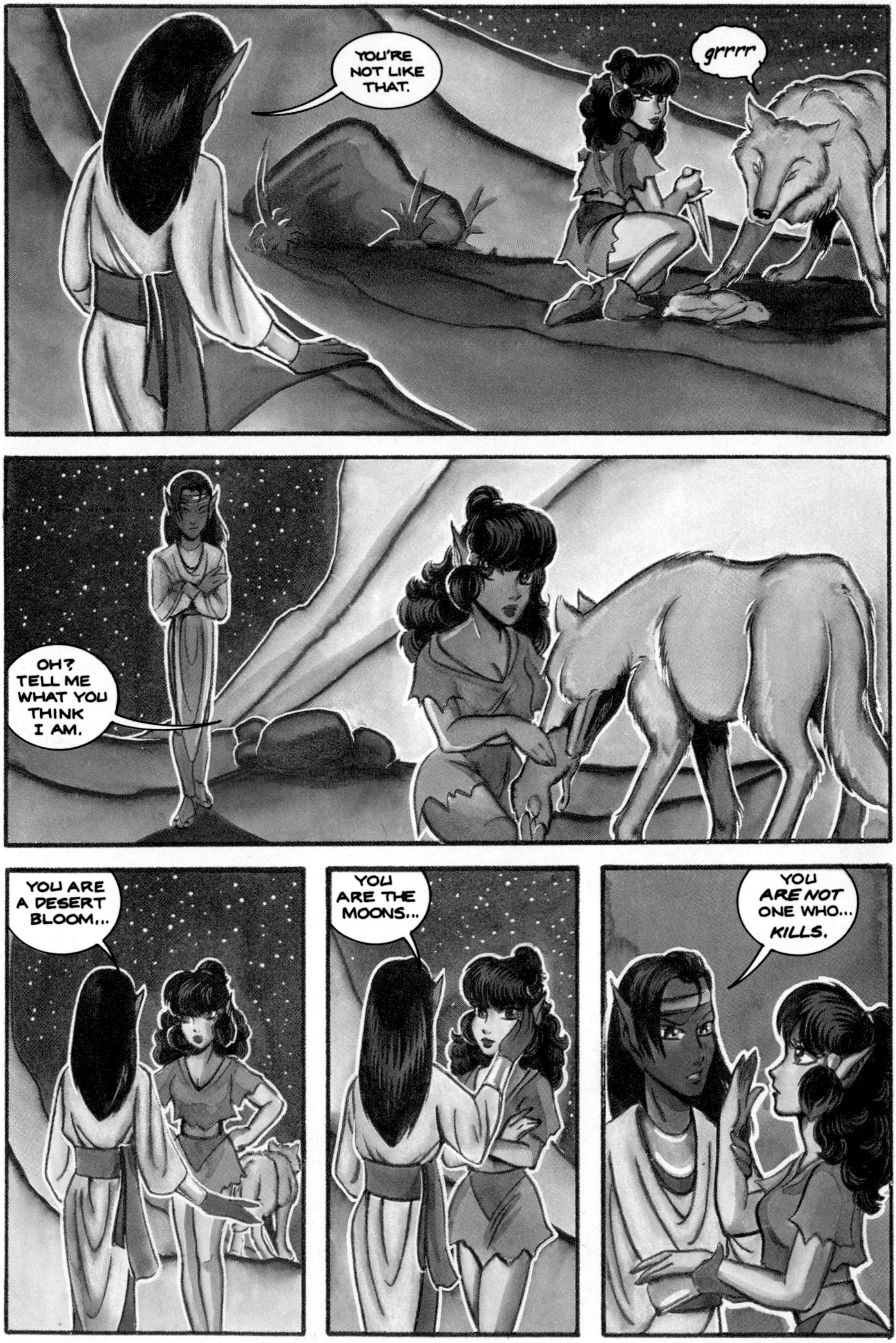
YOU'RE NOT LIKE THAT.
grrrr
OH? TELL ME WHAT YOU THINK I AM.
YOU ARE A DESERT BLOOM...
YOU ARE THE MOONS...
YOU ARE NOT ONE WHO... KILLS.

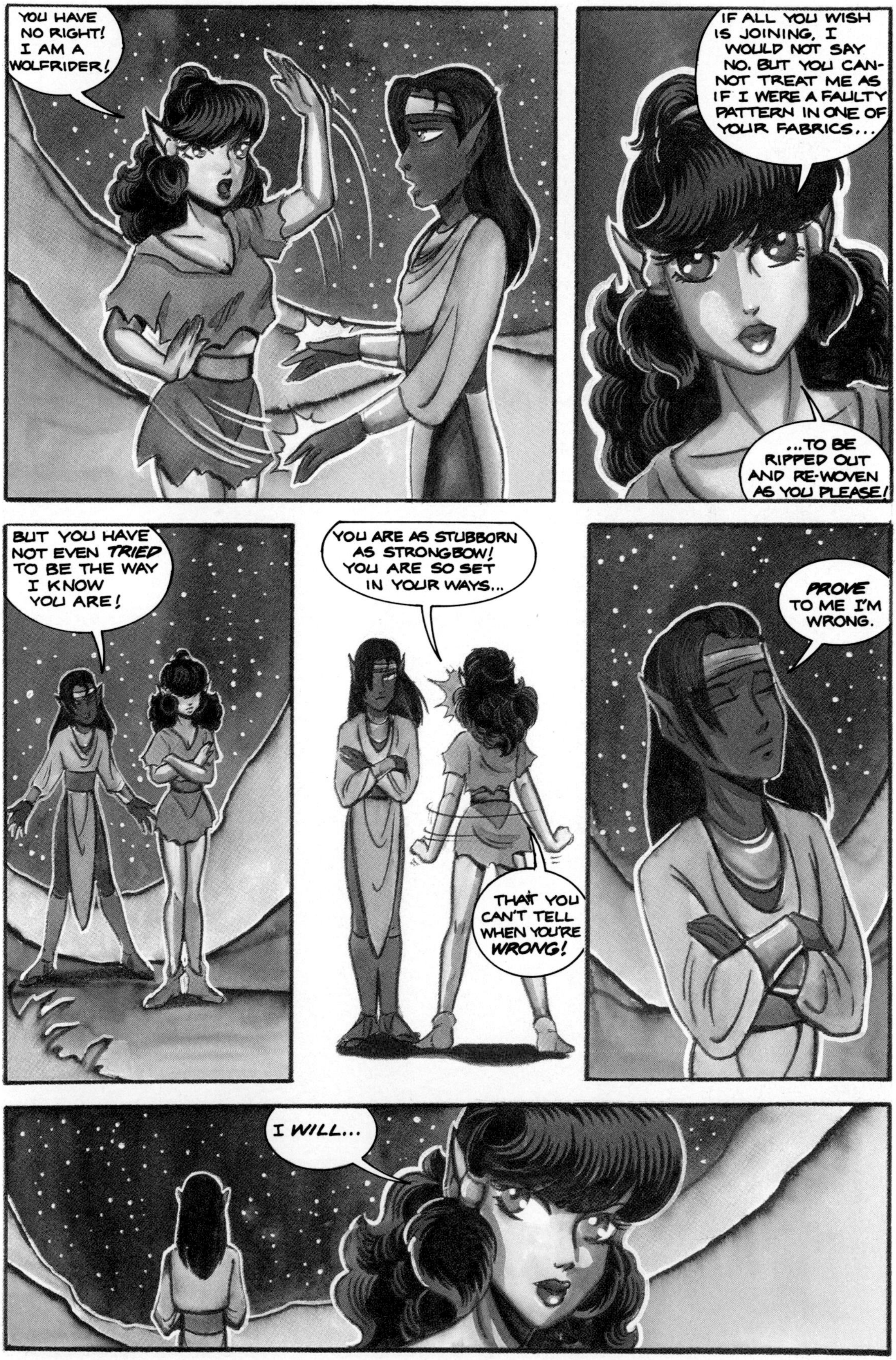
YOU HAVE NO RIGHT! I AM A WOLFRIDER!
IF ALL YOU WISH IS JOINING, I WOULD NOT SAY NO. BUT YOU CAN-NOT TREAT ME AS IF I WERE A FAULTY PATTERN IN ONE OF YOUR FABRICS...
...TO BE RIPPED OUT AND RE-WOVEN AS YOU PLEASE!
BUT YOU HAVE NOT EVEN TRIED TO BE THE WAY I KNOW YOU ARE!
YOU ARE AS STUBBORN AS STRONGBOW! YOU ARE SO SET IN YOUR WAYS...
THAT YOU CAN'T TELL WHEN YOU'RE WRONG!
PROVE TO ME I'M WRONG.
I WILL...

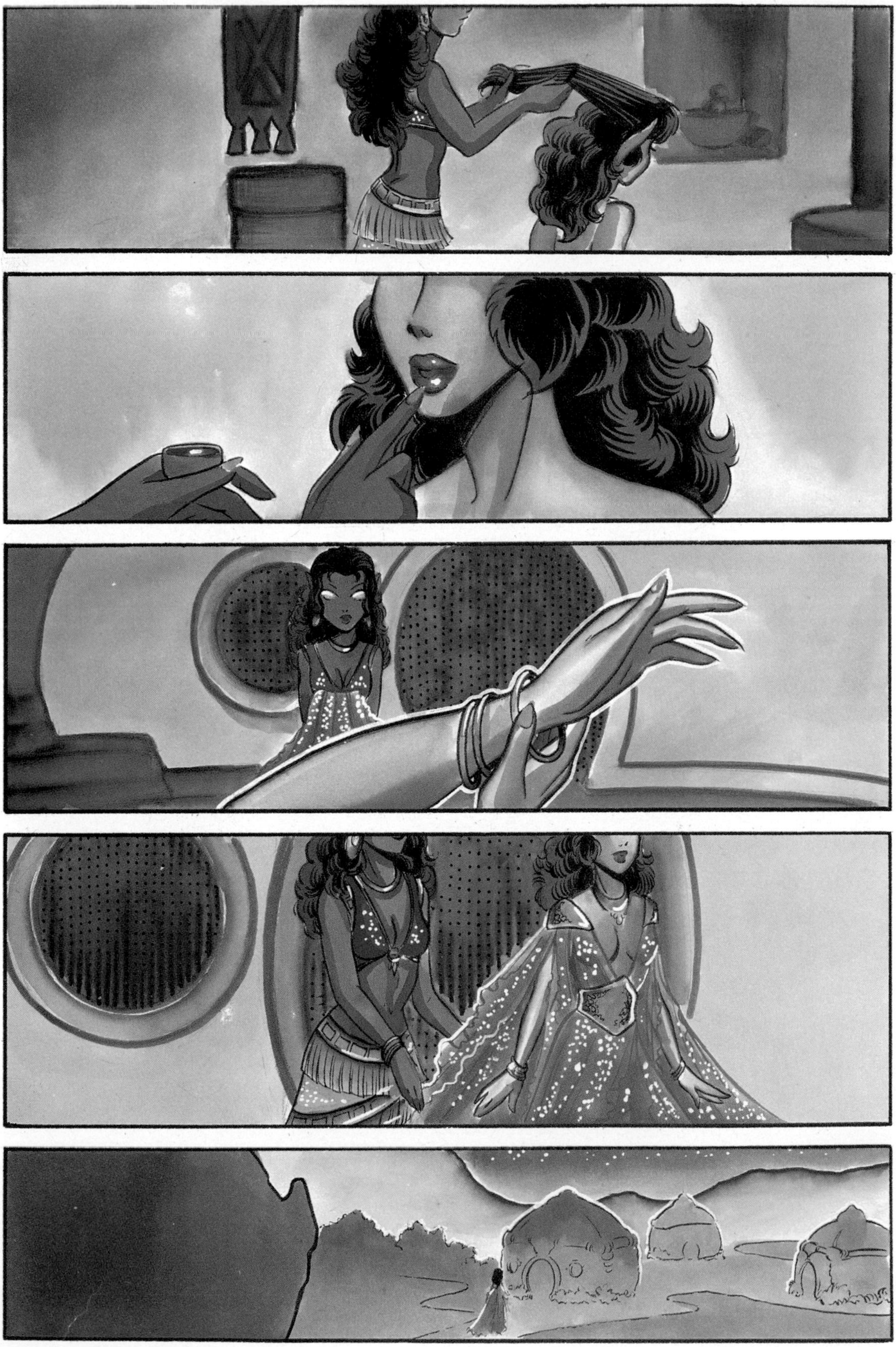

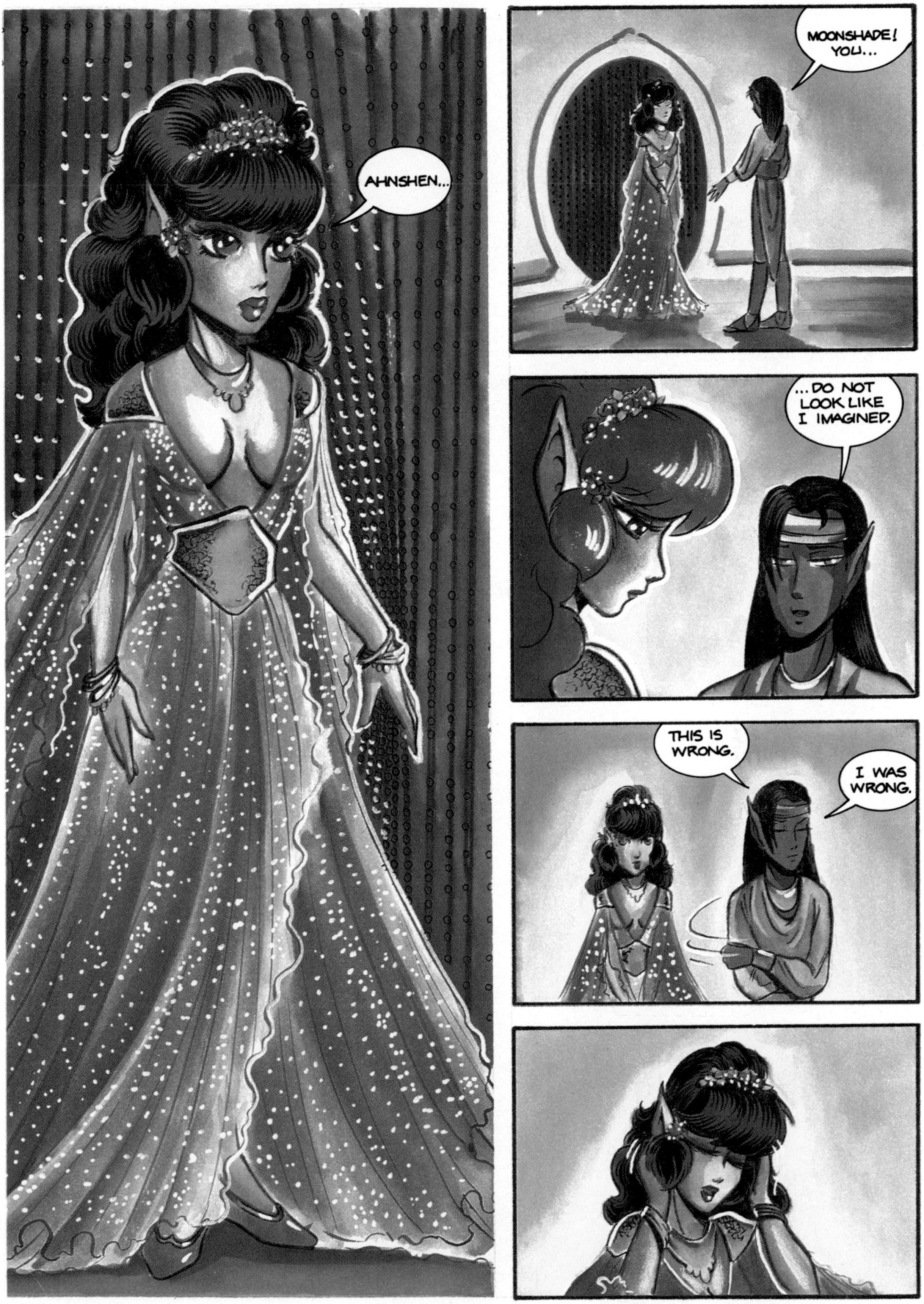
AHNSHEN...
MOONSHADE! YOU...
...DO NOT LOOK LIKE I IMAGINED.
THIS IS WRONG.
I WAS WRONG.

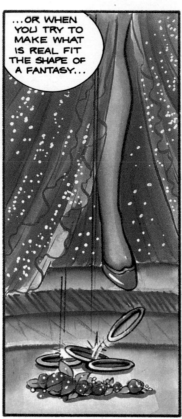

REMEMBER THIS IF YOU SEE ANOTHER HEAT-VISION...

...OR WHEN YOU TRY TO MAKE WHAT IS REAL FIT THE SHAPE OF A FANTASY...

...OR TRY TO MAKE A PRETTY SHELL...

"...TO CONTAIN A FEVER DREAM."

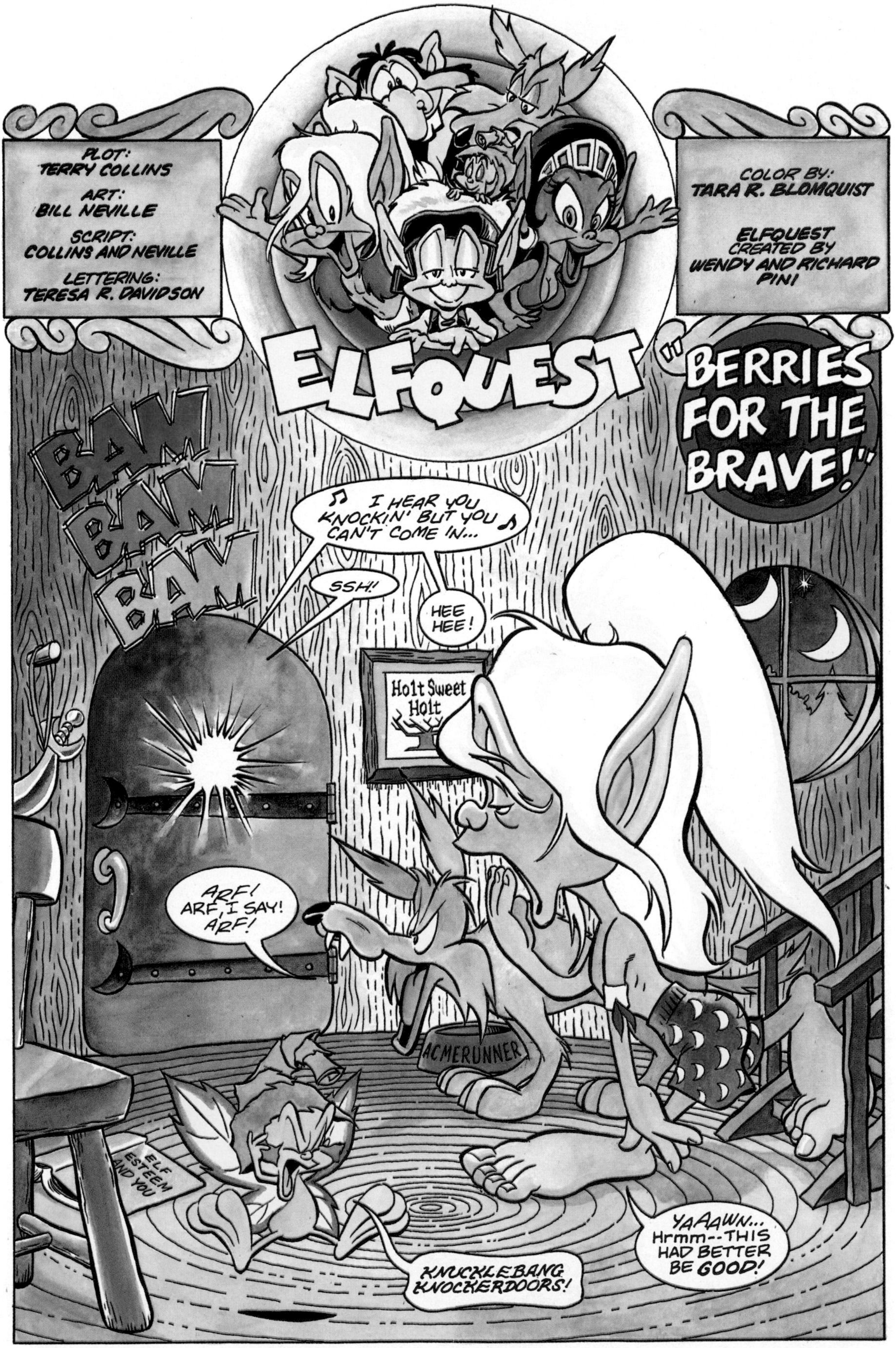
PLOT: TERRY COLLINS
ART: BILL NEVILLE
SCRIPT: COLLINS AND NEVILLE
LETTERING: TERESA R. DAVIDSON
COLOR BY: TARA R. BLOMQUIST
ELFQUEST CREATED BY WENDY AND RICHARD PINI
ELFQUEST
"BERRIES FOR THE BRAVE!"
BAM BAM BAM
♫ I HEAR YOU KNOCKIN' BUT YOU CAN'T COME IN... ♪
SSH!
HEE HEE!
Holt Sweet Holt
ARF! ARF, I SAY! ARF!
ACMERUNNER
ELF ESTEEM AND YOU
YAAAWN... Hrmm--THIS HAD BETTER BE GOOD!
KNUCKLEBANG KNOCKERDOORS!

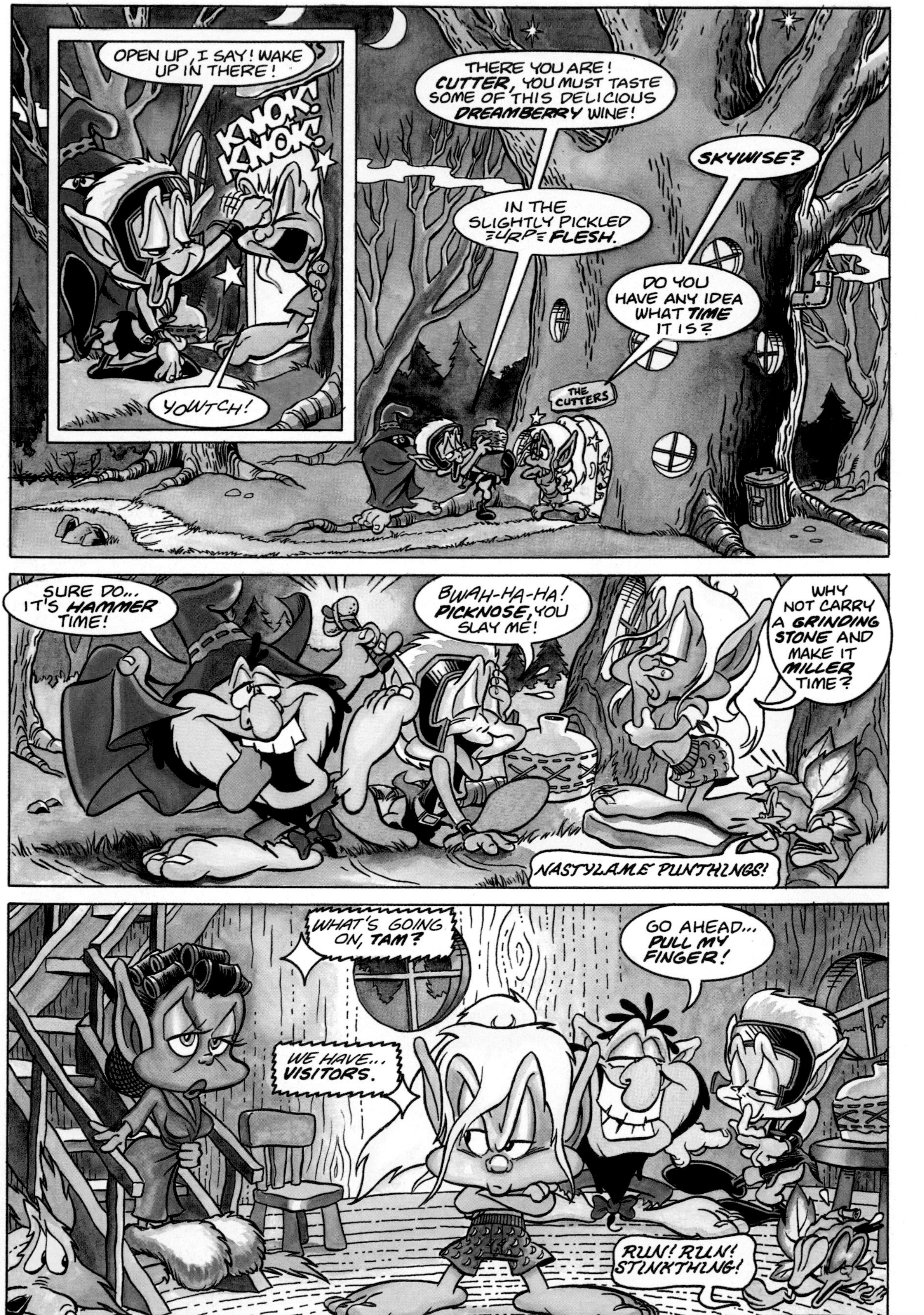
OPEN UP, I SAY! WAKE UP IN THERE!
KNOK! KNOK!
YOWTCH!
THERE YOU ARE! CUTTER, YOU MUST TASTE SOME OF THIS DELICIOUS DREAMBERRY WINE!
IN THE SLIGHTLY PICKLED URP FLESH.
SKYWISE?
DO YOU HAVE ANY IDEA WHAT TIME IT IS?
THE CUTTERS
SURE DO... IT'S HAMMER TIME!
BWAH-HA-HA! PICKNOSE, YOU SLAY ME!
WHY NOT CARRY A GRINDING STONE AND MAKE IT MILLER TIME?
NASTYLAME PUNTHINGS!
WHAT'S GOING ON, TAM?
WE HAVE... VISITORS.
GO AHEAD... PULL MY FINGER!
RUN! RUN! STINKTHING!

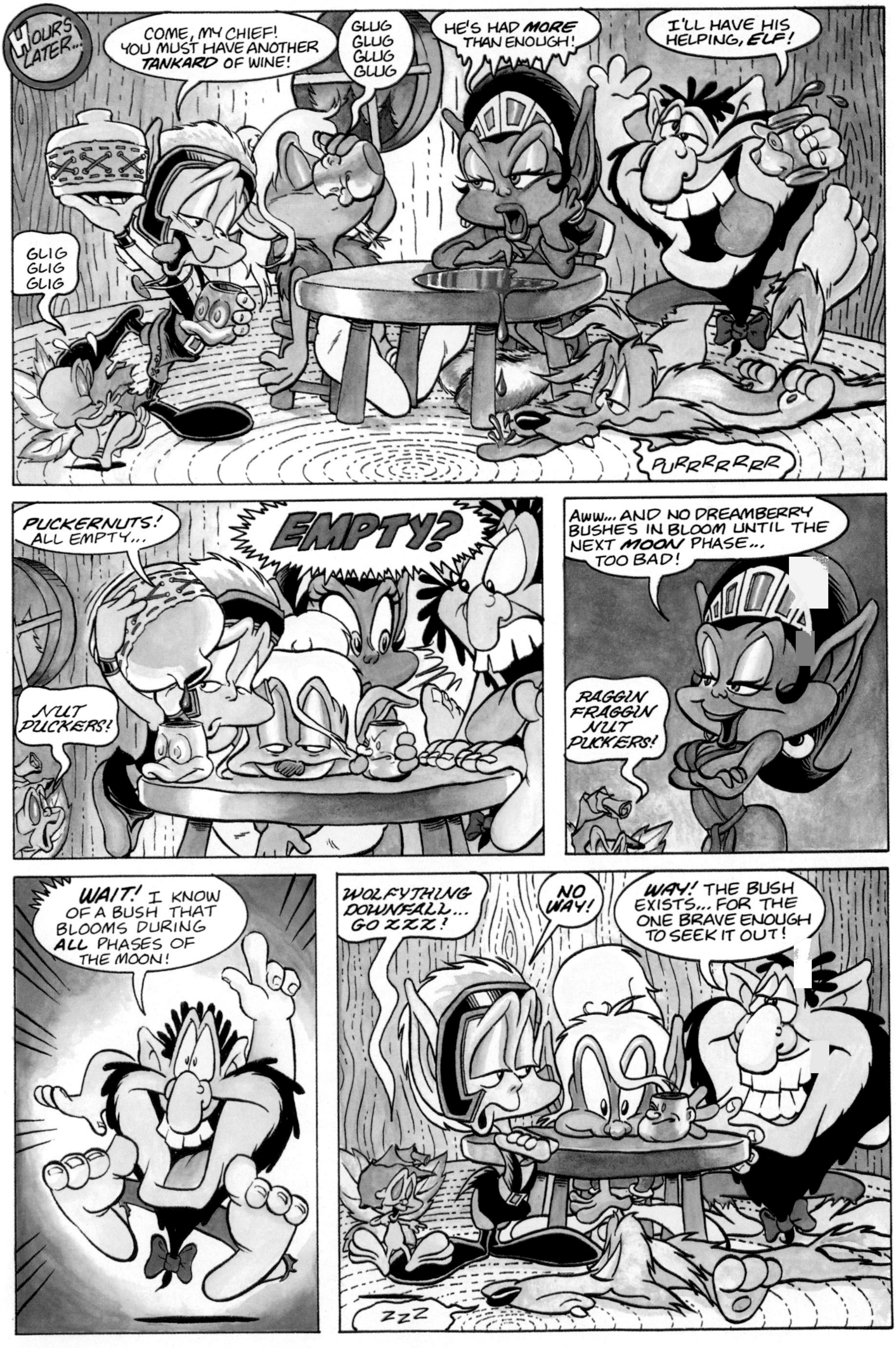

HOURS LATER...
COME, MY CHIEF! YOU MUST HAVE ANOTHER TANKARD OF WINE!
GLUG GLUG GLUG GLUG
HE'S HAD MORE THAN ENOUGH!
I'LL HAVE HIS HELPING, ELF!
GLIG GLIG GLIG
PURRRRRRRR
PUCKERNUTS! ALL EMPTY...
EMPTY?
NUT PUCKERS!
AWW... AND NO DREAMBERRY BUSHES IN BLOOM UNTIL THE NEXT MOON PHASE... TOO BAD!
RAGGIN FRAGGIN NUT PUCKERS!
WAIT! I KNOW OF A BUSH THAT BLOOMS DURING ALL PHASES OF THE MOON!
WOLFYTHING DOWNFALL... GO ZZZ!
NO WAY!
WAY! THE BUSH EXISTS... FOR THE ONE BRAVE ENOUGH TO SEEK IT OUT!
ZZZ

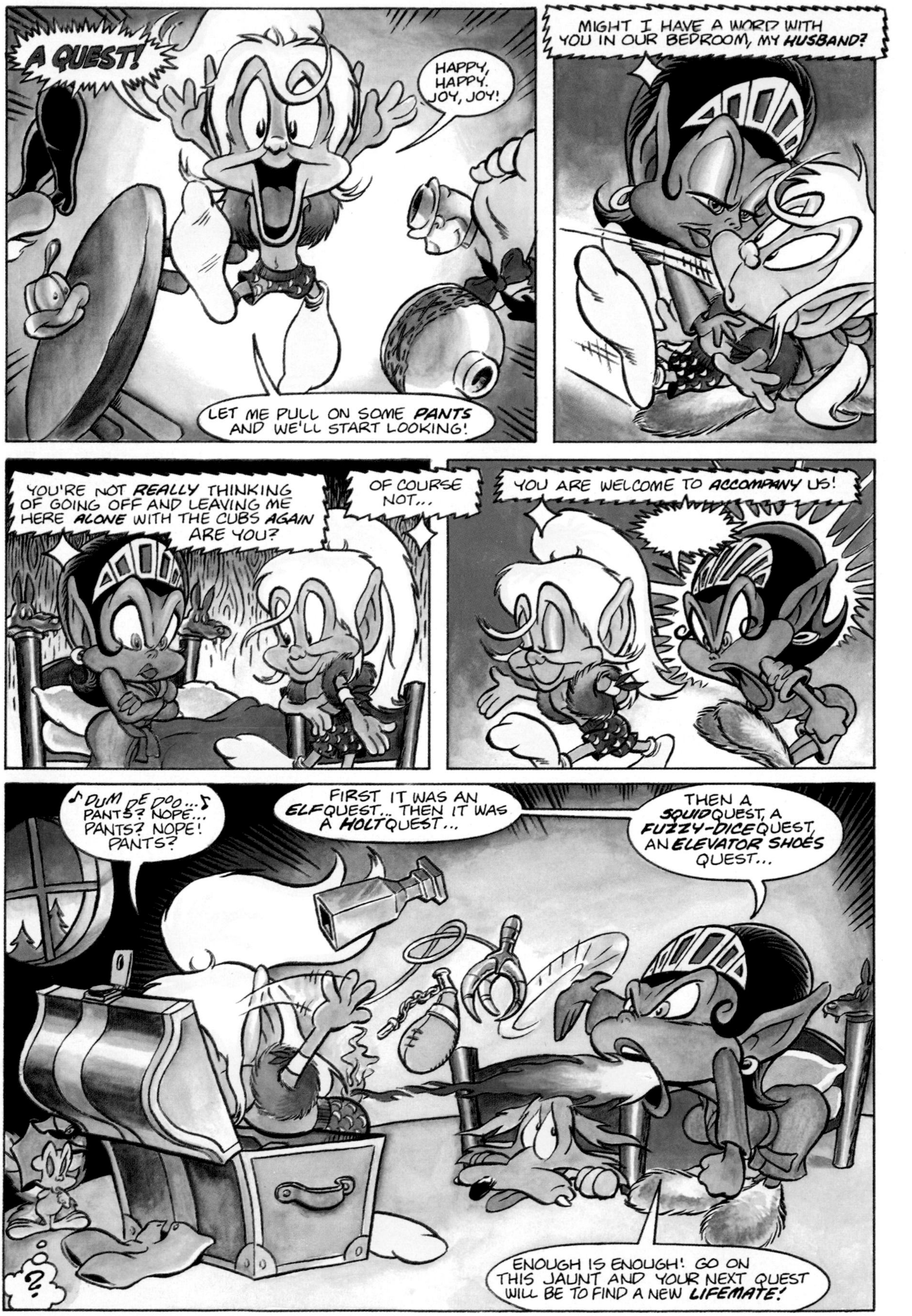
A QUEST!
HAPPY, HAPPY. JOY, JOY!
LET ME PULL ON SOME PANTS AND WE'LL START LOOKING!
MIGHT I HAVE A WORD WITH YOU IN OUR BEDROOM, MY HUSBAND?
YOU'RE NOT REALLY THINKING OF GOING OFF AND LEAVING ME HERE ALONE WITH THE CUBS AGAIN ARE YOU?
OF COURSE NOT...
YOU ARE WELCOME TO ACCOMPANY US!
♪ DUM DE DOO... ♪ PANTS? NOPE... PANTS? NOPE! PANTS?
FIRST IT WAS AN ELFQUEST... THEN IT WAS A HOLTQUEST...
THEN A SQUIDQUEST, A FUZZY-DICE QUEST, AN ELEVATOR SHOES QUEST...
ENOUGH IS ENOUGH! GO ON THIS JAUNT AND YOUR NEXT QUEST WILL BE TO FIND A NEW LIFEMATE!
?

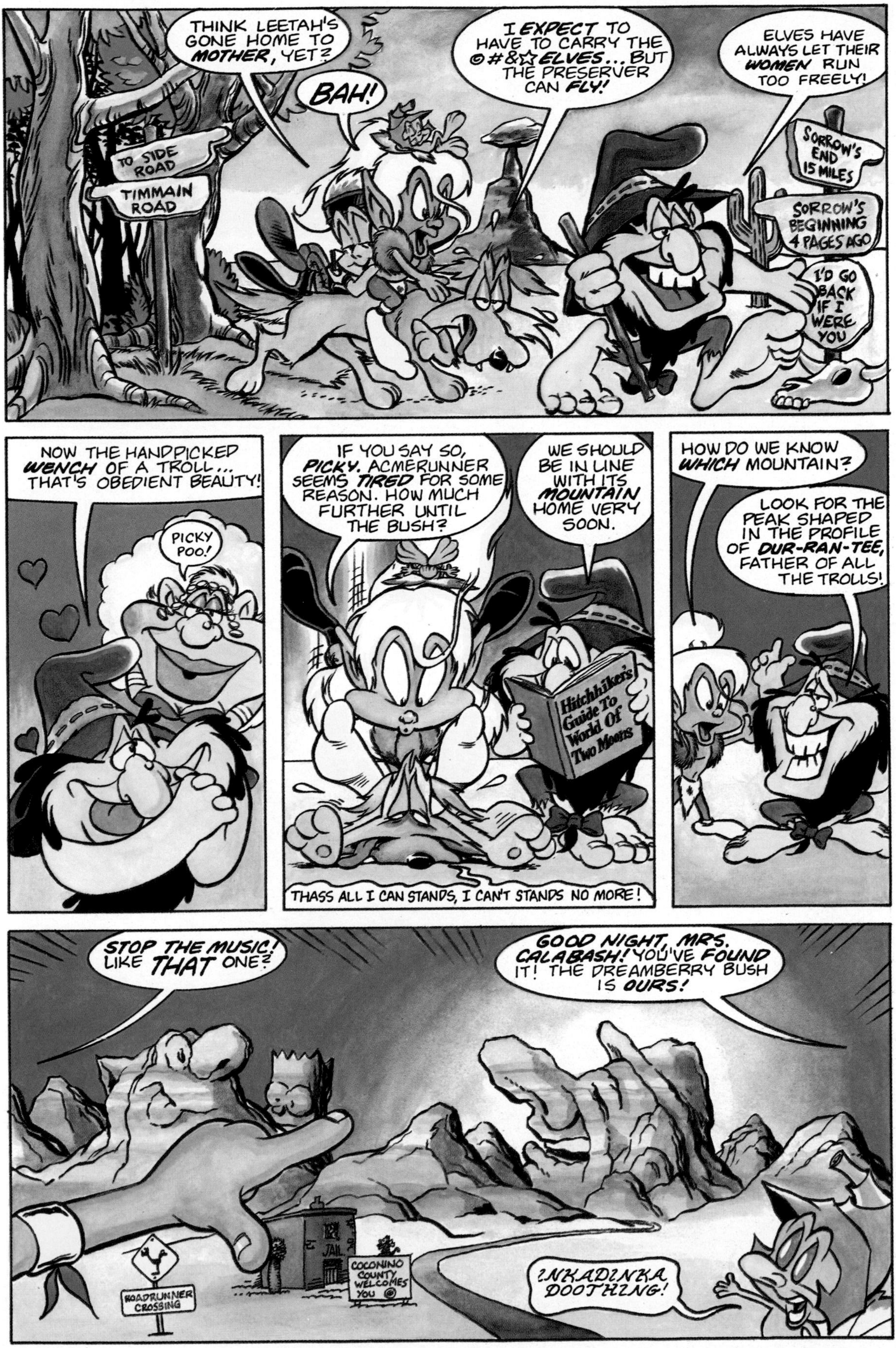

THINK LEETAH'S GONE HOME TO MOTHER, YET?
BAH!
I EXPECT TO HAVE TO CARRY THE ©#&☆ ELVES... BUT THE PRESERVER CAN FLY!
ELVES HAVE ALWAYS LET THEIR WOMEN RUN TOO FREELY!
TO SIDE ROAD
TIMMAIN ROAD
SORROW'S END 15 MILES
SORROW'S BEGINNING 4 PAGES AGO
I'D GO BACK IF I WERE YOU
NOW THE HANDPICKED WENCH OF A TROLL... THAT'S OBEDIENT BEAUTY!
PICKY POO!
IF YOU SAY SO, PICKY. ACMERUNNER SEEMS TIRED FOR SOME REASON. HOW MUCH FURTHER UNTIL THE BUSH?
WE SHOULD BE IN LINE WITH ITS MOUNTAIN HOME VERY SOON.
Hitchhiker's Guide To World Of Two Moons
THASS ALL I CAN STANDS, I CAN'T STANDS NO MORE!
HOW DO WE KNOW WHICH MOUNTAIN?
LOOK FOR THE PEAK SHAPED IN THE PROFILE OF DUR-RAN-TEE, FATHER OF ALL THE TROLLS!
STOP THE MUSIC! LIKE THAT ONE?
GOOD NIGHT, MRS. CALABASH! YOU'VE FOUND IT! THE DREAMBERRY BUSH IS OURS!
JAIL
COCONINO COUNTY WELCOMES YOU
ROADRUNNER CROSSING
?NKADINKA DOOTHING!

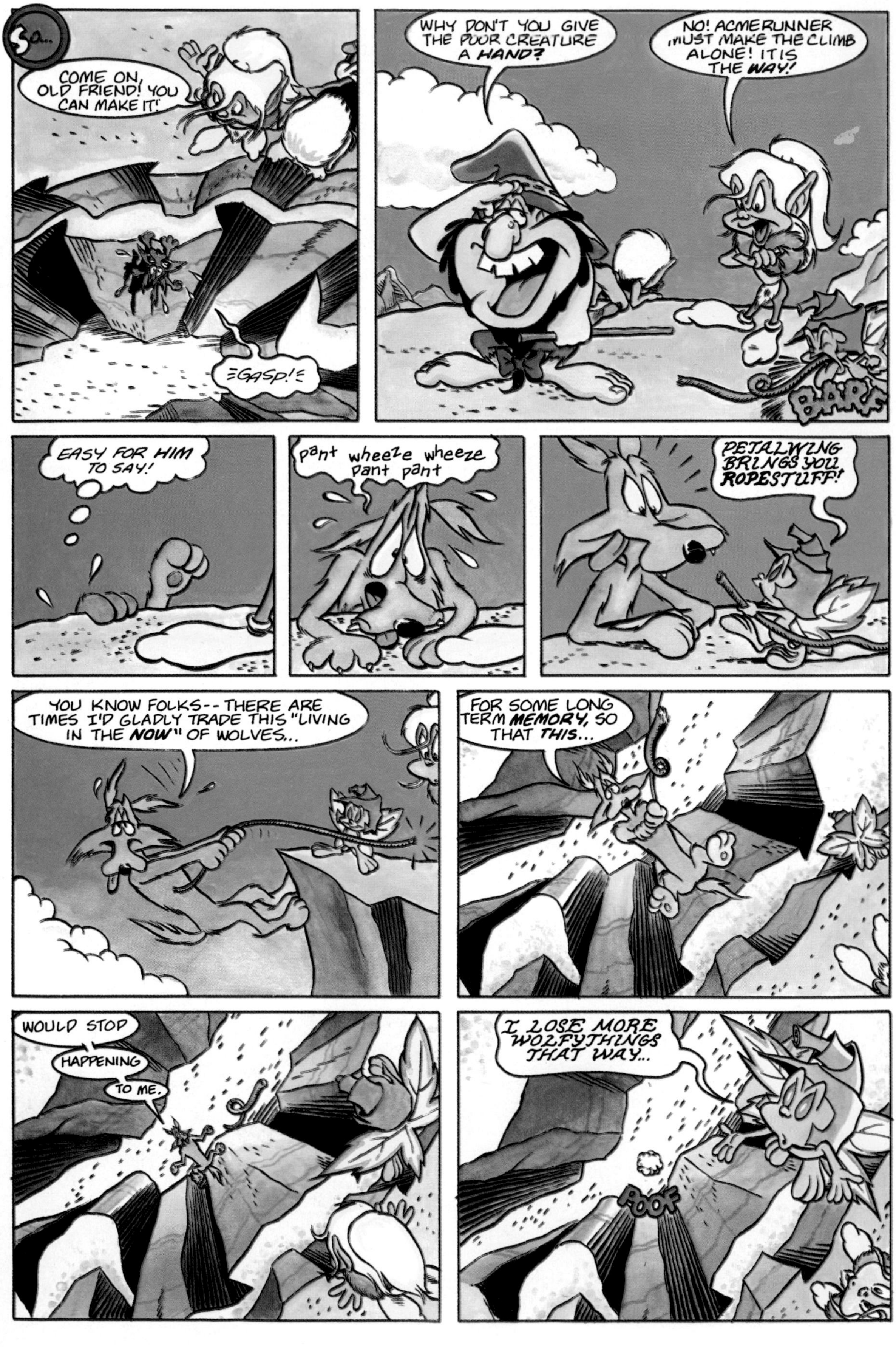
So...
COME ON, OLD FRIEND! YOU CAN MAKE IT!
GASP!
WHY DON'T YOU GIVE THE POOR CREATURE A HAND?
NO! ACMERUNNER MUST MAKE THE CLIMB ALONE! IT IS THE WAY!
BARF
EASY FOR HIM TO SAY!
pant wheeze wheeze pant pant
PETALWING BRINGS YOU ROPESTUFF!
YOU KNOW FOLKS-- THERE ARE TIMES I'D GLADLY TRADE THIS "LIVING IN THE NOW" OF WOLVES...
FOR SOME LONG TERM MEMORY, SO THAT THIS...
WOULD STOP
HAPPENING
TO ME.
I LOSE MORE WOLFYTHINGS THAT WAY...
POOF

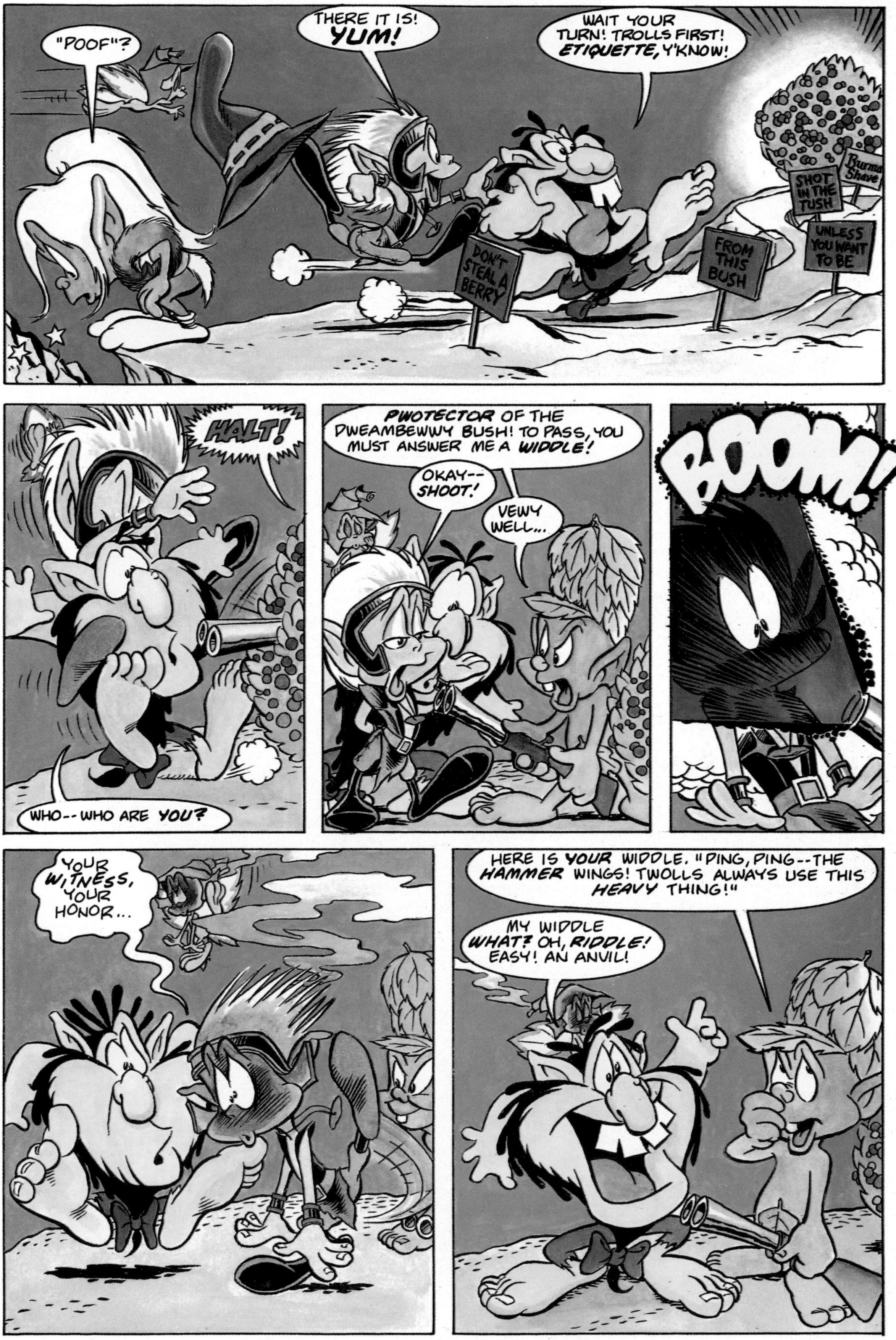
"POOF"?
THERE IT IS! YUM!
WAIT YOUR TURN! TROLLS FIRST! ETIQUETTE, Y'KNOW!
DON'T STEAL A BERRY
FROM THIS BUSH
UNLESS YOU WANT TO BE
SHOT IN THE TUSH
Burma Shave
HALT!
WHO-- WHO ARE YOU?
PWOTECTOR OF THE DWEAMBEWWY BUSH! TO PASS, YOU MUST ANSWER ME A WIDDLE!
OKAY-- SHOOT!
VEWY WELL...
BOOM!
YOUR WITNESS, YOUR HONOR...
HERE IS YOUR WIDDLE. "PING, PING--THE HAMMER WINGS! TWOLLS ALWAYS USE THIS HEAVY THING!"
MY WIDDLE WHAT? OH, RIDDLE! EASY! AN ANVIL!

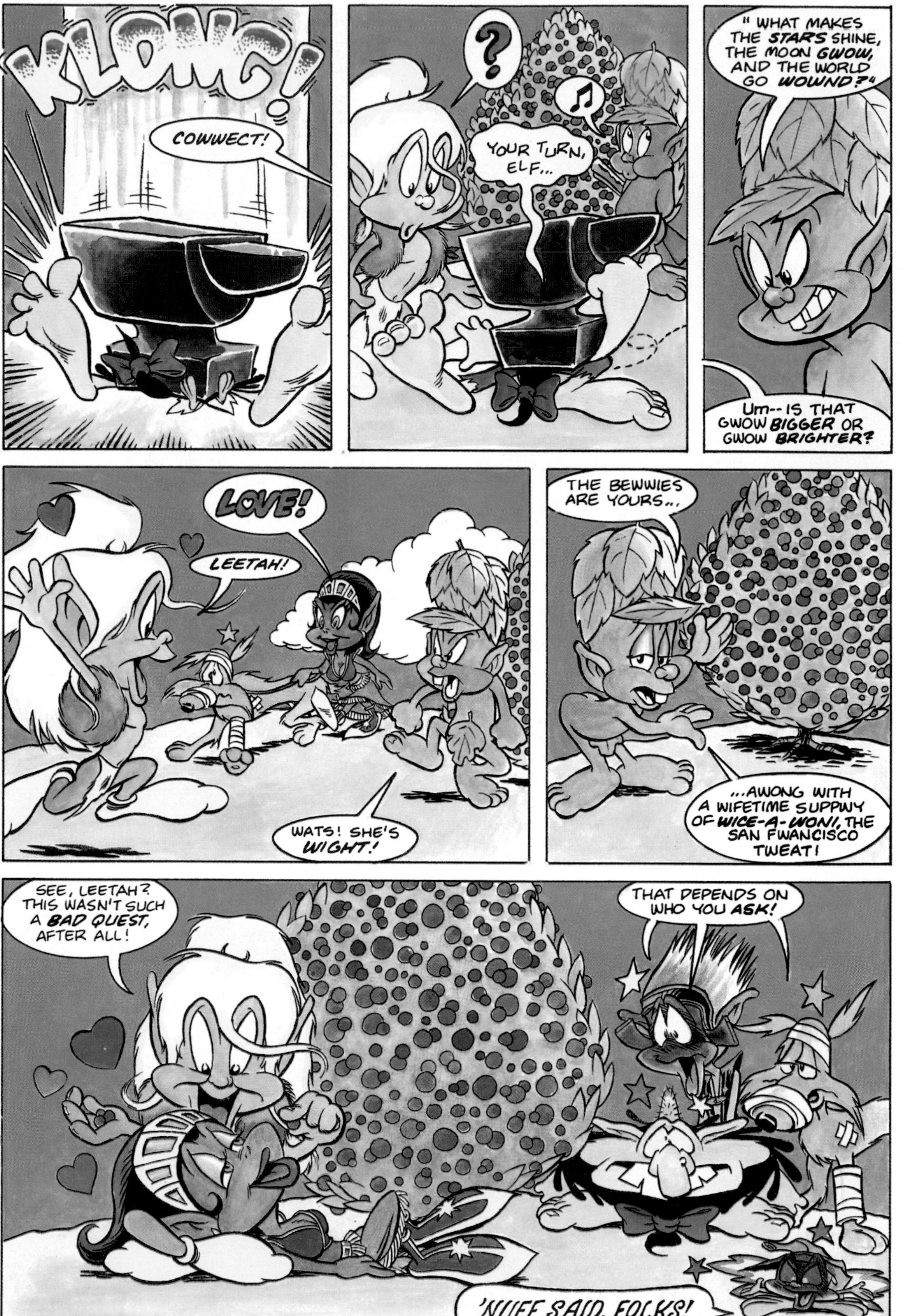
KLONG!
COWWECT!
?
♫
YOUR TURN, ELF...
" WHAT MAKES THE STARS SHINE, THE MOON GWOW, AND THE WORLD GO WOWND?"
Um-- IS THAT GWOW BIGGER OR GWOW BRIGHTER?
LOVE!
LEETAH!
WATS! SHE'S WIGHT!
THE BEWWIES ARE YOURS...
...AWONG WITH A WIFETIME SUPPWY OF WICE-A-WONI, THE SAN FWANCISCO TWEAT!
SEE, LEETAH? THIS WASN'T SUCH A BAD QUEST, AFTER ALL!
THAT DEPENDS ON WHO YOU ASK!
'NUFF SAID, FOLKS!

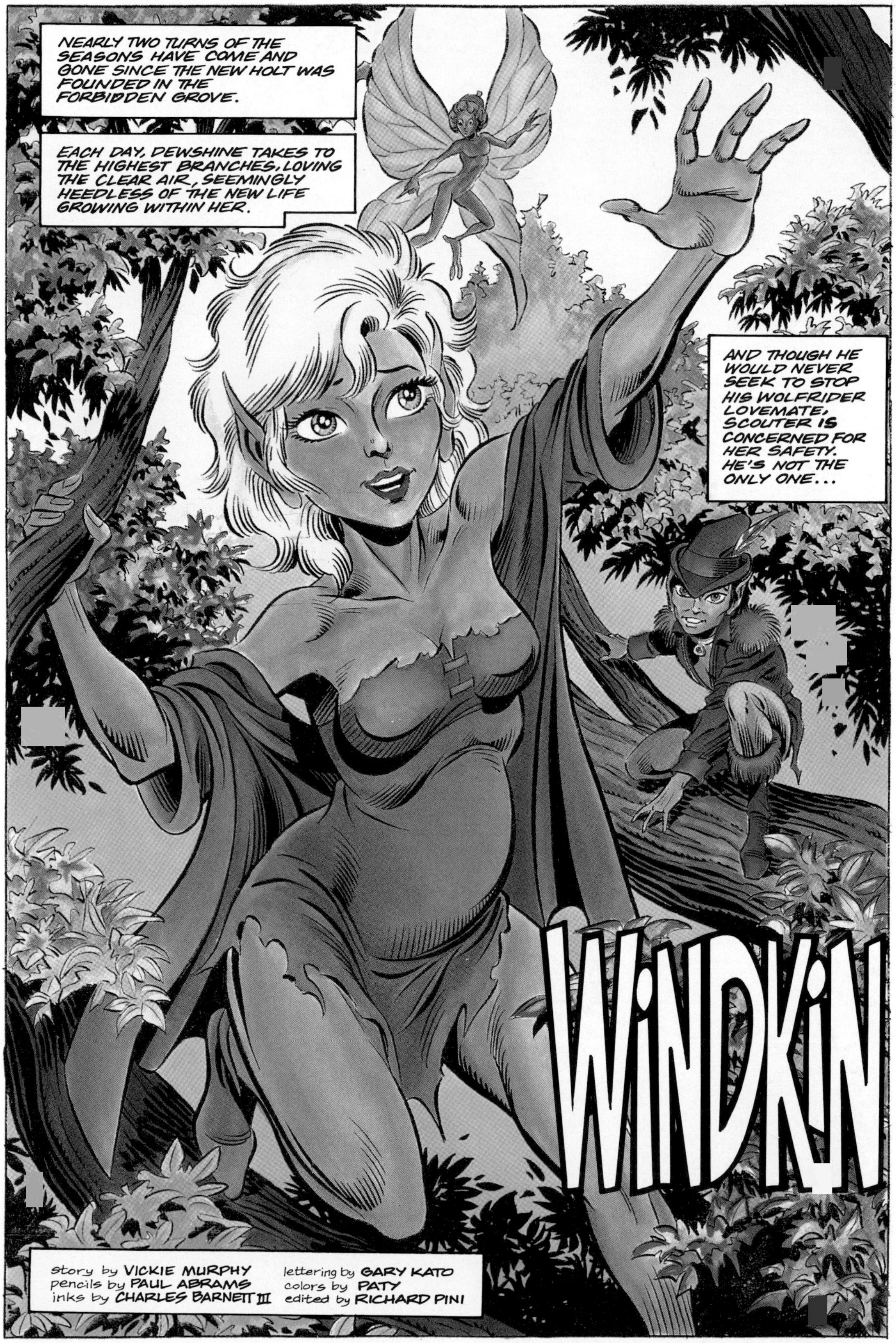
NEARLY TWO TURNS OF THE SEASONS HAVE COME AND GONE SINCE THE NEW HOLT WAS FOUNDED IN THE FORBIDDEN GROVE.
EACH DAY, DEWSHINE TAKES TO THE HIGHEST BRANCHES, LOVING THE CLEAR AIR, SEEMINGLY HEEDLESS OF THE NEW LIFE GROWING WITHIN HER.
AND THOUGH HE WOULD NEVER SEEK TO STOP HIS WOLFRIDER LOVEMATE, SCOUTER IS CONCERNED FOR HER SAFETY. HE'S NOT THE ONLY ONE...
WINDKIN
story by VICKIE MURPHY
pencils by PAUL ABRAMS
inks by CHARLES BARNETT III
lettering by GARY KATO
colors by PATY
edited by RICHARD PINI

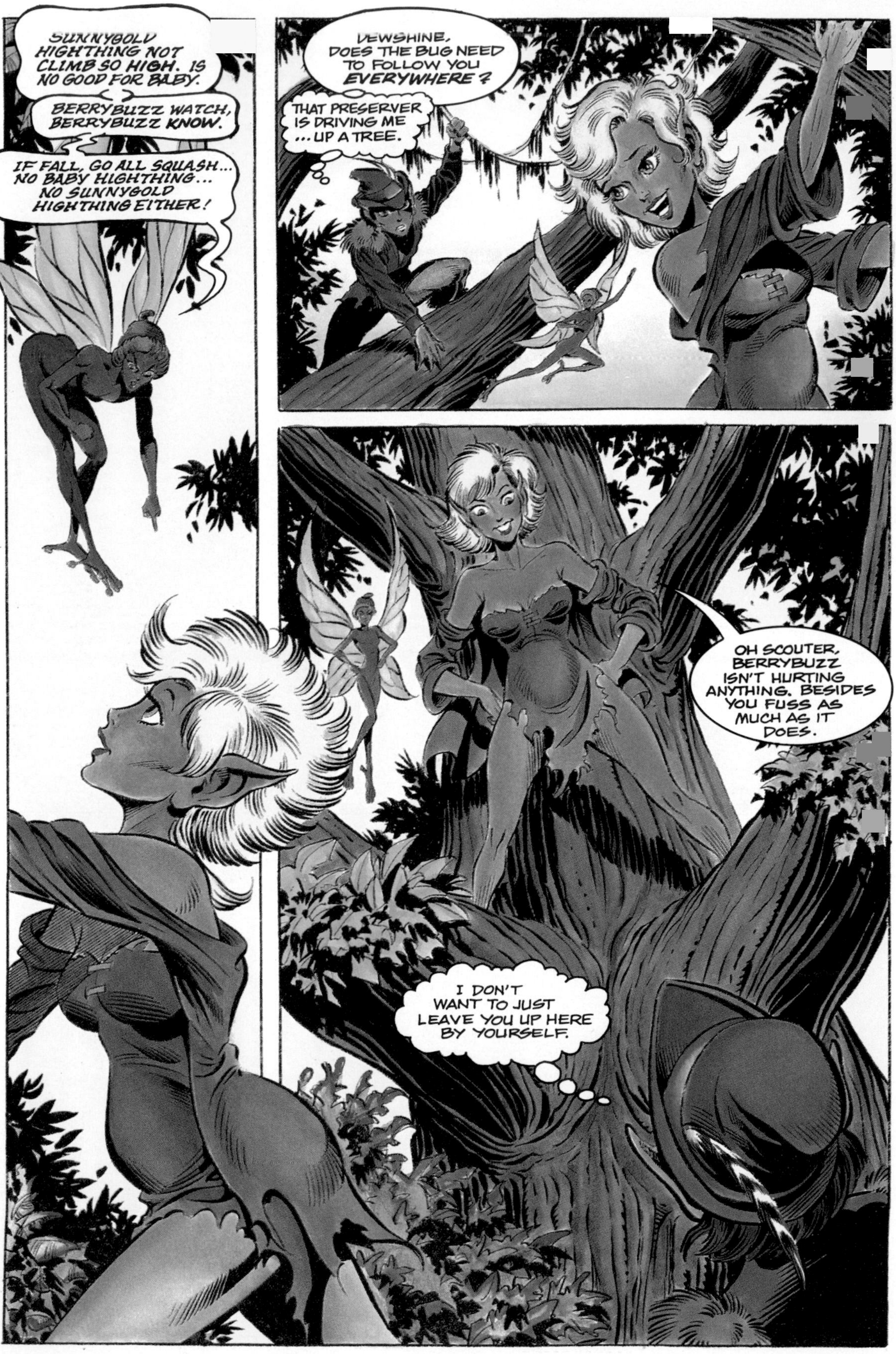
SUNNYGOLD HIGHTHING NOT CLIMB SO HIGH. IS NO GOOD FOR BABY.
BERRYBUZZ WATCH, BERRYBUZZ KNOW.
IF FALL, GO ALL SQUASH... NO BABY HIGHTHING... NO SUNNYGOLD HIGHTHING EITHER!
DEWSHINE, DOES THE BUG NEED TO FOLLOW YOU EVERYWHERE?
THAT PRESERVER IS DRIVING ME ...UP A TREE.
OH SCOUTER, BERRYBUZZ ISN'T HURTING ANYTHING. BESIDES YOU FUSS AS MUCH AS IT DOES.
I DON'T WANT TO JUST LEAVE YOU UP HERE BY YOURSELF.

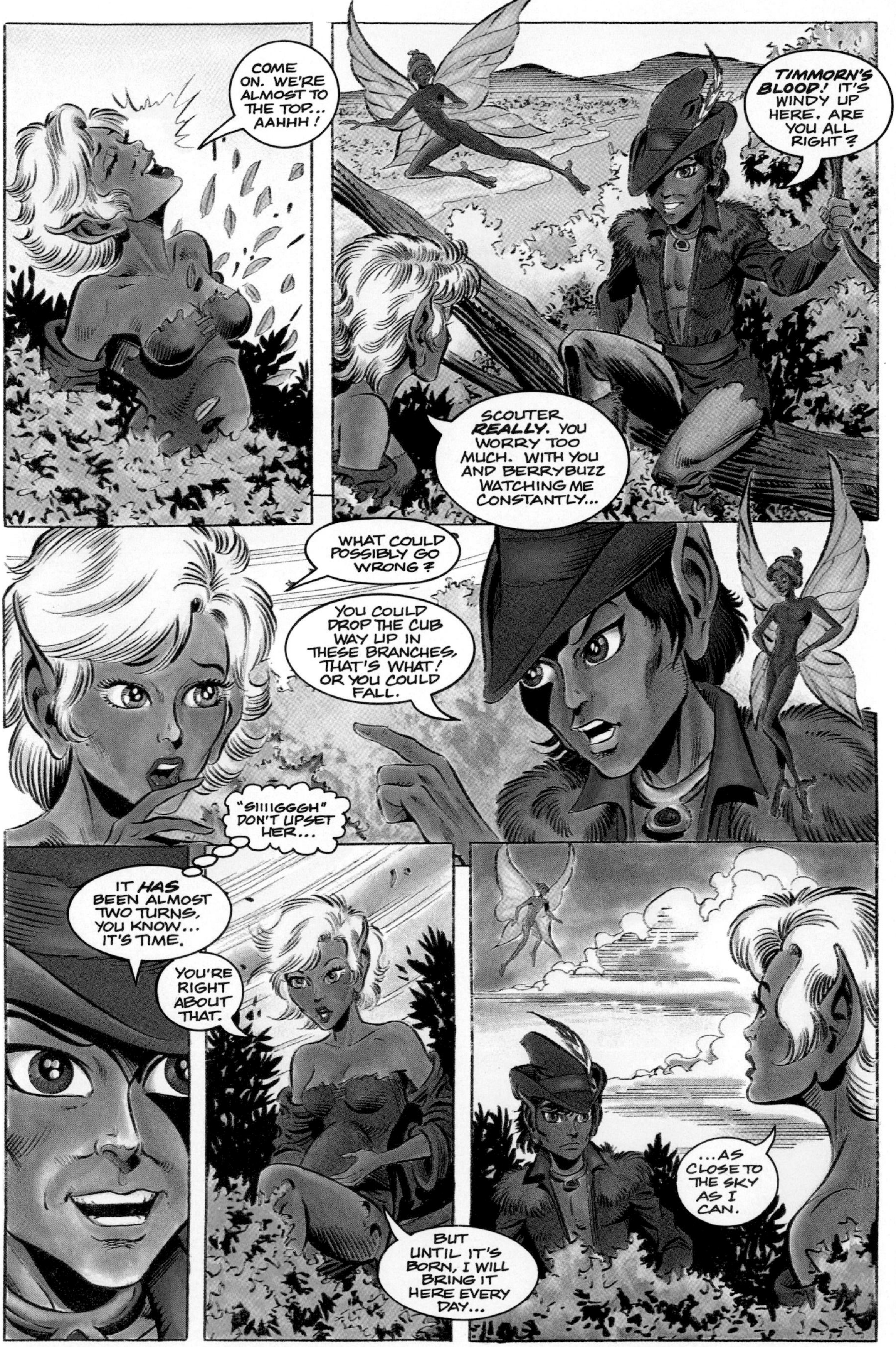
COME ON. WE'RE ALMOST TO THE TOP... AAHHH!
TIMMORN'S BLOOD! IT'S WINDY UP HERE. ARE YOU ALL RIGHT?
SCOUTER REALLY. YOU WORRY TOO MUCH. WITH YOU AND BERRYBUZZ WATCHING ME CONSTANTLY...
WHAT COULD POSSIBLY GO WRONG?
YOU COULD DROP THE CUB WAY UP IN THESE BRANCHES, THAT'S WHAT! OR YOU COULD FALL.
"SIIIIGGGH" DON'T UPSET HER...
IT HAS BEEN ALMOST TWO TURNS, YOU KNOW... IT'S TIME.
YOU'RE RIGHT ABOUT THAT.
BUT UNTIL IT'S BORN, I WILL BRING IT HERE EVERY DAY...
...AS CLOSE TO THE SKY AS I CAN.

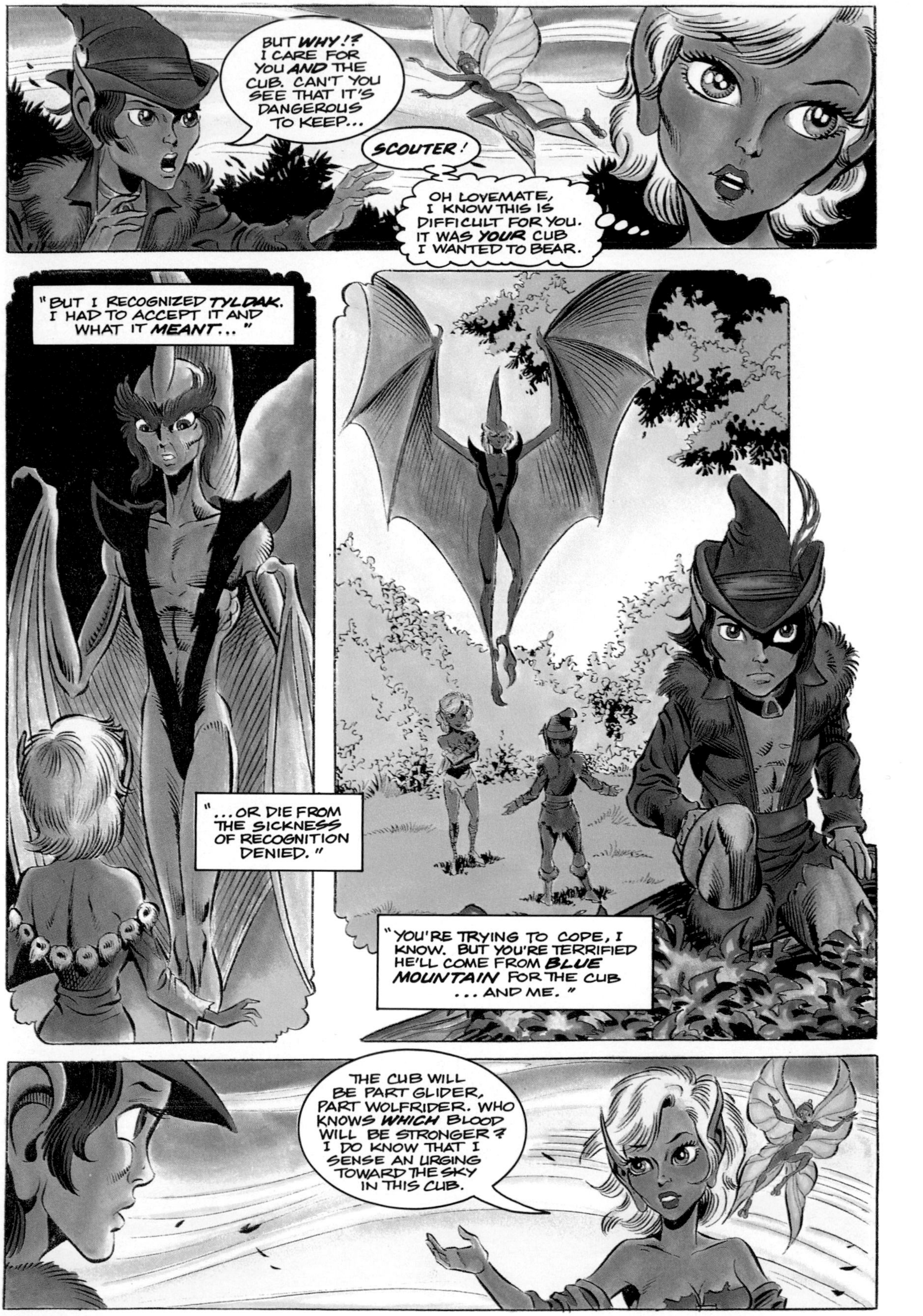
BUT WHY!? I CARE FOR YOU AND THE CUB. CAN'T YOU SEE THAT IT'S DANGEROUS TO KEEP...
SCOUTER!
OH LOVEMATE, I KNOW THIS IS DIFFICULT FOR YOU. IT WAS YOUR CUB I WANTED TO BEAR.
"BUT I RECOGNIZED TYLDAK. I HAD TO ACCEPT IT AND WHAT IT MEANT..."
"...OR DIE FROM THE SICKNESS OF RECOGNITION DENIED."
"YOU'RE TRYING TO COPE, I KNOW. BUT YOU'RE TERRIFIED HE'LL COME FROM BLUE MOUNTAIN FOR THE CUB ... AND ME."
THE CUB WILL BE PART GLIDER, PART WOLFRIDER. WHO KNOWS WHICH BLOOD WILL BE STRONGER? I DO KNOW THAT I SENSE AN URGING TOWARD THE SKY IN THIS CUB.

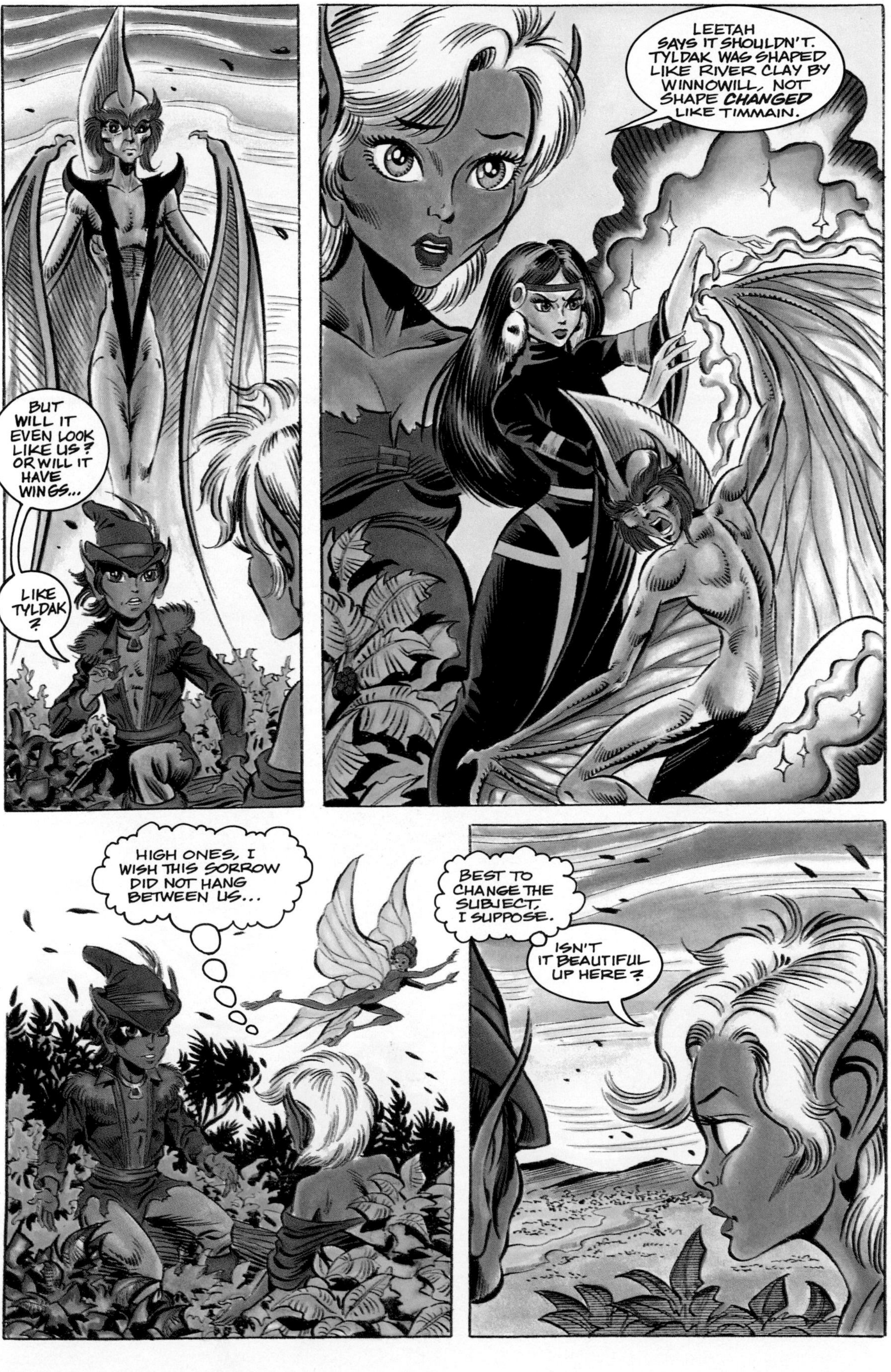
BUT WILL IT EVEN LOOK LIKE US? OR WILL IT HAVE WINGS...
LIKE TYLDAK?
LEETAH SAYS IT SHOULDN'T. TYLDAK WAS SHAPED LIKE RIVER CLAY BY WINNOWILL, NOT SHAPE CHANGED LIKE TIMMAIN.
HIGH ONES, I WISH THIS SORROW DID NOT HANG BETWEEN US...
BEST TO CHANGE THE SUBJECT, I SUPPOSE.
ISN'T IT BEAUTIFUL UP HERE?

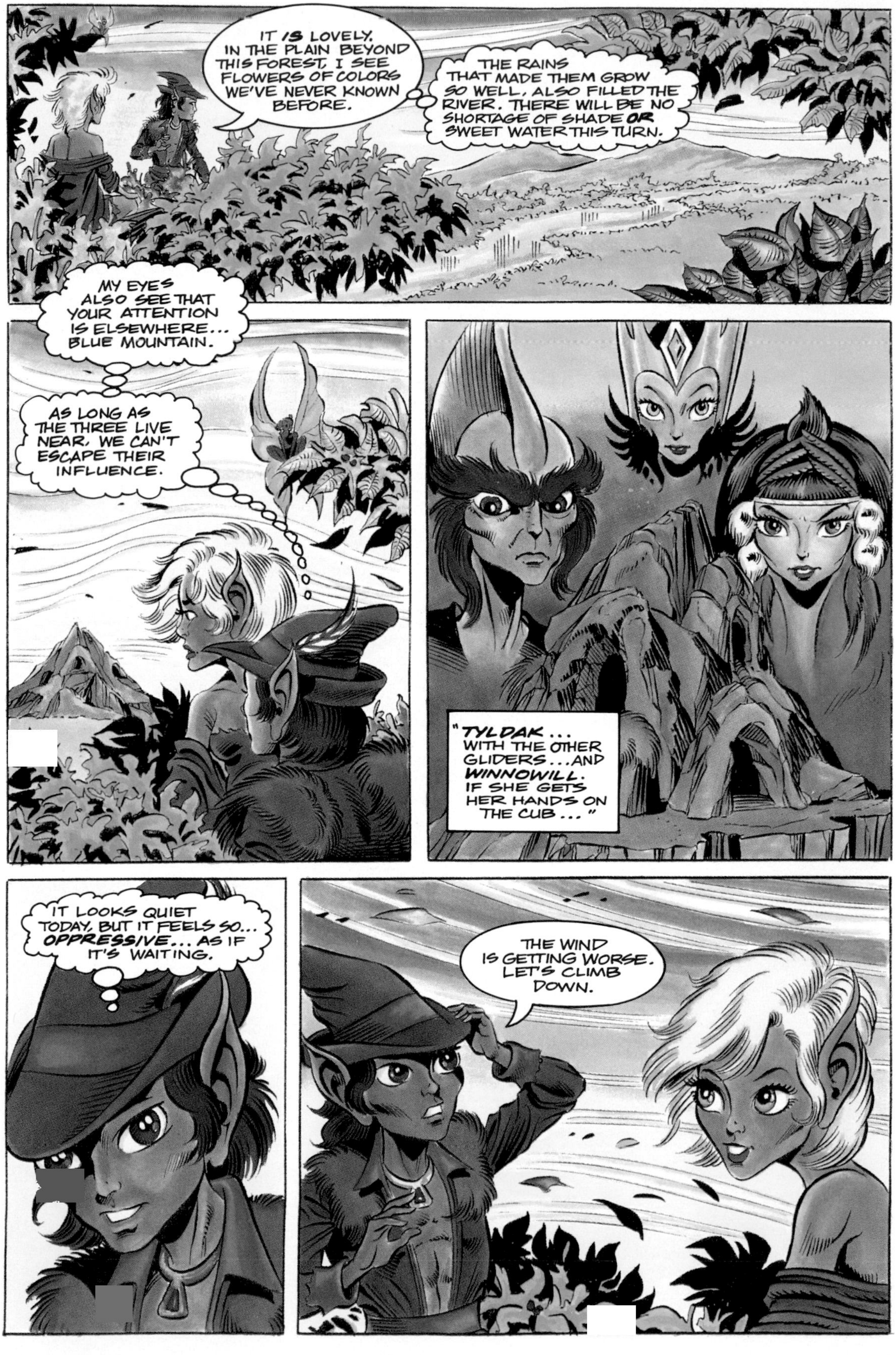
IT IS LOVELY. IN THE PLAIN BEYOND THIS FOREST, I SEE FLOWERS OF COLORS WE'VE NEVER KNOWN BEFORE.
THE RAINS THAT MADE THEM GROW SO WELL, ALSO FILLED THE RIVER. THERE WILL BE NO SHORTAGE OF SHADE OR SWEET WATER THIS TURN.
MY EYES ALSO SEE THAT YOUR ATTENTION IS ELSEWHERE... BLUE MOUNTAIN.
AS LONG AS THE THREE LIVE NEAR, WE CAN'T ESCAPE THEIR INFLUENCE.
"TYLDAK... WITH THE OTHER GLIDERS...AND WINNOWILL. IF SHE GETS HER HANDS ON THE CUB..."
IT LOOKS QUIET TODAY, BUT IT FEELS SO... OPPRESSIVE... AS IF IT'S WAITING.
THE WIND IS GETTING WORSE. LET'S CLIMB DOWN.

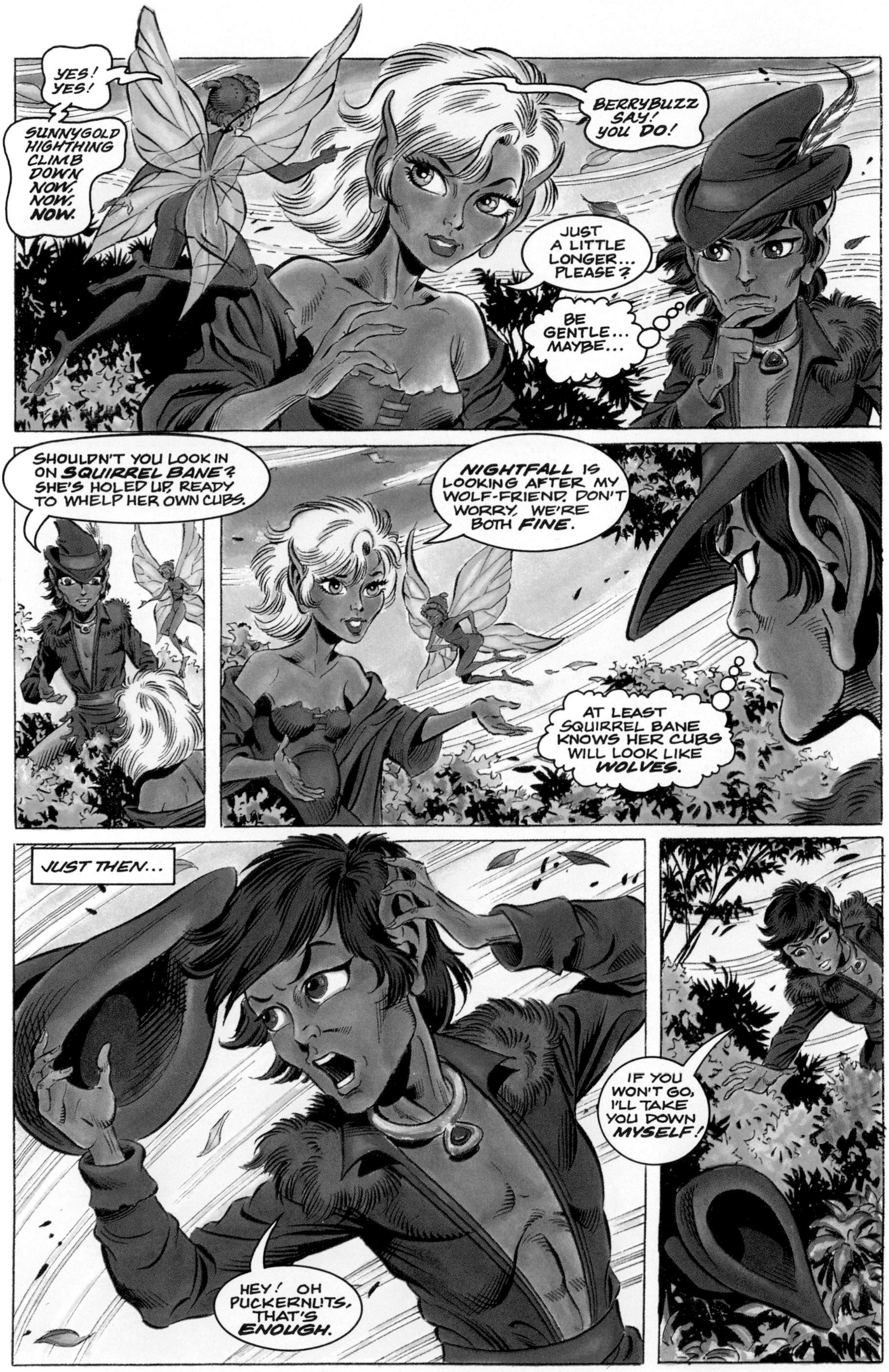
YES! YES!
SUNNYGOLD HIGHTHING CLIMB DOWN NOW, NOW, NOW.
BERRYBUZZ SAY! YOU DO!
JUST A LITTLE LONGER... PLEASE?
BE GENTLE... MAYBE...
SHOULDN'T YOU LOOK IN ON SQUIRREL BANE? SHE'S HOLED UP, READY TO WHELP HER OWN CUBS.
NIGHTFALL IS LOOKING AFTER MY WOLF-FRIEND. DON'T WORRY, WE'RE BOTH FINE.
AT LEAST SQUIRREL BANE KNOWS HER CUBS WILL LOOK LIKE WOLVES.
JUST THEN...
HEY! OH PUCKERNUTS, THAT'S ENOUGH.
IF YOU WON'T GO, I'LL TAKE YOU DOWN MYSELF!

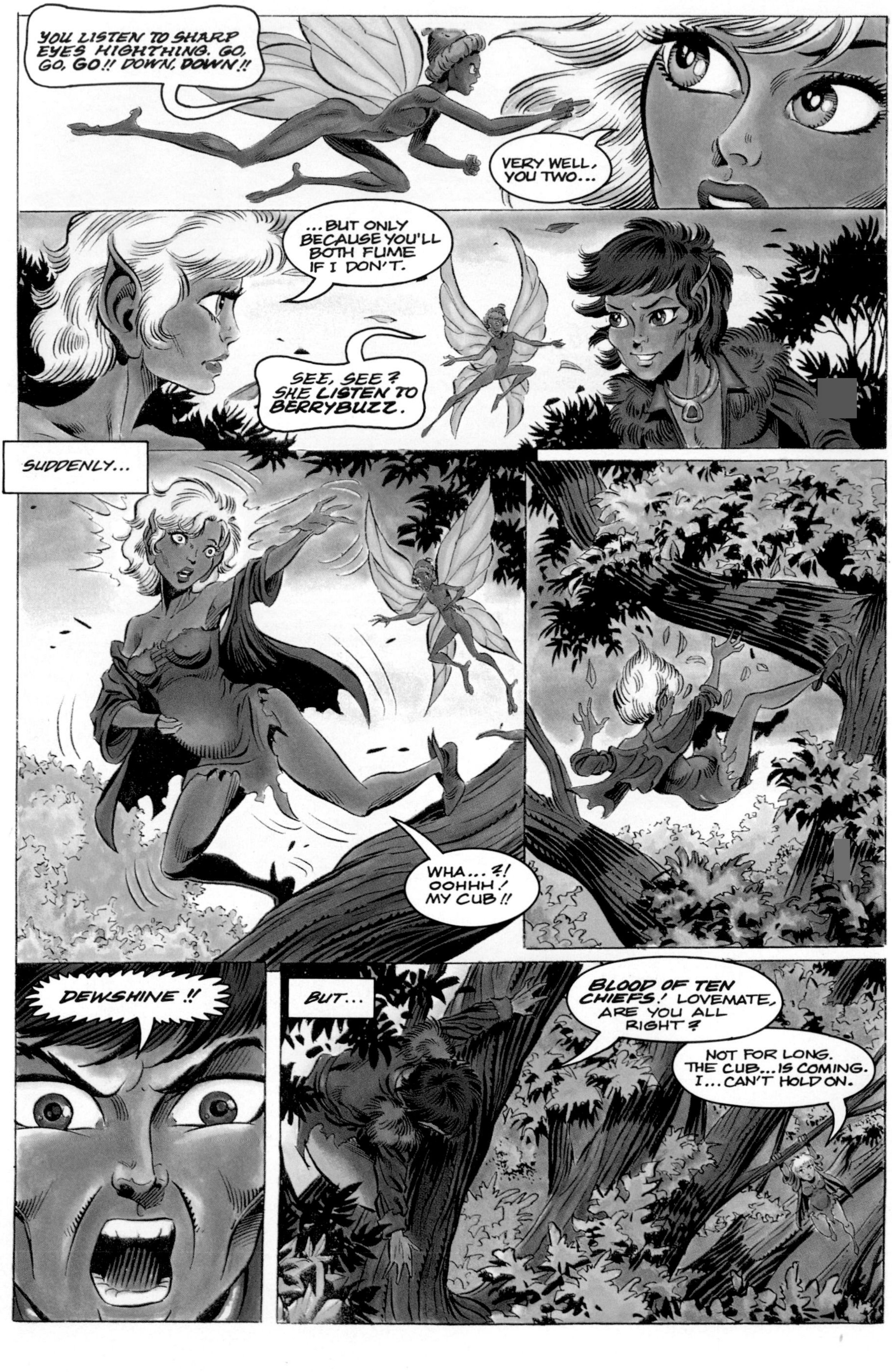
YOU LISTEN TO SHARP EYES HIGHTHING. GO, GO, GO!! DOWN, DOWN!!
VERY WELL, YOU TWO...
...BUT ONLY BECAUSE YOU'LL BOTH FUME IF I DON'T.
SEE, SEE? SHE LISTEN TO BERRYBUZZ.
SUDDENLY...
WHA...?! OOHHH! MY CUB!!
DEWSHINE!!
BUT...
BLOOD OF TEN CHIEFS! LOVEMATE, ARE YOU ALL RIGHT?
NOT FOR LONG. THE CUB...IS COMING. I...CAN'T HOLD ON.

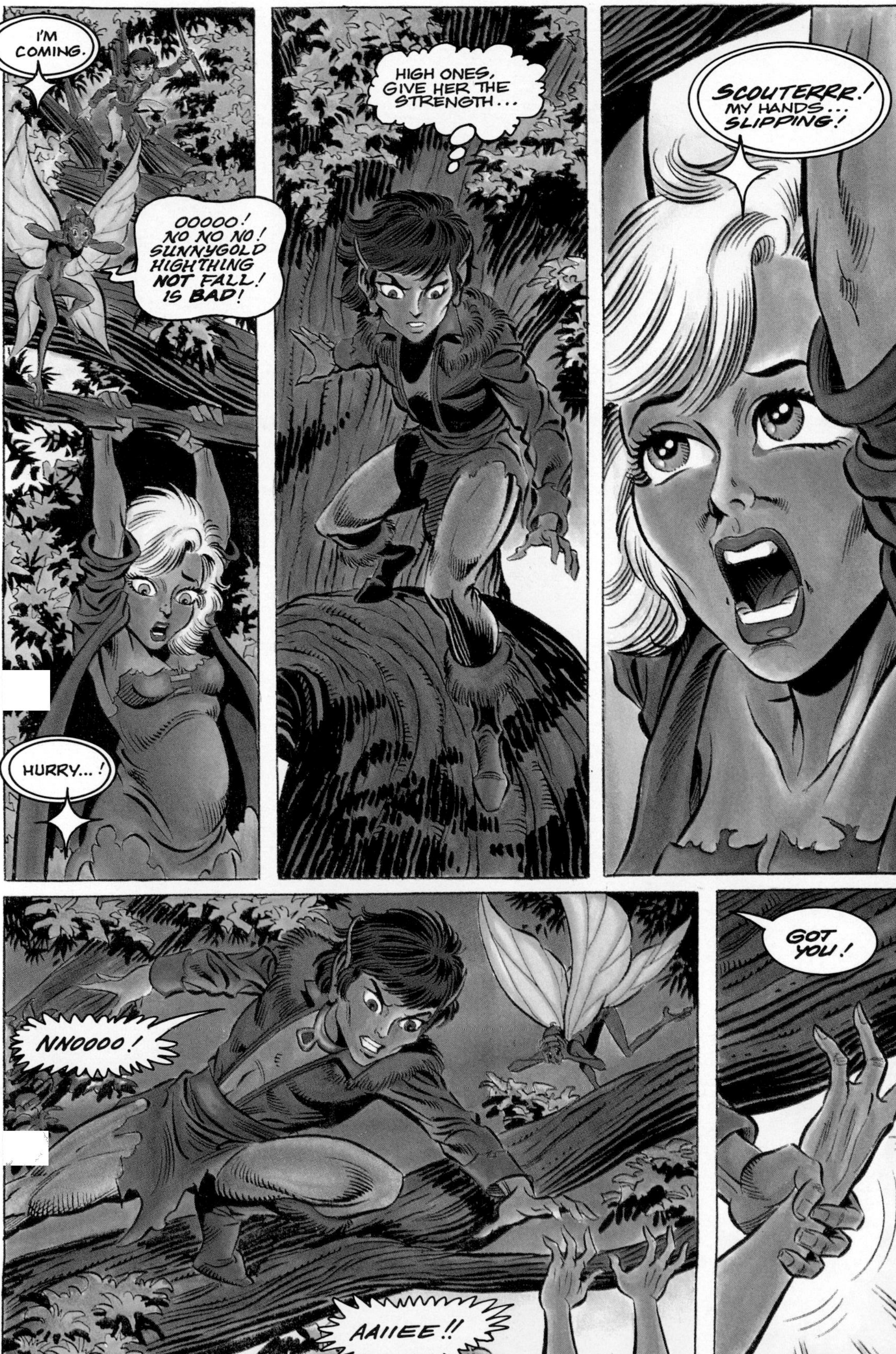

I'M COMING.
OOOOO! NO NO NO! SUNNYGOLD HIGHTHING NOT FALL! IS BAD!
HURRY...!
HIGH ONES, GIVE HER THE STRENGTH...
SCOUTERRR! MY HANDS... SLIPPING!
NNOOOO!
AAIIEE!!
GOT YOU!

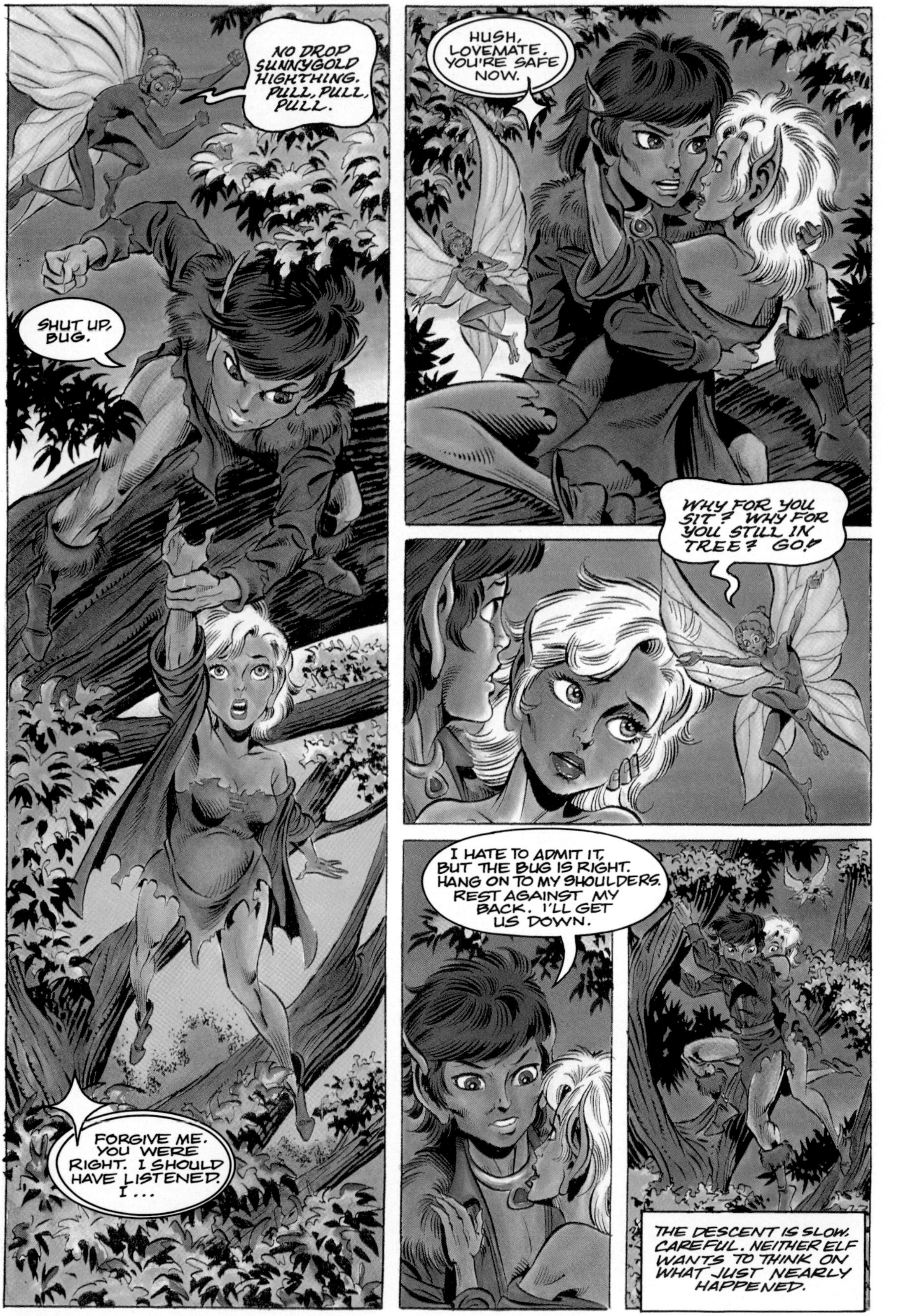

NO DROP SUNNYGOLD HIGHTHING. PULL, PULL, PULL.
SHUT UP, BUG.
FORGIVE ME. YOU WERE RIGHT. I SHOULD HAVE LISTENED. I...
HUSH, LOVEMATE. YOU'RE SAFE NOW.
WHY FOR YOU SIT? WHY FOR YOU STILL IN TREE? GO!
I HATE TO ADMIT IT, BUT THE BUG IS RIGHT. HANG ON TO MY SHOULDERS. REST AGAINST MY BACK. I'LL GET US DOWN.
THE DESCENT IS SLOW. CAREFUL. NEITHER ELF WANTS TO THINK ON WHAT JUST NEARLY HAPPENED.

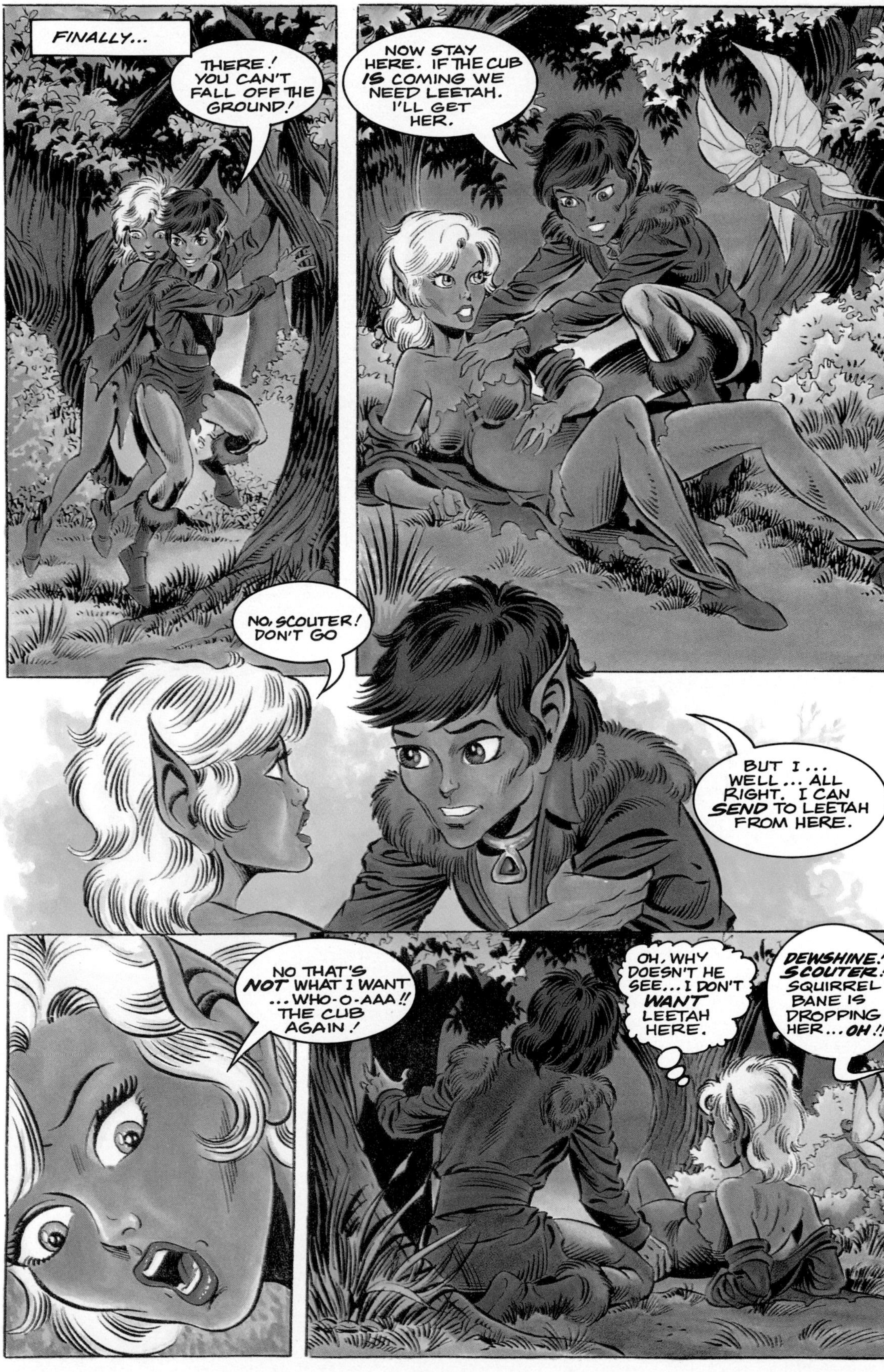
FINALLY...
THERE! YOU CAN'T FALL OFF THE GROUND!
NOW STAY HERE. IF THE CUB IS COMING WE NEED LEETAH. I'LL GET HER.
NO, SCOUTER! DON'T GO
BUT I... WELL... ALL RIGHT. I CAN SEND TO LEETAH FROM HERE.
NO THAT'S NOT WHAT I WANT ...WHO-O-AAA!! THE CUB AGAIN!
OH, WHY DOESN'T HE SEE... I DON'T WANT LEETAH HERE.
DEWSHINE! SCOUTER! SQUIRREL BANE IS DROPPING HER... OH!!

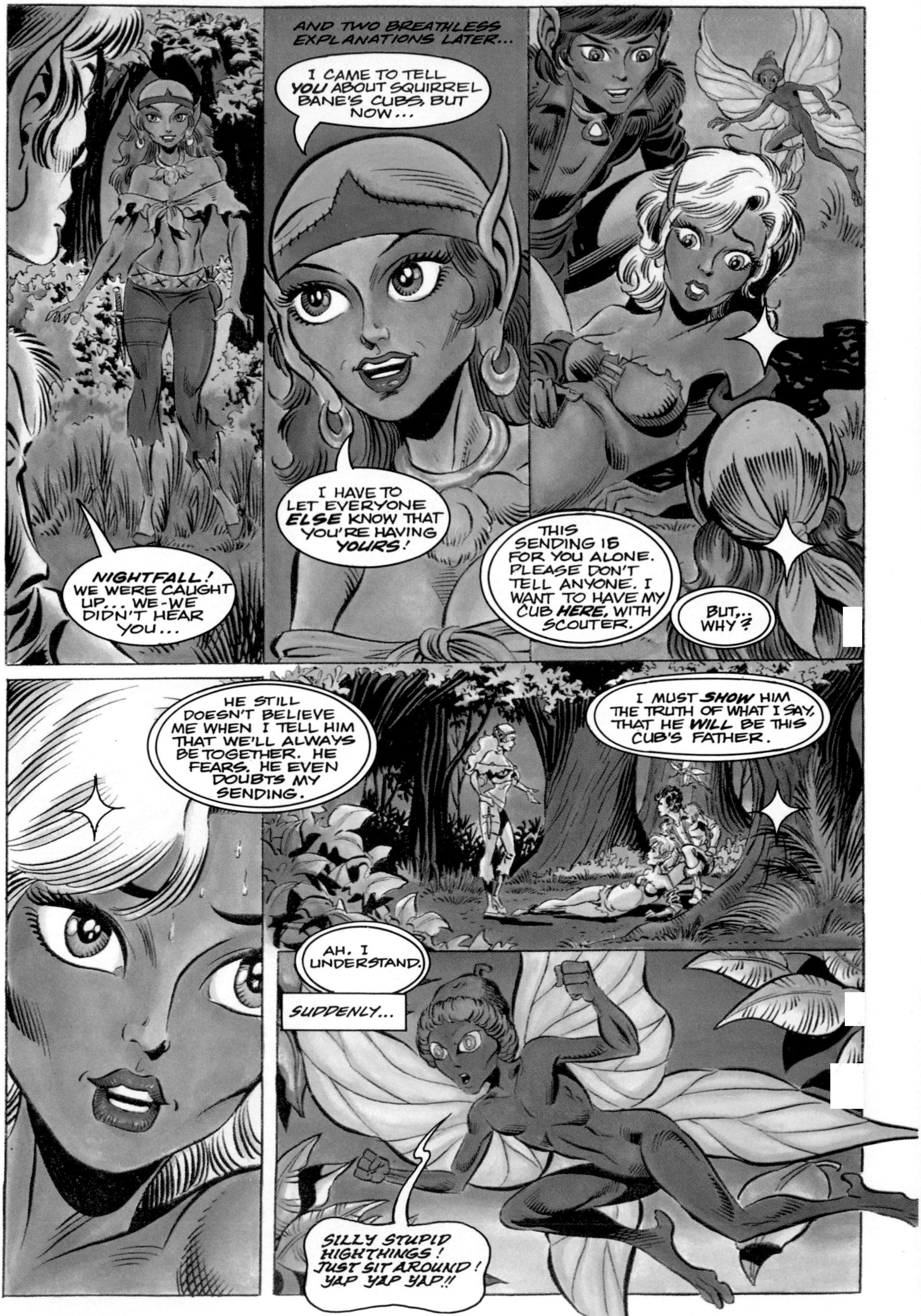
NIGHTFALL! WE WERE CAUGHT UP... WE-WE DIDN'T HEAR YOU...
AND TWO BREATHLESS EXPLANATIONS LATER...
I CAME TO TELL YOU ABOUT SQUIRREL BANE'S CUBS, BUT NOW...
I HAVE TO LET EVERYONE ELSE KNOW THAT YOU'RE HAVING YOURS!
THIS SENDING IS FOR YOU ALONE. PLEASE DON'T TELL ANYONE. I WANT TO HAVE MY CUB HERE, WITH SCOUTER.
BUT... WHY?
HE STILL DOESN'T BELIEVE ME WHEN I TELL HIM THAT WE'LL ALWAYS BE TOGETHER. HE FEARS. HE EVEN DOUBTS MY SENDING.
I MUST SHOW HIM THE TRUTH OF WHAT I SAY, THAT HE WILL BE THIS CUB'S FATHER.
AH. I UNDERSTAND.
SUDDENLY...
SILLY STUPID HIGHTHINGS! JUST SIT AROUND! YAP YAP YAP!!

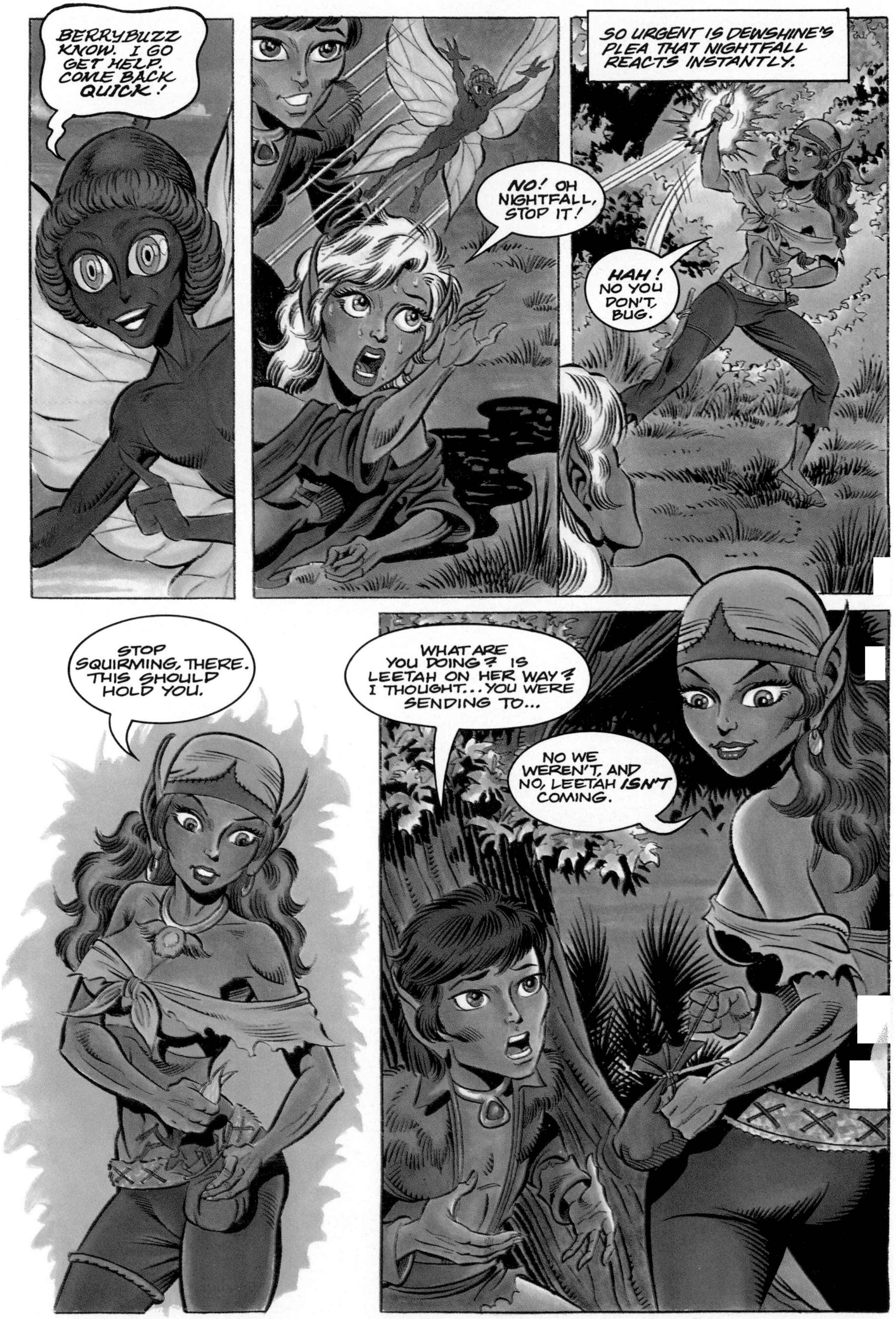
BERRYBUZZ KNOW. I GO GET HELP. COME BACK QUICK!
NO! OH NIGHTFALL, STOP IT!
SO URGENT IS DEWSHINE'S PLEA THAT NIGHTFALL REACTS INSTANTLY.
HAH! NO YOU DON'T, BUG.
STOP SQUIRMING, THERE. THIS SHOULD HOLD YOU.
WHAT ARE YOU DOING? IS LEETAH ON HER WAY? I THOUGHT...YOU WERE SENDING TO...
NO WE WEREN'T, AND NO, LEETAH ISN'T COMING.

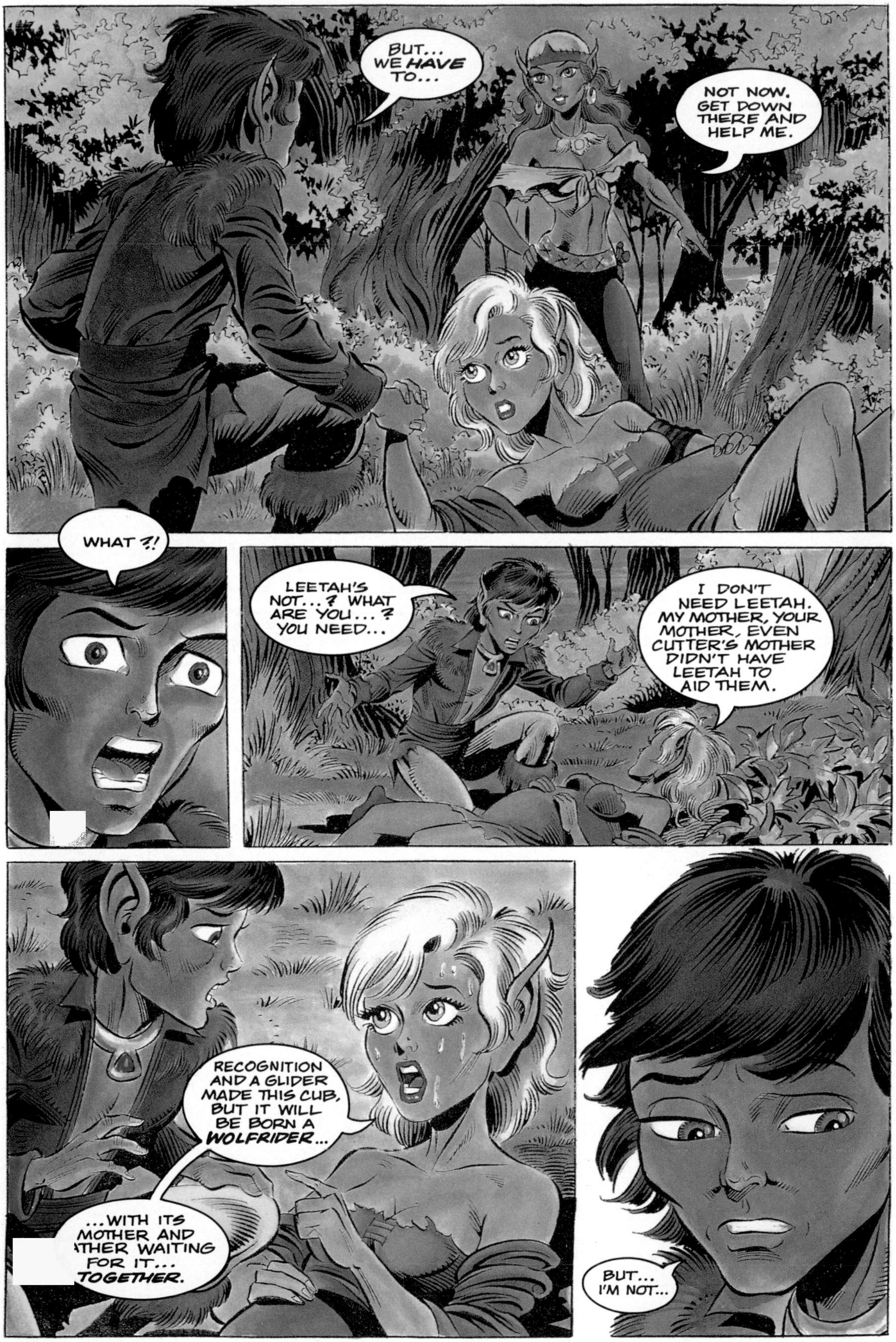

BUT... WE *HAVE* TO...
NOT NOW. GET DOWN THERE AND HELP ME.
WHAT ?!
LEETAH'S NOT...? WHAT ARE YOU...? YOU NEED...
I DON'T NEED LEETAH. MY MOTHER, YOUR MOTHER, EVEN CUTTER'S MOTHER DIDN'T HAVE LEETAH TO AID THEM.
RECOGNITION AND A GLIDER MADE THIS CUB, BUT IT WILL BE BORN A **WOLFRIDER**...
...WITH ITS MOTHER AND ATHER WAITING FOR IT... **TOGETHER**.
BUT... I'M NOT...

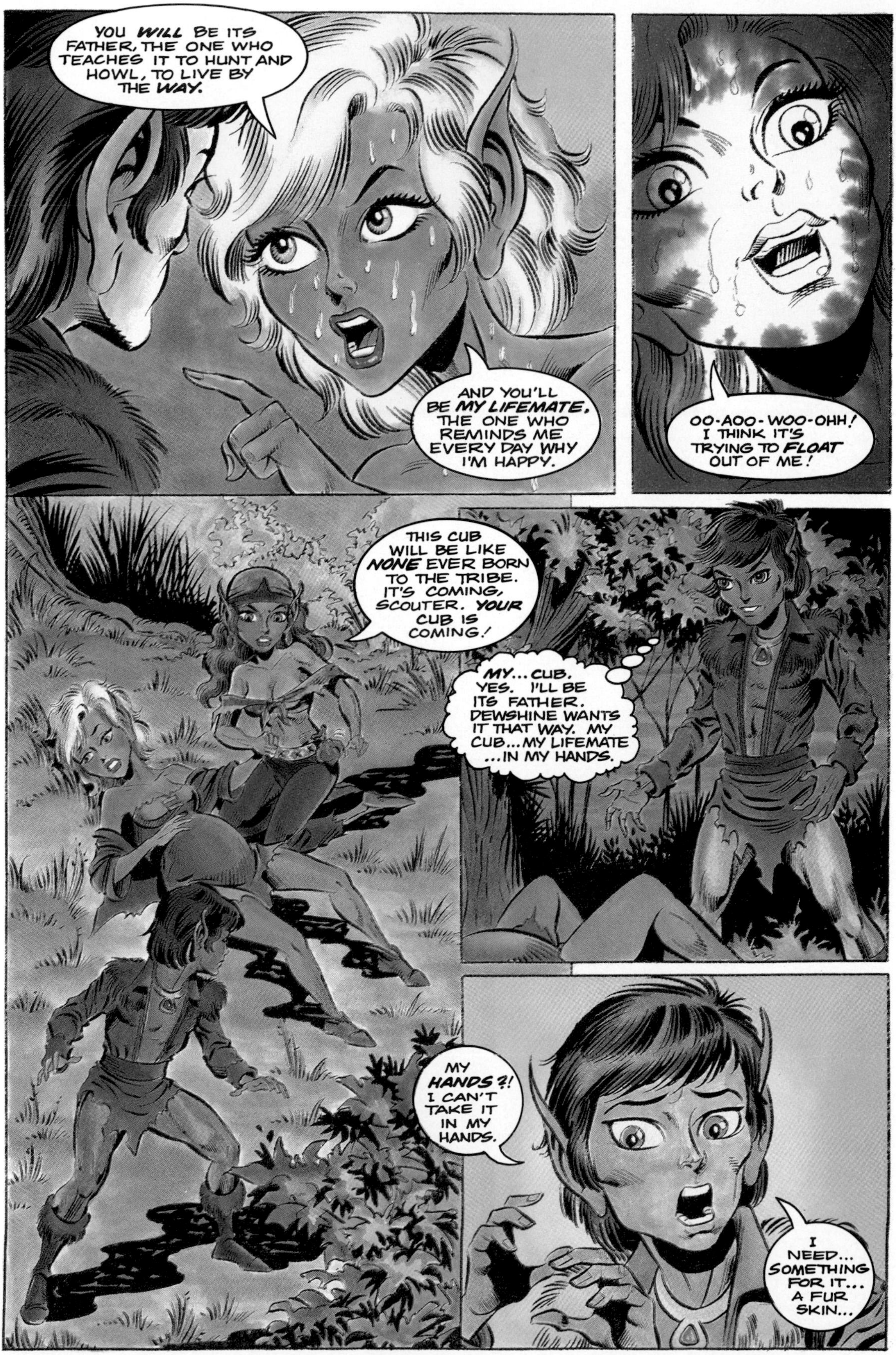
YOU WILL BE ITS FATHER, THE ONE WHO TEACHES IT TO HUNT AND HOWL, TO LIVE BY THE WAY.
AND YOU'LL BE MY LIFEMATE, THE ONE WHO REMINDS ME EVERY DAY WHY I'M HAPPY.
OO-AOO-WOO-OHH! I THINK IT'S TRYING TO FLOAT OUT OF ME!
THIS CUB WILL BE LIKE NONE EVER BORN TO THE TRIBE. IT'S COMING, SCOUTER. YOUR CUB IS COMING!
MY... CUB. YES. I'LL BE ITS FATHER. DEWSHINE WANTS IT THAT WAY. MY CUB... MY LIFEMATE ...IN MY HANDS.
MY HANDS?! I CAN'T TAKE IT IN MY HANDS.
I NEED... SOMETHING FOR IT... A FUR SKIN...

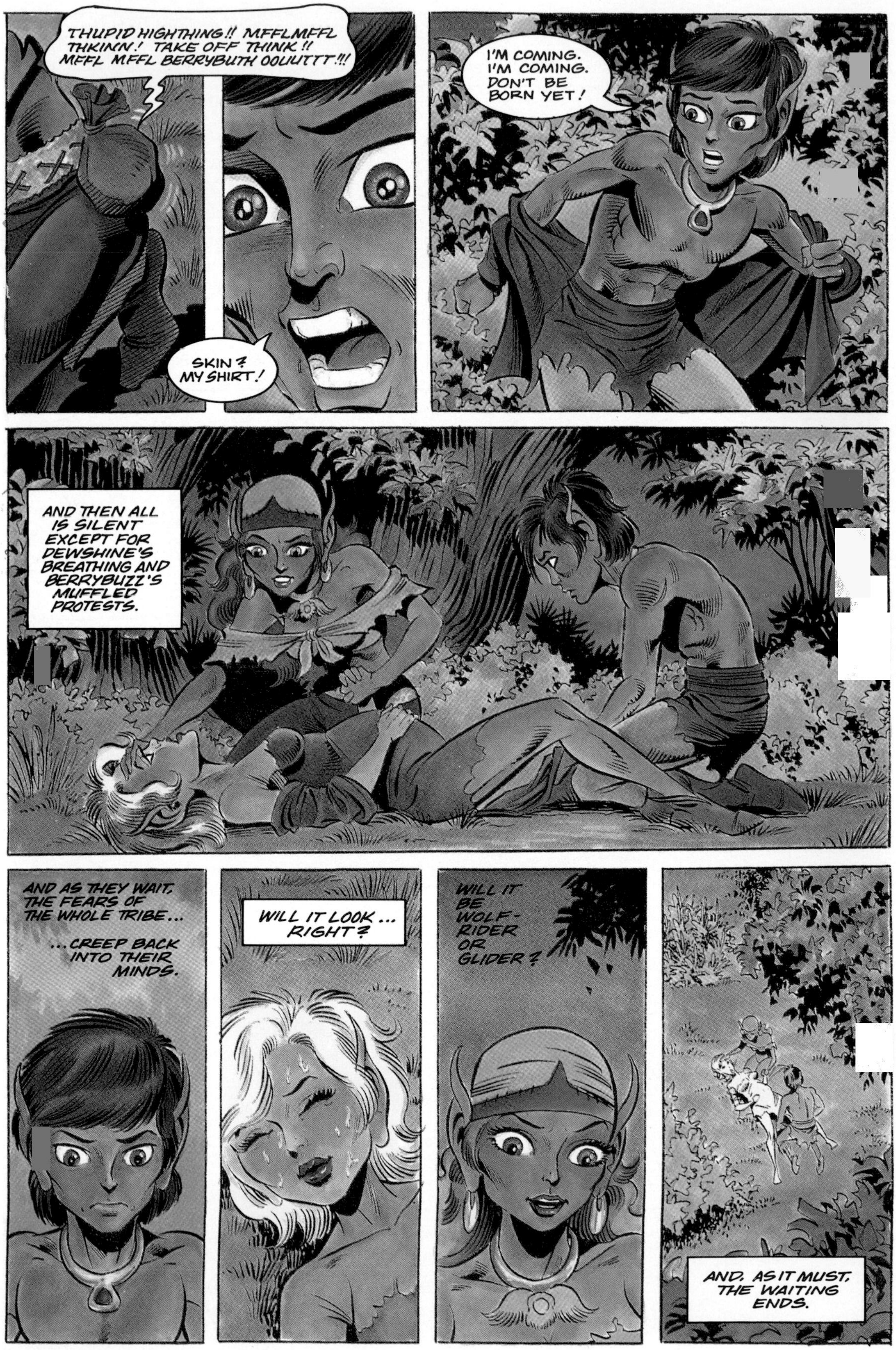
THUPID HIGHTHING!! MFFLMFFL THKINN! TAKE OFF THINK!! MFFL MFFL BERRYBUTH OOUUTTT!!!
SKIN? MY SHIRT!
I'M COMING. I'M COMING. DON'T BE BORN YET!
AND THEN ALL IS SILENT EXCEPT FOR DEWSHINE'S BREATHING AND BERRYBUZZ'S MUFFLED PROTESTS.
AND AS THEY WAIT, THE FEARS OF THE WHOLE TRIBE...
...CREEP BACK INTO THEIR MINDS.
WILL IT LOOK... RIGHT?
WILL IT BE WOLF-RIDER OR GLIDER?
AND, AS IT MUST, THE WAITING ENDS.

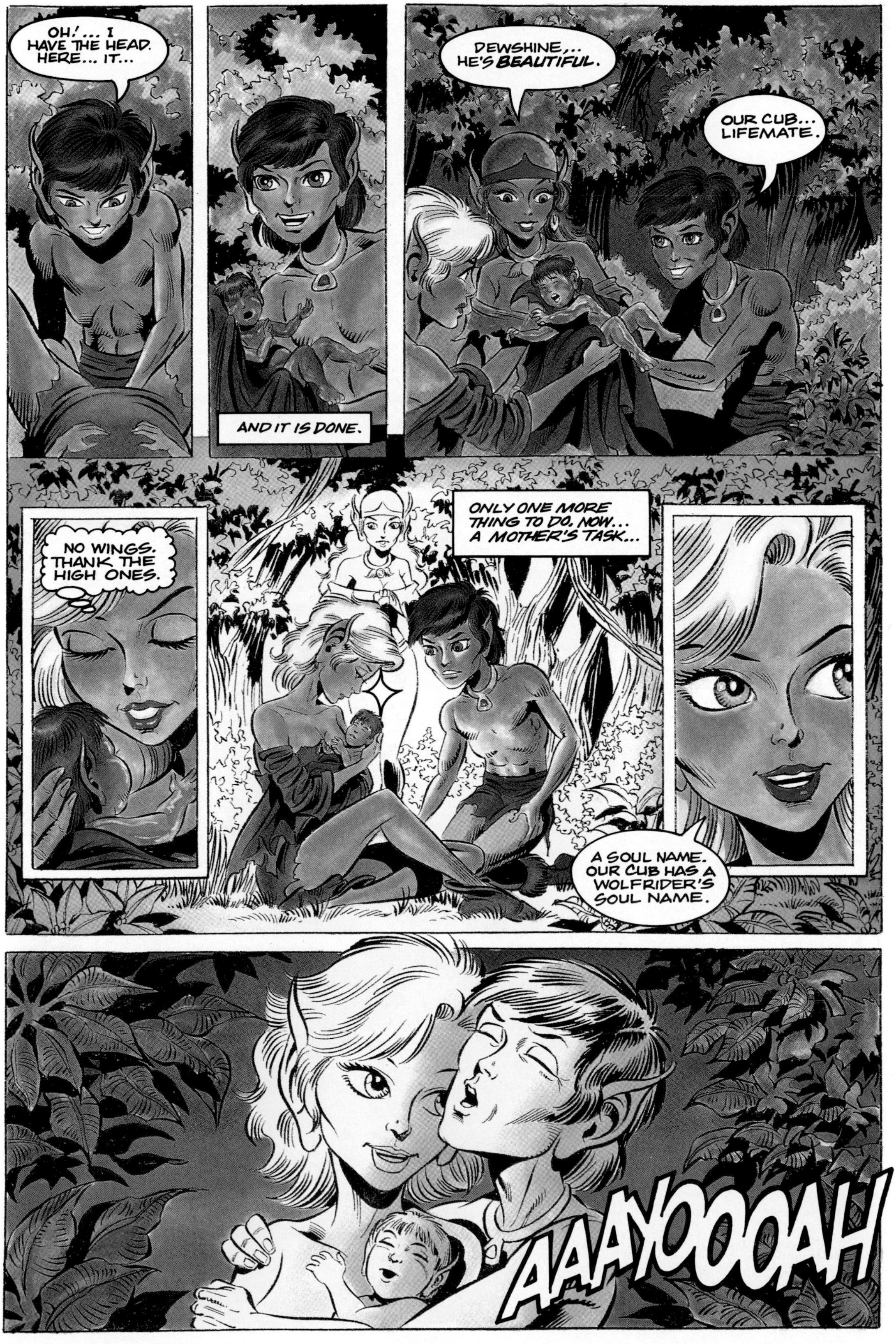
OH! ... I HAVE THE HEAD. HERE... IT...
AND IT IS DONE.
DEWSHINE,.. HE'S BEAUTIFUL.
OUR CUB... LIFEMATE.
NO WINGS. THANK THE HIGH ONES.
ONLY ONE MORE THING TO DO, NOW... A MOTHER'S TASK...
A SOUL NAME. OUR CUB HAS A WOLFRIDER'S SOUL NAME.
AAAYOOOAH

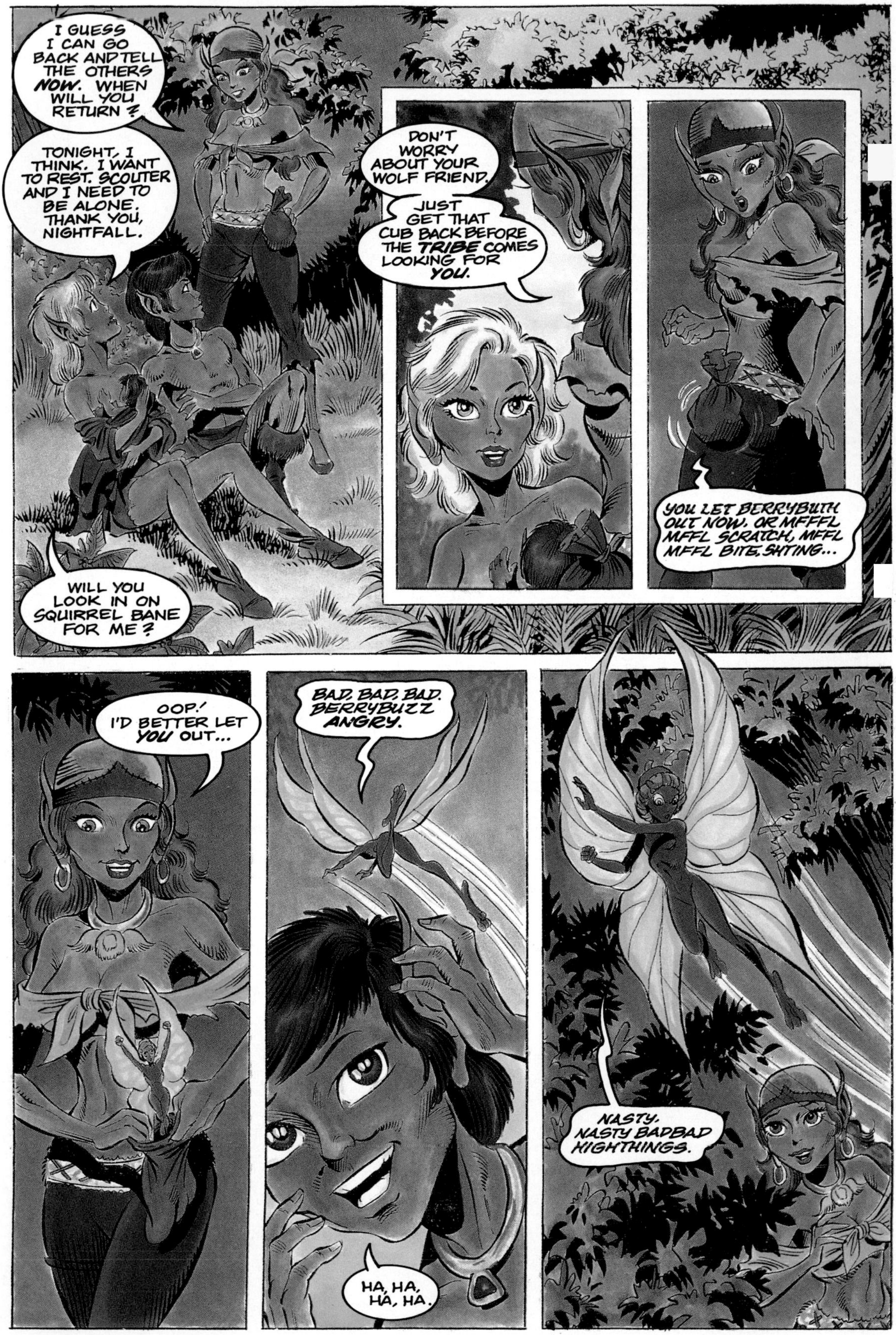
I GUESS I CAN GO BACK AND TELL THE OTHERS NOW. WHEN WILL YOU RETURN?
TONIGHT, I THINK. I WANT TO REST. SCOUTER AND I NEED TO BE ALONE. THANK YOU, NIGHTFALL.
WILL YOU LOOK IN ON SQUIRREL BANE FOR ME?
DON'T WORRY ABOUT YOUR WOLF FRIEND.
JUST GET THAT CUB BACK BEFORE THE TRIBE COMES LOOKING FOR YOU.
YOU LET BERRYBUTH OUT NOW, OR MFFFL MFFL SCRATCH, MFFL MFFL BITE, SHTING...
OOP! I'D BETTER LET YOU OUT...
BAD, BAD, BAD. BERRYBUZZ ANGRY.
HA, HA, HA, HA.
NASTY. NASTY BADBAD HIGHTHINGS.

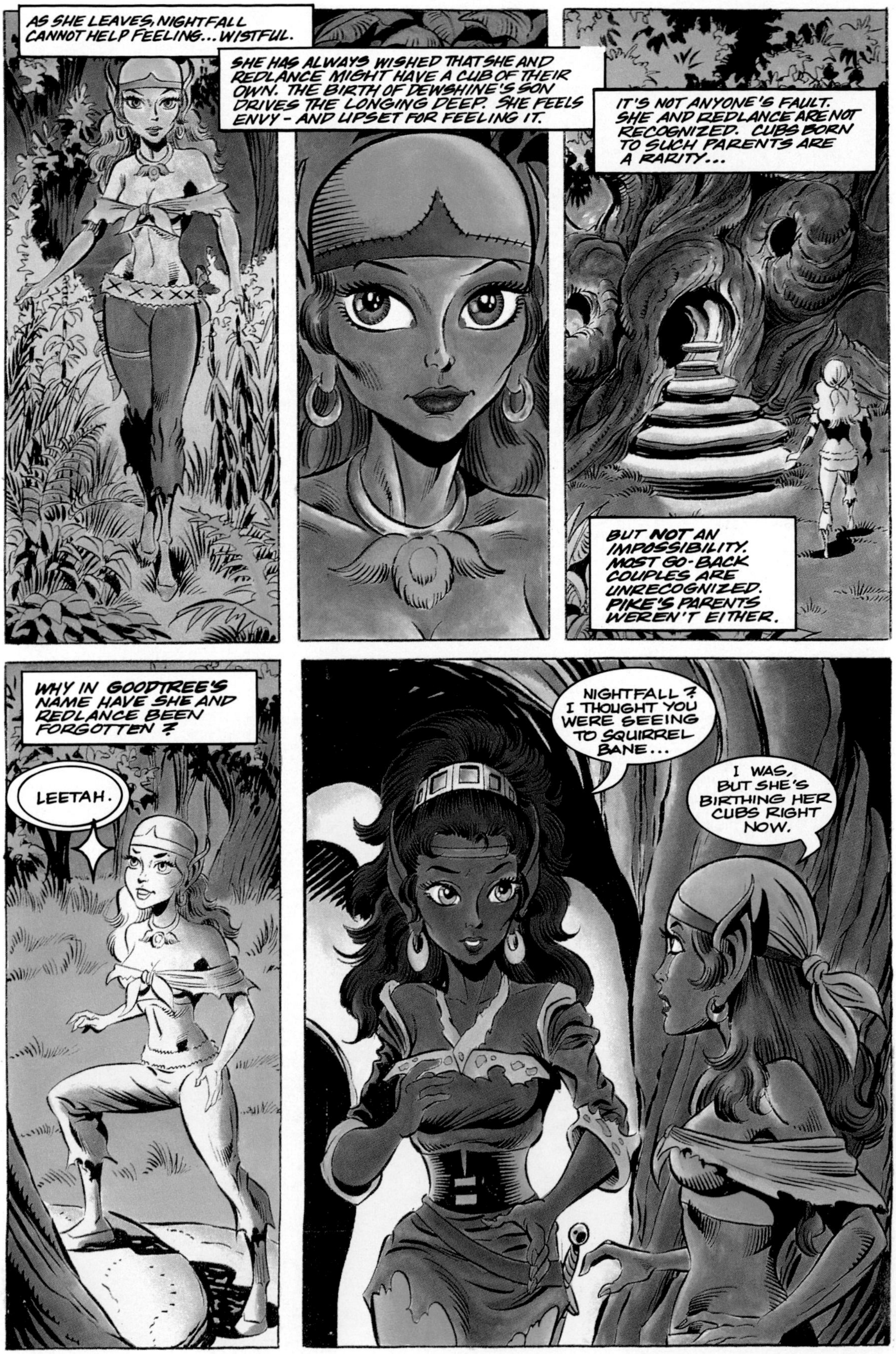
AS SHE LEAVES, NIGHTFALL CANNOT HELP FEELING... WISTFUL.
SHE HAS ALWAYS WISHED THAT SHE AND REDLANCE MIGHT HAVE A CUB OF THEIR OWN. THE BIRTH OF DEWSHINE'S SON DRIVES THE LONGING DEEP. SHE FEELS ENVY - AND UPSET FOR FEELING IT.
IT'S NOT ANYONE'S FAULT. SHE AND REDLANCE ARE NOT RECOGNIZED. CUBS BORN TO SUCH PARENTS ARE A RARITY...
BUT NOT AN IMPOSSIBILITY. MOST GO-BACK COUPLES ARE UNRECOGNIZED. PIKE'S PARENTS WEREN'T EITHER.
WHY IN GOODTREE'S NAME HAVE SHE AND REDLANCE BEEN FORGOTTEN?
LEETAH.
NIGHTFALL? I THOUGHT YOU WERE SEEING TO SQUIRREL BANE...
I WAS, BUT SHE'S BIRTHING HER CUBS RIGHT NOW.

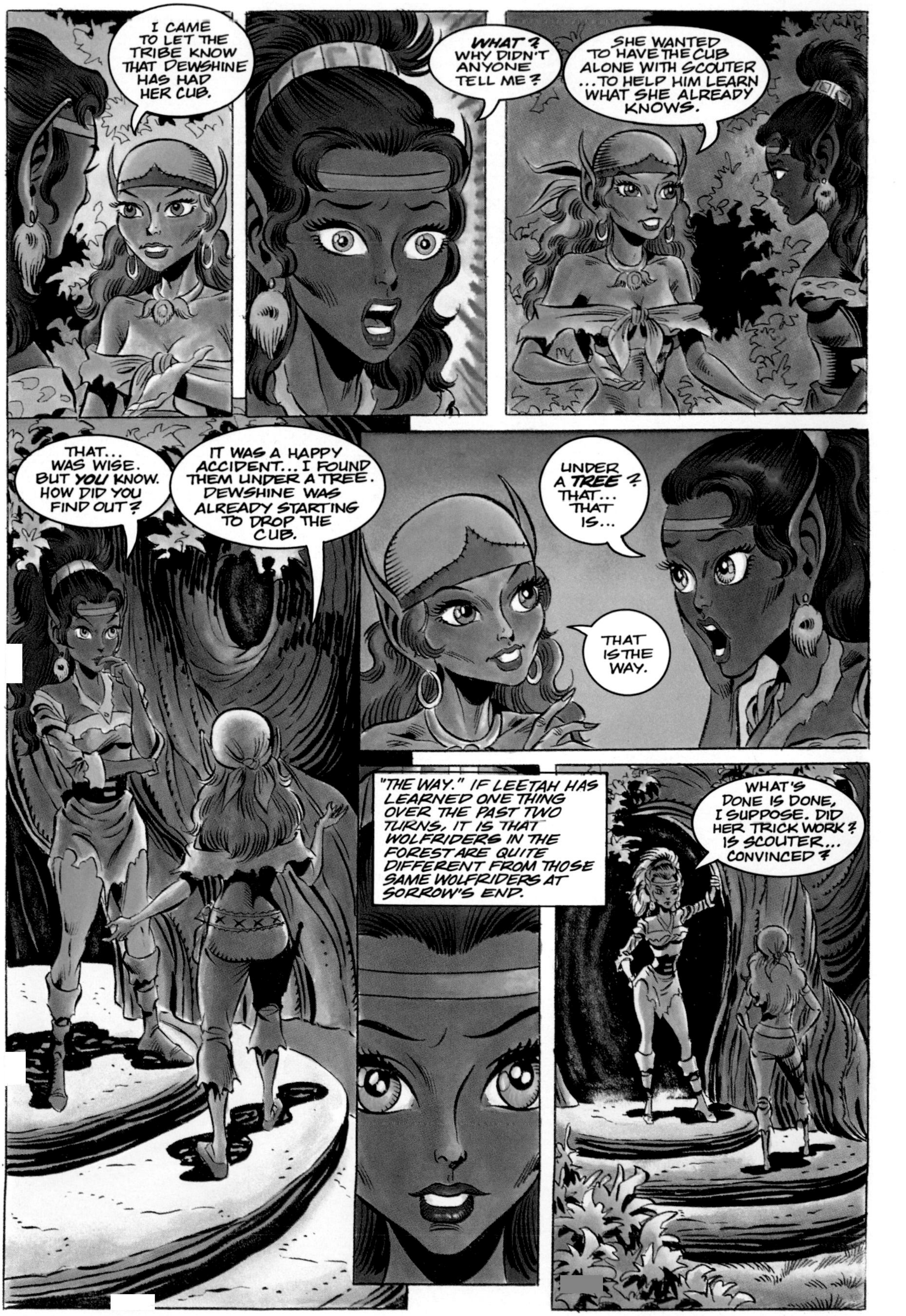
I CAME TO LET THE TRIBE KNOW THAT DEWSHINE HAS HAD HER CUB.
WHAT? WHY DIDN'T ANYONE TELL ME?
SHE WANTED TO HAVE THE CUB ALONE WITH SCOUTER ...TO HELP HIM LEARN WHAT SHE ALREADY KNOWS.
THAT... WAS WISE. BUT YOU KNOW. HOW DID YOU FIND OUT?
IT WAS A HAPPY ACCIDENT... I FOUND THEM UNDER A TREE. DEWSHINE WAS ALREADY STARTING TO DROP THE CUB.
UNDER A TREE? THAT... THAT IS...
THAT IS THE WAY.
"THE WAY." IF LEETAH HAS LEARNED ONE THING OVER THE PAST TWO TURNS, IT IS THAT WOLFRIDERS IN THE FOREST ARE QUITE DIFFERENT FROM THOSE SAME WOLFRIDERS AT SORROW'S END.
WHAT'S DONE IS DONE, I SUPPOSE. DID HER TRICK WORK? IS SCOUTER... CONVINCED?

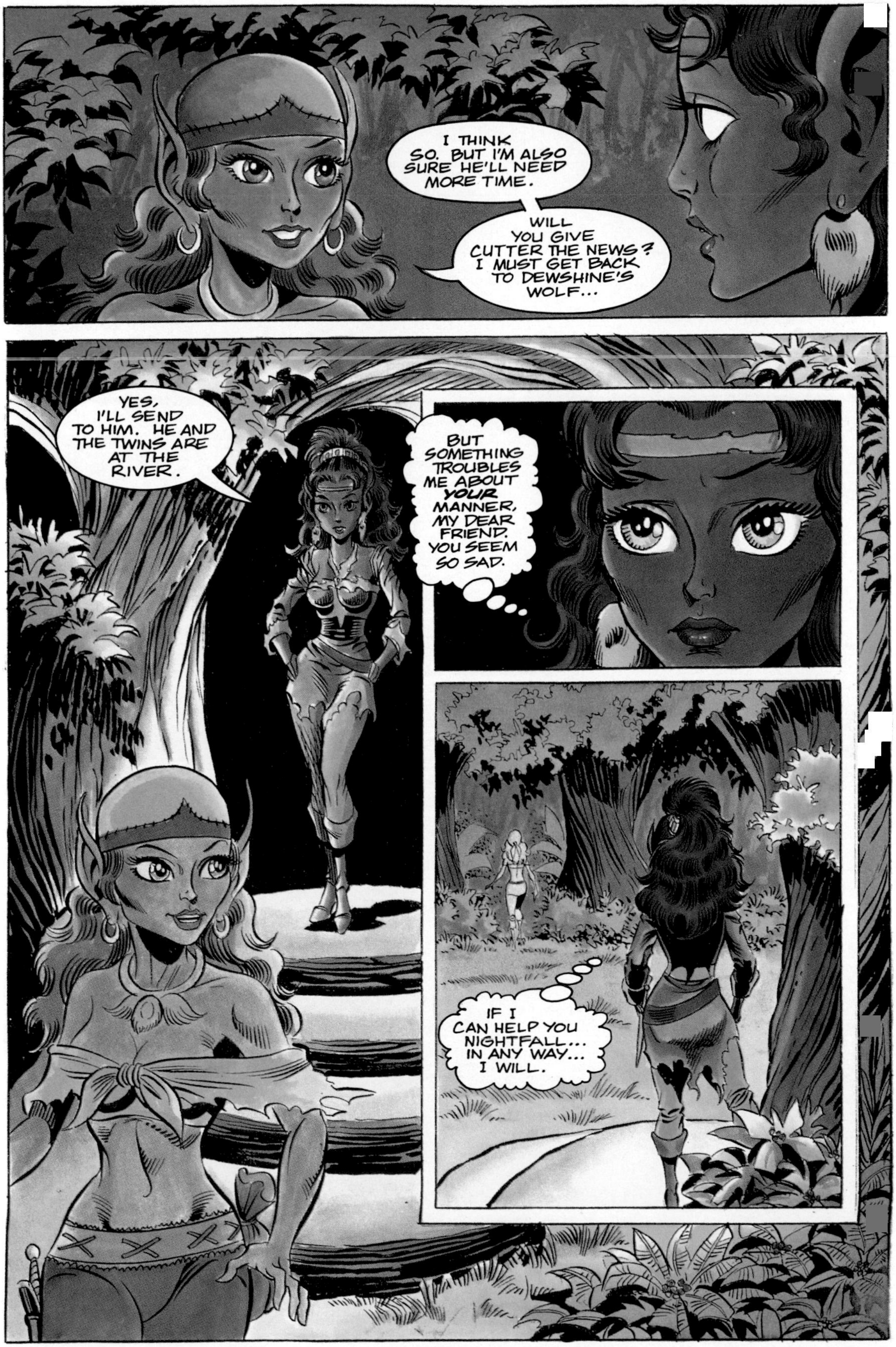
I THINK SO. BUT I'M ALSO SURE HE'LL NEED MORE TIME.
WILL YOU GIVE CUTTER THE NEWS? I MUST GET BACK TO DEWSHINE'S WOLF...
YES, I'LL SEND TO HIM. HE AND THE TWINS ARE AT THE RIVER.
BUT SOMETHING TROUBLES ME ABOUT YOUR MANNER, MY DEAR FRIEND. YOU SEEM SO SAD.
IF I CAN HELP YOU NIGHTFALL... IN ANY WAY... I WILL.

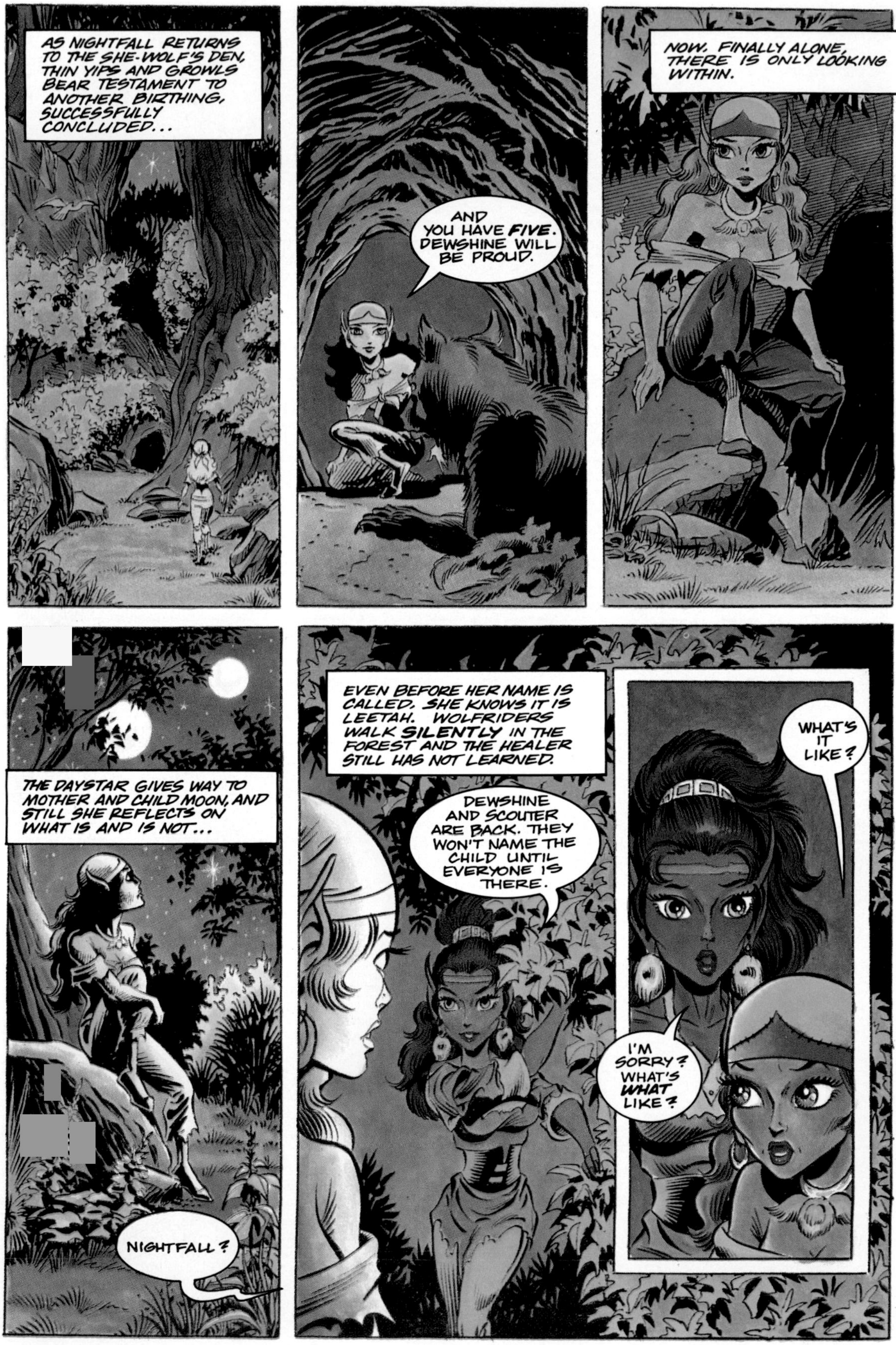
AS NIGHTFALL RETURNS TO THE SHE-WOLF'S DEN, THIN YIPS AND GROWLS BEAR TESTAMENT TO ANOTHER BIRTHING, SUCCESSFULLY CONCLUDED...
AND YOU HAVE FIVE. DEWSHINE WILL BE PROUD.
NOW. FINALLY ALONE, THERE IS ONLY LOOKING WITHIN.
THE DAYSTAR GIVES WAY TO MOTHER AND CHILD MOON, AND STILL SHE REFLECTS ON WHAT IS AND IS NOT...
NIGHTFALL?
EVEN BEFORE HER NAME IS CALLED, SHE KNOWS IT IS LEETAH. WOLFRIDERS WALK SILENTLY IN THE FOREST AND THE HEALER STILL HAS NOT LEARNED.
DEWSHINE AND SCOUTER ARE BACK. THEY WON'T NAME THE CHILD UNTIL EVERYONE IS THERE.
WHAT'S IT LIKE?
I'M SORRY? WHAT'S WHAT LIKE?

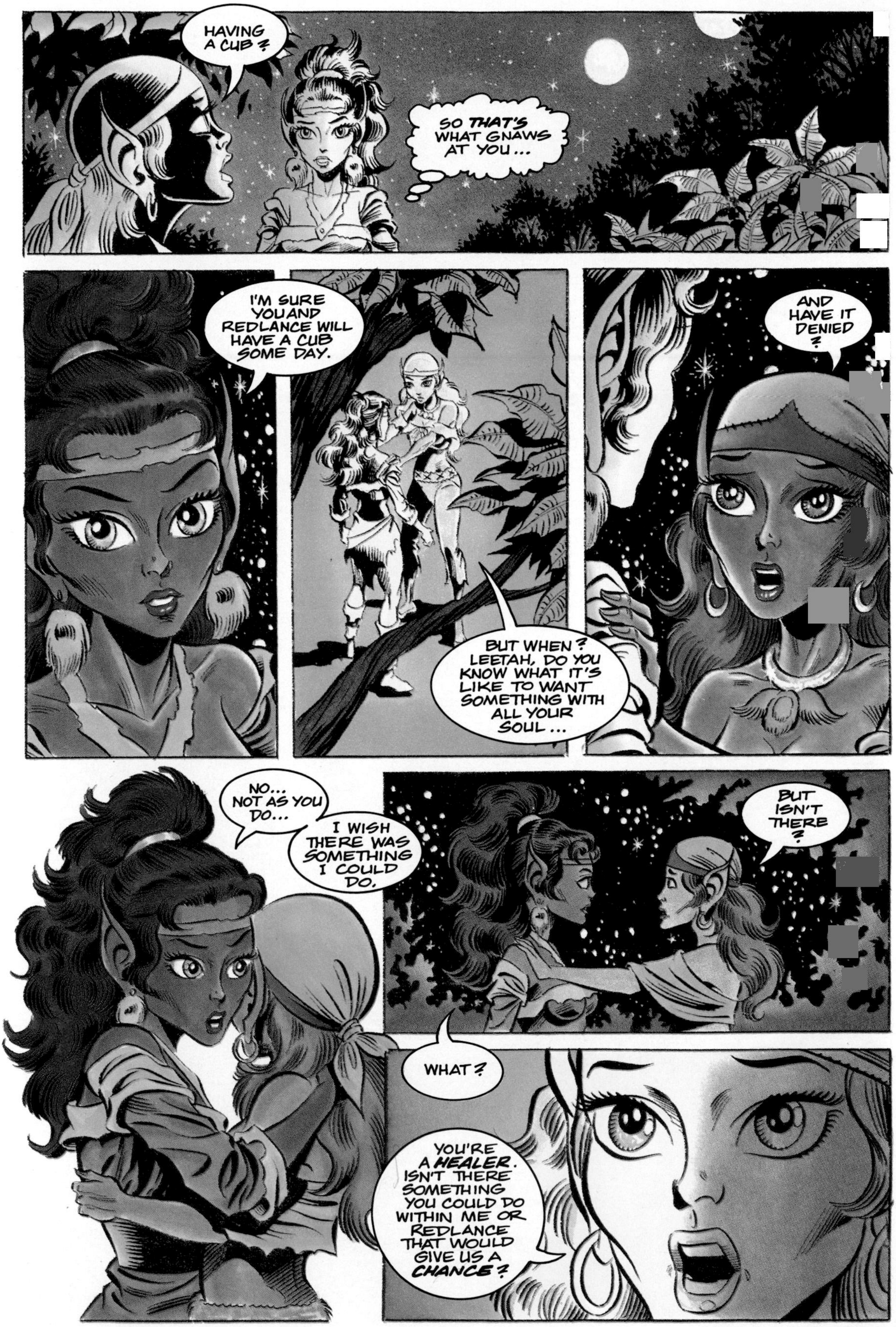
HAVING A CUB?
SO THAT'S WHAT GNAWS AT YOU...
I'M SURE YOU AND REDLANCE WILL HAVE A CUB SOME DAY.
BUT WHEN? LEETAH, DO YOU KNOW WHAT IT'S LIKE TO WANT SOMETHING WITH ALL YOUR SOUL...
AND HAVE IT DENIED?
NO... NOT AS YOU DO...
I WISH THERE WAS SOMETHING I COULD DO.
BUT ISN'T THERE?
WHAT?
YOU'RE A HEALER. ISN'T THERE SOMETHING YOU COULD DO WITHIN ME OR REDLANCE THAT WOULD GIVE US A CHANCE?

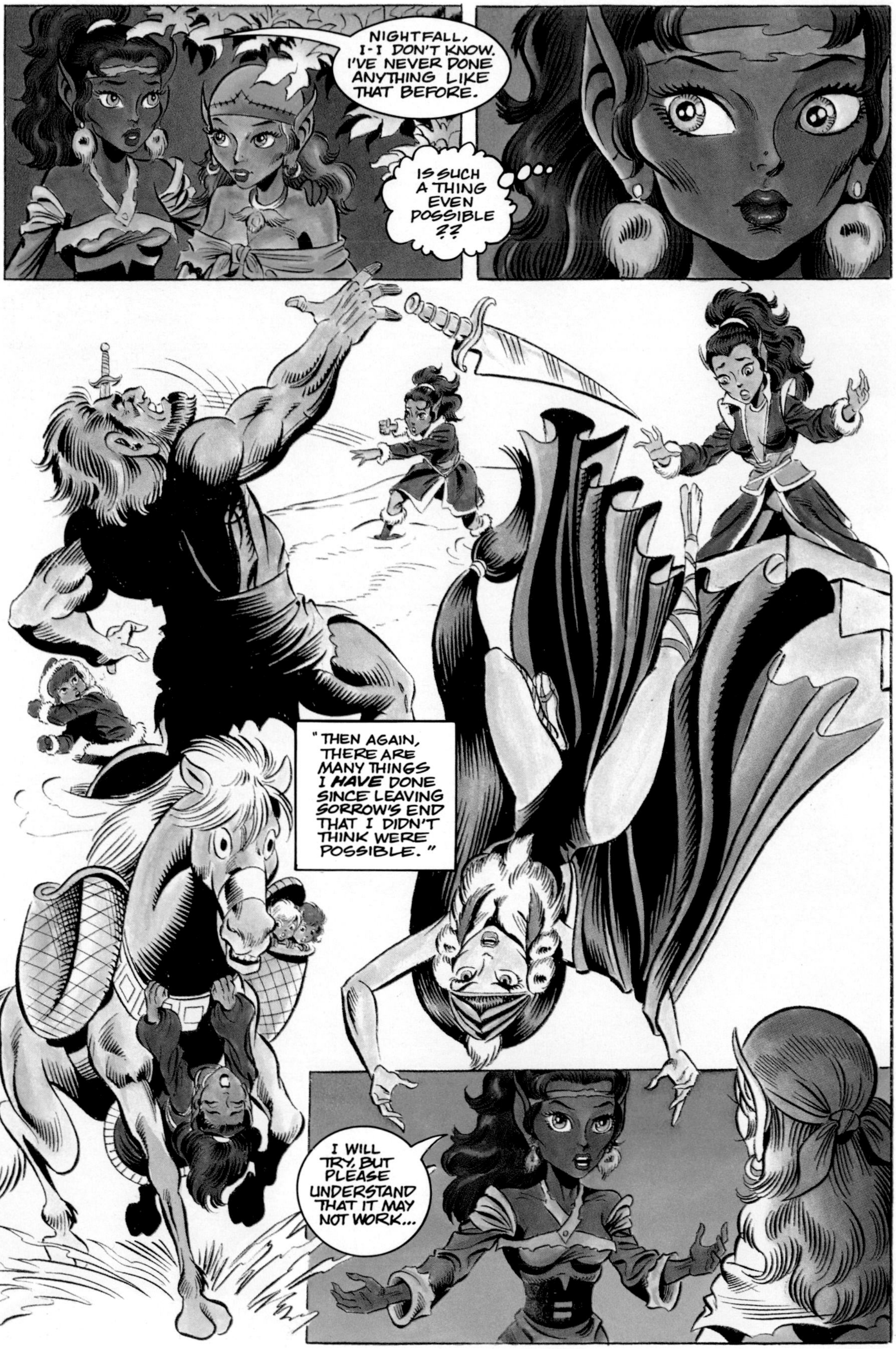
NIGHTFALL, I-I DON'T KNOW. I'VE NEVER DONE ANYTHING LIKE THAT BEFORE.
IS SUCH A THING EVEN POSSIBLE ??
"THEN AGAIN, THERE ARE MANY THINGS I HAVE DONE SINCE LEAVING SORROW'S END THAT I DIDN'T THINK WERE POSSIBLE."
I WILL TRY, BUT PLEASE UNDERSTAND THAT IT MAY NOT WORK...

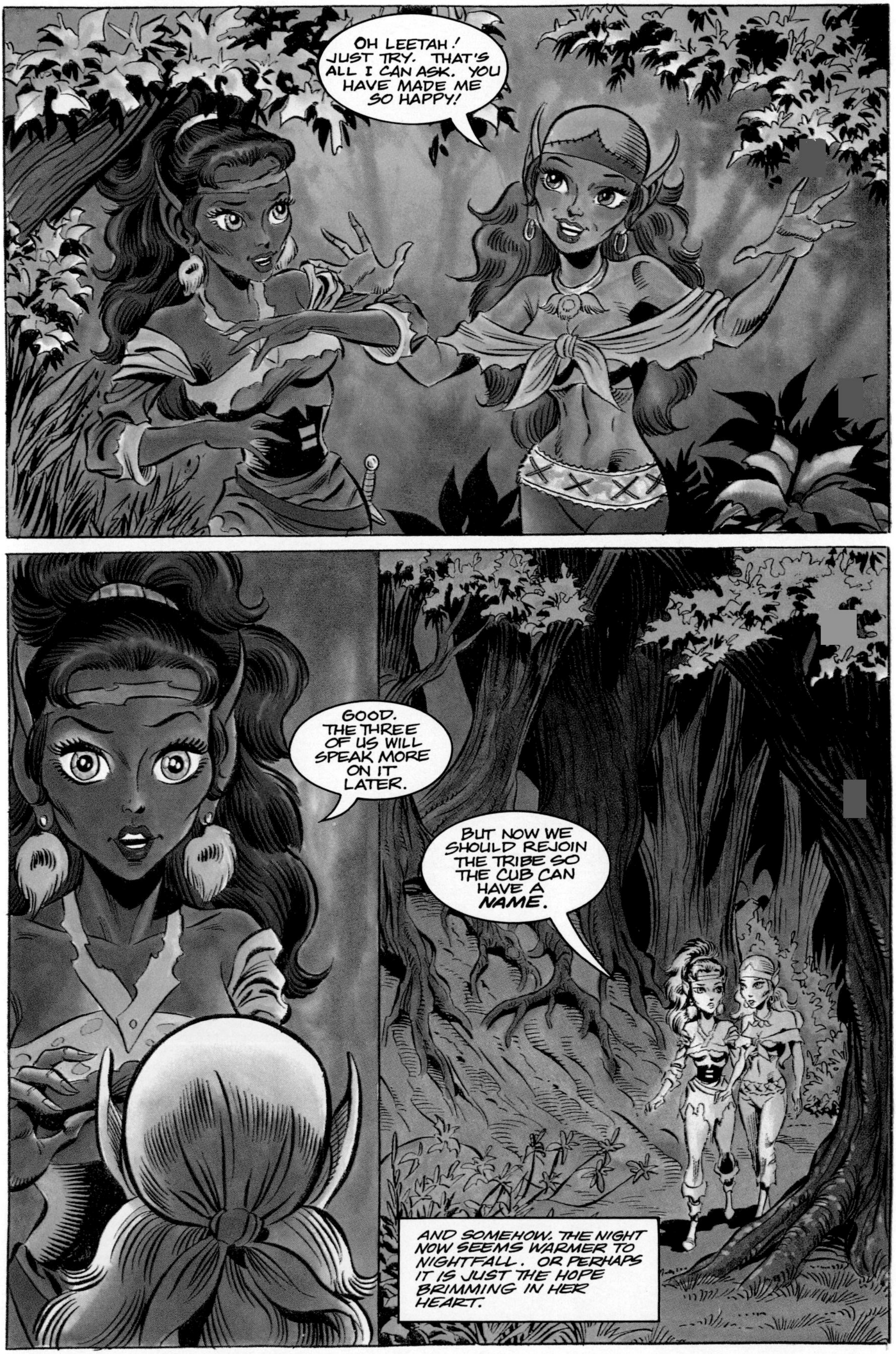
OH LEETAH! JUST TRY. THAT'S ALL I CAN ASK. YOU HAVE MADE ME SO HAPPY!
GOOD. THE THREE OF US WILL SPEAK MORE ON IT LATER.
BUT NOW WE SHOULD REJOIN THE TRIBE SO THE CUB CAN HAVE A NAME.
AND SOMEHOW, THE NIGHT NOW SEEMS WARMER TO NIGHTFALL. OR PERHAPS IT IS JUST THE HOPE BRIMMING IN HER HEART.

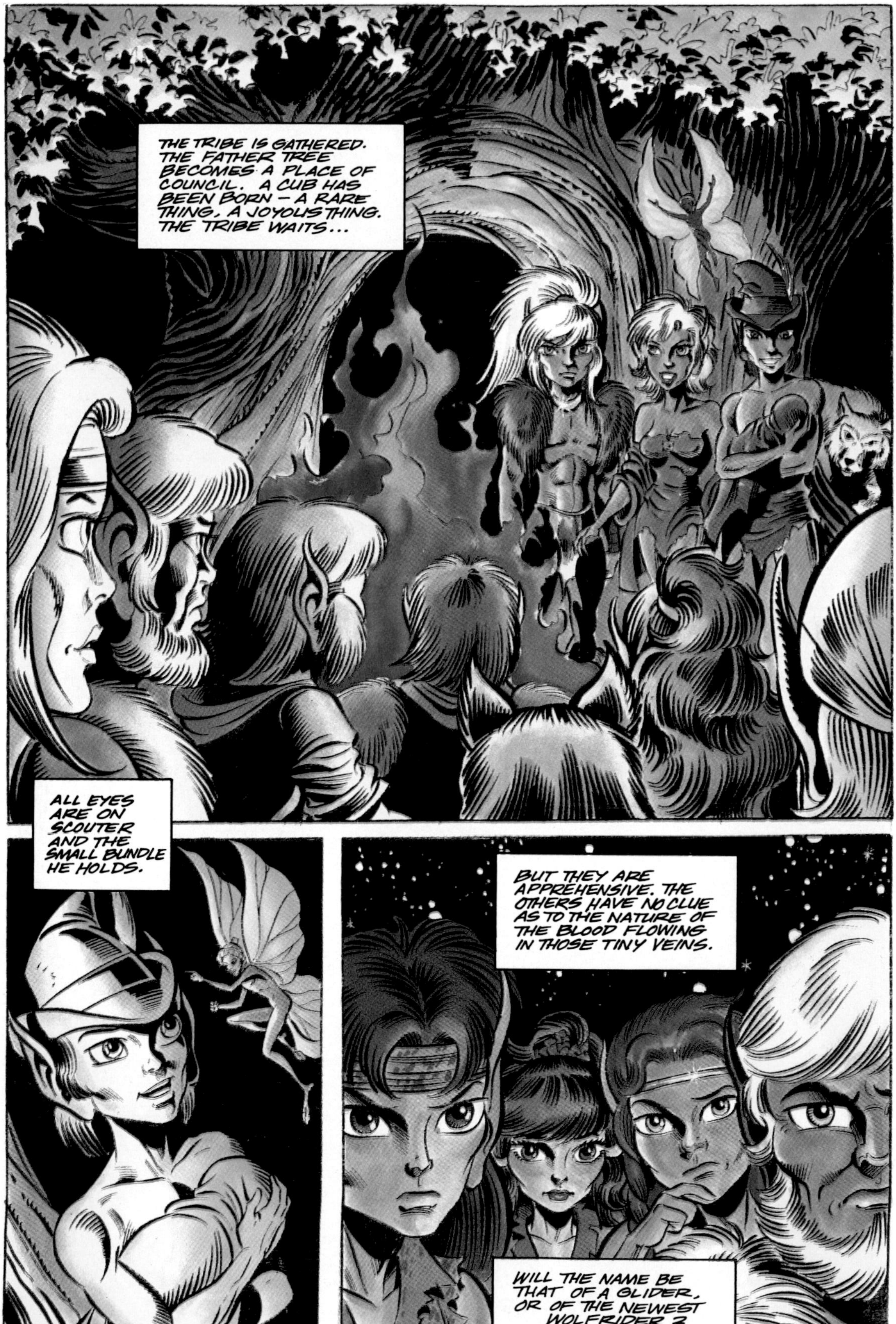
THE TRIBE IS GATHERED. THE FATHER TREE BECOMES A PLACE OF COUNCIL. A CUB HAS BEEN BORN — A RARE THING. A JOYOUS THING. THE TRIBE WAITS...
ALL EYES ARE ON SCOUTER AND THE SMALL BUNDLE HE HOLDS.
BUT THEY ARE APPREHENSIVE. THE OTHERS HAVE NO CLUE AS TO THE NATURE OF THE BLOOD FLOWING IN THOSE TINY VEINS.
WILL THE NAME BE THAT OF A GLIDER, OR OF THE NEWEST WOLFRIDER ?

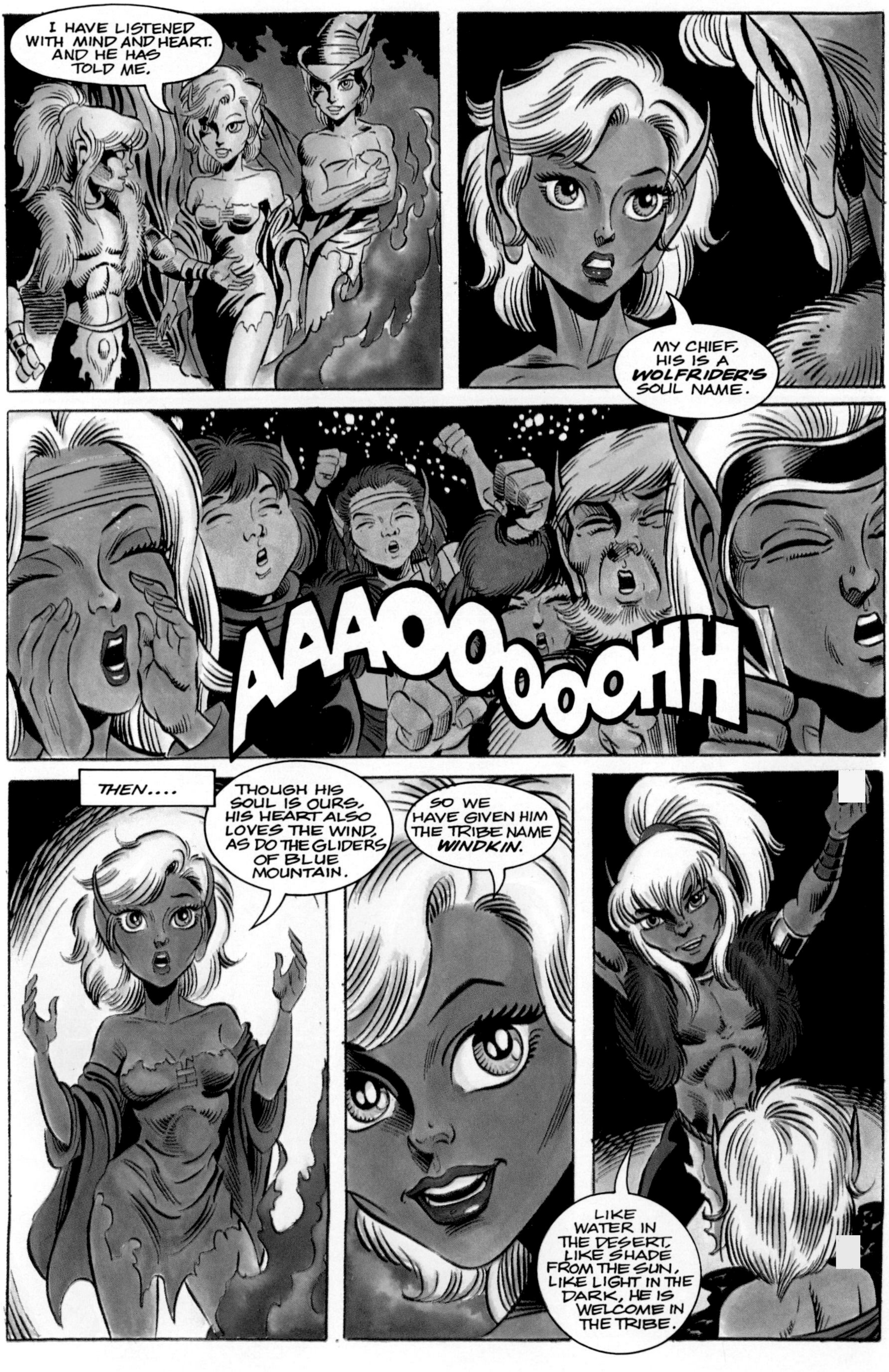
I HAVE LISTENED WITH MIND AND HEART. AND HE HAS TOLD ME.
MY CHIEF, HIS IS A WOLFRIDER'S SOUL NAME.
AAAOOOOOHH
THEN....
THOUGH HIS SOUL IS OURS, HIS HEART ALSO LOVES THE WIND, AS DO THE GLIDERS OF BLUE MOUNTAIN.
SO WE HAVE GIVEN HIM THE TRIBE NAME WINDKIN.
LIKE WATER IN THE DESERT, LIKE SHADE FROM THE SUN, LIKE LIGHT IN THE DARK, HE IS WELCOME IN THE TRIBE.

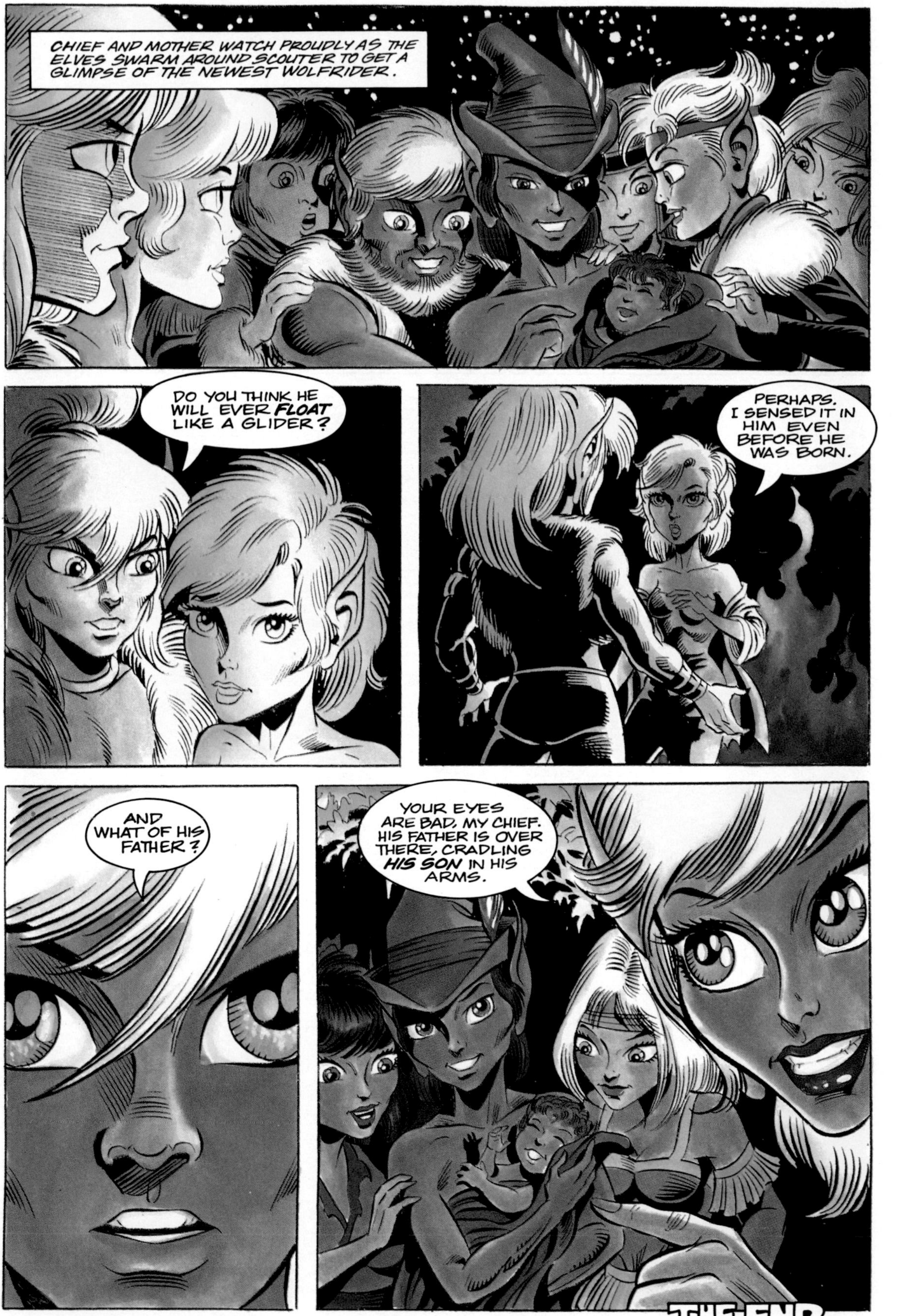
CHIEF AND MOTHER WATCH PROUDLY AS THE ELVES SWARM AROUND SCOUTER TO GET A GLIMPSE OF THE NEWEST WOLFRIDER.
DO YOU THINK HE WILL EVER FLOAT LIKE A GLIDER?
PERHAPS. I SENSED IT IN HIM EVEN BEFORE HE WAS BORN.
AND WHAT OF HIS FATHER?
YOUR EYES ARE BAD, MY CHIEF. HIS FATHER IS OVER THERE, CRADLING HIS SON IN HIS ARMS.
THE END

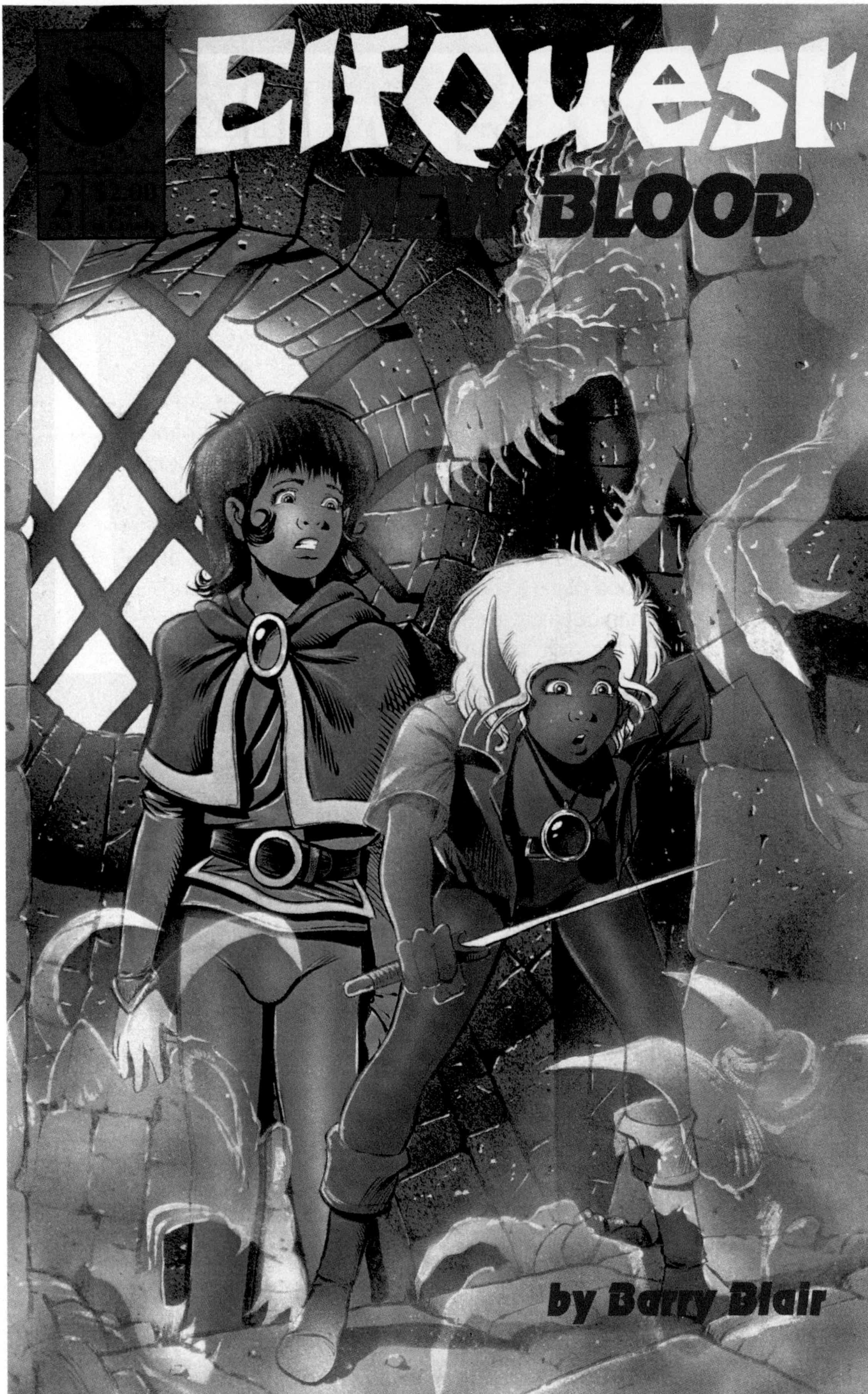

ElfQuest
NEW BLOOD
2
by Barry Blair

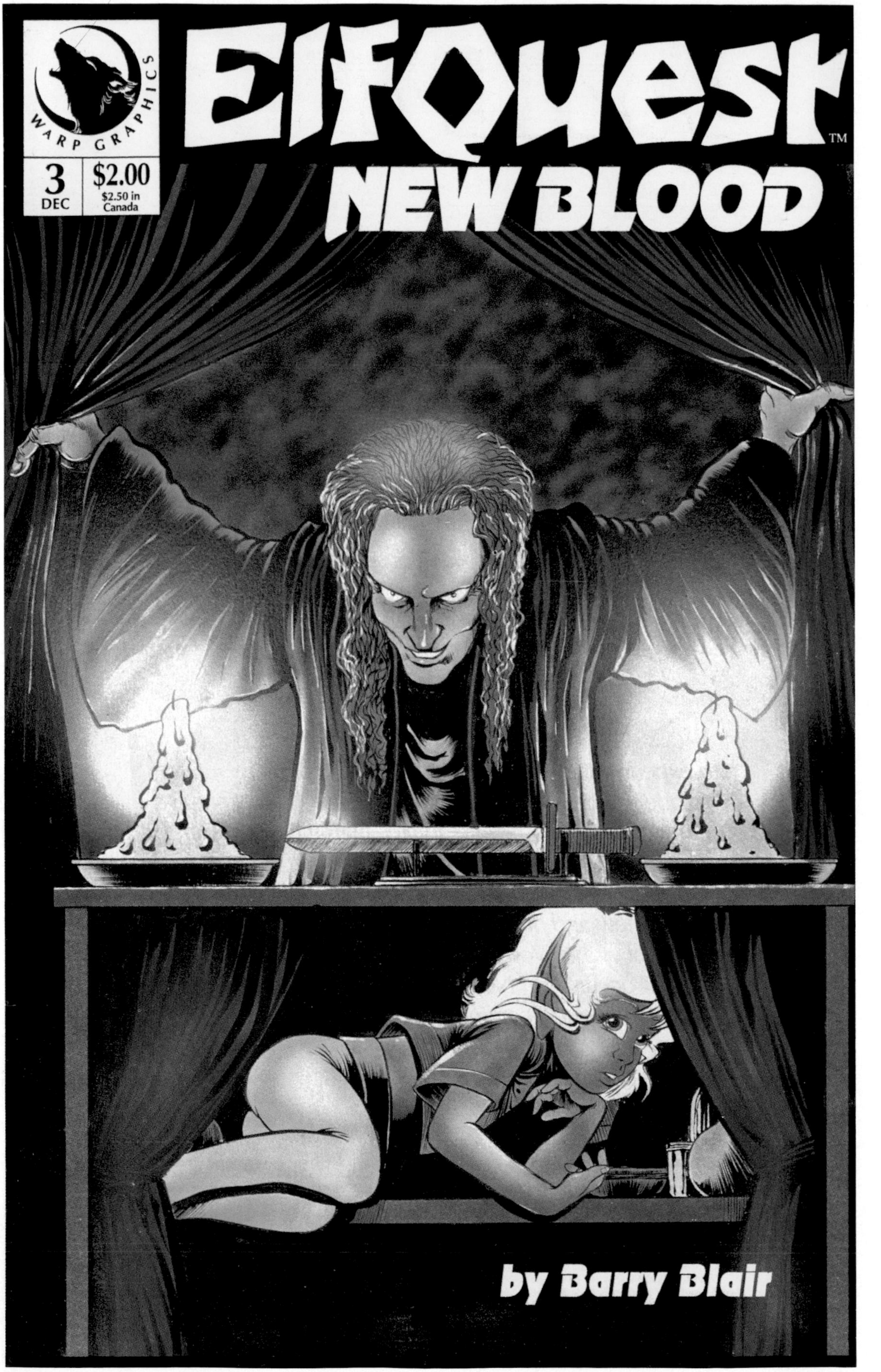
WARP GRAPHICS
3
DEC
$2.00
$2.50 in Canada
ElfQuest™
NEW BLOOD
by Barry Blair

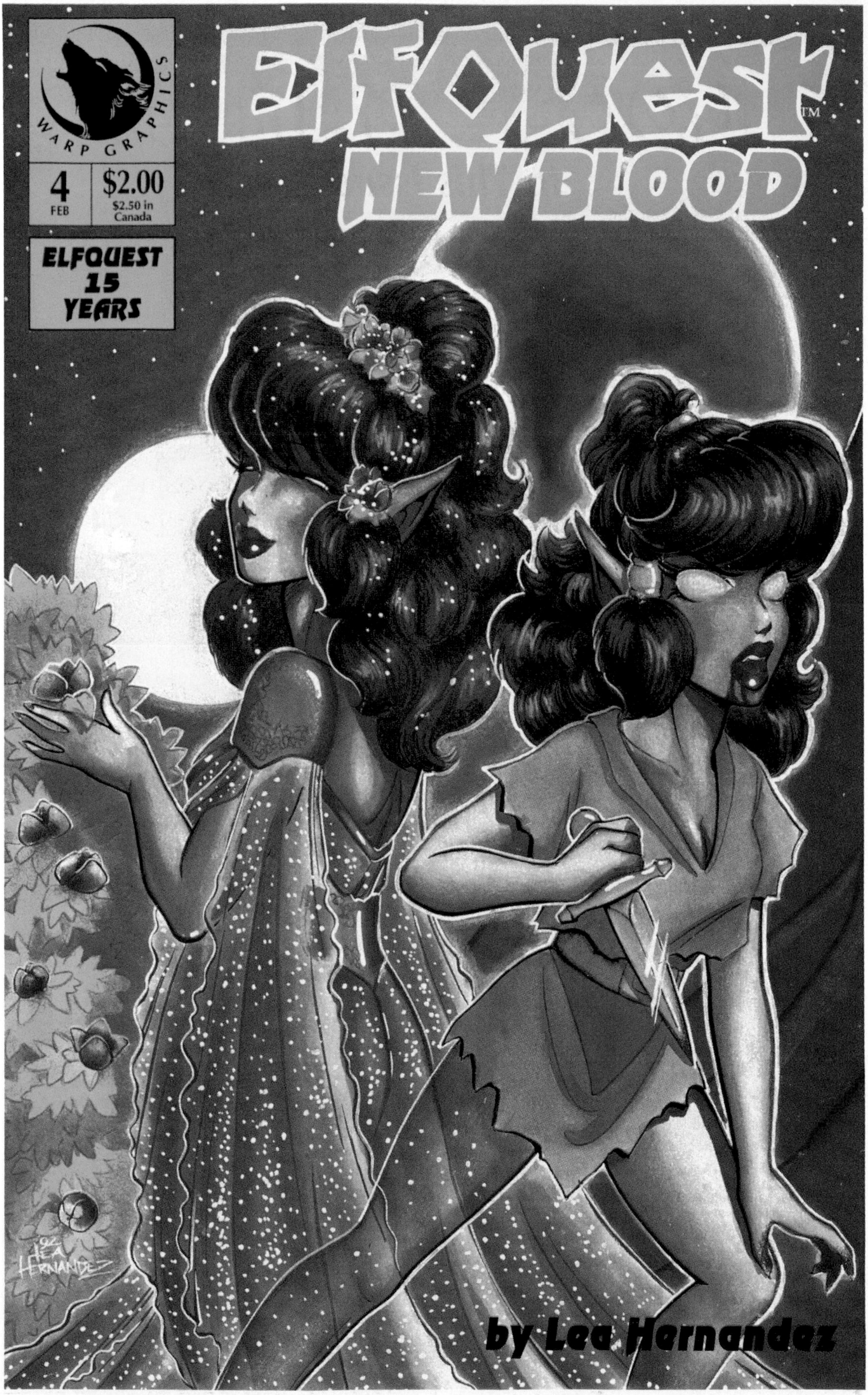
WARP GRAPHICS
4
FEB
$2.00
$2.50 in Canada
ELFQUEST 15 YEARS
ElfQuest™
NEW BLOOD
'92 LEA HERNANDEZ
by Lea Hernandez

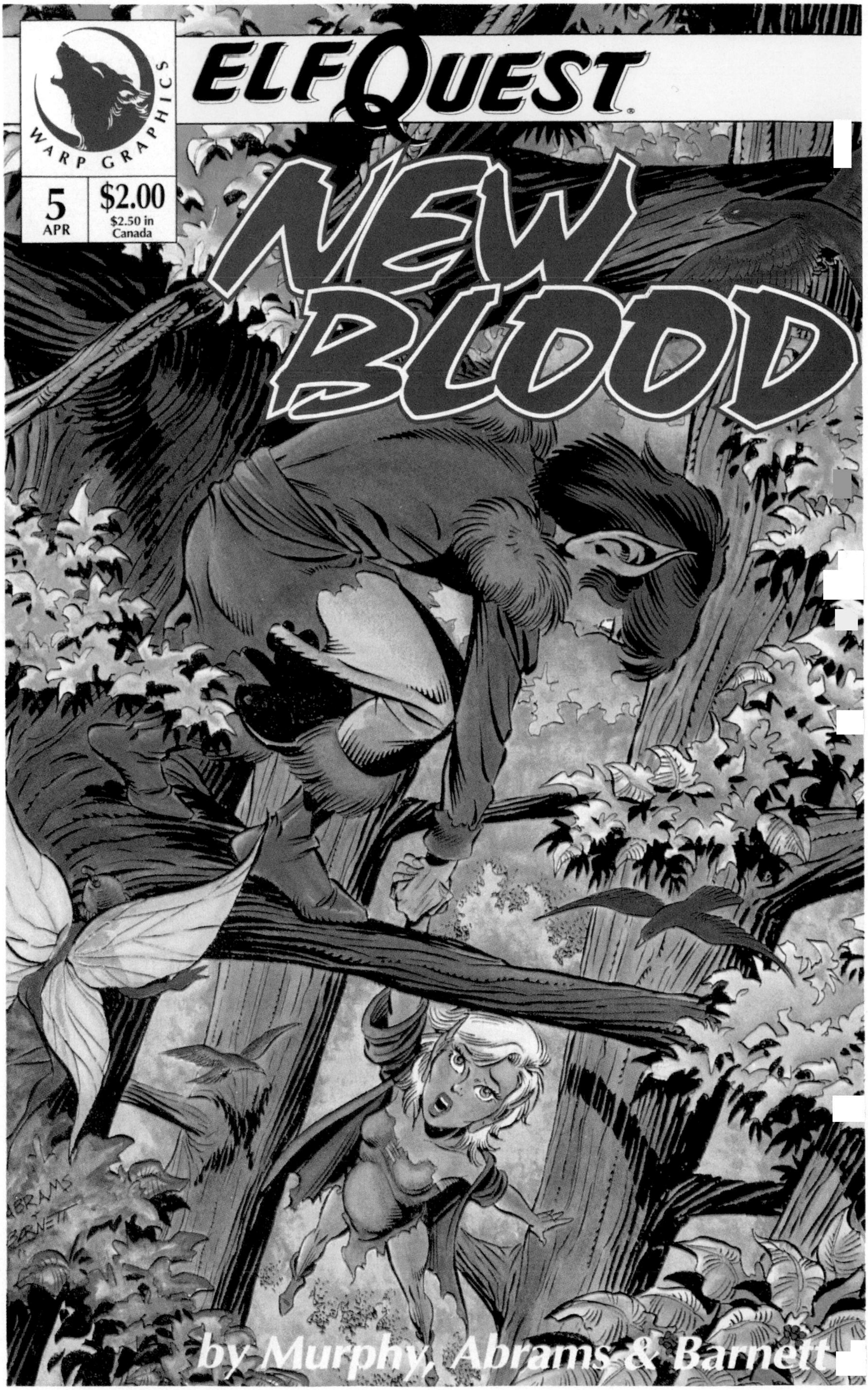

WARP GRAPHICS
ELFQUEST
5
APR
$2.00
$2.50 in Canada
NEW BLOOD
ABRAMS
BARNETT
by Murphy, Abrams & Barnett